Our Emily Dickinsons

Our Emily Dickinsons

*American Women Poets
and the Intimacies
of Difference*

Vivian R. Pollak

PENN

UNIVERSITY OF PENNSYLVANIA PRESS

PHILADELPHIA

A volume in the Haney Foundation Series, established in
1961 with the generous support of Dr. John Louis Haney

Published by
University of Pennsylvania Press
Philadelphia, Pennsylvania 19104-4112
www.upenn.edu/pennpress

Printed in the United States of America on acid-free paper
1 3 5 7 9 10 8 6 4 2

A Cataloging-in-Publication record is available
at the Library of Congress

ISBN 978-0-8122-4844-9

For my students
at Brandeis,
Cheyney University in Pennsylvania,
the University of Pennsylvania,
the University of Washington in Seattle,
Washington University in St. Louis

And for Mia and Alex

Contents

Abbreviations

Fr   *The Poems of Emily Dickinson: Reading Edition*. Ed. R. W. Franklin. Cambridge, MA: Harvard University Press, 1999. Citation by poem number.

L   *The Letters of Emily Dickinson*. Ed. Thomas H. Johnson and Theodora Ward. 3 vols. Cambridge, MA: Harvard University Press, 1958. Citation by letter number.

Dickinson and the Demands of Intimacy

In an emotionally tense poem written when she was still in her early thirties, Emily Dickinson expresses this haunting thought about her role during the Civil War: "It feels a shame to be Alive – / When Men so brave – are dead." Speaking as "one," "We," and "I" and as the possessor of a powerful conscience, she faults herself for escaping military martyrdom in "Battle's – horrid Bowl." Expanding the trope, she claims to envy the modern heroes who died for liberty, the ground that holds their bodies, and the stones by which they are memorialized. This remarkable confession prepares for an even more disturbing conclusion. Although any kind of living is an achievement, a sort of fame, it is not "Divinity." "Divinity," Dickinson suggests, is what the Union dead achieve by dying. Because the poem is not well known, I will quote it in full:

> It feels a shame to be Alive –
> When Men so brave – are dead –
> One envies the Distinguished Dust –
> Permitted – such a Head –
>
> The Stone – that tells defending Whom
> This Spartan put away
> What little of Him we – possessed
> In Pawn for Liberty –
>
> The price is great – Sublimely paid –
> Do we deserve – a Thing –

That lives – like Dollars – must be piled
Before we may obtain?

Are we that wait – sufficient worth –
That such Enormous Pearl
As life – dissolved be – for Us –
In Battle's – horrid Bowl?

It may be – a Renown to live –
I think the Men who die –
Those unsustained – Saviors –
Present Divinity – (*Fr* 524)

"It feels a shame to be Alive" inhabits several kinds of ambition. The first is the most sociable. It responds to a specific national emergency. The second is more personal, more complexly gendered. Unable to perform the heroic deeds associated with men, the speaker feels guilty. This emotion is partly displaced from the dead to the sacred ground in which they lie and to the headstones by which they are memorialized. By implication, the speaker who craves intimacy with the dead also wants to write words that are publicly recognized and that last. This speaker wants to disinter, to resurrect, and to give voice to an unlived life from which ugly feelings have been banished, but the dashes tell the story—they interrupt the flow.

Suppose, then, that you are a person who thinks deeply about identities that have not yet been fully constituted. Suppose, too, that you are a person who wants to spare herself humiliation. What would it be like to compose "It feels a shame to be Alive" and to keep it to yourself? What would it be like to copy these publicly oriented words onto a sheet of paper and to use that sheet to conclude a poem sequence in which you declare "This is my letter to the World" (*Fr* 519)? What would it be like to keep that twenty-poem sequence, that Fascicle 24, in a locked box or dresser drawer and to make yourself your only continuously attentive reader? What would it be like to go back over that poem sequence and to take a poem from another fascicle, a poem about rewards, to recopy it, alter it, and to insert it into this newer grouping, while leaving the old one in its place (*Fr* 375, Fascicles 18 and 24)? What would it be like to be that brilliantly conflicted, that partly repressed, that angry, loving, home-keeping person, that Emily Dickinson?

In this book, I begin with a Dickinson who was driven by a sense of unrealized potential. The daughter of a public man and the sister of another, she might well describe herself as "unsustained" in the heterodox services she performed for her country. In intellectually challenging, emotionally arduous poems that invite and repel intimacy, Dickinson links what affect theorist Sianne Ngai has taught us to think of as ugly feelings (such as shame and envy) to what I will call trace scenes, scenes that evoke collective experience but mystify important personal particulars.[1] The Dickinson I describe writes thinly descriptive poetry that refuses to satisfy the demands of her imagined audience for a fuller narrative of her life. If there is a center to what is by now the long history of Dickinson criticism, it is this: readers are curious about the person behind the poems. Although she did write, "When I state myself, as the Representative of the Verse – it does not mean – me – but a supposed person," the women poets who interest me most deeply have been reluctant to separate the life and the work so neatly (L 268). Reading for both text and context, they are interested not only in Dickinson's literary self-expression and fictionalized persona but also in her psychological intimacies and social sources.

Dickinson's psychological ambivalence about her relationship to her actual and potential readers has been well established and continues to be documented with precision. I argue that this ambivalence, however productive, has significantly influenced her reception. It has interrupted what we might think of as a coherent genealogy of American women's poetry. Such a genealogy would transmit ideas from one generation to the next. It would demonstrate incremental continuity and patient connections intimately forged. In all probability, it would disseminate an idealized version of mother-daughter relationships and would reinforce the romance of what a later poet (Muriel Rukeyser) calls "group culture."[2] I tell a somewhat different tale. The keenly observant Rukeyser, for one, believed that most Americans fear poetry because it takes us into unknown territory. It disorients us psychologically. It causes us to lose our emotional and intellectual equilibrium. With Rukeyser, I view Dickinson's achievement as an extended meditation on the risks of social, psychological, and aesthetic difference. In what follows, I will describe both neglected aspects of Dickinsonian difference and some of the social and psychological conflicts American women poets have encountered in her wake. To introduce my version of discontinuous, or "spasmodic" literary history, I will look more closely at Dickinson's role as

marked by the sexual politics of the mid-twentieth century. I will look more
closely at Muriel Rukeyser's hybrid manifesto, *The Life of Poetry* (1949).

In this underread classic of feminist critique, Rukeyser takes her time
before mentioning Dickinson. Indeed, she is about a third of the way through
the text when she glances at Dickinson's rhythms, which she compares to
those of the muscular Gerard Manley Hopkins (briefly) and to those of the
self-poised Walt Whitman (more extensively). "Emily Dickinson's strictness," she writes, "sometimes almost a slang of strictness, speaks with an
intellectually active, stimulated quick music." Yet it is Whitman who "offers
us the rhythms of resolved physical conflict. When he says, 'I have found the
law of my own poems,' he celebrates that victory."[3] From this perspective, it
is apparent that Dickinson has not yet found the law of her own poems; she
is still a poet in search of her fullest self. She is waiting to be liberated from
the anxieties of audience which arrest her. Her rhythms represent the problems of the confined female self and of its access to cultural power. My point
is that thinking about Dickinson makes Rukeyser uncomfortable. Recalling
her own professional frustrations, she moves quickly into an irate account of
her troubles as a biographer of J. Willard Gibbs, the nineteenth-century
American physicist who was one of her culture heroes and whose genius,
she believed, was overlooked. Like Dickinson, she was almost silenced, but
Rukeyser has other versions of Dickinson in reserve.

Some years earlier, in a distinctly unauthorized biography of Gibbs, who
never married, had no visible love life, and was content, Rukeyser had fas-
tened on an exemplary vignette: "Think of Edward Dickinson, the father of
the poet Emily Dickinson. . . . That father ran gasping up the steeple stairs
of the Baptist Church in Amherst, and pulled and pulled on the bell-rope
until the clanging startled the whole town, who turned to look, and saw the
sunset. That was the gesture of a poet who does what his daughter was later
to do : uses the old forms, pulls on the churchbell-rope, to call attention to
the vivid and changing moment in an unheard-of way."[4] Based on this episode, which embellishes a description in one of Emily Dickinson's early letters to her brother (*L* 53), what does her poetry effect? It empowers us to
believe in newly created selves and in desires extended into what Rukeyser
calls "our farthest range."[5] Under normal circumstances, Edward Dickinson
was a model of masculine discipline and self-restraint. He was celebrated for
his emotional reserve, but even *he* was capable of surprising turns and star-
tling gestures because of the poetry hidden in his nature. As Rukeyser suggests
in the passage from the Gibbs biography cited above, poets consolidate an

affective community by calling attention "to the vivid and changing moment in an unheard-of way." Breathing new life into the life of beauty, they encourage us to believe, as Rukeyser wrote at the conclusion of "Easter Eve 1945," "What fire survive forever / myself is for my time."[6] Poetry begins as personal passion. It is clarified by time and vulnerable to its passage.

From the beginning of her multifaceted career, Rukeyser was committed to what Richard Rorty has called "achieving our country."[7] In a continuing quest to alter national and global realities, she attended meetings, signed petitions, taught classes, worked for and against the U.S. government, and generally refused to conform to the expectations of her bourgeois Jewish parents and their friends. It is known that she had lovers of both sexes. It is known that she entered into a very brief marriage in 1945 to an artist whom she had met in San Francisco. Not at all well known is the fact that at this crisis in her erotic life, she read *Bolts of Melody*, the book of poems by Emily Dickinson just out. The journal she kept at the time states, "It seems impossible to go on completely by myself." What was the effect on her of this reading? On this point, her journal is silent.[8]

The Gibbs biography, however, provides some clues. Here is what she wrote: "She [Emily Dickinson] is a close expression of American self-destruction with all its powers of communication heightened. . . . There was always this wish . . . to be her own absolute. . . . Science could not overtake that, she felt. She had reached her only equilibrium; and that was the only law."[9] An emblem of American self-destructiveness. But why? Is it because in this telling, Dickinson wanted to live in her own world and risked madness as a consequence? Or was the madness wanting to live in her own world in the first place? Because this world has its own laws, its equilibrium, for the reader there is "clear joy, a gift in the hand that seemed nothing more bodied than broken light, as if one were to hold an invisible prism." But for the poet herself who is "cut off" and who has "made an image of that amputation," there is the "dry wine of logarithm."[10] How can such perilous self-sufficiency suffice? Influenced by traditions of lyric reading, in which the poet is isolated by history, Rukeyser is nevertheless determined to historicize Dickinson, to situate her in New England literary culture and in a tradition of intellectual women whose limited access to cultural power she deplores.

Rukeyser's response is exemplary for my study of Dickinson's contradictory and complex legacy for several reasons. The women poets I discuss engage with her episodically rather than continuously. Influenced by changes in their personal and professional relations and in their actual and potential

audiences, they exhibit a wide range of feelings toward Dickinson's achievement, and their attitudes toward her change over time. Consistently, however, they use Dickinson to clarify what is at stake in personal and
professional battles of their own. "If we are free," Rukeyser wrote in *The Life
of Poetry*, "we are free to choose a tradition, and we find in the past as
well as the present our poets of outrage—like Melville—and our poets of
possibility—like Whitman."[11] That same year, more tentatively, she also
wrote, "It seems to me that if we are in any way free, we are also free in
relation to the past, and that we may to some extent choose our tradition."[12]
These are very different statements, and between them I locate my project.
Whatever their differences, the women poets who interest me most deeply
have found sources of strength in Emily Dickinson, together with the problem of being cut off.

"Breathe-in experience," Rukeyser wrote in the first line of her first
book, "breathe-out poetry."[13] At twenty-one, she knew it was not that easy.
Between *Theory of Flight*, for which she won the Yale Younger Poets Prize in
1936, and 1949 when she published *The Life of Poetry*, *Orpheus*, and *Elegies*,
Rukeyser had experienced the ups and downs of a career which had gotten
off to a remarkably fast start. She was the author of seven books of poetry,
and in 1950 she would be one of the two women featured in John Ciardi's
anthology *Mid-Century American Poets* (the other was Elizabeth Bishop). At
mid-century, she was "a figure impossible to ignore," and she was working
tirelessly to bring poetry back into the mainstream of American life.[14] Yet the
Dickinson who spoke most poignantly in the wake of World War II was a
consummate elegist. Here are the only lines by Dickinson she quotes in *The
Life of Poetry*:

> The things that never can come back are several—
> Childhood, some forms of hope, the dead;
> But joys, like men, may sometimes make a journey
>   And still abide . . . .[15]

Affected by histories of Dickinson as a near miss, a poet who almost didn't
happen because of litigious heirs battling over her estate, Rukeyser deployed
Dickinson as a symbol of natural waste, loss, penalties, guilts. Under the
heading "Certain Misfortunes," she discusses the pathological secrecy of
Dickinson's legacy: "Emily Dickinson, whose unappeasable thirst for fame
was itself unknown for years after her death, had to fight through her

Figure 1. Emily Dickinson at age sixteen, in her senior year at Amherst Academy. Currently, this is the only authenticated photograph of the poet. Courtesy Amherst College Archives and Special Collections.

family—'Vesuvius at Home'—until a miserable lawsuit and the theft of a manure pile interrupted the posthumous publication of her work, and postponed for forty-nine years what may be her finest book."[16] Although Rukeyser idealized Dickinson as the victim of cultural sin (the suppression of a writer under the sign of private property), she viewed herself as a champion of "the rights of the reader," which she equated with "the rights of the people." These rights, she insisted, were ignored not only in the case of Dickinson but also of herself.[17] Thus, in *The Life of Poetry*, Rukeyser emphasized the link between

Figure 2. Poet and political activist Muriel Rukeyser in 1945. She was outraged by the publication history of Dickinson's poetry. Copyright © Imogen Cunningham Trust.

Dickinson's genius and her troubles. These troubles, as she explained elliptically in *Willard Gibbs*, included a tragic love affair (Rukeyser had known several).[18]

Taking roughly one hundred years as its focus, *Our Emily Dickinsons* describes changing conceptions of Dickinson and the problem for women poets of being cut off from the social experiences which consolidate an affective community, however that community is defined. In my book, I begin in the nineteenth century, dwell in the twentieth, and do not get very contemporary. Without attempting anything so ambitious as a complete history of the bold misreadings that have shaped Dickinson's reception from her time to ours, I describe some of the intimate reading practices through which women poets interrogate Dickinson, her literary culture, their literary cultures, and themselves. My unifying claims are these. Today's Dickinson is less "spasmodic" (*L* 265) than she used to be. She has more agency and she arouses less anxiety of gendered authorship. She is a poet who is no longer quoted most frequently as a supreme elegist because informed contemporary readers, and they are many, have fuller access to her variant voices. They are also more interested in the generic innovations of her prose. Inspired by brilliant theorists such as Susan Howe, we are learning to forget that there was ever a Dickinson who was considered shameful. I want to take us back to an earlier time, when skepticism about the relationship between text and context organized logics of sexed and gendered self-representation.

In the wake of feminist, New Historicist, and cultural materialist critical practices, Dickinson's public, semipublic, private, and semiprivate contexts continue to be clarified. For example, *A Historical Guide to Emily Dickinson*, which I edited, includes essays with the following titles: "'Is Immortality True?': Salvaging Faith in an Age of Upheavals," "Public and Private in Dickinson's War Poetry," "Dickinson and the Art of Politics," "Dickinson in Context: Nineteenth-Century American Women Poets," and "The Sound of Shifting Paradigms, or Hearing Dickinson in the Twenty-First Century."[19] Despite their different emphases, critics Jane Donahue Eberwein, Shira Wolosky, Betsy Erkkila, Cheryl Walker, and Cristanne Miller engage in a collaborative project. They demonstrate that Dickinson was not cut off intellectually. Extending their project of historical contextualization, I offer a fuller history of the social life of her emotions as interpreted by key interlocutors. I see this book as an intervention in that intersubjective history and as an experimental, collective psychobiography, organized around the themes of shame, envy, love, fame, and death, in which affective closure is not the goal. "Who writes these funny accidents, where railroads meet each other unexpectedly, and gentlemen in factories get their heads cut off quite informally?" Dickinson asked her friends Elizabeth and Josiah Gilbert Holland (he was an owner/editor of her favorite newspaper, the *Springfield Republican*). "The author, too, relates them in such a sprightly way, that they are quite attractive. Vinnie [her sister] was disappointed to-night, that there were not more accidents – I read the news aloud, while Vinnie was sewing. *The Republican* seems to us like a letter from you, and we break the seal and read it eagerly" (*L* 133).[20] Dickinson wrote this entertaining fan letter when she was twenty-two. In 1853, she had not yet reached either personal or poetic maturity, and only four of her poems can be dated before 1858, when she began making her manuscript books. While it is possible to argue that she became more self-absorbed intellectually and emotionally after 1864, when she stopped constructing these books ("fascicles"), the poets I discuss were not primarily concerned with periodizing Dickinson's oeuvre. In this regard, too, Rukeyser is exemplary. However much she wishes to locate Dickinson in history, there is a determination on her part to use the incomplete Dickinson for purposes of self-expression. Writing as both a poet and a critic, Rukeyser engages in a particular form of autobiographical self-representation or deflected lifewriting. Her critique throws into relief the close correspondence between impressionist literary criticism and biographical narrative.

I want to consider for a moment several discrete episodes in her use of Dickinson as the occasion for deflected lifewriting. In *Willard Gibbs* as in *The Life of Poetry*, Rukeyser quotes only part of a poem. She cuts the poem off. The excerpt from "How happy is the little Stone" (*Fr* 1570) shows us the upside of having no career to worry about. A stone has a "casual simplicity" lacking in human beings. A stone is complete in and of itself. It has no unrealized ambitions, no secret sorrows. A stone is

> . . . independent as the sun,
> Associates and glows alone,
> Fulfilling absolute decree
> In casual simplicity.[21]

Dickinson cuts the poem off too. Her syntax suppresses some ordinary connectives; she does not tell us anything about the formal or informal association to which the stone belongs; about the content of the law, the "absolute decree" the stone obeys; about the judge who has issued an "absolute decree" rather than a "decree nisi," which is a provisional court order, especially about divorce; or about why she seems to believe, at least for the moment, that happiness depends on being sentenced to associate with no one but one's self. Yet if we read "How happy is the little Stone" in the three-volume *Variorum* edited by R. W. Franklin, we discover that Dickinson sent the poem to her sister-in-law Susan, who was one of her literary advisors; to

Thomas Wentworth Higginson, who was another; to poet and novelist Helen Hunt Jackson, whose career I discuss in my first chapter; to Thomas Niles, an editor at Roberts Brothers with whom Dickinson was corresponding; to her cousins Louisa and Frances Norcross; and that she kept a copy for herself.[22] This publication history was not available in 1942 when *Willard Gibbs* was published. Had it been available, Rukeyser might have been less insistent on Dickinson as an exemplar of gendered self-reliance. Deflected lifewriting that is historically situated need not be narcissistically self-enclosed. Unlike stones, poet-critics can change and can respond to changes in the social construction of texts as collective enterprises. Unlike stones, they are not simple.

We see this greater complexity and responsiveness to changing times in my second example. In June 1959, along with several other poets, Rukeyser participated in a reading in New York City for the Library of Congress. She read four of her poems and six by Dickinson.[23] Rukeyser's evolving Dickinson was still an elegist, but she was more commanding and expansive, surer of her own choices. Oddly, Rukeyser's texts derive not, as we would expect, from the 1955 *Poems of Emily Dickinson: Including Variant Readings Critically Compared with All Known Manuscripts*, edited by Thomas H. Johnson, which was authoritative then, but from Martha Dickinson Bianchi's 1924 *Complete Poems*, which was both incomplete and discredited. Perhaps Rukeyser was concerned about copyright issues. More likely she had grown accustomed to the earlier versions and was reluctant to give them up.[24]

Several months later, in September 1959, Rukeyser published a review of Marianne Moore's *O to Be a Dragon*, in which she connects Dickinson more securely to a tradition of women's writing and to a specifically modernist tradition of women's spirituality. Moore, she explains, "has had in all her writing life a deep connection with the Psalms and with the hymns made out of their translated spirit. . . . [she] has a whole reach of followers to whom this relation with hymns will open up new fertilities, as does a similar relation in Emily Dickinson."[25] Demonstrating her knowledge of hymns, hymn meters, and Isaac Watts's hymnbook (1855 version), Rukeyser takes Moore to task for inaccurate citation of the Twenty-Third Psalm, which Rukeyser describes as a "document." In a longer draft of the review, Rukeyser developed the hymn context even more emphatically and mentions a family legend in which she herself is descended from the great Jewish scholar Akiba, "who was responsible for getting the Song of Songs included in the Bible."[26] In both the published and unpublished versions, Rukeyser mentions that Moore's reputation has been built on accuracy, that Elizabeth Bishop praises her on the book jacket as "the World's Greatest Living Observer," and that Moore's inaccurate footnote violates her own aesthetic scrupulosity. My claim is not that Rukeyser is deliberately (or only) engaged in feats of self-promotion. Her citation of Dickinson's relation to hymns and to Moore and to herself through hymnody registers real changes in Dickinson's reputation, changes which are easy to document in the contemporary reviews. In the Moore review, then, Dickinson is more connected than cut off.

The progressive phases of Dickinson's reputation I am tracking correspond to improvements in Rukeyser's personal and professional situation as well. She now has a child, a comparatively undemanding female lover, and a part-time position teaching creative writing at Sarah Lawrence College. This association provides her with an income, protects some of her own writing time, and gratifies her desire to nurture the young and to function as a public intellectual. She has not resolved her quarrel with the father, Lawrence B. Rukeyser, who disinherited her, but it now appears that Dickinson, like Moore, has deep roots and that her "fertilities" extend in many different directions.[27] Rukeyser's Vassar classmate Elizabeth Bishop is harder to transform, absorb, and recuperate, and I do not wish to exaggerate the degree to which Rukeyser has mellowed. Yet circa 1959, invoking Dickinson's name can strengthen Rukeyser's claim to literary authority. Rather than being an emblem of American self-destructiveness and feminized domesticity, Dickinson is associated with the feminist spiritual traditions of our country. So far as I have been able to determine, Rukeyser never wrote publicly about Dickinson again. With her own cultural authority more pronounced, to say nothing of Dickinson's, Dickinson seems to have interested her less. In terms of their mutual reputations, it was no longer the same appealing game of "loser wins," and it was no longer obvious that Dickinson needed to be rescued.

As Second Wave feminism took off, so too did Dickinson. Not only were her poems available in the three-volume Johnson edition which, we were taught, was definitive, but in 1958, Johnson and Theodora Van Wagenen Ward also had published an annotated, three-volume edition of her letters.[28] It was reassuring that Harvard University Press was behind both ventures, and it seemed that editing troubles were a thing of the past. Johnson, moreover, had published a well-received 1955 biography, in which a new but not *too* new Dickinson emerged. As the distinguished literary historian Perry Miller, himself a Harvard professor, explained in the *New England Quarterly*, "With Mr. Johnson we may rest assured that we are in safe and informed hands." Following New Critical protocols, Miller heaped praise on Johnson's

Interpretive Biography while suggesting that Dickinson, "a poet of authentic distinction," wrote many minor works. Miller also objected strongly to the enthusiasm of "cultists," whom Johnson's biography "quietly rebuke[s]."

> The biography is, refreshingly, an "interpretive" one, not the vulgarization of a myth of eccentricity. It is a study of Emily Dickinson as poet, drawing upon biographical facts only at points where these facts become relevant to appreciation of the verses. The whole quagmire of scandal, rumor, and recrimination in which for weary decades discussion of the artist has foundered is skillfully ignored. The result is that Emily Dickinson emerges as a poet of authentic distinction, a more serious and sophisticated craftsman than ever her admirers had supposed. Or rather, the enthusiasm of the cult is quietly rebuked so that we can clearly perceive just what she actually did accomplish.[29]

Although Miller does not name either the cultists or the critical snobs who react against them, informed readers might guess that the cultists were mainly women and the critical snobs mainly men.

On the definitiveness of the Johnson edition, there soon emerged an important dissenter, voicing her opinion in "'I am in Danger—Sir—,'" a poem which etched itself indelibly on the consciousness of graduate students such as myself back in the day. Referring to "your variorum monument," Adrienne Rich took the Dickinson industry to task for its sexist presumptions. Rich's Dickinson "choose[s] silence for entertainment" and is "determined to have it out at last on [her] own premises." To Rich, it seemed that "garbled versions" of Dickinson's life and work had been "mothballed at Harvard."[30] Beginning in 1963, Rich wrote trenchantly, brilliantly, poignantly about her own struggle to comprehend Dickinson without minimizing their differences. Rich's sustained engagement with a Dickinson who chose silence for entertainment and with other, less mysterious feminist heroines led to the landmark 1975 essay "'Vesuvius at Home': The Power of Emily Dickinson," which deeply influenced me and many of my closest women friends. Yet for the Rich who wrote in *Necessities of Life* that "whole biographies swam up and / swallowed me like Jonah," creating a new birth myth for herself included describing Dickinson as "masculine / in singlemindedness."[31] Both "'I Am in Danger'" and "'Vesuvius at Home'" employ emphatically gendered language, and Rich speculates in "'Vesuvius'" that

Dickinson was ambivalent about her powers: that being powerful, she risked experiencing herself as masculinized and consequently in some poems miniaturized herself.

Rich was angered by traditional characterizations of Dickinson's emotional dependence on a "Master" figure. In "'Vesuvius at Home,'" she does not appropriate Dickinson as a same-sex lover, unless we assume that the absence of an active sexual script encodes lesbian silence. Rather, she suggests that Dickinson, a poet of psychological compulsion, was remarkably self-sufficient and that her seclusion and presumed lack of an intimate erotic life was deliberately chosen to nurture her own genius. This idea was then and continues to be very appealing, especially for readers who value psychological autonomy as a desirable and/or achievable artistic goal.[32] The greater the original artist, the greater the autonomy and agency—that is Rich's implied theory. Dickinson, I think, rebuts or modifies that theory in "How happy is the little Stone" (*Fr* 1570), which is just one among many poems in which interdependency, complexity, and vulnerability are valued. Paradoxically, in "'Vesuvius at Home,'" Rich also suggests that Dickinson's deeply felt insights into psychological turmoil empower her. Rich thus avoids the trap (as I see it) of sourcing these insights primarily in secondhand experience. This part of her essay could not be clearer: Dickinson, a woman who suffered, in some way found the life she needed and fought the battle she needed to fight. In some way, she had a life-struggle "out at last on her own premises."

On this point, Rich engages the debate that also concerns Rukeyser, who writes that "if we are free we may *to some extent* choose our tradition" (italics mine). Yet Rukeyser's hero Whitman can suggest otherwise, as at times does Thoreau, who notes in his *Journal*, "It is vain to write on chosen themes. We must wait until they have kindled a flame in our minds. There must be the copulating and generating force of love behind every effort destined to be successful. The cold resolve gives birth to, begets, nothing. The theme seeks me, not I it. The poet's relation to his theme is the relation of love."[33] Whether or not Thoreau was sincere, his pose of passivity is nicely gendered. Enthusiastically, Rukeyser spoke of him as "this curious man who was like us in that he didn't 'match.'"[34]

Our Emily Dickinsons is based on reading for biographically precise, historically situated connections between women poets and their critics of both sexes. Chapter 1 focuses on the literary connections forged by Helen Hunt Jackson, whose stellar reputation as a poet has not been sustained by posterity. Jackson was born in the fall of 1830 in Amherst (as was Dickinson) and died in 1885 (Dickinson died the next year). Like Dickinson, she was encouraged by Thomas Wentworth Higginson, but unlike the Dickinson who circulated a portion of her handwritten verses to a coterie audience, Jackson successfully negotiated the demands of the literary marketplace. Choosing to "invest her snow," she did not find "Publication . . . the Auction / Of the Mind of Man" (*Fr* 788). Jackson knew Dickinson and her circle personally; an Amherst native, she was a successful poet, journalist, and fiction writer who is best known today for her protest novel *Ramona*. Jackson's earlier stories gratified the genteel public's hunger for romance and for wholesome literary heroines like Mercy Philbrick, whose "choice" of the life of the mind over a morally suspect lover reminded some inner circle, contemporary readers of—Emily Dickinson.[35] Jackson forced one Dickinson poem ("Success") into print and would have liked to print others. Barring that, she wanted to be Dickinson's literary executor. Although this role was foreclosed by her death (if nothing else), her enthusiastic response to the "stingy" friend she tried to reform exposes the competing logic of Dickinson's hesitations.

Chapter 2 provides a context for understanding the so-called war between the houses as it was negotiated by Mabel Loomis Todd, who while not herself a poet was Dickinson's most energetic national publicist in the 1890s. Todd came from a family with ties to Thoreau, and her desire to please her father (and a father substitute, the poet's brother Austin) took unexpected turns, implicating her in Dickinson's fate and Dickinson in hers. With Higginson, she launched Dickinson into the print public sphere in the 1890s. Both were engaged in editing practices which now seem scandalous. Moreover, because of her hostile relationship to the poet's close friend Susan Gilbert Dickinson, it is easy to understand why recent criticism has marginalized Todd and ignored the depth of her influence on Dickinson's reception. I seek to accord her a truer place, both for her sake and for the sake of a more historically responsible, less anachronistic literary critique. Todd viewed herself as a feminist who challenged personal and professional orthodoxy. Although the Dickinson she projected is a poet of many parts, the Dickinson she constructed most consistently is wonderfully self-poised and spiritually uplifting. In different ways, modernist poets such as Marianne Moore agreed with her.

For example, Moore's 1933 review of a new edition of Dickinson's letters, which is discussed in Chapter 3, helps us to understand what the term "wholesomeness" meant in Moore's occluded reflections on a social life turned inward. I argue that reconsidering Dickinson's life during this difficult period of personal and professional transition in the early 1930s helped the modernist Moore to reconnect with the strengths of her literary past. Moving closer to the present time, Chapter 4 uses Sylvia Plath's personal letters, journals, and other prose writings to understand the networks she was trying to mobilize for herself in which Moore had a central position. "Moore, Plath, Hughes, and 'The Literary Life' " offers an account of Plath's ambitions and provides an ampler context for understanding both her ambivalence toward Dickinson and the rivalrous energies that structured Plath's more comprehensive imagination of female authorship. This "female author" construct imagines writing as a bloody act. It was shaped in part by various versions of Rich's problem of the masculine, but Plath's problem of the masculine is also a problem of the feminine, of motherhood and daughterhood. In Barbara Antonina Clarke Mossberg's terms, "When a Writer is a Daughter," problems of intimacy and autonomy are foregrounded.[36]

Chapter 5 discusses Plath's early imitations of Dickinson and explores the roles of her mother, Aurelia Schober Plath, and of her husband Ted Hughes in shaping Plath's literary taste and posthumous reputation. Both Aurelia Plath and Hughes were Dickinson enthusiasts, and they appealed to Dickinson's fame to validate Plath's oeuvre. Hughes's prominence in the project may seem surprising, but the logic of this choice will become clearer as the narrative unfolds. Just as there is no public Dickinson without Thomas Wentworth Higginson (pace Alice James), there is no public Plath without Ted Hughes (pace Robin Morgan and all those Second Wave feminists who taught us to despise him).[37] "A Queer Interlude" shows Plath reading Bishop, whom she describes as Moore's goddaughter, only juicier. These transitional pages raise the question of whether Plath was beginning to construct a lesbian or bisexual identity for herself, her quest for (hetero)sexual normality notwithstanding.

Chapter 6 explains why Bishop, despite her admiration for the *Ariel* poet, couldn't complete her review of *Letters Home*, in which Plath performs the role of dutiful daughter. It offers an account of Bishop's deference dance with Moore, whom she reads in relation to personal and cultural mothers. I describe her responses not only to Dickinson as a self-caged bird but also to Whitman, who provides her with a "vista" she craves. For Bishop, the U.S.A. Schools of Writing are both ample and pathetically narrow, and her posthumously published story, "The U.S.A. School of Writing," touches on the homoeroticism and homophobia with which Dickinson is associated in Bishop's writings in the early 1950s. Bishop reviewed Rebecca Patterson's groundbreaking *The Riddle of Emily Dickinson*, and it infuriated her. She also reviewed a collection of Dickinson's letters to one of her closest women friends and wondered aloud about Dickinson's emotional neediness. "There is a constant insistence on the strength of her affections," Bishop wrote, "an almost childish daring and repetitiveness about them that must sometimes have been very hard to take."[38]

The writings about Dickinson I examine are fractured self-portraits; they are self-questioning and self-justifying. Todd emphasized Dickinson's ability to withstand social pressure; Jackson focused on her supposed failure to help others; Moore questioned the wholesomeness of Dickinson's life; early on, Plath attempted to neutralize Dickinson as a rival, while exaggerating the sadomasochistic erotics that inform Dickinson's "Master" construct; Bishop found her an overly demanding friend. Reading Dickinson, these poets affirmed particular versions of themselves, as Dickinson did when writing about her personal heroine, the witchy "Anglo-Florentine" Elizabeth Barrett Browning (*Fr* 600). Which is not to deny that effective self-representation in poetry is also gender performance, that gender performance in poetry is a form of choosing traditions.

Feminist critics of American poetry have tended to define masculine and feminine literary traditions as mutually exclusive, but given the robustness of Dickinson's critical heritage, I assume that the poetry of Moore, Plath, and Bishop—like that of Dickinson herself, and of Rukeyser, Rich, and Susan Howe—oscillates between gendered traditions, which are themselves hybrids of various emotions, forms, and allegiances. Increasingly, feminist literary critics describe gender as a social construction that, in Rukeyser's words, can be imaginatively neutralized "to some extent." Therefore, I follow through on a claim advanced by Sandra Gilbert and Susan Gubar, in their important *No Man's Land* trilogy. Emphasizing gendered anxieties of authorship as constitutive of literary modernism, Gilbert and Gubar show that modernist women writers in search of cultural authority responded powerfully to male voices, but they tend to minimize conflict among women.[39] Betsy Erkkila's *The Wicked Sisters* fills in this gap, and I build on the reconsideration of tradition announced in her subtitle, *Women Poets, Literary History, and Discord.*[40]

Moreover, I am indebted to other studies of the sexual poetic for which Dickinson serves as compass and chart, such as Cheryl Walker's *The Nightingale's Burden: Women Poets and American Culture Before 1900* (1982); Alicia Suskin Ostriker's *Stealing the Language: The Emergence of Women's Poetry in*

America (1986); Joanne Feit Diehl's *Women Poets and the American Sublime* (1990); Timothy Morris's *Becoming Canonical in American Literature* (1995); Cynthia Hogue's *Scheming Women: Poetry, Privilege, and the Politics of Subjectivity* (1995); Sabine Sielke's *Fashioning the Female Subject: The Intertextual Networking of Dickinson, Moore, and Rich* (1997); Elizabeth A. Petrino's *Emily Dickinson and Her Contemporaries: Women's Verse in America, 1820–1885* (1998); Lesley Wheeler's *The Poetics of Enclosure: American Women Poets from Dickinson to Dove* (2002); Zofia Burr's *Of Women, Poetry, and Power: Strategies of Address in Dickinson, Miles, Brooks, Lorde, and Angelou* (2002); Paula Bernat Bennett's *Poets in the Public Sphere: The Emancipatory Project of American Women's Poetry 1800–1900* (2003); Mary Loeffelholz's *From School to Salon: Reading Nineteenth-Century American Women's Poetry* (2004); and Thomas Gardner's *A Door Ajar: Contemporary Writers and Emily Dickinson* (2006). Despite the uniqueness of each of these works, in all of them, Dickinson signifies (more or less) because of her critique of the traditional gendering of literary history, in which women are objectified, spoken for, and culturally silenced.

Yet unlike the Walt Whitman who was obsessed with his legacy and who explicitly addressed himself to poets to come, Dickinson more typically emphasizes the affective power of language as it concerns herself, rather than her readers in an actual present or imagined future. "What would the Dower be," she writes, "Had I the Art to stun myself / With Bolts – of Melody!" (*Fr* 348). And of her archetypal poet, whom she casually marks as male,

> The Poet – it is He –
> Entitles Us – by Contrast –
> To ceaseless Poverty –
>
> Of Portion – so unconscious –
> The Robbing – could not harm –
> Himself – to Him – a Fortune –
> Exterior – to Time – (*Fr* 446)

Contemporary critics such as Virginia Jackson have reacted strongly against New Critical constructions of Dickinson as a lyric poet "Exterior – to Time," and generalizations about her relationship to time are, to say the least, notoriously difficult to sustain.[41] In "This was a Poet," for example, from which I quoted, the speaker does not claim to *be* exterior to time; rather, she posits exteriority as a utopian goal. Reading poetry, she suggests, insulates her against an impoverished present. But if in reading poetry she feels connected to the immortals, it is less clear that she feels connected to other readers, even if those readers are reading her. Whether they be good, bad, or indifferent interpreters of her language, Dickinson's imagined readers would have the power to violate her "ceaseless Poverty." "Ceaseless Poverty" appeals to her; it disciplines and reorganizes confusion. In this poem, though certainly not always, its gendered contrasts are generative.

That Dickinson ever experienced herself as disorganized is hard to credit today, when none of her markings on paper are readily accepted as casual, accidental, or unimportant. Visually and linguistically, even her "scraps" signify.[42] To avoid confusion, and because of my focus on earlier readers and patterns of response, I usually cite R. W. Franklin's 1999 *The Poems of Emily Dickinson: Reading Edition*, which condenses his 1998 *The Poems of Emily Dickinson: Variorum Edition*. Yet even the *Variorum* is far from universally accepted, and a new Harvard website (edickinson.org) allows visitors to create immediate, individual hypertexts of her handwritten manuscripts.

Given this condition of textual indeterminacy, what would it mean to be an heir or heiress to Dickinson's "experimental method"?[43] Addressing this issue, and anticipating Jackson's *Misery*, Zofia Burr argued in 2002 that "the haunting legacy of Emily Dickinson's life and work has shaped a romantic conception of women's poetry as private, personal, and expressive that has governed the reception of subsequent American women poets." Burr's *Of Women, Poetry, and Power* claims to demonstrate "how the canonization of Dickinson has consolidated limiting assumptions about women's poetry in twentieth-century America."[44] Although her analysis is reductive in its understanding of a sharp distinction between public and private audiences, she raises a question that the women writers in my study address, both directly and indirectly. Is Dickinson's influence a good thing?

Leaving aside the question of Dickinson's rich borrowings from popular and elite transatlantic traditions, it is clear to me that her history of the social life of emotions was grounded in an experience of psychological difference. "I never consciously touch a paint, mixed by another person" (*L* 271), she explained during her most artistically active years, cautioning her correspondent (in this instance Higginson) against locating her in a predictable or predictably gendered literary tradition. He had called her "'Wayward'" (*L* 271). Over time, as she gained confidence in her ability to reorganize and so to sustain those connections that mattered to her most deeply, she found herself needing to write less and, in a particularly lighthearted mood, once signed herself "America" (*L* 1004). Notwithstanding this aberration, her formative, ego-based experience of social and psychological isolation enabled a powerful critique of collective suffering, while the unpredictability of her language has made her available to writers whose subsequent relationships to more multicultural poetries she could not have imagined. To emphasize this point, I invoke the figure of Gwendolyn Brooks, some of whose early poems sound a good deal like Dickinson's and whose attention to female anger and social deviance can also be understood as Dickinsonian. Brooks has acknowledged her early debt to Dickinson, while also insisting, "Emily Dickinson and I are absolutely different in the details of our lives." In 1986, she explained, "I loved her poetry when I was young. I still go back to it from time to time. She was a good poet. She knew how to make a little powerhouse out of a phrase. She would string common words together and make magic. I can appreciate that."[45] Lesley Wheeler insightfully links Brooks and Dickinson through an idiom of enclosure, and Brooks is on record as imagining herself invading Dickinson's space. After the first shock, she writes, Dickinson would have appreciated her hairstyle, her "natural."[46] Detailing these appealing, multicultural connections between Dickinson and African American women poets is part of another project to which I hope to contribute in the future.[47]

In her own time, and as a poet exemplifying the power of strangeness, Dickinson was ambiguously positioned in relation to sentimental structures of feeling that had deep roots in Puritan culture and were sustained with particular vigor in women's writing in the antebellum period. As interpreted by Dickinson, literary sentimentalism reaffirmed family ties, and Dickinson warned Higginson against reading her in this way. "I never had a mother," she told him, "I suppose a mother is one to whom you hurry when you are troubled" (*L* 342b). Describing her aggressive alienation from her family and its religious practices, she further stated, "They are religious – except me – and address an Eclipse, every morning – whom they call their 'Father.' But I fear my story fatigues you – I would like to learn – Could you tell me how to grow – or is it unconveyed – like Melody – or Witchcraft?" (*L* 261).[48]

Granted that some measure of egotism is a precondition for writing poetry and for literary writing in general, Dickinson's "'shunning Men and Women,'" as Higginson phrased it, posed problems for her early readers, as it posed problems for Dickinson herself. Rebuffing his curiosity, she explained, "They talk of Hallowed things, aloud – and embarrass my Dog" (*L* 271).

This attempt to deflect the conversation from her person to her poetry failed to satisfy him. She had already told him about a "terror – since September" she identified as the source of her "palsy" (her nervousness) and her "Verses" (*L* 261, *L* 265). Whether or not Dickinson was exaggerating to get his attention—a distinct possibility—in letters to Higginson and to other members of her small contemporary audience, she frequently emphasized her social isolation and too intimate acquaintance with death. In the new century, Dickinson's supposed self-absorption remained a central problematic of her reception. For example, critic Ella Gilbert Ives, a Mount Holyoke graduate who wrote the first extended essay on Dickinson in the twentieth century, explained in the *Boston Evening Transcript* in 1907 that Dickinson was "arrogantly shy." Although Ives declared that her curiosity was satisfied by a visit to "'the house behind the hedge,'" it turns out that Ives had not ceased to wonder why, not really. Despite her wit, Dickinson was "the loneliest figure in the world of letters."[49]

In *Our Emily Dickinsons*, my goal is less to unsettle the claims about Dickinsonian physical, mental, and emotional isolation—in Rukeyser's terms, her problem of being cut off—than to demonstrate their importance in constituting the myths of identity through which Dickinson has been read by American audiences and by women poets in particular. Moore, I will suggest, had a conversion experience; Plath died before she had time, but her interest in Dickinson's inner strength was growing; Bishop liked Dickinson better after meeting her in the Johnson edition, but as she explained to her friend Robert Lowell, Dickinson could still set her teeth on edge. There was a lot at stake for Bishop in identifying herself with the Dickinson to whom she was frequently compared, as was Moore, as was Plath. Moore did not seem to mind at all, Bishop resented the comparison, and Plath was thrilled. Yet at journey's end, versions of Rukeyser's question reverberated for all these poets with special urgency. To what extent are we free to choose our own traditions? Let me rephrase the question. If we read for both text and context, is it still possible to "dwell in Possibility – / A fairer House than Prose?" (*Fr* 466). Reading for biographically precise connections, in Chapter 1, I will show that for women poets in Dickinson's sphere, there existed the immediate possibility of cultural relevance, especially if they also committed themselves to prose. But what did it take to organize a multigenre literary career in which cultural relevance was no shame? I turn now to Helen Hunt Jackson, whose canny example has much to teach us about the inner workings of the networks Dickinson both mobilized and didn't.

Chapter 1

Helen Hunt Jackson
and Dickinson's Personal Publics

I hope some day, somewhere I shall find you in a spot where
we can know each other. I wish very much that you would
write to me now and then, when it did not bore you. I have a
little manuscript volume with a few of your verses in it—and
I read them very often—You are a great poet—and it is a
wrong to the day you live in, that you will not sing aloud.
When you are what men call dead, you will be sorry you were
so stingy.

—March 20, 1876

What portfolios of verses you must have.—

It is a cruel wrong to your "day & generation" that you
will not give them light.—If such a thing should happen as
that I should outlive you, I wish you would make me your
literary legatee & executor. Surely, after you are what is called
"dead," you will be willing that the poor ghosts you have left
behind, should be cheered and pleased by your verses, will you
not?—You ought to be.—I do not think we have a right to
with hold from the world a word or a thought any more than
a *deed*, which might help a single soul.

—September 5, 1884

In a strongly gendered literary culture, what did it take to become a writer who used her personal traumas for the greater good? Helen Hunt Jackson thought she knew. In the letters quoted above, she urges Dickinson to be more compassionate and fully present. Eerily, she suggests that a dead Dickinson will regret her miserliness, her stubborn social isolation, her public silence. But what aspects of Dickinson's poetry did Jackson admire and why? To understand what was at stake for each of them in their mainly long-distance friendship, I turn now to the beginning of Jackson's career and to her interactions with the readers who were potentially Dickinson's as well.

Becoming "H. H."

In the bitterly cold winter of 1866, Helen Hunt met Thomas Wentworth Higginson in Newport, Rhode Island, where she was trying to put the pieces of her life back together. War widow and war hero, they bonded quickly, watching for signs of spring. Higginson kept assiduous records of the weather and, in her own way, so did Helen. He was handsome, gregarious, and eminently well-connected; she seemed cheerful (unlike his invalid wife Mary) and was certainly outspoken; in her youth, she had been a belle. As their friendship deepened, the pace of her literary productivity quickened. Drawing on Higginson's energies and on her own connections, she published poems of sorrow, domestic advice columns, regionalist travel sketches, book reviews, and a free-standing little book for children that reworks the prodigal son motif. *Bathmendi: A Persian Tale* is a pun-filled prose fable about a family of four brothers, among them the poet "Sadder," who roams the Orient looking for "Bathmendi," or happiness. After many horrific adventures, Sadder and his brethren discover that happiness is best found at home.[1]

"Home" was a problematic concept for "H. H.," whose childhood losses (she was an orphan) were compounded by the more recent bereavements. But her efforts paid off in 1869 when the *Atlantic Monthly*, which had rejected poem after poem, published her verse fable "Coronation," in which a beggar teaches a king how to live. In this dreamscape, power does not buy happiness, and kings, who arouse anxieties about powerful men, can be replaced.[2] Emerson admired both the poem and her persistence, and she returned the favor with "Tribute," which speaks back to his "Days," in which a humbled speaker fails to realize his "morning wishes." In Jackson's mid-summer "Tribute," a deferential daughter of time determines to do better:

> Midway in summer, face to face, a king
> I met. No king so gentle and so wise.
> He calls no man his subject; but his eyes,
> In midst of benediction, questioning,
> Each soul compel. A first-fruits offering
> Each soul must owe to him whose fair land lies
> Wherever God has his. No white dove flies
> Too white, no wine too red and rich, to bring.
> With sudden penitence for all her waste,
> My soul to yield her scanty hoards made haste,
> When lo! they shrank and failed me in that need,
> Like wizard's gold, by worthless dust replaced.
> My speechless grief, the king, with tender heed,
> Thus soothed: "These ashes sow. They are true seed."
> O king! in other summer may I stand
> Before thee yet, the full ear in my hand![3]

In "Tribute," Jackson's identification not only with "speechless grief" but with the power to compel is evident. As an astute reviewer noted in the *Springfield Republican*, "This author . . . does not find in equality and individuality all that her soul prompts her to seek."[4]

Encouraged by her publications in middlebrow and elite periodicals, and by her personal popularity in genteel literary circles in Newport and New York, by 1870 "H. H" was eager to consolidate her gains in poetry, the art she prized most highly at the time. Thus, when the Boston publisher James T. Fields tried to dissuade her from gathering her periodical publications into a book, she agreed to pay for the stereotype plates herself. Her gamble paid off and *Verses* went into a second edition. When the *Nation*'s reviewer found the volume, despite some merits, "fatiguing" because of "a tension of feeling incompatible with prettiness," she abandoned her mask of feminine humility and attempted to publish a rebuttal.[5] Higginson, who remained her most sympathetic reader, welcomed this "new poetess" in the *Woman's Journal*, where he classified her variety of subjects and tones. Far from faulting her want of feminine "prettiness," he praised her as "a feminine knight."[6]

To the extent that "H. H." was a woman warrior, however, her politics remained paradoxically tied to middle-class norms of respectability, and she devised aesthetic strategies to test their limits. An allegory published in *Scribner's Monthly* in December 1870 demonstrates her skill at both preserving and troubling the patriarchal status quo. "The Abbot Paphnutius" extends and complicates the wanderlust of *Bathmendi*, of "Coronation" (in which a king sheds his heavy burdens by eloping with a beggar), and of the subversive subplot of "Tribute." "The Abbot" takes a self-scourging, sensitive intellectual into the (disguised, literary) marketplace, where he hopes to find a brother. Instead, he is desperately confused by what he sees and hears. "Cunning night" has "spread and lit her snares / For souls made weak by weariness and cares," and the fastidious Abbot's defenses against temptation and more specifically against lust begin to crumble:

> With secret shudder, half affright, half shame,
> Close cowled, he mingled in the babbling throng,
> And with reluctant feet was borne along
> To where, by torches' fitful glare and smoke,
> A band of wantons danced, and screamed, and spoke
> Such words as fill pure men with shrinking fear;
> "Good Lord deliver me! Can he be here,"
> The frightened Abbot said, "the man I seek?"

From out of this nightmarish crowd there emerges a drunken flute player who accosts the fearful abbot "with ribald laughter, clutching him by gown / And shoulder." Finding renewed courage in conversation, the abbot refuses to believe that the musician is as bad as he seems. With some prodding, the musician reveals that he once rescued a woman from captivity and gave her "three hundred pieces of good gold to free / Her husband and her sons from *slavery*" (italics mine). Nevertheless, the flute player remains faithful to his lurid past and the downcast, failed reformer returns to the cloister to go about his "patient, silent ways." Three days later, he hears a low rapping on the cloister door. Enter the chastened musician, at which miraculous sight "Paphnutius rose, / His pale face kindled red with joyful glows." Although the other monks are angered by the presence of a vagabond, brotherhood prevails. The moral is that "publicans and sinners may be saints" and that saints may be secret sinners.[7] Again, the prodigal son, again the assimilation of an unruly sexual past. Again, the partial reconstruction of a decimated family. In one sense, patriarchal religious authority is validated; in another, it is democratized and transformed.

For "H. H." in the early stages of her career, patriarchal authority, feminized and liberalized, was incarnated not only by Emerson but also by Higginson, an unchurched Unitarian minister who tended toward the even more liberal Universalist creed.[8] In 1849, he had been forced out of his Newburyport, Massachusetts, pulpit because of his extreme abolitionism; he resigned to avoid being fired. Higginson explained, "I do not wish to *be* a fanatic,—but I have no fear of being called so. There are times and places where Human Feeling is fanaticism,—times and places where it seems that a man can only escape the charge of fanaticism by being a moral iceberg."[9] In 1854, he tried to rescue the fugitive slave Anthony Burns from a Boston courthouse, and Thoreau praised him as "the only Harvard Phi Beta Kappa, Unitarian minister, and master of seven languages who has led a storming party against a federal bastion with a battering ram in his hands."[10] In 1857, he headed the list of eighty-nine men who called for a Massachusetts Disunion Convention to consider "the practicality, probability and expediency of a separation between the free and slave states."[11] Like most members of her New Englandish social circle, Jackson had been a Unionist and her husband, Major Edward Hunt, had given his life for the cause. Higginson nevertheless explained, "She was by temperament fastidious, and therefore conservative. On the great slavery question she had always, I suspect, taken regular-army views; she liked to have colored people about her as servants, but was disposed to resent anything like equality."[12]

In the first decade of her poetry career, "H. H." repeatedly troped on various forms of servitude and of slavery (as she did in "The Abbot Paphnutius"), but with several exceptions she rarely wrote about the racial politics of the Civil War or the racial injustices of Reconstruction. Thus, the new and expanded *Verses* of 1873 does not complicate the repressed racial politics of the earlier volume; rather, it demonstrates her continuing eagerness to export the problem—to locate it in a vaguely mythological past.[13] In 1874, however, the orientalism of *Bathmendi*, the story of the wandering poet, became significantly more complex when she published *The Story of Boon*, which is loosely grounded in her encounters with Anna Leonowens, who taught the wives and children of Mongkut, King of Siam. As Virginia Jackson explains, "*The Story of Boon* is an especially interesting example of [her] attempt to appeal to a female readership at the same time that she rather exhibitionistically portrayed depths of sadomasochistic passion and transcendental literary

Figure 3. Thomas Wentworth Higginson in an 1865 photograph taken in Newport, Rhode Island, where Helen Hunt met him during the dark days of her bereavement. They became close friends.

ambition—all in the form of a postbellum, post-abolitionist, postcolonial, Reconstruction verse narrative about sexual slavery in tetrameter couplets."[14]

This twenty-six-page verse drama was not appreciated by *Scribner's Monthly*. In "Some Recent Women Poets," an anonymous reviewer assessed Jackson's place in "the republic of letters," explaining that her strength lay elsewhere. "What H. H., as we think, ought to have asked herself, and what we, in explaining to ourselves her failure, *have* asked, is: 'Were her powers of a kind adapted to the dramatic narration of a very dramatic event in a poem of this length?' Judging from her collected poems, we should have concluded that they were not." Comparing Jackson to her only American rival, Julia Ward Howe, the reviewer contended that her poems were both "stronger" and more "distinctively feminine": those "which arise from the events of women's and children's life, possess an intense, indefinable aroma which could not have been exhaled from any masculine mind." Unlike many women poets, Jackson, having entered deeply "into the vicissitudes of womanly life, the joys and griefs of wifehood and maternity," was able to see beyond her suffering. Quoting her poem "Joy," he explained,

> There is a deep and sustaining joy in her poetry which is not found elsewhere in women's poetry—a joy, nevertheless, that recognizes its own foundations as being based

> "On adamant of pain,
>   Before the earth
> Was born of sea, before the sea,
> Yea, and before the light."[15]

Cast as a dialogue between an "I" who is searching for peace and Joy itself, the poem emphasizes the value of willful forgetting. Yet the *Scribner's* reviewer noted that "to pick flowers to pieces, even in the interests of critical science, is not a grateful task." An overreaching and a lack of self-restraint threatened Jackson's "high philosophy of life."

The review I have been quoting clarifies the standards by which women poets were judged in the middlebrow periodical press, as represented by *Scribner's* and its powerful editor, J. G. Holland, who was an early friend of Emily Dickinson and her family. Strong but not too strong, delicate but not too delicate—this was evidently a conversation not only about poetry and personality but also about woman's sphere. Whereas *Scribner's* faulted Jackson for her lack of self-restraint, the more liberal *Galaxy* found her too high-minded, too educated, too genteel. "To be popular," the reviewer advised,

> Poetry must stir the blood, make the pulse beat quicker, and kindle some of those feelings which are common to ordinary humanity into a temporary conflagration. It is not this kind of poetry which "H. H." writes. It is not the love which maddens the brain, or fires the blood, or makes the heart faint, which she likes to describe; it is the love which renounces its own happiness for something higher. . . . In speaking of the poems of love in the volume, we must not be understood as implying that there are no others; for "H. H." includes in her range most human emotions—always with the limitation, that they are the emotions of the educated, the refined, and of those who are born so, rather than of those who obtain or ought to obtain both education and refinement against their wiles, like most of us.[16]

Jackson's poetry could not be expected to appeal to "the dark, morose, dreamy, determined, ambitious, and dangerous classes." Nevertheless, the *Galaxy* found the verses well worth reading "for their finish and delicacy of sentiment." Other reviewers agreed that Jackson's appeal was more to the head than to the heart, that unlike Elizabeth Barrett Browning, to whom she was frequently compared, there was less "range of imagination." On the other hand, remarked a reviewer who classified Jackson's poetry into seven types, Jackson was "more compact and symmetrical."[17]

Although there was some general recognition that Jackson excelled at sonnets, readers such as Higginson understood that beneath the poetry's formal finish and delicacy of sentiment there was something passionate and untamed. The "Dedication" to both of the books called simply *Verses* hints at an unconventional erotic life, as the speaker shuttles between loss and desire, which "will always be / One more sweet secret thing 'twixt thee and me." Did she have him in mind when she wrote it?

> When children in the summer weather play,
> Flitting like birds through sun and wind and rain,
> From road to field, from field to road again,
> Pathetic reckoning of each mile they stray

They leave in flowers forgotten by the way;
Forgotten, dying, but not all in vain,
Since, finding them, with tender smiles, half pain,
Half joy, we sigh, "Some child passed here to-day."
Dear one,—whose name I name not lest some tongue
Pronounce it roughly,—like a little child
Tired out at noon, I left my flowers among
The wayside things. I know how thou hast smiled,
And that the thought of them will always be
One more sweet secret thing 'twixt thee and me.[18]

Exploiting the authority of motherhood, Jackson positions a playful, child-identified woman on the margins of domesticated, middle-class discourse. The secret sorrows of her past can be contained through the sublimations of form, her voice insists, as she dedicates a poem, a book, and a career to a reader-lover needing protection from the world's rough tongues. "In these verses," Higginson wrote in the *Atlantic*, "there is great freshness of imagination, and an intensity of feeling unsurpassed by any woman since Elizabeth Barrett Browning. There is never any diffuseness, but more commonly an excess of concentration."[19] Jackson's intensity disturbed him, and we can only speculate about how that "excess of concentration" affected their intimate friendship. At first she found him "lacking in the truest flavor of manhood."[20] Then, as biographer Kate Phillips explains, "She seems to have developed intense feelings for her mentor, feelings that Anna Mary Wells, the one Higginson biographer who has looked into this matter, believes were reciprocated."[21] After her death, he wrote, "There was an utterly exotic and even tropical side of her nature, strangely mingled with the traits that came from her New England blood."[22] And in a commemorative poem, he announced that here was a poet who could "Teach new love-thoughts to Shakespere's Juliet fair, / New moods to Cleopatra."[23] She was, he summarized, "the most brilliant, *impetuous*, and thoroughly individual woman of her time" (italics mine).[24]

An Everlasting Talker

Helen Maria Fiske Hunt Jackson's individuality was hard won. She was born in Amherst in the fall of 1830, as was Dickinson. An "everlasting talker" who was "inclined to question the authority of everything," as a child Helen was mischievous, boisterous, and robust, whereas Dickinson, although noted for her wit, was already frailer and more self-contained.[25] Both were the daughters of professional men: Edward Dickinson was a successful lawyer; Nathan Welby Fiske a proselytizing minister-professor. On the subject of career, Nathan's loving wife Deborah tried to console him. "'I am as sick as you are of your connection with Amherst College,'" she wrote, "'You work very hard, and get *no thanks*, nothing but your daily bread and *insults*.'"[26] At the Fiskes, the alphabet of love was more fully revealed than it was at the Dickinsons, and Nathan and Deborah were openly affectionate with each other. "To have a companion, an equal, whom you love & by whom you are loved, who is one with yourself in every dear interest for time & eternity," Nathan wrote, is "blessedness." "As to prayer for you," wrote Deborah, "I shall as soon forget to pray for myself."[27]

The cherished only child of a well-to-do Boston merchant, Deborah Vinal Fiske was compassionate, playful, and "sincerely pious." Quite unlike Emily Norcross Dickinson, she was a sparkling letter writer who published children's stories in the *Youth's Companion*, in which, as biographer Kate Phillips puts it, her "comic sensibility and sympathy for children almost entirely overwhelm the moral lessons she wishes to impart."[28] Yet Deborah Fiske contended with tuberculosis, a disease rampant in New England at the time, and her life was cut short before she was forty. As her strength failed, she became concerned about her ability to educate Helen at home, and in the fall of 1841, when she was ten, Helen was sent to the first of several boarding schools, this one in nearby Hadley. In a variety of living arrangements away from home, Helen was adaptable and comparatively carefree until the loss of the mother whom she remembered as "good and wise," "loving, caressing, overflowing," beloved by the whole town and herself loving "the whole world."[29] Then, after her mother's death in 1844, thirteen-year-old Helen began to live with her mother's cousin Martha Hooker, whose husband was an austere Calvinist. Desperately unhappy, she learned to despise the housework demanded of her, was frightened into a temporary religious conversion ("an actual submission of my own will"), and threw herself into her studies.[30] An intellectually precocious student who hated the insistent practical and psychological demands of the Hookers' household, Helen hoped to attend Mount Holyoke Female Seminary, but her critical and demanding father, whom she revered, concluded that Ipswich Female Seminary would be better for "the training of [her] heart & dispositions."[31]

At Ipswich, she chose her courses because she hoped to be useful to him in his work, learning German, improving her Latin, and reading widely in philosophy, but she was unable to experience the sustained religious conversion for which he so ardently prayed. Following the advice of colleagues and physicians, at the end of Helen's first year at the seminary, her father embarked on a trip to Palestine to restore his health, promising that on his return, as Phillips explains, "he would take her back home with him to Amherst and there personally supervise the completion of her education."[32] Fiske began to recover from the tuberculosis and depression that had plagued him since his wife's death when he suddenly succumbed to dysentery in the house of a British medical missionary in Jerusalem. According to Ruth Odell, "He bore his suffering as another evidence of the will of God, who had appointed as a final test that he should suffer and die far from home and friends and relatives."[33] Professor of moral philosophy and metaphysics, Nathan Welby Fiske gave up his earthly fight on May 27, 1847, and was buried on Mount Zion. Years later, Dickinson remembered the words of the tribute published by the former president of Amherst College in his honor: "In Jerusalem he died; on Mount Zion, and near the tomb of David was he buried. . . . Who at death would not love to go up from Jerusalem below, to Jerusalem above?" (*L* 1042n).

Orphaned at sixteen of both parents, Helen dressed in mourning throughout her adolescence. "No words can describe the sensations of loneliness, disappointment and discouragement which weighted down my spirit," she explained to her empathic guardian Julius Palmer, "I felt that I had now no motive to *do*, or even to *live*."[34] Despite her depression, she completed a second year at Ipswich (Dickinson left Mount Holyoke after one) and, beginning in January 1849, attended the Abbott Institute in New York City, a school for the higher education of women. Its directors, the Reverend John S. C. Abbott and his brother Jacob, were graduates of her father's alma mater, Andover Theological Seminar, and John was a graduate of the Bowdoin College class of 1825, which included Nathaniel Hawthorne and Henry Wadsworth Longfellow. They were both prolific authors, and John's example and encouragement inspired Helen to consider a literary career.[35] After graduating, Helen moved to Charlestown, Massachusetts, where she lived in a boardinghouse with her grandfather Vinal, who supported her financially but was only vaguely interested in her welfare, and her sister Ann, who resembled her physically but was less robust. Solitary and at loose ends, she was elated when the Abbotts invited her back to teach, but she lost her position when they decided to devote themselves to full-time writing. After an interval of uncertainty, in the fall of 1851 she moved to Albany to live in the home of her guardian's brother, the Reverend Ray Palmer, who was an important mentor and with whom she continued to correspond in later years. Reading avidly, she translated French, wrote lively letters, and continued to study under his supervision. At a ball that winter, she met the governor's brother, Edward Bissell Hunt, and got married in October 1852, shortly after her twenty-second birthday. As she exulted in her most memorable nature poem, later cited by both Sylvia Plath and Elizabeth Bishop, "O suns and skies and clouds of June, / And flowers of June together, / Ye cannot rival for one hour / October's bright blue weather."[36]

Edward Hunt was a West Point–educated engineer, an intellectual, and a workaholic. Emily Dickinson met him in 1860 and found him fascinating, as did Helen's slightly younger friend Sarah Woolsey, who published poems and the *Katy-Did* books for children under the name "Susan Coolidge."[37] According to Woolsey, Hunt was "an unusually handsome man," endowed with "a nature just, temperate, and kindly."[38] At first Helen was blissfully happy in her marriage, but in 1854 she was devastated by the death of their eleven-month-old son Murray. A second son, Warren Horsford, called "Rennie," was born in 1857, and Helen was a doting mother. During the long periods when she was separated from her husband, who was often stationed in places where she could not or would not join him—in unhealthful Florida, for example—she pursued an aggressive program of self-education, made friends easily, and continued to pride herself on her writing. The Hunts were reunited in 1863, but Edward died that fall in an accident in the Brooklyn Navy Yard while working to perfect a "Sea Miner," a missile of his own design. Eighteen months later, on the day before Lincoln's assassination, Helen lost her beloved Rennie to diphtheria. Turning emphatically to literature to assuage her multiple griefs, that June she published two poems in the *New York Evening Post* under the pseudonym "Marah," the Hebrew word for "bitter," and "the name that the biblical Naomi assumes after the death of her own husband and two sons. 'Call me Mara: for the Almighty hath dealt very bitterly with me,' Naomi says in Ruth 1: 20–21. 'I went out full, and the LORD hath brought me home again empty.' "[39]

After an interval of intense mourning, in which she was haunted by thoughts of self-destruction, the multiply bereaved Helen Hunt moved to Newport, which was already familiar to her from an earlier stay. There she met Higginson and became his protégée; he emphasized the importance of

Figure 4. Major Edward Bissell Hunt in uniform in about 1860. Emily Dickinson said he was the most interesting man she ever saw *(L 342b),* a remark that formed the basis of Josephine Pollitt's unreliable centennial biography, *Emily Dickinson: The Human Background of Her Poetry.* Courtesy Special Collections, Tutt Library, Colorado College, Colorado Springs, Colorado.

Figure 5. The social and self-confident Helen Maria Fiske Hunt in a photograph taken when she was about twenty-five.

"revision and care and conformity to rules of grammar and traditional rhyme schemes." She took his advice seriously and "studied his *Out-door Papers*, a book she described as one of the 'most perfect specimens of literary composition in the English language.'"[40] Faithful John Abbott continued to interest himself in her career and others helped too, including the radical Unitarian clergyman Moncure Conway, whom she knew in Washington and Newport, as well as Charles Dudley Warner, who liked her *Scribner's* review of his essay collection, *My Summer in a Garden*. She wrote to Warner personally, telling him "'how heartily, how tenderly' she had enjoyed his book."[41]

Less than a decade after her literary debut, Jackson was considered by some the leading woman poet in America, and Emerson included five poems by "H. H." ("Thought," "Joy," "Ariadne's Farewell," "Coronation," and "My Legacy") in his 1874 *Parnassus* anthology, the volume that famously excludes Whitman. He mentioned her in the preface as "a lady who contents herself with the initials H. H.," noting that her poems "have rare merit of thought and expression, and will reward the reader for the careful attention which they require."[42] Emerson also told friends that he considered "H. H." not just the leading woman poet but the leading *poet* on the continent. Higginson repeated this anecdote in an 1879 essay in the *Literary World*, which he reprinted and revised for his *Short Studies of American Authors*, noting that Emerson particularly admired her sonnet "Thought," which captures "the uncontrollableness of thought by will."

> O Messenger, art thou the king, or I?
> Thou dalliest outside the palace gate
> Till on thine idle armor lie the late
> And heavy dews: the morn's bright, scornful eye
> Reminds thee; then, in subtle mockery,
> Thou smilest at the window where I wait,
> Who bade thee ride for life. In empty state
> My days go on, while false hours prophesy
> Thy quick return; at last, in sad despair,
> I cease to bid thee, leave thee free as air;
> When lo, thou stand'st before me glad and fleet,
> And lay'st undreamed-of treasures at my feet.
> Ah! messenger, thy royal blood to buy,
> I am too poor. Thou art the king, not I.[43]

I will return to this theme of the uncontrollableness of thought by will later on but will note in passing that the poem's structure is highly controlled, its syntax and word choice somewhat ponderous.

Given the anticolloquial archaisms Jackson chooses to invoke ("art thou," "Thou dalliest," "Thou smilest," "thou stand'st," and so forth), together with the vaguely medieval scene, all of which contribute to the sound of an armored voice, it may come as no surprise that Jackson's aversion to personal publicity was unusually marked. She told Joseph B. Gilder, editor of the *Critic*, that she refused to be "vivisected for the gratification of a vulgar curiosity." Reacting to a newspaper profile, a genre she particularly abhorred, she complained to Charles Dudley Warner, "They are sickening; insuperable; one is ready to disappear from the face of the earth altogether, to escape them. . . . There is no punishment severe enough for those who write & journals that publish such things."[44] She never read her poems in public, and when she rejected an invitation to speak before the New England Women's Club in 1873, she not only pleaded cowardice but also added, to a woman friend, "You would no doubt quite despise me if you had the least idea, how foreign to my instincts and tastes, such a thing would be. It is often almost more than I can bear the slight publicity which I have brought upon myself by saying—behind the shelter of initials, and in the crowded obscurity of print—a few of the things I have felt deeply."[45] The friend was Abigail Williams May, a leader among Boston's social reformers and a cofounder of the Women's Club. Even as an Indian rights activist with a government commission, Jackson never gave speeches, and despite the excellence of her own education, she was conflicted about higher education for women. When her favorite niece suffered a nervous breakdown at Vassar, Jackson wrote to her sister Ann Banfield, "Give a woman a good strong healthy body, to be a wife & mother, & bring forth healthy strong children—& you have done not only more for *her*, but more for the world, than if you give her all the languages, sciences, &c on the Vassar programme."[46]

Meanwhile, Jackson's fiction writing career advanced. In a review of her *Saxe Holm Stories*, the *Springfield Republican*'s editor Samuel Bowles announced that "Mrs Hunt stands on the threshold of the greatest literary triumphs ever won by an American woman." Bowles speculated that "one reason why Mrs Hunt does not yet consent to associate her name with the book may be this very intimacy of relation that it holds to herself. She perhaps shrinks from appearing before the world as the originator of characters

which recall so vividly the life of the past."⁴⁷ Ladylike scruples notwithstanding, Jackson drove a hard bargain and believed in getting fair market value
for her wares, explaining to editors that while she wrote for love, she printed
for money. Eventually, she was one of the most financially successful writers
of her day, and as Ruth Odell observes, "When it came to money-making,
she was an ardent feminist."⁴⁸

Although Jackson was not "delicate" in doing what she called "very
serious literary labor," she often drove herself to the breaking point and was
apprehensive about illness, fearing especially tuberculosis, the disease that had
killed her mother.⁴⁹ In November 1873, accompanied by her physician, she
set out for Colorado which, as Phillips explains, was becoming famous "as a
healthful sanctuary for people with respiratory infections and also as a tourist
destination. Jackson hoped to recover there and to find fresh subjects for a
new collection of travel essays."⁵⁰ By January she was writing to William
Hayes Ward, editor of the *Independent*, from a hotel in Colorado Springs,
where she planned to spend the winter and where she met her second husband, William Sharpless Jackson—a banker, railroad executive, and community leader. He was six years younger than she, and Helen was reassured by
his robustness. They married in 1875 in "October's bright blue weather."
Her commemorative poem was published in the *New York Independent* in
November 1878:

> O Suns and skies and clouds of June,
>   And flowers of June together,
> Ye cannot rival for one hour
>   October's bright blue weather,
>
> When loud the bumble-bee makes haste,
>   Belated, thriftless vagrant,
> And Golden-Rod is dying fast,
>   And lanes with grapes are fragrant;
>
> When Gentians roll their fringes tight
>   To save them for the morning,
> And chestnuts fall from satin burrs
>   Without a sound of warning;
>
> When on the ground red applies lie
>   In piles like jewels shining,

And redder still on old stone walls
  Are leaves of woodbine twining;

When all the lovely wayside things
  Their white-winged seeds are sowing,
And in the fields, still green and fair,
  Late aftermaths are growing;

When springs run low, and on the brooks,
  In idle golden freighting,
Bright leaves sink noiseless in the hush
  Of woods, for winter waiting;

When comrades seek sweet country haunts,
  By twos and twos together,
And count like misers hour by hour,
  October's bright blue weather.

O suns and skies and flowers of June,
  Count all your boasts together,
Love loveth best of all the year
  October's bright blue weather.[51]

The Lecture That Changed Her Life

In the next year, Jackson heard a lecture that changed her life even more than did her remarriage. Visiting Boston and listening to the leader of a group of starving Ponca Indians who had been tragically dispossessed from their tribal home in the Dakota Territory and removed against their wishes to Indian Territory (present-day Oklahoma), she found the spiritually uplifting cause for which she felt she had been destined. At the deepest level, she identified with Chief Standing Bear's story of homelessness and bereavement—he had watched helplessly "as over one hundred of his tribe died, including his son."[52] On a smaller scale, she too had watched helplessly over dead children. The woman who had earlier scoffed at reformers explained to Higginson, "I have become what I have said a thousand times was the most odious thing in life, 'a woman with a hobby.'"[53]

As an Indian rights advocate, Jackson was praised by the *New York Times* for her "ripe scholarship" and "facile pen," and for exhibiting "an enthusiasm and a sympathy with the wronged which none but a tender-hearted and just woman can possess."[54] Yet her views were controversial to the extent that they were not ignored, and even her husband was slow to be converted by her crusading zeal. "Dear heart," she wrote, "you ought to be as strong for *justice* to the Indian as you were for *justice* to the Negro. I can't write a word, or work with any heart, if you are not going to feel with me in it all—& I do feel as earnest & solemn a 'call' as ever a human being felt to work for this cause."[55] Whatever his reservations about her politics, William loved her enough to realize that this was work his "excited" wife needed to do, and he did not object when, several weeks later, she moved to New York City to begin research on *A Century of Dishonor: A Sketch of the United States Government's Dealings with Some of the Indian Tribes*, which she completed in four months.[56] Inspired as she had not been since the early days of her poetry career, in writing this account of "national shame," Jackson worked herself into a state of nervous exhaustion. After completing it, she left for a European tour with old friends from the days of her first marriage. Higginson read proof in her absence.[57]

During this recuperative interval, Jackson was far from idle. As she explained in a letter written from Bergen, Norway, thanking her friend Anne Lynch Botta for sending along a big batch of newspaper clippings "about my beloved Indians," "Nothing puts the Indians out of my mind. Except I know that there is nothing to be done this summer." Proposing "unless William objects" to fight it out "til something is accomplished," she explained, "I have great hopes of [President James A.] Garfield."[58] Over the course of the next four years, her forays into the wilderness of American Indian politics took many forms. For example, in 1883 she went to Southern California as a "special agent" for the Commissioner of Indian Affairs and completed a *Report on the Condition and Needs of the Mission Indians of California*.[59] But her appeals to Congress, to government officials, and to the American public were having less of an impact than she would have liked. Still "excited . . . on this matter," in December she began *Ramona*, the novel in which, as she explained to *Californio* friends and to Higginson, "I have sugared my pill, and it remains to be seen if it will go down."[60] Jackson further explained, "The success of it—if it succeeds—will be that I do not even suggest any Indian history,—till the interest is so aroused in the heroine—and hero— that people will not lay the book down. There is but one Indian in the story."[61] By "Indian," she meant the full-blooded Indian, Alessandro; the surviving hero, Felippe, is of Spanish descent.

"It was sheep-shearing time in Southern California; but sheep-shearing was late at the Señora Moreno's. The Fates had seemed to combine to put it off."[62] Thus opens *Ramona*, Jackson's most enduring work. Sentimental and realistic, regional and national, the novel "sugarcoats" its multicultural ambitions in ways that are familiar to readers of Jackson's literary model *Uncle Tom's Cabin*. Like Eliza and Cassy, Ramona is light skinned. She has "just enough of olive tint in her complexion to underlie and enrich her skin without making it swarthy. Her hair was like her Indian mother's, heavy and black, but her eyes were like her father's, steel-blue. Only those who came very near to Ramona knew . . . that her eyes were blue, for the heavy black eyebrows and long black lashes so shaded and shadowed them that they looked black as night."[63] Her beloved Alessandro is physically tall, strong, only somewhat literate, sexually inexperienced, and emotionally vulnerable. He and Ramona are made for each other, but her deceitful guardian, who "looked simply like a sad, spiritual-minded old lady, amiable and indolent," has other plans:

> Her voice heightened this mistaken impression. She was never heard to speak either loud or fast. There was at times even a curious hesitancy in her speech, which came near being a stammer, or suggested the measured care with which people speak who have been cured of stammering. It made her often appear as if she did not know her own mind: at which people sometimes took heart; when, if they had only known the truth, they would have known that the speech hesitated solely because the Señora knew her mind so exactly that she was finding it hard to make the words convey it as she desired, or in a way best to attain her ends.[64]

Although Jackson's ambivalent identification with this insincere "genius" who has "unlimited power over all persons around her" is evident throughout the novel, the compelling romance plot hinges on the sufferings of the younger generation: Ramona, whose marriage is delayed and then destroyed; Alessandro, who is maddened by the strain of being unable to provide for his family and his people; and the Señora's son and heir Felipe, the character with power to tame his mother, if only he would use it. In an uncomfortably incestuous moment, the Señora kisses the sword-belt he is about to buckle on, which he inherited from his father, "a Mexican officer and gentleman," whom he greatly resembles. From broken treaty promises to subtler, privatized larcenies that betray a motherless daughter, the novel weaves together multiple fates and nationalities in its critique of what happens "In the Name of the Law" (the original title).[65] The reviews were generally favorable, and as Phillips notes, Jackson studied them eagerly.[66]

"Pity me," Dickinson wrote her long-distance ally in March 1885, "I have finished Ramona," adding hyperbolically, "Would that like Shakespere, it were just published," which both underscores and unsettles the praise (*L* 976). *Ramona*, Dickinson suggests, is of its time—mutable and mortal, whereas her beloved Shakespeare is eternally new. Yet this fateful political romance has impacted many lives and has never been out of print. As early as 1887, Cuban poet José Marti translated the novel into Spanish; according to one count, it exists today in most known languages. Michele Moylan explains,

> Not only have library patrons read copies of the novel into tatters, but the variety of films, plays, and pageants the novel inspired further reflects the story's popularity. After D. W. Griffith's first film adaption of the novel in 1910, *Ramona* was dramatized on film three more times. One film (1928, starring Dolores Del Rio and Warner Baxter) ushered in the age of talkies, and one (1936, starring Loretta Young and Don Ameche) the age of Technicolor. By 1914 Carlyle Channing Davis and William A. Alderson, authors of *The True Story of "Ramona,"* could account for fifty-three theater versions, and many others have since appeared. And a springtime "Ramona pageant," described in a 1984 full-page *Newsweek* article as a "breathtaking piece of entertainment," has played to sell-out crowds in California almost every year since 1923.[67]

To this list can be added "Ramona," the memorable lyric which topped the charts in 1928, and a Mexican telenovela. What is interesting, then, is the feeling that motivates Dickinson's "Pity me" complaint.

In fact, Dickinson had already used the double-edged Shakespeare metric when she suggested to Higginson in 1871 that although "Mrs. Hunt's" poems were "stronger" than any written by women since "Mrs – Browning" and "Mrs Lewes" (George Eliot), no one could rival Shakespeare. "Literature," she pronounced oracularly, remains "firm," and "truth like Ancestor's Brocades can stand alone" (*L* 368). Using Shakespeare as the benchmark of immortality, as she was to do in her letter praising *Ramona*, Dickinson barely disguises her contempt for contemporary culture. Under these circumstances, why should anyone write, including herself? Her contempt may also imply that she aspires to be Shakespeare's only begotten daughter.[68] Analyzing how and why Jackson became the catalyst for some of Dickinson's more extreme denials of ambition will further illuminate the historic specificity of gendered literary practices, Jackson's skill at negotiating those practices, and Dickinson's emerging reputation as a poet whose supposed insularity isolated her from the life of her time.

A Little Manuscript Volume

Helen Maria Fiske Hunt and Emily Elizabeth Dickinson knew each other as children but were not close friends. Richard B. Sewall explains, "[Helen's] parents . . . took her out of Amherst Academy when she was eleven and sent her away to school. This was the beginning of an unsettled and knockabout youth."[69] After her mother's death when she was thirteen, she was rarely in "dear old Amherst," and as one of Dickinson's school friends remembers, she was not part of the literary circle at Amherst Academy that produced *Forest Leaves*, the magazine to which Dickinson contributed droll bits, nor of the Shakespeare Club to which Emily Dickinson belonged.[70] She did return for occasional visits, especially at the August commencement, and Henry Root, an Amherst College student whom she met in 1851 before her move to Albany, became a close friend.[71] Additionally, Helen and her first husband, Edward Hunt, dined with the Dickinson family in August 1860, and Emily Dickinson was impressed by his wit—he told her that her dog, who was waiting for table scraps, understood gravitation. She visited Amherst again in December and in July 1861, but after the July visit, she wrote to her sister, "I saw little of the Amherst people except just to speak to them on the street or in the exercises."[72] Since Dickinson was no longer attending public functions and her parents did not have their usual Commencement party, they are unlikely to have met.

Higginson reintroduced them as writers some time after "H. H." moved into Mrs. Dame's boarding house in Newport in early 1866. He showed her the poems he had received from his (as yet unmet) Amherst correspondent.

He was curious about Dickinson's life and ambitions, but "H. H." "could not tell [him] much." She was, however, "deeply interested" in the letters and copied some of the poems into "a little manuscript volume."[73] She may have contacted Dickinson when she was visiting Amherst in 1868, and Dickinson may have responded. There is an envelope in Dickinson's handwriting of about 1868 addressed to her in Amherst but never sent. Another unsent envelope is addressed, about 1872, to Bethlehem, New Hampshire, where "H. H." was spending the summer. In the summer of 1873, when she was hoping that a move would help to restore her physically and mentally, Dickinson recommended an Amherst boardinghouse. Since "H. H." knew that Dickinson never left her home, it is surprising that she would have trusted her recommendation. After the brief visit, a distressed Helen wrote to her sister, "Dearest Annie":

> I myself have had a most disastrous week at Amherst—but am grateful to have escaped with my life.—It is the only step I have taken this summer for which I reproach myself—the going there. But I was so uncomfortable here [in New Hampshire] & thought I had gained enough to make it safe to try this change—& I wrote to Emily Dickinson who has two cousins boarding in the house, & she wrote me that they said there was no dampness there at all!—and they were "timid themselves" she added—But it was not only damp—it was close and stifling.

After more complaints about the "positive miasm about the house" and fears that her maid had cholera "brought from Amherst," she concluded, "Luckily I could get back into my old room [in New Hampshire]—& so comfortable does the frying pan feel after the fire. . . . I can't help wondering why I was permitted to go to A.—I have lost all I had gained here—& more too, I am afraid."[74]

There seems to have been no further direct contact between them until October 1875, when Dickinson suddenly congratulated her on her remarriage to William Sharpless Jackson, which was reported in the national press. She wrote, "Have I a word but Joy," signed it "E. Dickinson," and then added, "Who fleeing from the Spring / The Spring avenging fling / To Dooms of Balm" (L 444). Jackson responded, "I do wish I knew just what 'dooms' you meant," and then, "I hope some day, somewhere I shall find you in a spot where we can know each other. I wish very much that you would write to me now and then, when it did not bore you. I have a little manuscript volume with a few of your verses in it—and I read them very often—You are a great poet—and it is a wrong to the day you live in, that you will not sing aloud. When you are what men call dead, you will be sorry you were so stingy" (*L* 444a). Given the thinness of the friendship up to this time, it is all the more remarkable that Jackson took it upon herself to chastise Dickinson for her difference.

The little manuscript volume has disappeared, but we can make some progress toward reconstructing it, given that it was drawn from Higginson's collection. Higginson remembered her copying it around 1866, but his memory may have been faulty. (He later asked Mabel Loomis Todd whether he had visited Dickinson once or twice, having no distinct memory of the second visit.) Erring on the side of caution, let us assume that Jackson's copying extended until she left the East in November 1873. By then, Higginson had received some fifty-five poems. Many address the theme of physical, metaphysical, social, and psychological compulsion. For example, consider "That after Horror – that 'twas *us*" which Higginson received in about late 1862. Dickinson sent only the second stanza:

> The possibility to pass
> Without a Moment's Bell –
> Into Conjecture's presence –
> Is like a face of steel
> That suddenly looks into our's
> With a Metallic Grin –
> The Cordiality of Death
> Who Drills his welcome – in – (*Fr* 243)[75]

Grammatically, this is a single sentence and can be repunctuated as follows:

> The possibility to pass
> Without a Moment's Bell
> Into Conjecture's presence
> Is like a face of steel
> That suddenly looks into our's
> With a Metallic Grin:
> The Cordiality of Death
> Who Drills his welcome in.

Figure 6. Helen Hunt Jackson at around the time of her 1875 remarriage to William Sharpless Jackson, a Colorado businessman. Courtesy Special Collections, Tutt Library, Colorado College, Colorado Springs, Colorado.

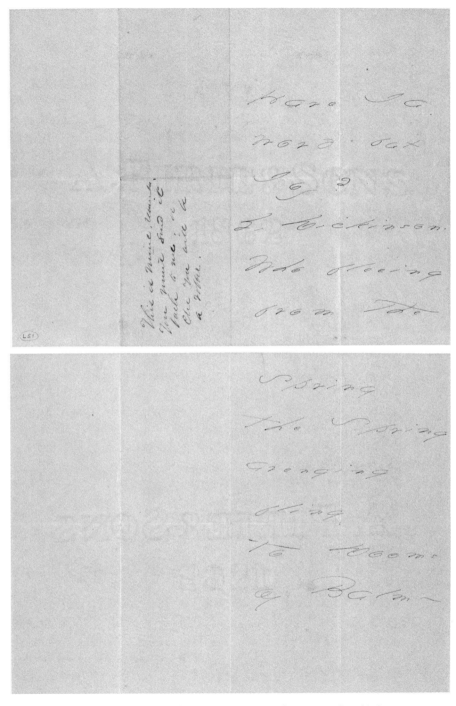

Figure 7. Reading about Jackson's remarriage, Dickinson sent her this letter-poem. A puzzled Jackson sent it back and asked her to explain what kind of dooms she had in mind. By permission of the Houghton Library, Harvard University, Ms Am 1118.4.

Dickinson's dashes serve to arrest the rush of thought, and the complicated play of forward and backward movements is likely to have caught Jackson's attention. In both versions, the shortness of the lines emphasizes the rush of thought, in this case the uncontrollableness of the thought of death, which is both welcomed and feared. No notice, the dislocated voice announces, no notice when the sentries depart, which is what happens in Jackson's "Coronation," when a king lets down his guard to admit a beggar who teaches him how to live. In Freudian terms, the id (figured as a beggar) accosts the superego (figured as a king) precisely because the beggar discerns that the king is an imposter.

> At the king's gate the subtle noon
>   Wove filmy yellow nets of sun;
> Into the drowsy snare too soon
>   The guards fell one by one.
> . . . .
> At the king's gate, the crafty noon
>   Unwove its yellow nets of sun;
> Out of their sleep in terror soon
>   The guards waked one by one.
>
> "Ho here! Ho there! Has no man seen
>   The king?" The cry ran to and fro;
> Beggar and king, they laughed, I ween,
>   The laugh that free men know.
>
> On the king's gate the moss grew gray;
>   The king came not. They called him dead;
> And made his eldest son one day
>   Slave in his father's stead.[76]

I mentioned earlier that "Coronation" was the first of Jackson's poems to be published in the *Atlantic Monthly* and that it was included in Emerson's *Parnassus*. Jackson, I speculate, saw Dickinson as extending the dark romantic compulsions of her own project.

We can gain further insight into Jackson's taste as a reader-editor by examining their later correspondence. After Dickinson sent her the "Dooms of Balm" letter, Jackson boldly sent it back, asking for an explanation. When

Dickinson did not return the missing letter, Jackson objected, "You did not send it back, though you wrote that you would. Was this an accident, or a late withdrawal of your consent? Remember that it is mine—not yours—and be honest." Jackson also thanked her for "not being angry with my impudent request for interpretations" (*L* 444a). Honesty was important to Jackson, as it was to Dickinson, and when Jackson let the correspondence lapse, Dickinson became concerned about having offended her. Rather than assuming that Jackson was busy, Dickinson personalized the silence, the averted face. Most of us have been there—filling the silence with fears that a cherished relationship is about to end. Dickinson expressed those apprehensions in many of her best-loved poems, for example in "My life closed twice before it's close," extant only in a transcription made by Mabel Loomis Todd. Its date cannot be established, and there is something appropriate in that temporal dislocation:

> My life closed twice before it's close;
> It yet remains to see
> If Immortality unveil
> A third event to me,
>
> So huge, so hopeless to conceive
> As these that twice befell.
> Parting is all we know of heaven,
> And all we need of hell. (*Fr* 1773)

Admiring Dickinson for her honesty and for her unpredictable representations of strength and vulnerability, Jackson is likely to have been seduced by "There came a Day at Summer's full," in which inner and outer weathers converge at last:

> There came a Day at Summer's full,
> Entirely for me –
> I thought that such were for the Saints,
> Where Resurrections – be –
>
> The Sun, as common, went abroad,
> The flowers, accustomed, blew,
> As if no soul the solstice passed
> That maketh all things new –

The time was scarce profaned, by speech –
The symbol of a word
Was needless, as at Sacrament,
The Wardrobe, of Our Lord –

Each was to each The Sealed Church,
Permitted to commune this – time –
Lest we too awkward show
At supper of the Lamb.

The Hours slid fast – as Hours will,
Clutched tight, by greedy hands –
So faces on two Decks, look back,
Bound to opposing lands –

And so when all the time had leaked,
Without external sound
Each bound the Other's Crucifix –
We gave no other Bond –

Sufficient Troth, that we shall rise –
Deposed – at length, the Grave –
To that new Marriage,
Justified – through Calvaries – of Love – (*Fr* 325)[77]

The poem's emotional realism is grounded in biblical imagery to which Jackson would have responded. Although she had moved away from the orthodoxy of her youth, the promise of perfect love symbolized by the ritual of communion was part of her heritage, as was the hope that "the Grave" could be "Deposed," or dethroned. "Emigravit," the heroine of Jackson's first novel, proclaims when her life's work is done, "Oh, write of me, not,—'Died in bitter pains / But, Emigrated to another star!'" "Emigravit": Jackson had the word carved on her tombstone.[78]

Still very much alive and several years away from the lecture by Standing Bear to which she responded so deeply, in August 1876 Jackson wrote from Princeton, Massachusetts, where she was staying with her new husband,

My dear Miss Dickinson,
    How could you possibly have offended me? I am sorry that such an idea should have suggested itself to you.

I have often and often thought of sending you a line, but there are only sixty minutes to an hour. There are not half enough.

I enclose to you a circular which may interest you. When the volume of Verse is published in this series, I shall contribute to it: and I want to persuade you to. Surely, in the shelter of such *double* anonymousness as that will be, you need not shrink. I want to see some of your verses in print. Unless you forbid me, I will send some that I have. May I? . . . .

Thank you for writing in such plain letters! Will you not send me some verses?

Truly your friend
Helen Jackson (*L* 476a)

Jackson had come east to see friends and family, to complete arrangements for the publication of *Mercy Philbrick's Choice*, and to conduct research for her next major project. Odell recounts, "She was planning a book to be called *Explorations* which would depict familiar places and scenes under fictitious names, and in which only a map appended would gradually reveal, through its new local phraseology, what the places really were."[79] As the trip was winding down, she spent a "clear but very cold" night on Mount Holyoke, and on her way north, on a "lovely day" in October, she visited Dickinson. Except for the comment on the weather, her diary is laconic: "Drove back to Ashfield by way of Amherst—left Mrs. Warren there—called on E. Dickinson."[80]

During the brief visit, Jackson, who had not seen Dickinson for many years, commented impulsively on her appearance. Afterward, she apologized for her intrusiveness and justified it:

I feel as if I had been very impertinent that day in speaking to you as I did—accusing you of living away from sunlight,—and told you that you looked ill, which is a mortal piece of ill-being, at all times, but truly you seemed so white and mothlike. Your hand felt like such a wisp in mine that you frightened me. I felt like a great ox, talking to a white moth and begging it to come and eat grass with me to see if it could not turn itself into beef! How stupid.—[81]

A comedy of errors ensued. Dickinson wrote Higginson a few days later, asking him what he thought of Jackson's request, but without making it clear that Jackson wanted poems. Thinking that Jackson was inviting her to write fiction, he responded, "It is always hard to judge for another of the bent of inclination or range of talent; but I should not have thought of advising you to write stories, as it would not seem to me to be in your line. Perhaps Mrs. Jackson thought that the change & variety might be good for you: but if you really feel a strong unwillingness to attempt it, I don't think she would mean to urge you" (L 476b). Dickinson was relieved. Interpreting his advice liberally, she felt he had authorized her to say no, and she sent Mary Channing Higginson a Christmas gift of Emerson's *Representative Men*. It was "a little Granite Book you can lean upon" (L 481).

Still, Dickinson felt anxious about letting the other woman down. Apparently their correspondence lapsed in 1877 (or some letters have been lost), but when Dickinson wrote in April 1878 to inquire why Jackson's face was "'averted,'" Jackson apologized and sought to reassure her: "I have never forgotten that you kindly wrote one day, asking if all were well with me: and I have all along meant to write and say 'yes,' if no more." After some amiable chitchat about the difficulties she had been having in fixing up her very "picturesque and cozy little house" in Colorado Springs, she returned to the matter of the poems, though she was lowering her sights and asking now for only "one or two." She also returned to the matter of Dickinson's health, mentioning her friend, the physician Hamilton Cate, who had accompanied her on her arduous journey to Colorado when she was ill years earlier. Jackson wrote, "I wish you would give my love to Doctor Cate—I was about to say 'when you see him,' but you never see anybody! Perhaps however you have improved" (L 573a).[82]

A Masque of Poets

That October, when she was spending several enjoyable months traveling in the East, Jackson returned to the Connecticut Valley, visited friends including Cate and Dickinson, introduced Dickinson to her husband, and again raised the subject of *A Masque of Poets*. Writing the next day from Hartford where she was staying with Charles Dudley Warner, she asked permission to submit "Success" (Fr 112), which she knew by heart. Apparently she and Dickinson had discussed another poem during the forenoon visit, but by the next day Jackson had given up on waiting for her. "Now—will you send me the poem? No—will you let me send the 'Success'—which I know by heart—to Roberts Bros for the Masque of Poets? If you will, it will give me a great pleasure. I ask it as a personal favor to myself—Can you refuse the only thing I perhaps shall ever ask at your hands?" (*L* 573b).

What happened next is unclear, except that Jackson submitted "Success" to Thomas Niles in the nick of time for the book's publication in late November. By then she was back in Colorado Springs and in early December wrote the reluctant author,

> My dear friend,
>   I suppose by this time you have seen the Masque of Poets. I hope you have not regretted giving me that choice bit of verse for it. I was pleased to see that it had in a manner, a special place, being chosen to end the first part of the volume. (*L* 573c)

Whatever the sequence—and Dickinson may have sent her "that choice bit of verse" after Jackson had submitted it in her own handwriting—this poignant and puzzling interchange, which took so long to produce the desired result, opened possibilities for Dickinson with publisher Thomas Niles, with whom she began to correspond. In January, Niles wrote Dickinson that Emerson was being credited with fathering her poem, "wh. as you have doubtless perceived was slightly changed in phraseology" (*L* 573d). Indeed. Either Niles or someone else, most likely the book's editor, George Parsons Lathrop, changed three words, added one, and subtracted one: "clear" became "plain," "burst" became "break," "agonized" became "agonizing"; "the" in line 4 is his, while Dickinson's "and" in line 12 is omitted. In a poem that almost asks us to *count* its words, that's a lot:

> SUCCESS is counted sweetest
>   By those who ne'er succeed.
> To comprehend a Nectar
> Requires the sorest need.
> Not one of all the Purple Host
> Who took the flag to-day,
> Can tell the definition,
> So plain, of Victory,
> As he defeated, dying,
> On whose forbidden ear
> The distant strains of triumph
> Break, agonizing clear. (*A Masque of Poets*)

It goes without saying that house style demanded further changes in punctuation and capitalization. These Niles did not even bother to mention. Yet Dickinson often changed line breaks, words, punctuation, and capitalization in sending poems to friends, and these versions might differ from the version she chose to save for herself.[83] As was her habit, Dickinson wrote a thank you note to Niles. She may have called the book "delightful."[84]

In rapid order and without any further permission, Jackson began to function as Dickinson's editor. Without revealing either her own identity or her friend's, she reviewed *A Masque of Poets* for the *Denver Daily Tribune* and reprinted "Success." As to phraseology, her word choice is identical with the 1862 copy Dickinson sent to Higginson, except that Jackson, following the *Masque* version, also changed "clear" to "plain" in line 8. Evidently neither editor was satisfied with the repetition of "clear," and Jackson unfortunately altered the rhythm by inserting a comma at the end of the penultimate line.

Of the enterprise as a whole, she explained, "It is a book of tantalizing interest. . . . If any one had told us beforehand that in a volume containing poems from nearly all the well known American, and many of the well known English poets of to-day, it would be next to impossible to determine with any degree of accuracy the authorship of the poems, the statement would have seemed preposterous. But such is the fact. Here are seventy-five poems, all of them published now *for the first time*" (italics mine).[85] On this last point, she was incorrect. All her efforts had been devoted to securing a poem that had been published in the *Brooklyn Daily Union* in April 1864, when Dickinson had "lost the use of her eyes." Probably Dickinson herself was unaware of the anonymous publication in a paper to which Amherst had ties, and Jackson would not have appreciated the joke had she known it.[86] Moreover, a note of fatigue crept into her unofficial, post-publication report to Dickinson when she stated, "On the whole, the volume is a disappointment to me" (*L* 573c). In the next year, the correspondence lapsed.

When this happened, Dickinson reminded her that friendship was one of the joys of her life. "Spurn the temerity – / Rashness of Calvary – / Gay were Gethsemene, / Knew we of thee," she wrote in April, hyperbolically comparing herself to Jesus or to one of his followers (*Fr* 1485). In the meantime, Jackson had finished a children's novel, begun a novel she never finished, and lapsed into a depression. But among the poems Jackson might have committed to memory and then selected to publish and to publicize and edit, why the special emphasis on "Success"? Higginson recalled that "H. H. did not know of her poems till I showed them to her (about 1866) and was very little in Amherst after that. But she remembered her at school."[87] If we assume that "H. H." had copied most of the poems for her "little manuscript book" before she sailed for Europe on November 5, 1868, where she remained for fourteen months, she still had a goodly number from which to choose. Based on Ralph Franklin's approximate chronology, Dickinson sent only one poem to Higginson in 1867, none in the period 1868–69, and only one in 1870. Using 1867 as the cutoff point, Jackson had a potential anthology of thirty-three poems. (Before the publication of *A Masque of Poets*, the only poem Dickinson had sent directly to *her* was the quatrain congratulating Jackson on her marriage [*Fr* 1368].) Again I ask, why "Success"?

First, it complements the poems by which Jackson was represented in *A Masque*: "A Woman's Death Wound," "Quatrains," and "Horizon." "Quatrains," for example, reworks the public/private motif in which both she and Dickinson were invested, as does "A Woman's Death Wound" to a lesser degree. "Horizon" hovers between philosophical reflection and nature appreciation and is another outsider poem, a genre in which Dickinson specialized. "Horizon" puns on "dearth" and "death," and asks what the future holds. Post-Christian in tone, it describes a life in quest of a center and offers as an imagined possibility a traditional consolation Dickinson's "Success" forecloses. Jackson: "For threescore years from gray to rose, / From rose to gray, it [the sweet center] shines and saves / Our lives from dearth. / Who knows, who knows / If we shall see it in our graves."[88] Dickinson: "defeated – dying . . . agonized and clear."

Second, Jackson knew that her chances of being allowed to publish anything with a strong confessional effect were slight. On that basis she would rule out a poem such as "Before I got my eye put out" (*Fr* 336), which seems to be revisiting a personal trauma. Indeed, Higginson rarely got such poems, most of which Dickinson kept for herself.[89] Engaging in a severe act of self-editing, she did not send him her most psychologically traumatized poems. His cache consisted of poems that can loosely be classified as spiritual, meditative, and religious, on the one hand, and responses to nature on the other. ("Before I got my eye put out" can be read as an anti-nature poem, in that the persona is excluded by her loss of vision from the creaturely natural order.) Nor did she send him love poems, which is one of the reasons he was later shocked by the eroticism of "Wild Nights" (*Fr* 269). There is one notable exception to her rule against sending him love poems. Because its occasion bears directly on Dickinson's definition of success for her art, I will examine it further.

Higginson's Cache

During the years between April 1862 and May 1886, years in which they met just twice, Dickinson sent Higginson over seventy letters and ninety-eight poems. She drafted five more, which were never sent. Numerically speaking, he was the second most important member of her carefully chosen personal public, the first being her sister-in-law Susan, whose knowledge of the practical politics of literary editing in no way equaled his. Addressing Higginson not only as "Dear friend" but as "Sir" and "Preceptor" and "Master," at times Dickinson expressed transparently anxious feelings, minimizing her ambitions to deflect criticism but also, as she imagined, to please him and to keep him interested. She was concerned that he would desert her, which did not stop her from experimenting with her role in their relationship, signing herself "Your friend," "Your Gnome," "Barabbas," "Your Scholar," "E. Dickinson," and just plain "Dickinson," employing the latter for the first time in 1866, in a letter beginning "Whom my Dog understood could not elude others" (L 316). Carlo had understood her, even if he had not.[90] And there were letters with no signature, such as the following, in response to one of his many essays in the *Atlantic*,

> Bringing still my "plea for Culture,"
> Would it teach me now? (L 323)[91]

With her eleven-word letter, Dickinson enclosed a poem she had sent in one form or another to her cousins Louisa and Fanny Norcross and to her sister-in-law Susan several years before. "The Luxury to apprehend" (*Fr* 819) indulges those riotous appetites that Jackson's poetry tends to suppress.

When Higginson visited Amherst in 1870, he was almost overwhelmed by the force of Dickinson's personality. Trying to defend himself against her intensity, he wanted to read her as a character in a novel, for example a novel about dysfunctional New England families by Elizabeth Stoddard, "where each member runs his or her own selves" (L 342a). And he jotted down sayings such as the following:

> "Could you tell me what home is"
> "I never had a mother. I suppose a mother is one to whom you
> hurry when you are troubled."

"I never knew how to tell time by the clock till I was 15. My father
thought he had taught me but I did not understand & I was afraid
to say I did not & afraid to ask any one else lest he should know."
(*L* 342b)

On the basis of this interview and of what he already knew, Higginson concluded that emotional vulnerability prevented Dickinson from sharing her
poems widely. Several years later, he told Lydia B. Torrey in Newport that
"occasionally he has letters from Emily Dickinson . . . containing the loveliest
little delicate bits of poetry imaginable—he said they always reminded him
of skeleton leaves so pretty but *too delicate*,—not strong enough to publish."[92]
An opportunity to meet again arose on December 3, 1873, when he gave
an evening lecture at Amherst College. The announced topic was "After
High School, What?" but the *Record*, the town newspaper, noted sardonically
that the talk "proved to be an argument in favor of woman suffrage."[93] During the day, Higginson, a physical culture buff, was impressed by the Amherst
athletes who struck him as healthier than their Harvard peers. In the afternoon, he spent time at the Homestead. This second interview did not inspire
him to take the careful notes that have come down to us from his earlier visit.
On the whole, though, he enjoyed the trip, the weather was unseasonably
warm, and as he explained to his sisters, "I saw my eccentric poetess Miss
Emily Dickinson who *never* goes outside her father's grounds & sees only
me & a few others. She says, 'there is always one thing to be grateful for—
that one is one's self & not somebody else['] but Mary thinks this is singularly
out of place in E.D.'s case. She (E.D.) glided in, in white, bearing a Daphne
odora for me, & said under her breath 'How long are you going to stay.' I'm
afraid Mary's other remark 'Oh why do the insane so cling to you?' still
holds. I will read you some of her poems when you come."[94]
Preserving the exquisite courtesies on which their relationship depended,
he nevertheless wrote to her on December 31, "I hope you will not cease to
trust me and turn to me; and I will try to speak the truth to you, and with
love" (*L* 405a). She wrote back in January 1874, stating in her own inimitable
way that when she was a child, she never had a mother, but that she found
"Awe" nurturing and that "Awe" was her shelter "after you left me the other
Day." In effect, Higginson, she thought, had become her good literary
mother. To smooth over whatever awkwardness there had been, an awkwardness she tried to forestall by staging her entry in white bearing a Daphne
odora, Dickinson enclosed a poem beginning "Because that you are going /

And never coming back." And he never did come back until her funeral. This is the love poem that stands as the exception to the No Love Poems rule she had imposed on herself in her correspondence with her mentor. It echoes "Because I could not stop for Death" (*Fr* 479), defines death as "Treason" in a draft version, and emphasizes that love does not know treason. It is one of the longest poems she ever wrote, and I quote only its first stanzas:

> Because that you are going
> And never coming back
> And I, however absolute
> May overlook your Track –
>
> Because that Death is final,
> However first it be
> This instant be suspended
> Above Mortality.
>
> Significance that each has lived
> The other to detect
> Discovery not God himself
> Could now annihilate
>
> Eternity, Presumption
> The instant I perceive
> That you, who were Existence
> Yourself forgot to live – (*Fr* 1314)[95]

Pursuing her great theme of the unlived life, Dickinson urges Higginson to live more fully, and with her. He did, but perhaps not in the ways she had in mind.

On November 29, 1875, Higginson read several of Dickinson's poems aloud to members of the Women's Club on Tremont Street in Boston without giving her name. We don't know which ones. The 3:30 event was advertised on the front page of the *Woman's Journal*, which later noted that Higginson read poems by his recently deceased sister Louisa and "also some of another friend, of remarkable strength and originality."[96] He explained to his other sister, Anna, that Dickinson's "weird & strange power excited much interest."[97] Higginson introduced both "Unknown Poetesses" to a sizable group of about eighty as "port-folio" poets. This was not treason because, as Karen Dandurand suggests, "He evidently regarded his reading of the poems as 'private' . . . so long as the event was closed to the general public and the press."[98]

Dickinson did not hear about this event from him, just as she did not know how widely he was sharing her poems and letters with others. By that time she may have suspected as much, given that he had shared her poems with Jackson. For example, as Dandurand observes, "The membership of the New England Women's Club in the mid-1870s included many writers, reform activists, and women distinguished in other fields. Indeed, a partial listing of the club's members reads like a compendium of notable women. . . . Some of the less-well-known names on the New England Women's Club membership rolls may be significant, too, for a different reason." She notes two consecutive entries for the period 1870–78, "both of them reading simply 'Norcross, Miss.'" It is possible that Dickinson's cousins Louisa and Fanny were in the audience at 3 Tremont Street when Colonel Higginson, who was known to promote women writers, commanded his usual good crowd.[99]

Be that as it may, in February 1876, when Dickinson wrote him "The Treason / of an accent Might / Ecstasy transfer," how might he have felt? "The Treason of an accent": could she be referring to his talk on "Two Unknown Poetesses," the blow softened by an allusion to the happiness he might have conveyed to the audience or even to her? Two additional lines are lineated as follows in the letter: "Of her / effacing / Fathom Is no / Recoverer" (*L* 450, *Fr* 1388).[100] Perhaps she was suggesting that once ecstasy is effaced and buried deep as the ocean bottom, it cannot be retrieved even by deep divers. Or did she mean that once something is said, it can't be taken back?

Whatever her intention, Higginson is unlikely to have spent much time trying to decode the message. If he felt guilty about his treason, it was a transitory mood. In the same letter, she stated, "Candor—my Preceptor—is the only wile." But this could have been maddening; did she have to address him as her teacher when she so rarely took his advice? Higginson understood what she meant, though, in referring to the "Prelude" to his novel *Malbone*, which discussed the problem of sincerity in literature. They both understood that the sincerity effect he promoted was not easy to achieve, human emotion itself being so difficult to control. "Candor . . . is the only wile" because art distinguishes and prioritizes. It balances freedom and self-control.

Dickinson's choice of Higginson as an unofficial editor and confidant was to some extent fortuitous. When she first approached him, "Letter to a Young Contributor" had just been extravagantly praised by the *Springfield Republican*, which was owned by two of her friends, Samuel Bowles and J. G. Holland, with Bowles at that point the more actively involved of the two. Moreover, the *Republican* had just published the much revised "Safe in their Alabaster Chambers" (*Fr* 124), which was in all probability given to Bowles by Dickinson's ambitious sister-in-law, Susan. Comparing their strategy to a military move, Susan sent this excited note across the lawn: "*Has girl read Republican?* It takes as long to start our Fleet as the Burnside."[101] Although the Burnside Expedition was stalled off the coast of North Carolina, it looked as though the Dickinson ship was about to set sail. Several months later, however, Dickinson insisted to Higginson that she was not ambitious for fame or reputation (*L* 265). She wrote him, "Two Editors of Journals came to my Father's House, this winter – and asked me for my Mind – and when I asked them 'Why,' they said I was penurious – and they, would use it for the World" (*L* 261). "Penurious": but Dickinson would not be commodified. And then: "If fame belonged to me, I could not escape her – if she did not, the longest day would pass me on the chase – and the approbation of my Dog, would forsake me – then – My Barefoot-Rank is better" (*L* 265). Coupled with the "terror – since September" (*L* 261) she described previously, Higginson advised her to "delay 'to publish.'"

Although she had written to Susan, "Could I make you and Austin – proud – sometime – a great way off – 'twould give me taller feet" (*L* 238), Dickinson's publication horizon included eternity. In "Letter to a Young Contributor," Higginson explained, "If our life be immortal, this temporary distinction is of little moment, and we may learn humility, without learning despair, from earth's evanescent glories."[102] She knew that story well and was acutely aware of the fluctuation in literary reputations. "Sic transit gloria mundi" begins a satiric Valentine poem of her youth—thus passes earthly glory. At sixty-eight lines, it is the longest poem she ever wrote (*Fr* 2). Later, at about the time that she read Higginson's "Letter to a Young Contributor," she explained to the audience in her mind,

> I had the Glory – that will do –
> An Honor, Thought can turn her to
> When lesser Fames invite –
> With one long "Nay" –

> Bliss' early shape
> Deforming – Dwindling – Gulphing up –
> Time's possibility – (*Fr* 350)

Dickinson saved this poem for herself. Its speaker refuses to negotiate with time, which betrays an early bliss, a primal Eden. She copied it into one of her fascicles, and it may have been inspired by her initial correspondence with Higginson. Ralph Franklin's dating ("about summer 1862") permits this reading.[103] By early 1862 Dickinson had about 335 poems ready to go, most of which had been copied into fascicles. Few of these poems had been shared with anyone other than herself. Based on the chronology Franklin provides, Dickinson's productivity was at its peak when she was keeping her manuscripts to herself, as she did in 1862 and 1863. As she became more sociable in later years—sociability here defined as the sharing of poems—her rate of composition slackened. Did she write fewer poems because thinking of herself as friendless liberated her to speak more freely than she otherwise could have done?

Theorizing Fame

Throughout her adult life, Dickinson theorized fame, warned against it, anticipated and remembered its sweetness. Understood as a debased version of success, fame collapsed readily into mere popularity, its conspicuous honors and glittering presentism devoid of past and future. Yet she wanted to believe that under some circumstances—rare, to be sure—fame's steadfast honey could be tasted in this life, to which it peculiarly belonged. And so fame was different from the maddeningly elusive lover of her unshared poem "I cannot live with you," which she copied into her Fascicle 33 in "about the second half of 1863," the lover of whom she writes, "And were You lost, I would be – / Though my name / Rang loudest / On the Heavenly fame" (*Fr* 706). Measuring her love by sacrifice, Dickinson suggests that true fame corresponds to a powerful positive emotion which, paradoxically, does not stay.

> It would never be Common – more – I said –
> Difference – had begun –
> Many a bitterness – had been –
> But that old sort – was done –

Or – if it sometime – showed – as 'twill –
Opon the Downiest – morn –
Such bliss – had I – for all the years –
'Twould give an easier – pain –

I'd so much joy – I told it – Red –
Opon my simple Cheek –
I felt it publish – in my eye –
'Twas needless – any speak –

I walked – as wings – my body bore –
The feet – I former used –
Unnescessary – now to me –
As boots – would be – to Birds –

I put my pleasure all abroad –
I dealt a word of Gold
To every Creature – that I met –
And Dowered – all the World –

When – suddenly – my Riches shrank –
A Goblin – drank my Dew –
My Palaces – dropped tenantless –
Myself – was beggared – too –

I clutched at sounds –
I groped at shapes –
I touched the tops of Films –
I felt the Wilderness roll back
Along my Golden lines –

The Sackcloth – hangs opon the nail –
The Frock I used to wear –
But where my moment of Brocade –
My – drop – of India? (*Fr* 388)

Dickinson's moment of brocade is a moment of truth. Out of this moment, true generosity emerges. She publishes it, or rather her body does. She is elated almost beyond description. And then, as in so many other poems, her moment of brocade disappears. That's the trouble with love and with literary success: you can't count on its steadfastness.

In examining Dickinson's antagonistic relationship to what she understood to be the risks not only of print publication but also of communication in general, I have suggested some of the ways in which she was reassured by Jackson, who called her, unequivocally, a great poet. I have also suggested some of the ways she was reassured by Higginson, who did not try to make her feel guilty or to insist that she publish. As we have seen, clergymen such as Higginson were important strategic allies for literary women. They, too, were trained to minimize the importance of worldly success while seeking it, and in all probability Higginson was not the first minister outside of her immediate Amherst circle whom Dickinson had tried to interest in her poems. Earlier, she had approached another Worcester Unitarian clergyman, the Reverend Edward Everett Hale, to inquire about the last days of her friend Benjamin Franklin Newton. Hale, who went on to write "The Man Without a Country," assured her that Newton had died a peaceful death and Dickinson thanked him for his letter. After a lapse of several years, Dickinson wrote again. She sent Hale "a Rose" and promised to "pluck you buds serener" upon "a purer morn." She may have enclosed rose petals, but it is even more likely that she enclosed a poem.[104] Hale was less responsive than Higginson and seems not to have replied. Then there was the "Master" to whom she sent poems and who was most likely the Reverend Charles Wadsworth, the Philadelphia minister she characterized as her "dearest earthly friend" (L 807).[105] Whatever their religious differences, these men were invested with spiritual authority and had official positions that were denied to most literary women.

Like Jackson, Higginson was aware of this disadvantage. In "Saints and Their Bodies," he stated, "The vocation of a literary man is far more perilous than that of a frontier dragoon." What then, he asked, of "the superhuman efforts often made by delicate women."[106] From the start, Dickinson told Higginson that she was not physically strong, adding for good measure that her poetry derived from a "terror – since September" (L 261). Under these circumstances, he advised her to "delay 'to publish'" (L 265). Notwithstanding, he soon realized that she had her own kind of mental toughness and for at least a decade he respected the limits of their relationship, which she insistently cast in a pedagogical mode. Signing herself "Your scholar," she ignored

his advice except on the crucial point, that she "delay 'to publish'" (*L* 265).
Delay she did.

Helen Hunt Jackson wanted to speed things up. Like Higginson, she
believed that poetry had an important public function. Like him, she was
aware of Dickinson's desire to preserve her privacy, and she knew from her
own experience that to publish was to risk the censure of strangers. In poem
after poem, though, she suggests that success is something individuals should
define for themselves:

> Not he who rides through conquered city's gate,
> At head of blazoned hosts, and to the sound
> Of victors' trumpets, in full pomp and state
> Of war, the utmost pitch has dreamed or found
> To which the thrill of triumph can be wound;
> Nor he, who by a nation's vast acclaim
> Is sudden sought and singled out alone,
> And while the people madly shout his name,
> Without a conscious purpose of his own,
> Is swung and lifted to the nation's throne;
>
> But he who has all single-handed stood
> With foes invisible on every side,
> And, unsuspected of the multitude,
> The force of fate itself has dared, defied,
> And conquered silently.
>   Ah that soul knows
> In what white heat the blood of triumph glows![107]

Describing a neat recompense for narcissistic wounds, this extended sonnet
is directed toward anyone who has ever felt undervalued, a large group to be
sure. More specifically, both in Jackson's "Triumph" and in Dickinson's
"Success," spiritual aristocracy is privileged and military victory devalued.
But while Jackson endorses spiritual toughness, Dickinson concentrates on
the psychological cost of losing. Both poems operate at a considerable remove
from a closely observed social scene and seek to empower outsiders. For
Dickinson's defeated and dying soldier, revelation is agonizing and the "ear"
oddly segmented and surreal. Jackson's more upbeat "Triumph" explores a
fantasy of limitless personal power. She writes for anyone who can stand

alone, conquer silently, and thrill to secret success. The problem, though, is that her voice carries forward smoothly and is too knowing. Read back through Dickinson, it is the rare ear that will find her language memorable.

The Problem of Collective Memory

Jackson acknowledged this weakness in the next phase of the intermittent correspondence she was conducting with Dickinson, to whom she wrote in May 1879,

> I know your "Blue bird" by heart—and that is more than I do of any of my own verses.—
>
> I also want your permission to send it to Col. Higginson to read. These two things are my testimonial to its merit.
>
> We have blue birds here—I might have had the sense to write something about one myself, but I never did: and now I never can. For which I am inclined to envy, and perhaps hate you. (*L* 601a)[108]

She also suggested that Dickinson try her hand "on the oriole," and Dickinson responded enthusiastically. "Dear friend," she wrote, sending two poems she seems to have written to order, "To the Oriole you suggested I add a Humming Bird and hope they are not untrue" (*L* 602). These persona poems circumvent the problem of self-revelation with which both Dickinson and Jackson were so deeply concerned. Despite her unsettled state at the time, the likelihood is that Jackson responded to Dickinson's letter, but there is an unexplained gap in the correspondence until April 1883, when Dickinson wrote, hoping to prod her neglectful friend into speech. "To be remembered what?" she asked. "Worthy to be forgot, is their renown" (*L* 816). Anyone can be remembered, she seems to say. My distinction is that I can be so easily forgotten. Consumed with her own writing, Jackson was probably not eager to continue the conversation with a friend she was inclined to envy and almost to hate. The correspondence picks up again in September 1884, while *Ramona* was being serialized in the *Christian Union*. Health problems aside, the heart of Jackson's letter is this passage, which I quoted as an epigraph:

> What portfolios of verses you must have.—
>
> It is a cruel wrong to your "day & generation" that you will not give them light.—If such a thing should happen as that I should

outlive you, I wish you would make me your literary legatee &
executor. Surely, after you are what is called "dead," you will be
willing that the poor ghosts you have left behind, should be cheered
and pleased by your verses, will you not?—You ought to be.—I do
not think we have a right to with hold from the world a word or a
thought any more than a *deed*, which might help a single soul.
(*L* 937a)

Without responding directly to this heated language—the earlier "wrong"
(*L* 444a) has become a "cruel wrong"—Dickinson deftly deflected the request. Whereas Jackson had called her "stingy" in 1876, Dickinson now suggested that hoarding (or self-control) has its virtues. Figuring the release of
poetic power as assaultive in its intensity, she justified her thrifty logic with a
witty quatrain demonstrating her "natural" outlays as follows:

> And then he lifted up his Throat
> And squandered such a Note –
> A Universe that overheard
> Is stricken by it yet – (*L* 937)[109]

Gendering poetic power as profligate and male, Dickinson in effect warned
Jackson against typecasting her as just another cheering and pleasing poetess.
The idea that language might wound as well as soothe was almost clichéd.
Jackson herself had demonstrated the idea in one of the three poems by
which she was represented in *A Masque of Poets* (four if we count "Success").
In "A Woman's Death Wound," someone, presumably a brutal husband,
tortures someone, presumably his loving wife, with "but a word. A blow had
been less base."[110] But where Jackson's sonnet condemns the wielder of the
fatal word as a murderer, Dickinson's more outrageous singer revels in power
alone.

Each in her own way, both Jackson and Dickinson sought to rationalize
their achievements and to redefine success in terms that the other might
understand. Quite unlike Mercy Philbrick, the impossibly high-minded heroine of Jackson's first novel who writes poems, dresses in white, and lives in
a small town in western Massachusetts, Dickinson chose to "unwind the
solemn twine" of tradition and of region without committing herself to the
hazards of a public career (*Fr* 1). Writing, as noted by an early critic, "almost
in a new language," she committed herself to resisting official logics of belief,

to affirming the individual, specifically herself, and to confirming doubt.[111]
This led her to "justify – Despair," to prove its compulsive illogic (*Fr* 355).
She started from a position of greater certainty, when in 1852 she produced a
pastiche of male sentimental and patriotic rhetorics, which concludes with
an elaborate farewell to conventional citizenship:

> Good bye, Sir, I am going;
> My country calleth me;
> Allow me, Sir, at parting,
> To wipe my weeping e'e.
>
> In token of our friendship
> Accept this "Bonnie Doon,"
> And when the hand that plucked it
> Hath passed beyond the moon,
>
> The memory of my ashes
> Will consolation be;
> Then, farewell, Tuscarora,
> And farewell, Sir, to thee! (*Fr* 2)

"Sic transit gloria mundi" meditates not only on the fame-is-dust motif but
also on the fleetingness of romantic friendships. It was published anonymously in the *Springfield Daily Republican* on February 20, 1852, with the
preface, "The hand that wrote the following amusing medley to a gentleman
friend of ours, as 'a valentine,' is capable of writing very fine things, and there
is certainly no presumption in entertaining a private wish that a correspondence, more direct than this, may be established between it and the Republican."[112] We now know that when it came to conventional print publication,
direct correspondence was not in Dickinson's line. "Sic transit gloria mundi"
was sent first to William Howland—an Amherst College graduate who studied law with Edward Dickinson and who courted the poet's sister Lavinia.
He passed the manuscript along to Samuel Bowles and/or Josiah Gilbert
Holland. By 1852, although still in her early twenties, Dickinson was bidding
farewell not only to "Tuscarora" but also to instrumental political and religious rhetoric.[113] Invoking the charged trope of the vanishing Indian, the
emerging and retreating poet adopts a postmortem perspective on the doings
of this frantically busy world. Consoling those she is about to leave behind,

she imagines the disintegration of her physical and social body. *Her* consolation? The pastiche persona is silent on that subject, but it sounds as though she's having a glorious time.

Although Dickinson's journeys into the unknown helped to shape modernist aesthetics, when she died her passing was noted only as a local event. By way of contrast, Helen Hunt Jackson's death in a posh San Francisco boarding house inspired obituary tributes from coast to coast. Yet as soon as Dickinson's poems began to circulate in print in 1890, their names were linked. In general, reviewers did not compare Dickinson's poems to Jackson's but contented themselves with noting the shared scene of their childhood in a small New England town and their later literary friendship, coupled with Jackson's desire to see her friend's poetry into print. That she had succeeded with one poem ("Success") was widely noted, as was the "cruel wrong" letter in which Jackson had volunteered to be Dickinson's literary executor if she outlived her. (The letter was quoted in the "Preface" to the 1891 *Poems*.) There were repeated mentions as well of the supposed collaboration of Dickinson on Jackson's *Saxe Holm* stories, and on Dickinson as a model both for Mercy Philbrick and for another of Jackson's poetess heroines, Draxy Miller.[114] In June 1895, however, Jackson's belief in Dickinson's failure to do her duty, her "civil wrong" (as one reviewer put it), was complicated by a reference to Dickinson's assessment of Jackson.[115] Writing in the *Midland Monthly*, Mary J. Reid explained,

> Personally, [Helen Hunt Jackson] was one of the most popular
> authors in America. Not only Emerson but hundreds of obscure
> men and women in farmhouses and factories culled her poems from
> the newspapers, memorizing them while at work, pasting them in
> home-made scrap-books or pinning them to the leaves of the family
> Bible. . . . Emily Dickinson's opinions of Mrs. Jackson's works are
> of value as the estimate of a loving friend who never judged a book
> without having first mastered its contents.[116]

Reid then turned her attention to Dickinson's achievement, and Jackson's poetry is already surrounded with an elegiac glow.

In this chapter, I have emphasized that a literary career did not come easily to a nineteenth-century American woman, not even a woman such as Jackson, who was confident in the social value of her own convictions. Dickinson's career evidently demanded a different kind of self-confidence, and I should like to conclude this chapter with a look at a poem unseen in its entirety by any member of Dickinson's private audience before her death. One stanza was recast in a letter to her sister-in-law, but the poem as a whole exists today only in a transcript made by Mabel Loomis Todd, the subject of our next chapter. It is a poem about mystery, and it resists single-minded rationality. It interrogates surfaces and depths, gently probing the inconceivable mystery, the poignancy and terror, of all disappearances, but it ends with a kind of sermon, in that the last stanza sounds as though it is drawing a moral. At first it seems the speaker wants to know what lies at the bottom of her emblematic well. She also fears her own curiosity. The poem negotiates beautifully between precise knowledge—but of what?—and the abyss. For Dickinson and for her publics, is nature's well cozy, or forbidding, or eerily both?

> What mystery pervades a well!
> The water lives so far –
> A neighbor from another world
> Residing in a jar
>
> Whose limit none have ever seen,
> But just his lid of glass –
> Like looking every time you please
> In an abyss's face!
>
> The grass does not appear afraid,
> I often wonder he
> Can stand so close and look so bold
> At what is awe to me.
>
> Related somehow they may be,
> The sedge stands next the sea
> Where he is floorless
> And does no timidity betray –
>
> But nature is a stranger yet;
> The ones that cite her most
> Have never passed her haunted house,
> Nor simplified her ghost.

To pity those that know her not
Is helped by the regret
That those who know her, know her less
The nearer her they get. (*Fr* 1433)

At first a "neighbor" and then an "abyss," the water, uncontainable, is troped as "the sea," and when the speaker contemplates the relationship between the boundless "sea" and the "sedge" at the edge or shore, her confident voice falters; the word "betray" jars us with its surprise. Here is an intersubjective development for which the poem had not prepared us, which implies a ghostly audience. Yet Dickinson does not suggest that concealing her fears is socially useful. Rather, "What mystery" invites us to forgive ourselves our inevitable timidities, to let some sleeping ghosts lie, but also to take comfort in the fact that unlike too many of our neighbors, we are not smug.

Perhaps symbolizing the power of the unconscious, the unfathomable sea takes care of itself, while well water, the grass, the sedge, and the people Dickinson knew had their limits and were more vulnerable to betrayal. Those limits and betrayals became an integral part of her story, and they shaped her posthumous career. "What mystery contains a well" may suggest that Dickinson did not understand her own very human nature. However emphatic her denials of ambition, she was deeply conflicted about her private vocation and longing to be remembered. But by whom and for what? Until she could settle that question in her mind, her "Barefoot-Rank" was, as she told Higginson, "better" (*L* 265).

Chapter 2

Mabel Loomis Todd
and Dickinson's Art of Sincerity

In about 1879, Dickinson penciled this poem on a sheet of stationery and may have sent it next door to the Evergreens, the home of her brother Austin and sister-in-law Susan:

> A Counterfeit – a Plated Person –
> I would not be –
> Whatever Strata of Iniquity
> My Nature underlie –
> Truth is good Health – and Safety, and the Sky –
> How meagre, what an Exile – is a Lie,
> And Vocal – when we die – (*Fr* 1514)

For complex reasons, late nineteenth-century Americans were anxious about sincerity and fascinated by fraud. Dickinson herself thought about poetry both as a deceiver's art and as a place for truth. This conflict is enacted in "A Counterfeit," where a dominant voice says that whatever else she or he is, he or she is sincere. An undervoice seems less sure. Dickinson signed the unaddressed poem with the name of a local minister, "Lothrop," who had been charged in the court of public opinion and in his church with brutalizing his family several years earlier. When she adopted this pseudonym, she was indulging in a private joke and would be surprised to discover that we share it too, especially since the manuscript is headed "In petto," a legal term meaning "in secret."

"A Counterfeit" engages local history and has a big range. In dialogue with late nineteenth-century anxieties about confusing social realities, it suggests that a new day is coming in which purer, truer voices will be heard. But what is the "Strata of Iniquity" to which the text alludes? Is the poem's dominant voice operating on the theory that human nature is corrupt and that there is some wickedness in everyone, as orthodox religionists still taught, or does it reflect a more liberal point of view that privileges tolerance and diversity? "A Counterfeit" is evidently open to multiple interpretations, not all of which would have been accessible to Dickinson's immediate audience. For example, it may suggest that the truth is "Vocal" *only* when we die, and in this chapter, I will pursue a version of that theory, namely that the truth about Emily Dickinson's life and about her life in poetry became visible only after her death, but I will not suggest that this collective life is independent of its specific historical context. Whereas Roland Barthes has suggested that the ideal reader is "without history, biography, psychology," the process of dissemination I describe is more contingent on individuals with specific histories, biographies, and psychologies.[1] In particular, Dickinson's death created imperfect reader-allies without whom the versions of Dickinson as we know her would not exist. One such reader-ally was Mabel Loomis Todd, who became the focus of the so-called War Between the Houses, in which both sides accused each other of being counterfeits and ended up in a courtroom claiming fraud. Working alone and with others, at times with almost maniacal energy, it was she who first transformed Dickinson from a virtually anonymous coterie poet into a writer who clarified for wider publics both the terrors and the pleasures of what became a collective social and literary text. Mabel's story is thus integral with Dickinson's, and the stages of her developing personal and literary alliances deserve close attention. In what follows, I refer to this important historical actor as Mabel, as Mabel Loomis Todd, and eventually in her professional capacity as Todd or Mabel Todd. That is to say, I have not been able to solve the problem of consistent naming for this literary woman in crisis.

Family Romances

Mabel Loomis Todd moved to Amherst in time for the fall semester when her husband David became an instructor in astronomy at Amherst College in 1881. Together, the Todds set about the business of making a home for

themselves in the community in which both Susan and Austin were prominent figures. At first the Dickinsons took the Todds (and especially Mabel)
under their wing, but in late 1883, Mabel became Austin Dickinson's lover
and unofficial wife. In some ways, it was a conventional story: at twenty-
four, she was young enough to be his daughter. The official wife, Susan, was
furious but was unable to reclaim her husband's affection or to get David to
intervene. Strangely, the Todds continued to function emotionally and sexually as an empathetic, sympathetic couple, and David considered Austin, who
was the treasurer of Amherst College and active on the board of trustees, his
best friend. Together with Austin, the Todds were intent on keeping up
appearances, and Mabel succeeded in concealing her affair from most, but
not all, members of the Amherst community. Throughout this period of
intense sexual experimentation, she was eager to fulfill herself through a professional career and in late 1887 found what she hoped might be her life's
work in editing Dickinson. "The poems were having a wonderful effect on
me, mentally and spiritually," she later wrote. "They seemed to open the
door into a wider universe than the little sphere surrounding me which so
often hurt and compressed me—and they helped me nobly through a very
trying time."[2] The very trying time had to do with the humiliations she
suffered as Austin Dickinson's mistress rather than his wife, and Dickinson's
poems were her "sky," her world elsewhere. As a recent biographer (Lyndall
Gordon) has emphasized, she devoutly wished that the false wife (Susan
Dickinson) would disappear. That didn't happen, nor did anything come of
the suicide pact she proposed to Austin. He wasn't interested and in her heart
of hearts, neither was she. Having been schooled by her idealistic poet-father
Eben Jenks Loomis in Transcendental higher laws, she scorned her enemies
in the petty conventional world she inhabited while at the same time being
sensitive to real and imagined slights. In response to this split between true
and false identities, she deflected depression by working at painting, at music,
and at literature, by publishing stories and travel writings, but also yearning
to accomplish something more ambitious that would make her name and
cause her to be as admired in public as she was in private by the men who vied
for her clandestine favors. Only slightly less interested in pleasing women, she
tried to defer to her mother and grandmother, and when they were in town,
there were no more of the long, leisurely afternoons she spent with Austin,
or for that matter of the long, leisurely evenings enjoyed by the excitable
threesome: Mabel, Austin, and David. Independently, David, whose earlier

infidelities had helped to propel Mabel into Austin's arms, was enjoying sexual adventures of his own.

Be that as it may, in the summer and fall of 1889, Mabel hoped to accompany David (and her father) on an eight-month trip to West Africa to observe a solar eclipse, but at the last moment, the U.S. Navy insisted that it would not permit a woman on board a combatant ship. Responding to this disappointment and to the prospect of her husband's extended absence, she decided to move to Boston to study music and to get out of the town where she was feeling persecuted by Susan's aura, which she invested with almost mystical authority. In early November, she arranged to visit with Thomas Wentworth Higginson, whom she had met briefly at Dickinson's funeral. By then Mabel had spent the better part of two years selecting and transcribing poems, sometimes with help, more often alone, sometimes by hand, more often on a typewriter. She was looking for a publisher, and when she read Higginson some of her favorite poems, he had a conversion experience. Mabel recalled of this historic reading, "He was greatly astonished—said he had no idea there were so many in passably conventional form . . . if I would classify them all into A B and C he would look them over later in the winter."[3] Classify them she did, at the white heat, and on December 26 she wrote to Austin, who was far from enthusiastic about her efforts, "Work is my only salvation, & the first leisure shows me (unpityingly) the horror of my life, which goes on without the slightest interest from the Almighty, a life absolutely deserted by Him and left to swing for itself in space, unhelped & uncared for. Prayers are no more than so much extra breath wasted, or as Emily says, no more than if a bird stamped its foot on the air. I am utterly alone." Slipping into Dickinson's idiom came easily to her, and she knew many of the poems by heart. "Of Course – I prayed," Dickinson wrote, "And did God Care?"

> He cared as much as on the Air
> A Bird – had stamped her foot –
> And cried "Give Me" –
> My Reason – Life –
> I had not had – but for Yourself –
> 'Twere better Charity
> To leave me in the Atom's Tomb –
> Merry, and nought, and gay, and numb –
> Than this smart Misery. (*Fr* 581)

Confessing to Austin that their love-religion was on the verge of collapse, a smarting Mabel concluded her letter, "I shall never try to acquire any leisure again. It is fatal. Work to the last, breaking point, is all that is left for me."[4]

Whatever her identification with emotional numbness, remaining entombed was not in Mabel's nature, nor was it in Higginson's to sit idly by waiting for a gift that might or might not come. Despite some difference over particulars, these two near-strangers worked well together; Mabel's energy and enthusiasm carried them along on a daily basis, while Higginson brought experience of the publishing world and personal probity to the project. Of course he was squeamish about Dickinson's prosodic abnormalities (as he thought them), but he shrewdly realized that her position as a literary outsider contributed to the sincerity effect valued by 1890s readers. As I will show further, Mabel was both an outsider and an insider, and the uncertain balance between these roles eventually caused her to identify with psychological martyrdom and to "seek in Art – the Art of Peace" (*Fr* 665).

Mabel began her life quietly enough in Cambridge, Massachusetts, on November 10, 1856, and in her youth did not cause her parents trouble. Her maternal grandfather was a Congregational minister in Concord during its Transcendental prime, but Mabel never knew the Reverend John (d. 1852). Rather, it was her youthful maternal grandmother Mary Wales Fobes Jones Wilder, a founder and first president of the Concord Female Anti-Slavery Society, whom she admired and knew well. (Other founders were Lidian Emerson and Thoreau's mother and sisters.)[5] The intensity that characterized Mabel throughout her life was to some extent inherited from both of her parents, but especially from her father, a polymath who tried to translate his knowledge of nature into a scientific career that, as Polly Longsworth suggests, never fully enabled him to realize his talents. Longsworth, however, represents Eben as something of an intellectual impostor, and this seems to me unduly harsh, as was the fate of his youngest sister Collette, a well-educated poetess who began publishing in the *Springfield Republican* when she was twelve but who died young. Another sister painted. Mabel barely knew her father's parents, and her paternal grandmother Waitie Jenks Barber died in 1860, a year after Collette Loomis published "Only a Shadow" in the *Republican*, where Dickinson might have read it. As Paula Bernat Bennett suggests, "Only a Shadow" is an erotic poem influenced by Tennyson and Whitman, in which a "lonely" woman's desire is gratified by and in the night: "The hand of the night is very dear to her, / The arm of the night is about her form, / The lips of the night are very near to her, / And the breath of the summer night is warm." Poesque as well, with an atmosphere of beating, beating hearts and weary and dreary gloom, "Only a Shadow" blurs the line between erotic fantasy and a more confusingly amorphous social reality, as Mabel's imagination was to do.[6]

Like Collette, his painting sister, and his other siblings, including his brother Mahlon, who persuaded some members of Congress that he had invented the wireless telegraph before Marconi, Eben spent some of his youth near Washington, DC, where his father was engaged in the scientific work that was recognized when Amherst College awarded him an honorary degree in 1851. Following in his father's footsteps, Eben studied at the Lawrence Scientific School associated with Harvard and worked in the American Ephemeris and Nautical Almanac Office in Cambridge, living some of this time in Concord. According to John Burroughs's biographer Clara Barrus, he was a man who had "boarded with Thoreau's mother, [eaten] at the same table with Thoreau, roamed the woods with him, and bathed with him in Walden Pond."[7] It was in Cambridge, though, that he met the sister of a colleague, and he married lively and energetic Mary ("Mollie") Alden Wilder in 1853. Mabel was a charming only child.

In sum, the Loomises were a talented and quirky family, although less is known about both the talents and the quirks of the women. As a group they valued education, and Grandfather Nathan, who graduated from a demanding western Massachusetts academy, a private high school, knew Greek. Marrying young, he followed his Baptist-minister-father to New York State, where he farmed and taught school and where Mabel's father, the fifth of nine children, was born. Grandfather Nathan was the head of a boys' school in northern Virginia before he began working as a "computer" or mathematician in Washington and was known as "Professor Loomis," as was his son Eben, although he seems to have had no official academic affiliation. In 1861 and 1864, when Nathan was a member of the Massachusetts legislature, representing West Springfield and the Republican Party, he was listed in the official record as a "Civil Engineer." As a group, the Loomises were staunch Unionists, including Judge George Loomis, Eben's brother, a West Virginia attorney who was "a past master of political debate . . . a man of deep and firm convictions, and always fearless in their advocacy."[8]

A Unionist whose particular politics have not come down to us, in 1866 Eben sold the house on Sacramento Street in Cambridge where Mabel had spent most of her young life to the recently hired assistant editor of the

Atlantic Monthly, William Dean Howells, who describes it and the neighbor-hood in "Suburban Sketches." It was a "carpenter's box," Howells writes, and beautifully planted, in "a poor suburb of a suburb."[9] The house at 41 Sacramento Street, now a short distance from Harvard, was on an unpaved and unlighted street and it bordered on a field with cows when Eben bought it new in 1857. It was the last house he and Molly would own during Mabel's youth. The reason for the sale was this: Eben needed money to invest in a cotton plantation near Jacksonville, Florida, an adventure that proved disas-trous from a financial point of view. He was part of a cohort that included Henry James's brothers Wilky and Robertson and many other well-intentioned northerners, whose numbers Lawrence N. Powell estimates as between twenty and fifty thousand. In *New Masters: Northern Planters During the Civil War and Reconstruction*, Powell states that "the northern planting class was, in fact, as numerically significant as any group of Reconstruction actors. Members of this group probably outnumbered Yankee schoolmarms . . . for the simple reason that profit has usually been a stronger motive than philanthropy." Thus Eben was not acting alone. He had a partner and the enterprise was funded by Molly's wealthy cousin, Herbert Wilder. Nor was he alone in that he had a Vermont overseer whose hard treatment "at the height of the hoeing season" caused the field hands to desert him. Powell adds, "Loomis lost almost one hundred acres of cotton to weeds as a result."[10] Molly and Mabel remained in Massachusetts, with the prospect of moving to Florida if the plantation flourished. When falling cotton prices, a disastrous drought, adversarial relationships with white southerners, and insoluble labor problems rendered Eben nearly penniless, he returned to the Cambridge Nautical Office shortly before the Office moved its work to Washington. Eben was compelled to follow, and Molly and Mabel remained in Boston, where Mabel had begun attending school for the first time, delighting in the companionship of children her own age. A year later, a somewhat reluctant Molly joined him, and twelve-year-old Mabel, a precocious student like her aunt Collette, settled comfortably into a new school.

In Gilded Age Washington, Walt Whitman's circle considered Eben Jenks Loomis "a distinguished man."[11] He wrote poetry of his own, recited reams of Shakespeare to himself and others, and Mabel writes in a memoir that the house was frequented by distinguished literary visitors such as John James Piatt and his "brilliant" wife Sarah, whose name she does not men-tion.[12] Nevertheless, the Loomises lived in cramped boarding houses and had to sacrifice for Mabel's education. She was already keeping a journal, and as Longsworth explains,

> Mabel clearly emulated her father when it came to writing, the pursuit that tied them most closely. "Is it presumptuous to say my style is improving in the direction of yours?" she inquired hopefully when she was sixteen. A few days later she announced, "I was never so happy in my life as I am now. Not from anything that happens, but because I feel in me the possibility of great things in the way of writing." This was a sense she bore all her life, so that during her girlhood she published seven essays (and wrote another twenty), and in her lifetime wrote or edited twelve published books and some two hundred articles.[13]

After three winters at the Georgetown Female Seminary, Mabel returned to her New England roots to study piano and voice at the prestigious Boston Conservatory of Music. She had an unsatisfactory romance that year and then, while visiting her parents in Washington, she caught the eye of David Peck Todd, her father's colleague and an ambitious Amherst College graduate, whom Mabel described as "very good looking, a blond with magnificent teeth, pleasant manners, and immense, though innocent enough, powers of flirting." She added in her journal, "Well, so also have I."[14]

Although the multitalented Mabel wasn't sure what she wanted to do with her life, she knew that David Peck Todd supported her desire to make an uncommon name for herself, but after they were engaged in 1878, something happened that caused her to want to flee. She couldn't write about it even in her diary, which is nevertheless highly attentive to physical detail and to her own body. She explains, for example, that as her anxiety increased, she found it difficult to eat and that her weight dropped precipitously. Mabel may have discovered that David was having an affair, or he may have pressed her for sexual favors she was unable to grant. Whatever it was, the couple worked through it and developed a strong, loving, and unconventional partnership. After their marriage in March 1879, they lived with her parents in a boardinghouse and the newlywed Mabel tried unsuccessfully to practice birth control, firm in the conviction that she could not become pregnant if she had an orgasm before her husband's. In an astonishingly frank, unpublished essay, "Millicent's Life," written after she arrived in Amherst, she describes her attempts first to deny and then to end the pregnancy. (She consulted a female physician who advised her to take hot baths, long walks, and the like, and Mabel added a few methods of her own.)[15]

When the Todds arrived in Amherst in the late summer of 1881 without their toddler Millicent (she was being cared for by the Loomises until they got settled), Mabel was hoping for a warmer welcome than she received, but before long she was forming friendships and was welcomed into the Dickinson homes—the beautiful houses on Main Street side by side, with their gardens and socially prominent people. Except for Emily Dickinson. She was a recluse and couldn't be said to be socially prominent, although she was intellectually prominent, and Mabel was excited: "All the literary men are after her," she wrote her parents.[16] It was the other house, the house belonging to Dickinson's brother, where the parties were and where the young people came. At first Susan liked Mabel, having no premonition that this charming and ambitious young woman would cause her grief. And so it happened that on February 8, 1882, Mabel and Susan shared a pleasant afternoon together. Mabel kept a diary, and this is what she wrote. "Went in the afternoon to Mrs. Dickinson's. She read me some strange poems by Emily Dickinson. They are full of power."[17] This moment changed her life.

With her vivid imagination, Mabel felt as though she were living in a novel, one she hoped some day to write. She was enthralled by Dickinson's handwriting, courage, and reputation, to say nothing of her family connections. "I told you I admired Mrs. [Susan] Dickinson at first," she wrote her parents, "but I am thoroughly captivated with her now." "She does, as I supposed, live very handsomely, & she is so easy and charming, & sincere. . . . She has a beautiful new upright piano, & her young daughter & I played some duetts, & then I sang . . . Her husband was not at home last night—but I was very much impressed with him in various ways. He is fine (& very remarkable) looking—& very dignified & strong and a little odd."[18] Mabel liked odd people as long as they were successful, and "queer" is an honorific in her 1883 short story, "Footprints," whose heroine is not conventionally pretty but able to find rare flowers in coy hiding places. With luck and pluck, she evades the "alleged modern artificiality" of life, which Mabel's description of Susan as "so easy and charming and sincere" also underscores.[19] It seems that sincere people were not all that common, and perhaps sincere women in her experience were rarer. "Footprints" is told from the perspective of a disenchanted middle-aged hero who finds renewed vigor with the considerably younger Mildred Elton. She is clear-eyed and frank; her step is elastic and free. She saves her shy, nature-loving suitor from chronic joylessness, and the story, with its elaborated seaside setting, contains echoes of Whitman's poem of psychological and artistic exhaustion, "As I Ebb'd with the Ocean of Life." In Mabel's story, the male point of view predominates, but the self-confident woman takes the lead, as "Henry Arnold" follows her footprints to a happy ending, two together and the right two at that. The plot turns on a romantic ruse, a deliberately contrived scene that provokes jealousy. The heroine succeeds by remaining calm, while Arnold, her discouraged suitor, suffers the torments to which literature has accustomed us.

Intent on self-culture and social success, Mabel used her talents (she was an artist too) not only to give Susan and Austin's daughter piano lessons but also to ingratiate herself with the Dickinson sisters. She wrote her parents, "This morning I practiced [Chopin] an hour & then went by request to call at the big house, the family mansion, where now live in solitary state Mr. Dickinson's two sisters, the unique Emily & Miss Lavinia." That she could not see Dickinson face to face added to the fun.[20]

Mabel coordinated talents and people, and with her boundless energy was writing about the Dickinsons in both a diary and a journal. Here is what she wrote in her journal on September 15, 1882, after visiting the big house, the family mansion, the Homestead:

Last Sunday I went over there with Mr. Dickinson. Miss Vinnie, the other sister who does occasionally go out, told me that if I had been otherwise than a very agreeable person she should have been dreadfully tired of my name even, for she says all the members of her brother's family have so raved about me that ordinarily she would hate the sound of Mrs. Todd. But when I left her on Sunday she took my hand in the shyest, quaintest way, and said she saw plainly that she should have to yield to the same fascination which had enthralled her family; & when I come back [*from Washington*] she wants me to have stated & regular days for coming there to sing & play. It was odd to think, as my voice rang out through the big silent house that Miss Emily in her weird white dress was outside in the shadow hearing every word, & the mother, bedridden for years was listening up stairs. When I stopped Emily sent me in a glass of rich sherry & a poem written as I sang.[21]

The poem may not have been written as she sang, but it is most likely this one. The only copy is in pencil, on a folded sheet of stationery:

Elysium is as far as to
The very nearest Room
If in that Room a Friend await
Felicity or Doom –

What fortitude the Soul contains,
That it can so endure
The accent of a coming Foot –
The opening of a Door – (*Fr* 1590)

Assuming, however, that "Elysium" was written to order, it can be read as emphasizing the danger of Mabel's coming choice. It underscores the uniqueness of her situation by universalizing it, and Mabel is likely to have applied its hyperbolic opposition of "Felicity or Doom" to herself. She is also likely to have enjoyed the poem's syntactic ambiguity, which makes it hard to distinguish active from passive roles. Is Mabel, for example, taking the emotional and somatic initiative or is she merely waiting to see what will happen? "Elysium" conflates language and poetry: "The accent of a coming Foot – / The opening of a Door – ," uniting the pain of passion with its prospect of bliss. For the speaker, there is no middle ground, though the poem unites them.

Rubicon

Be that as it may, Mabel had fortitude, and a restless husband. Her eye began to stray too and, after a flirtation with Susan and Austin's son Ned, landed on Austin, whose family connections, wealth, and commanding presence made him an undisputed leader in his church and community. He was the college treasurer, influential with the board of trustees on whom David's tenure depended, and he set David's salary. Austin was old enough to be Mabel's father and like her father was an ardent nature lover. After that, their paths diverged. While Eben Jenks Loomis bore his burdens gracefully and believed in the power of the Soul to right ephemeral wrongs, Austin Dickinson had little faith in cosmic justice. Rather, he was a successful man of the world who was bitter about his marriage and the confinements of small-town life. Whatever his personal dissatisfactions, however, Austin was a conscientious husband and father, until he fell hopelessly in love with Mabel. When

Figure 8. Mabel Loomis Todd in 1882, some months after her arrival in Amherst. She loved beautiful clothes and beautiful things. Courtesy Todd-Bingham Picture Collection, Yale University. MS 496E, Series I, Box 4, Folder 59.

he wrote "Rubicon" in his diary on September 11, 1882, he meant that there could be no turning back. Technically speaking, the couple did not become full-fledged lovers on that day in September when they looked deeply into each others' eyes and assented to their fate. Soon, in the New England antinomian, Transcendental, and higher law tradition, they considered themselves spiritually wed. Another year passed and then, without warning, Austin and Susan lost their "deare childe," eight-year-old Gilbert, to typhoid.[22] He was the golden boy who had been holding the marriage together. Susan retreated, and several months later, Austin and Mabel were making love at the Homestead, "the wild life current" throbbing "back and forth from one to the other."[23] Methodically, Austin noted the date in his diary, December 13, 1883, and he drew a pair of lines to indicate that he and Mabel had had sexual intercourse. For her part, Mabel believed that in giving herself to Austin, she was saving the life of the man whom she viewed as her king, her God, her Christ. She was also saving herself from drudgery and the suspense of being dependent on David's moods. He slept very little and there was insanity in his family. He soothed himself with other women.

How much did Emily Dickinson know about the tangled web of hatreds, deceits, and desires that was so deeply to influence the future of her work and literary reputation? As with so much else about her erotic experience, we can't be sure. After her nephew's untimely death, by which she was prostrated for months, she wrote to Susan, "Gilbert rejoiced in Secrets – His Life was panting with them – With what menace of Light he cried 'Dont tell, Aunt Emily'!" (L 868), and "Aunt Emily" has not told. Even if we read "Elysium" as a comment on Mabel's momentous choice, and on Austin's, it does not adopt a moral position on either official or unofficial marriages. Rather, it sets up oppositions that it then deconstructs, for example the opposition between voice or "accent" and poetic or bodily feet. "Elysium" is then what you make of it; psychologically, it may be heaven and it may be hell.

Before Austin and Mabel crossed their "Rubicon," however, Dickinson wrote a letter to her friend and fantasy-lover Judge Otis Phillips Lord about gender hierarchies, body and spirit, trespass and forgiveness, time and timelessness—all wrapped up in "Tenderness" that has "not a Date – it comes – and overwhelms." Did Dickinson want Lord to overwhelm her in the flesh? Yes, at least in theory, and no, for " 'No' " is the "wildest word" in the English language (L 562). "The trespass of my rustic Love upon your Realms of Ermine, only a Sovereign could forgive," she wrote Lord, "I never knelt to other" (L 750). Strictly speaking, this was not true, if we include her

Figure 9. Susan Gilbert Dickinson and her son Gib in July 1882. The image is excerpted from a group photograph titled "Shutesbury School of Philosophy," an inside joke commemorating a large-scale picnic in which Mabel Loomis Todd and her husband David also participated. Courtesy Todd-Bingham Picture Collection, Yale University. MS 496E, MADID 8368.

erotic imagination in our story. Lyndall Gordon argues that the poet clearly sided with Sue, yet given her sympathy for Austin's predicament and perhaps for Mabel's, the reality is likely to have been more complex. True, Dickinson never became curious enough about Mabel to overcome her fear of strangers, to endure "the accent of a coming Foot," even if she was the one opening the door. In her social relationships, Dickinson was self-protective. In this particular relationship, she did not want to offend either Sue or Austin, whom in happier times she had called her "crowd" (L 212). True, she wrote to her nephew Ned, "Ever be sure of me, Lad," but this statement, on which Gordon leans heavily, is perfectly consistent with her longstanding social practice.[24] Not to overemphasize the point, but Emily Dickinson had excused herself from many interpersonal, social obligations in a life that was drawing to its close. She was not looking for extra trouble.

We know, though, that Austin Dickinson's love for Mabel Loomis Todd and hers for him implicated others in their secrets. For example, Emily's sister Lavinia definitely encouraged the clandestine correspondence that fueled the fires when Austin and Mabel could not be together. She helped them to arrange meetings in the Homestead, in the dining room and in the library, and she cautioned her faithful housekeeper Maggie Maher not to disturb them, as she is likely to have cautioned Emily. She got Maggie to pack picnic lunches for the country drives that Austin and Mabel took in fine weather, where they enjoyed the privacy of a carriage. And she sent Maggie to the Dell, the house Austin had helped to build for the Todds, where Maggie saw Mr. Dickinson on his way up to the stairs, where he retreated with Mabel behind a closed door for the long afternoons they spent together, circumstances permitting.[25] These were occasions that frightened Millicent, who recalled

> A tall lean man, sitting rigidly erect in his chair. His clean-shaven face, except for red sidewhiskers, was without a smile. I could not have imagined how he would look if he should smile. It would never have occurred to me to try to imagine. . . . Aristocratic, contemptu-ous, yes, but to me just the somewhat terrible center of the universe, though why he was such I could not have said. He was. No human being ever mentioned his name to me, nor did I ever mention his. I doubt whether he would have acknowledged my presence by so much as a nod had I met him on the street.[26]

Millicent had no way of knowing that Austin and Mabel were trying unsuc-cessfully for a child of their own. They called it "the experiment."[27]

For his part, Mabel's husband David, as I have suggested, had his own erotic agendas. These have been amply described by historian Peter Gay, in *The Bourgeois Experience Victoria to Freud: Education of the Senses*, as "incestu-ous, polygamous, probably homosexual."[28] In less hyperbolic theoretical terms, David enjoyed Mabel's infidelity, or at least some of it, admired Austin as a civic leader, and considered him his best friend. Tragedy, comedy, or farce? It depends on your point of view.

Despite its complexity, Mabel did not regret her choice of Austin as a lover. We recall her heightened anxiety before her marriage, which seems not to have been fully or permanently resolved. Her arrangement with both David and Austin kept it in check by diversifying her emotional risks. She did not want a divorce from David, and it is not clear that she wanted Austin to divorce Susan, given the attendant loss of social status a divorce would have entailed. In "Sexuality, Class and Role in 19th-Century America," historian Charles E. Rosenberg notes that "any historical consideration of sexuality necessarily involves a problem in method. Most would-be students are concerned with behavior, but must satisfy themselves with the materials of myth and ideology; such scholars must somehow extrapolate a relationship between the content of this ideology and the behavior it, presumably, reflected and legitimated." But Mabel was sensitive to multiple ideologies, and that was part of her dilemma. She wanted to be a good wife and mother, and she wanted to be faithful to her husband. Her main commitment, however, was to actualizing her own potential, to opening doors for herself. Commenting on the discrepancy between what is good for society as a whole and what is good for the individual, Rosenberg suggests that the sexually repressive ideology operative in Victorian America was indeed functional in an increasingly bureaucratized society. It helped to create a "social discipline" appropriate to a "middle class of managers, professionals, and small entrepreneurs," while stifling basic human needs.[29] More recently, in "Sin, Murder, Adultery, and More: Narratives of Transgression in Nineteenth-Century America," Ann Schofield comments that "respectability infused most cultural narratives," while in *Criminal Conversations: Sentimentality and Nineteenth-Century Legal Stories*, Laura Hanft Korobkin describes the emergence in fiction, in the courtroom, and in the court of public opinion of an erotically autonomous wife.[30] This label describes Mabel in some ways but not in others.

In Amherst in the 1880s and 1890s, both Mabel and Austin wanted to conceal their sexual relationship and to some extent succeeded in doing so. While Mabel wrote about the affair in her diary, employing a sexual code to track her somatic life, what is more unusual is that she hoped to publish the many passionate letters she and Austin exchanged at some future time without, apparently, sacrificing her claim or his to American Victorian respectability. Like other powerful men, Austin came to believe that the rules that applied to other people were not made for him, and Mabel to some extent shared this elite perspective. The heart, she knew, has its reasons, and why wouldn't Sue just go away?

Here it is useful to recall that Mabel's adored father was an acquaintance of Walt Whitman's, that Whitman sent him copies of *Two Rivulets* in 1877 and of *Leaves of Grass* in 1882, that Mabel is likely to have read poetry by her father's friend before she had ever heard of Emily Dickinson, and that as indicated in her diary Mabel herself was reading *Leaves of Grass* in that year. In several senses, though, she was not a Whitmanian woman. As mentioned before, she had no desire to be the mother of a large brood, although she was tempted to become pregnant again with David in order to produce a son. Not so much reproaching herself as acknowledging her own limits, Mabel wrote, "I have not the quality of motherhood sufficiently developed. I do not in general care for children."[31] The question she was asking herself was whether she could make an exception for Millicent. Then, too, Mabel was attracted to the power differentials that Whitman's project works to negate. Consider the figure of the so-called Twenty-Ninth Bather, in Section 11 of "Song of Myself," who is the most erotically differentiated of his more usually anonymous cast of characters.

> Twenty-eight young men bathe by the shore,
> Twenty-eight young men and all so friendly;
> Twenty-eight years of womanly life and all so lonesome.
>
> She owns the fine house by the rise of the bank,
> She hides handsome and richly drest aft the blinds of the window.
>
> Which of the young men does she like the best?
> Ah the homeliest of them is beautiful to her.
>
> Where are you off to, lady? for I see you,
> You splash in the water there, yet stay stock still in your room.[32]

This emblematic figure, a classic instance of American Victorian sexual repression, desires *young* men whose economic status is either unmarked or inferior to hers, whereas Mabel's *amours* tended upward. She encouraged and then rejected the attentions of a vulnerable young man, Sue and Austin's son Ned, in favor of his older, wealthier father, and it was not until her husband's nervous collapse years later that Mabel turned to a younger man, an artist, for companionship. To think of her at age twenty-eight as not only handsome and richly drest and erotically desirous but also as intellectually, socially, and economically ambitious is accurate.

The *Century* and the Poetess

Thus in early December 1884, when she had just turned twenty-eight, Mabel's admirably detailed diary contains the following entry: "In the evening Mr. Dickinson came in like a brilliant north west breeze & read us a sparkling little story in the current *Century*."[33] The story, excerpted from "a still unpublished book," was titled "An Adventure of Huckleberry Finn: With an Account of the Famous Grangerford-Shepherdson Feud." To introduce this work to the public, Twain was splicing forward and back. Huck's beloved Jim soon disappears, but after several pages, he is replaced by Emmeline Grangerford. The poor dead poetess. The careless female artist. The sadful elegist. Reading aloud to the Todds, Austin could not have recited Emmeline's bathetic "Ode to Stephen Dowling Bots, Dec'd," for that had been excised, and it is remarkable how smoothly the narrative moves along without it.[34] This moment in Amherst and this episode in Twain's great novel together open up questions about women poets in the public sphere that reinforced Mabel's understanding of Dickinson's project. For that reason, I will take a closer look at Emmeline.

As Walter Blair and Barton Levi St. Armand have observed, Emmeline Grangerford is a composite figure, and no single source stands behind her.[35] In the novel's seventeenth chapter, Twain/Huck describes a supposed Emmeline who is herself imitating verse obituaries such as those she copies into her scrapbook out of the *Presbyterian Observer*. The effect of the caricature is to suggest that generic conventions exist and that Emmeline has failed to master them, which raises the further question of whether the conventions are themselves flawed, insofar as they are identified with gender. Myra Jehlen, calling Emmeline a sentimental silly, concludes that "on the whole in this story, being a woman is not a proud thing."[36] Huck thinks otherwise. "If Emmeline Grangerford could make poetry like that before she was fourteen," he remarks, "there ain't no telling what she could a done by and by."[37] Twain could count on his audience to recognize the genteel stereotype. He was reading the poetess tradition in broad terms as second rate. This was the normalizing association that Mabel Loomis Todd determined to disrupt.

Before proceeding, I should note that Dickinson herself had ample opportunity to read the *Century* excerpt that captivated Mabel, David, and Austin—the excerpt featuring Huck, Jim, Buck, Emmeline, the other Grangerfords, and Harney Shepherdson—but she doesn't mention Twain in any of her surviving writings. She too would have recognized the stereotype, though whether she would have enjoyed it is another question. According to Huck, Emmeline died for want of a rhyme and was quickly forgotten. In terms developed by literary theorist John Guillory, by sociologist Alvin Gouldner, and by philosopher Pierre Bourdieu, Emmeline Grangerford lacks cultural capital. That women writers might be useful to each other is something that Twain blocks out of his analysis, and I have come to think of the collaboration between Emily Dickinson and other women, including Mabel Loomis Todd, as Emmeline Grangerford's revenge.

From the moment she arrived in Amherst, Loomis Todd was ready to discover a woman of genius with whom she could identify, and in this eagerness, she was not alone. Many late nineteenth-century readers were eager to discover an American woman poet who could rank with the revered Elizabeth Barrett Browning or even the immortal Sappho. The desire to discover an American woman writer of genius extended far back in the nation's history of cultural competition, and it extended into Dickinson's own family. In 1826, when the poet's father Edward was still a bachelor, he described meeting the celebrated novelist Catharine Maria Sedgwick at a party he had attended. Edward was writing to his future wife, Emily Norcross, the poet's mother. He explained,

> I passed Tuesday Evening of this week, in company with Miss Sedgwick, the Authoress of "Redwood" & "New England Tale", at a party at Judge Lyman's. She has an interesting countenance—an appearance of much thought, & rather masculine feautures [sic]. And I feel happy at having an opportunity of seeing a female who has done so much to give our works of taste so pure and delicate a character—and a conscious pride that women of our own country & our our [sic] own State, too, are emulating not only the females, but the men of England & France & Germany & Italy in works of literature—& we are warranted in presuming that, if they had opportunities equal to their talents, they would not be inferior to

our own sex in improving in the sciences. Tho' I should be sorry to
see another Madame de Stael—especially if any one wished to make
a partner of her for life. Different qualities are more desirable in a
female who enters into domestic relations—and you have already
had my opinions on that Subject—More when we meet.[38]

For national pride, producing a distinguished woman author was advanta-
geous. For family pride, something else was needed. Edward was looking for
a True Woman and thought that he had found one in Emily Norcross. In
theory, he honors books; in practice, he distrusts their influence. As Emily
Dickinson later explained to Thomas Wentworth Higginson, "He buys me
many Books – but begs me not to read them – because he fears they joggle
the Mind" (L 261). Early biographers thought that she had a father complex,
and her relations with her father were considered "peculiar." She said on one
occasion, "I am not very well acquainted with father."[39] Meeting Edward
Dickinson in 1870, Higginson wrote, "I saw Mr. Dickinson this morning a
little—thin dry & speechless—I saw what her life has been. Dr. S. [the college president] says her *sister* [italics mine] is proud of her" (L 342b).

No one doubts that Lavinia was proud of Dickinson's mind and art.
What about Austin? As noted by his daughter Martha, Austin feared publicity for the family and had a "morbid horror" of any suggestion that his
sister Emily had suffered a "love disappointment."[40] Martha, in her carefully
scripted and still unpublished *Recollections of a Country Girl*, remarks that her
father "never liked and would not even hear those of her poems sent over to
my mother that were sad or suggested anything of the kind." Because Martha
was herself not only musical but also literary, as she matured she was warned
by her father against "solitude and introspection. . . . There were to be no
more solitary poets in his family."[41] Nevertheless, Martha Dickinson Bianchi's title for the volume she edited as a memorial to the friendship of her
mother and aunt was *The Single Hound*, a phrase from the last stanza of a
poem in which Dickinson reflects on cosmic loneliness, comparing life to an
almost posthumous experiment in facing death without the benefit of spiritual belief.

> This Consciousness that is aware
> Of Neighbors and the Sun
> Will be the one aware of Death
> And that itself alone

Figure 10. Austin Dickinson in 1890. Passionate about Mabel, he was unenthusiastic about the publication of his sister's poems. Courtesy Todd-Bingham Picture Collection, Yale University. MS 496E, MADID 196.

Is traversing the interval
Experience between
And most profound experiment
Appointed unto Men –

How adequate unto itself
It's properties shall be
Itself unto itself and None
Shall make discovery –

Adventure most unto itself
The Soul condemned to be –
Attended by a single Hound
It's own identity. (*Fr* 817)[42]

This was precisely the kind of existential loneliness, with its residual Puritanism, that did not concern Mabel. She had been raised to believe that God, or a world spirit Oversoul, was on her side and that concerns about hell and damnation were old-fashioned. Mabel reveled in the power and genius she recognized in herself; these were *her* hounds, and she welcomed them. It was time, she thought, for gifted women in American society to shine and reign. How, though, to do it, or more precisely, what was to be her medium? Teaching piano was all to the well and good, and she occasionally sold some of her small flower paintings, but these were not the heroic public feats of which she knew herself capable.

A Literary Career Is My Only Relief

Mabel's heroism emerged slowly and unevenly after Dickinson's death. Dressed in black at the funeral, she was observed looking "haggard, as if she had lost a dear friend."[43] Because her powers of recovery were formidable, later that day she confided to her diary,

> Just after dinner my dear Mr. Dickinson came in with his hands full of apple-blossoms to tell me his final arrangements for the afternoon . . . At 2:30 David came & we went across to Emily's funeral. The most deliciously brilliant sunny afternoon. Simple "services"—Col.

Higginson read Emily Bronte's poem on Immortality. Then we all
walked quietly across the sunny fields, full of innocents & buttercups to the cemetery.[44]

And to her mother, days later,

The funeral—if so ghastly a name could apply to anything so poetical as the service of last Wednesday afternoon—was the most beautiful thing I ever saw. Several clergymen were there, & Col. Higginson
came up from Cambridge. . . . The few words that he spoke to
preface his reading [of Brontë's poem] were simply exquisite. Then
President Seelye [the Amherst College president], Dr. Hitchcock [a
professor] & the other honorary pall-bearers took out the dainty,
white casket into the sunshine, where it was lifted by the stout arms
of six or eight Irish workmen, all of whom have worked about the
place or been servants in the family for years, & all of whom Emily
saw & talked with, occasionally, up to the last. They carried her
through the fields, full of buttercups, while the friends who chose,
followed on irregularly through the ferny footpaths to the little
cemetery.[45]

Despite the observation that Mabel looked haggard, in her writing she sounds
as though she is enjoying herself. Writing provided Mabel with a safe haven
from the Amherst gossips, and besides, wasn't the well-organized funeral so
like a book, so poetical? Her tears dried quickly.

Mourning the loss of his beloved mother and theorizing grief, Roland
Barthes observes that "as soon as someone dies, [there is a] frenzied construction of the future (shifting furniture, etc.): futuromania."[46] It was the more
deeply bereaved Vinnie who was frenzied and whose futuromania had important consequences. Marietta Jameson, the neighbor who observed Mabel at
the funeral, recorded Vinnie's disconsolate words: "Yesterday AM [May 15,
the day Emily died] when I went over Vinnie said, 'How can I live without
her? Ever since we were little girls we have been wonderfully dear to each
other—and many times when desirable offers of marriage have been made to
Emily she has said—I have never seen anyone that I cared for as much as you
Vinnie.'" Mrs. Jameson continued, "Sometimes I feel as if Vinnie would not
long survive her—she is very thin, & white and this winter's anxiety [Emily's
health] has told fearfully upon her—Perhaps there is a Providence in Emily's
thus being taken as she could not very well be left alone."[47] Despite her tart

tongue, Vinnie was not alone. She had her house and grounds and garden, her friends, her remaining family (a mixed blessing to be sure—she and Sue were not natural soulmates), her family pride, her servants, her cats, her dreams of romance—were they memories?—and Emily's poems.

Shortly after the poet's death, Vinnie began an aggressive campaign to make her sister's genius known to the world. She turned first to Susan and, when Susan delayed, to Mabel, who was interested in helping but who had other, more pressing commitments. Mabel first copied a few poems at Lavinia's request in February 1887, but in June she and David left for Japan, where he planned to photograph a total solar eclipse and she planned to write about it. Leaving Millicent with her parents in Washington, she enjoyed the train trip across Canada to Vancouver and tolerated seasickness with the physical resilience and good humor that defined all of her travels. She spent long days painting and socializing while David was away from dawn to dusk preparing to photograph the corona of the sun that she was preparing to draw. At the last minute, the corona was obscured by clouds, and writing to Austin the next day, Mabel exclaimed, "Oh! my dear, my dear! How can I find words to tell you of yesterday's disappointment!"[48] A few weeks later, she became the first woman to climb Mount Fuji on foot. Her account of this historical event, published in the *Nation* on October 13, 1887, explains, "Until the revolution of 1868, which changed so many old customs and prejudices, foreigners were not allowed to ascend this great peak, as they were looked upon in the light of mere beasts. Neither were women permitted to go higher than the sixth station [of ten]."[49] Mabel mined this trip for all it was worth, and that fall two other articles in the *Nation* were reprinted in the *New York Post*, the *Springfield Republican*, and the *Amherst Record*. By then she was a local celebrity.

The poetry work began in earnest only in November, and David helped with some of the transcriptions. In *Ancestors' Brocades: The Literary Discovery of Emily Dickinson: The Editing and Publication of Her Letters and Poems*, their daughter Millicent Todd Bingham quotes David's recollection, " 'We used to spend hours and hours . . . just looking at the poems. Vinnie would bring over a basketful which she would dump on the floor in front of the fireplace in the back parlor at night. After your mother had finished copying them, I compared them with the originals and then she went all over them again. It took hours and hours of my time.' "[50] Whereas David was doing his duty and perhaps atoning for his infidelities, Mabel found the work uplifting. It eased her pain.

Self-pityingly, she could view her life as a tragedy, and because the social pressures were intense, she left Amherst when she could. She and David spent Christmas visiting his family in New Jersey; she was in Washington in March; and fortunately Sue, whom she and Austin referred to as "the Great Black Mogul," was away in August with her children.[51] Torn by her two identities and still emotionally dependent on David, Mabel derived both intense pleasure and intense pain from her affair with Austin, all the while continuing to transcribe Dickinson's poems and to attend to her other writings. Travel remained important in transporting her out of a town, Amherst, where her actions were minutely scrutinized, and she had an admirable fund of curiosity about the world and its ways. Consequently, in the fall of 1889, she was planning to accompany David on an eight-month trip to West Africa, but the plan fell through at the last minute. And so, it will be recalled, having spent the better part of two years selecting and transcribing Dickinson's poems, she was looking for a publisher and met with Higginson. Vinnie had already spoken to him, but he was dubious. When the magnetic Mabel read him some of her favorite poems—they were in her cousin Caro's luxurious apartment—he had a transformative experience. Almost. Higginson had many other critical agendas, whereas Mabel was thoroughly committed to the project. "I feel more and more," she noted in her journal, "that I must write or die. A literary career is my only relief."[52]

Months passed. In early January, she attended a lunch party in her honor at the Charles Street home of Annie Adams Fields, who prided herself on her "eminent friendships." Willa Cather explains, "For a period of sixty years Mrs. Fields's Boston house, at 148 Charles Street, extended its gracious hospitality to the aristocracy of letters and art and to an aristocracy of charming personalities rarer still. During that long stretch of time there was scarcely an American of distinction in letters or art or public life who was not a guest in that house; scarcely a visiting foreigner of renown who did not pay his tribute there."[53] Fields, the widow of "gentleman" publisher James T. Fields, wrote poetry herself, and Mabel must have mentioned her work on Dickinson; perhaps Higginson facilitated the introduction. The party was a sign of progress, although as she explained in a long letter to Austin, she was nursing her mother and grandmother who were down with the flu and "got over there just *barely* in time to be decent. . . . It was a very pleasant occasion, but I had to come back & fly upstairs again, & then get the two dinners, & carry up; & then I arranged them for the night, & went to the Symphony concert."[54] Then, in February, there was a drawing room talk on climbing Mt. Fuji that initiated a lecturing career in which Mabel Loomis Todd eventually covered some 160 towns, mainly in New England and the Midwest. Her mother was in the audience and, by her own account, overjoyed—"she is a tremendous critic, & she said I had at last found my genius—she never heard anything so cultivated and ladylike and bright & perfect." By her own account, Mabel was "a brilliant success."[55]

That winter, Higginson was ill, but not too ill to select about two hundred poems from Mabel's typescripts and to attempt to interest Houghton Mifflin in them. They declined. When Higginson recovered, Mabel was in Chicago, visiting a wealthy and very social cousin who introduced her around, although Mabel felt that she was being snubbed by one of cousin Lydia's friends because of Sue—she was mistaken. In Chicago, she gave well-attended drawing room talks on Japan and planned for her return to Boston and Amherst, where she and Austin were to be reunited. "I dont know what you mean about 'the poems' and their possibly delaying you somewhere," he wrote. "That is of no consequence."[56] All in all, the Chicago trip was a triumph. Cousin Lydia, herself a feminist and a poet, applauded Mabel as "the brightest & most versatile woman she ever knew."[57] When she got back to Amherst on May 15, Lavinia's faithful housekeeper Maggie Maher was in the basement cooking supper, and Austin, who was impatient with her work on his sister, was by the fireplace.

Returning to Boston at the end of May, Mabel Loomis Todd met with Higginson and they agreed on a manuscript of two hundred poems, which she took to Roberts Brothers, a firm with a history of developing and supporting women writers. In mid-June, Thomas Niles signed on, though not without some resistance. "Dear Mr. Higginson," he wrote, "It has always seemed to me that it would be unwise to perpetuate Miss Dickinson's poems. They are quite as remarkable for defects as for beauties & are generally devoid of true poetical qualities. If, however, Miss Dickinson [Lavinia] will pay for the plates, we will publish them . . . a small ed."[58] Niles's memory was imperfect, his "always" inaccurate. But now, on the advice of his editor Arlo Bates, who as Niles acknowledged was not inclined to be overly generous, he insisted that the number be cut almost in half. Despite these setbacks, by August Mabel was reading proofs and Higginson was drafting an essay he hoped to place in the *Century*. When the *Century* could not offer an immediate publication date, he turned to the *Christian Union*, a publication that elicited this response from Austin, in the form of a personal letter dated October 10:

My Dear Col Higginson

    It is inexcusable that I have not sooner acknowledged, in even the briefest manner, my appreciation of your notice of my sister and her work. . . .

    Whether it was, on the whole, advisable to publish is yet with me, a question, but my Sister Vin, whose knowledge of what is, or has been, outside of her dooryard is bounded by the number of her callers, who had no comprehension of her sister, yet believed her a shining genius, was determined to have some of her writing where it could be read of all men, and she is expecting to become famous herself thereby, and now we shall see.[59]

Despite his lack of enthusiasm, Austin ordered "a dozen copies" of Higginson's essay. The train was about to start and he did not want to miss it.

Sincerity and the Reviews

Sincerity, originality, intensity, poetic power—the terms run together in nearly six hundred reviews collected in Willis J. Buckingham's invaluable documentary 1890s history. "Herein is the note of every line that she penned," enthused a New York weekly, "sincerity." "Absolute sincerity can be felt even in the most astonishingly odd or original remarks and views," praised the *Hartford Courant*. The *San Francisco Sunday Call* explained, "Early in life she revolted from the orthodox creed, but she was none the less dominated by her austere Puritan ideals. Strongest among these was an intense craving for sincerity, together with a loathing for cant and social hypocrisy." The politically oriented Chicago weekly *America* announced, "Whatever else may be said of Miss Dickinson's verse there is not room for doubting the sincerity of its origin."[60] The new sincerity did not mean that nothing was withheld, and many reviewers commented on the poet's biographical elusiveness. For example: "Emily Dickinson was a strange creature. None of her friends knew that she wrote verse: the secret did not come out until after her death." And "Tales of thwarted love naturally were invented by gossiping imaginations, and some of Miss Dickinson's poems strongly deepen the impression that there may have been some foundation for the idea. But if her life really had its tragic romance the secret had been so loyally guarded by her friends that the inquisitive public does not yet and probably never will know it as an acknowledged fact."[61]

As both of these pioneering editors anticipated, reviewers also commented on the poet's seeming lack of technical skill, formal sophistication, and polish. Even Mabel's father had his doubts. Shortly after the book appeared on November 12, 1890, he wrote her, "The book is dainty beyond description, but in reading the poems I am mad (in country vernacular) all of the time. Why didn't she pay some attention to rhythm & rhyme? The thoughts are too strong and beautiful to be wasted, and half of their beauty is concealed, and to the majority of readers will be forever, under the rough exterior."[62] And this from Whitman's friend, a man who could reassure the Whitman circle that Emerson had not lost faith in the poetry, even if the poet himself was a shameless self-promoter. "Dainty" was perhaps a compliment to Mabel's artwork, since the flowers on the cover were copied from her design.

To deflect doubt about rough exteriors and other strangenesses, Higginson had crafted a widely cited "Preface," in which he classified Dickinson as a "portfolio" or journal-keeping poet, drawing the term from an 1840 Emerson essay that described a "revolution in literature." "Only one man in the thousand may print a book," Emerson had suggested, "but one in ten or one in five may inscribe his thoughts, or at least with short commentary his favorite readings in a private journal."[63] Although Emerson's language refers to men, portfolio keepers in the nineteenth century were often women, and since their journals were usually meant for private consumption, they need not be faulted for fragmentary form.[64] Furthermore, Higginson's essay "An Open Portfolio" appeared in the *Christian Union*, a nonsectarian religious and literary family weekly, on September 25, 1890, as part of the "dainty" book's advance publicity campaign. Its first word was "Emerson."[65] He knew Emerson personally and had been writing about him for years. Although he never forgot the radical reformer, his later Emerson was "to sit, like Socrates, beneath the plane-trees, and offer profound and beautiful aphorisms, without even the vague thread of the Socratic method to tie them together . . . he remained still among the poets, not among the philosophic doctors, and must be permanently classified in that manner."[66]

Reviewers immediately picked up on the Emerson connection. One explained, "Her poems in their apparent wilfulness of intonation often recall Emerson's, but also as much by the character of their thought, for she was a transcendentalist by native essence, and her intuitions were her reasons."

Another: "Her poetry is cast, for the most part, in a single mould; but that is wholly original and of a fine rugged beauty. The influence of Emerson is apparent in it."[67] Another: "Some of the poems on different aspects of nature would have delighted Ralph Waldo Emerson. They are akin to him in spirit—such as his feminine counterpart might have written." The author of this comment, Louise Chandler Moulton, began by noting, "If one were to judge the book by the theories of poetic art, one would hardly call most of its contents poems at all," but that "there is about the book a fascination, a power, a vision that enthralls you, and draws you back to it again and again." This sympathetic reader, who was herself a poet, fiction writer, and journalist, argued, "Dickinson felt the pitilessness of nature as . . . Emerson never felt it" and that "she meant that these leaves torn from her heart should be her legacy to the world when she herself had passed beyond its reach."[68] Mabel noted in her journal that the review was "strong and appreciative."[69]

Of course Emerson had enemies, the comparisons were not always flattering, and at least one was downright sexist:

> Her limitations show plainly in her work and much study of Emerson has colored and shaped her vision; it has also cramped her methods of expression. It will not do to say that the "discipline of public criticism and the enforced conformity to accepted ways" could have broadened Miss Dickinson to the stature of a first-class poetical genius. Her lack was intrinsic and constitutional. Mere functional derangement of the organ of expression is curable; but here was organic lesion of the most unmistakable type. Her vision was clear and surprisingly accurate, but her touch was erratic and at frequent intervals nerveless, while her sense of completeness was singularly dull. She exaggerated the faults of Emerson's verse-style into absurdity. She rhymes *tell* and *still*, *book* and *think*, *own* and *young*, *denied* and *smiled*, *gate* and *mat*, *care* and *hour*, and so on into hundreds of the like, perhaps, with the singular misfortune of failing often just at the point where a perfect rhyme is absolutely necessary to complete the turn of grace or the point of lyrical surprise.[70]

The reviewer, Maurice Thompson, was quoting the "Preface" authored by Higginson but in a letter he was kinder: "I appreciate the fine originality of the poems and honor the forthright sincerity of expression that marks them as coming from a strong, independent soul."[71]

Let me pause for a moment to suggest that sincerity has deep roots in histories of American feeling and that the localized crisis of gender to which Mabel was responding made it impossible for her to satisfy the sincere ideal. As Jay Fliegelman explains in *Declaring Independence: Jefferson, Natural Language, and the Culture of Performance*, the essence of sincerity is "the demand that private and public character cohere in a single, externalized self."[72] In fact, Mabel made that argument about her "startlingly original" poet in a little known essay that she published in *Home Magazine*, a Washington, DC women's monthly. Modestly titled "Bright Bits from Bright Books," Dickinson, she wrote, "lived out her own ideas—a thing for which most of us have not the courage. . . . Finding as her life went on that society grew more distasteful, that the hollowness and insincerity of its forms hampered and annoyed her more than anything it bestowed could compensate, she withdrew more and more into herself."[73] For Mabel, this was an emotionally satisfying reason for Dickinson's reclusion, as it was for many of her contemporaries and as it still remains. I see versions of this argument almost every day.

Never having met Dickinson or corresponded with her extensively, Moulton was confident that Dickinson had a vision of the future of poetry in which she herself would figure. Higginson was much less sure and emphasized that the poetry was produced "absolutely without the thought of publication, and solely by way of expression of the writer's own mind." The quotation is from the first sentence of the 1890 "Preface," which was written by Higginson alone. The opening sentence thus brings together several of Higginson's main themes: Emerson, portfolio poetry, and sincerity. He distanced his poet from a perhaps "tainted" field of literary production, even as "she" entered the fray. Higginson further stated that "in the case of the present author, there was absolutely no choice in the matter; she must write thus, or not at all."[74]

In "Bright Bits," Mabel says nothing about Dickinson's intentions for her poetry, and we do not have copies of the many lectures on Dickinson that she delivered between 1890 and 1896, when the War Between the Houses stopped her public readings of this material. Turning, however, to the three prefaces she wrote (to the 1891 *Poems*, to the 1894 *Letters*, and to the 1896 *Poems*), as well as the very interesting comments interspersed in the *Letters*, it is apparent that her Dickinson is a self-conscious and deliberate artist who united public and private selves by repressing the desire to publish and other varieties of ordinary self-extension and circulation.[75] For example, in 1891 she

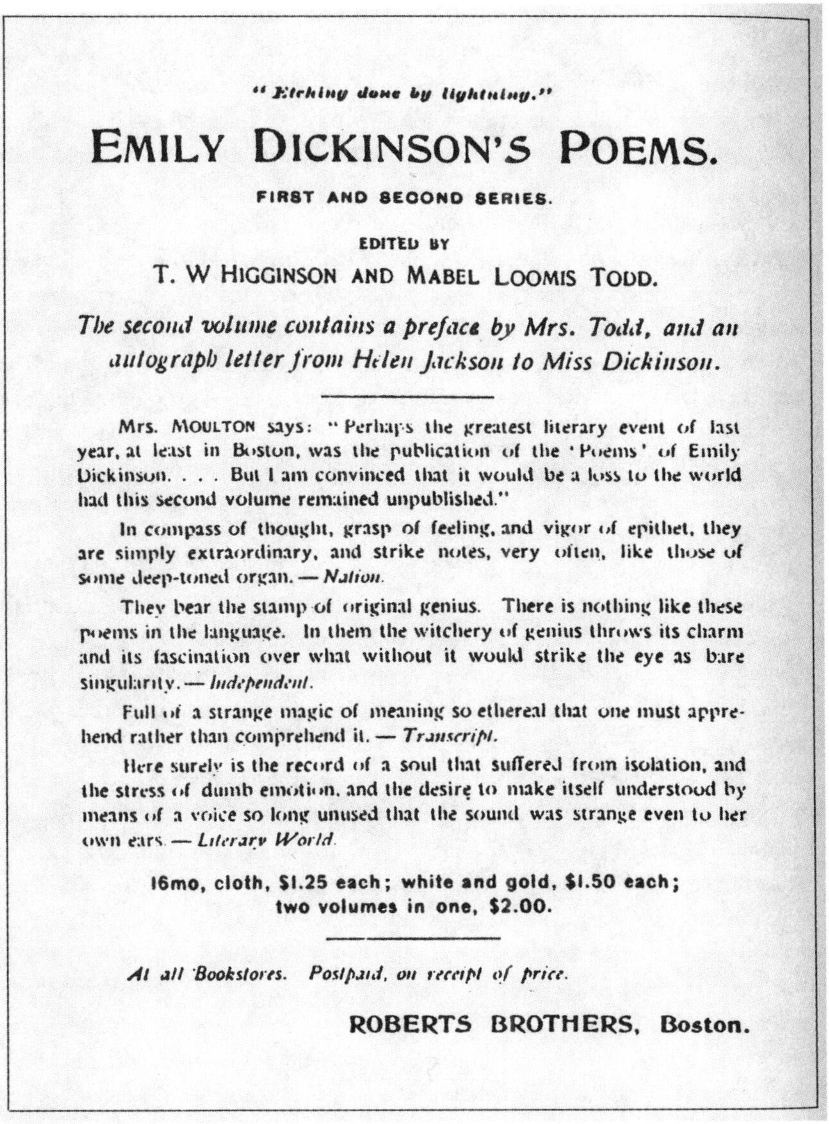

" Etching done by lightning."

EMILY DICKINSON'S POEMS.

FIRST AND SECOND SERIES.

EDITED BY

T. W HIGGINSON AND MABEL LOOMIS TODD.

The second volume contains a preface by Mrs. Todd, and an autograph letter from Helen Jackson to Miss Dickinson.

———

Mrs. MOULTON says: " Perhaps the greatest literary event of last year, at least in Boston, was the publication of the ' Poems ' of Emily Dickinson. . . . But I am convinced that it would be a loss to the world had this second volume remained unpublished."

In compass of thought, grasp of feeling, and vigor of epithet, they are simply extraordinary, and strike notes, very often, like those of some deep-toned organ. — *Nation.*

They bear the stamp of original genius. There is nothing like these poems in the language. In them the witchery of genius throws its charm and its fascination over what without it would strike the eye as bare singularity. — *Independent.*

Full of a strange magic of meaning so ethereal that one must apprehend rather than comprehend it. — *Transcript.*

Here surely is the record of a soul that suffered from isolation, and the stress of dumb emotion, and the desire to make itself understood by means of a voice so long unused that the sound was strange even to her own ears. — *Literary World.*

16mo, cloth, $1.25 each; white and gold, $1.50 each; two volumes in one, $2.00.

———

At all Bookstores. Postpaid, on receipt of price.

ROBERTS BROTHERS, Boston.

Figure 11. An 1892 advertisement for the first two books of Emily Dickinson's poems, from one of Mabel Loomis Todd's many scrapbooks in the Mabel Loomis Todd Papers, Yale University.

strongly disputes the view that all of Dickinson's poetry was tossed off at the white heat. While this may be true of some poems, "still more had received thoughtful revision": "There is the frequent addition of rather perplexing foot-notes, affording large choices of words and phrases. And in the copies which she sent to friends, sometimes one form, sometimes another, is found to have been used. . . . To what further rigorous pruning her verses would have been subjected had she published them herself, we cannot know." Although she stops short of saying that Dickinson had thought about future publication, she does state that "many of the poems had been carefully copied on sheets of note-paper, and tied in little fascicles, each of six or eight sheets." And in 1894, she concludes the "Introductory" by saying, "Warm thanks are due the friends who have generously lent letters for reproduction. That they were friends of Emily Dickinson, and willing to share her words with the larger outside circle, waiting and appreciative, entitles them to the gratitude, not merely of the Editor, but of all who make up the world that Emily 'never saw,' but to which, nevertheless, she sent a 'message.'" The vocabulary replicates the intimacy of a domestic scene, and readers who never knew Dickinson are constructed as a "shy" poet's friends. Gesturing toward a separate spheres vocabulary that served to shore up threatened class, racial, and ethnic boundaries, Mabel Todd's strategy suggests that whatever Dickinson's intentions, the "gentle, wide-eyed" values of a woman-centered private sphere may be extended into the public arena without violating ethical principles. "The sanctities were not invaded," she asserts disingenuously.

In some of the comments interspersed throughout the 1894 volume, Mabel Todd is bolder and refuses to commit to the no-thought-of-publication narrative: "Whether, in writing her poems, the joy of creating was sufficient, or whether a thought of future and wider recognition ever came, it is certain that during life her friends made her audience. She cared more for appreciation and approval from the few who were dear than for any applause from an impersonal public. She herself writes, 'My friends are my estate.'"[76] Thus we cannot know whether Dickinson at times thought about wider recognition, but as a young woman her stories were the focus of her school friends' admiration, while "intellectual brilliancy of an individual type was already at seventeen her distinguishing characteristic." Todd does acknowledge that "Emily was often besieged by different persons, literary and otherwise, to benefit the world by her 'chirrup'" and that she steadily refused their entreaties. The word "chirrup" may suggest that some of Dickinson's admirers, however sincere, were lacking in intellectual gravitas. Dickinson entertained that opinion herself, writing to her cousin Louisa Norcross, "Of Miss P—I know but this, dear. She wrote me in October, requesting me to aid the world by my chirrup more. Perhaps she stated it as my duty, I don't distinctly remember, and always burn such letters, so I cannot obtain it now. I replied declining. She did not write to me again – she might have been offended, or perhaps is extricating humanity from some hopeless ditch" (L 380). Todd quoted this letter too.[77]

Not surprisingly, there is some slippage in Todd's various representations of Dickinson's private self, which the very short 1896 preface does nothing to resolve. It consists of three short paragraphs, refers readers to what has already been said about Dickinson's "intellectual activity [which] was so great that a large and characteristic choice is still possible among her literary material," and dodges the problem of interpretation, claiming that "the surroundings in which any of Emily Dickinson's verses are known to have been written usually serve to explain them clearly, but in general the present volume is full of thought needing no interpretation to those who apprehend this scintillating spirit." Even before the War Between the Houses put an end to her Dickinson project, Mabel was being distracted by other matters.

I have been arguing that Mabel Todd's Dickinson is distinct from Higginson's, but as we might expect, there are important points of convergence. The American audience projected by Todd and Higginson valued "sincerity," which represents the convergence of a public and a private self, or in the absence of such a convergence the refusal of public performance. But this audience also demanded worldliness in the form of formal self-restraint. Thus if Dickinsonian sincerity is one unifying theme of 1890s criticism, so too is the assumption that sincerity alone is a weak aesthetic value, and some 1890s critics were perfectly willing to believe that Dickinson was sincere about her emotions but to be pitied; although "a person of power which came very near to that indefinable quality which we call genius . . . she never learned her art."[78] When Houghton Mifflin rejected the manuscript of the first edition, "The poems, they said, were much too queer—the rhymes were all wrong. They thought that Higginson must be losing his mind to recommend such stuff."[79] For 1890s readers, technical competence might go some distance toward compensating for ideological incoherence. Almost everyone could spot a faulty rhyme, even if *metrical* competence (not to say subtlety) remained the purview of an elite. Higginson therefore asked, "When a thought takes one's breath away, who cares to count the syllables?" (The question demonstrates the problem, since English verse rhythms are not merely syllabic.[80]) Mabel Todd used the wonderful term "'thought-rhymes,'" "appealing, indeed, to an unrecognized sense more elusive than hearing." The appeal was lost on many, including her father Eben Loomis, even if, as Todd stated, "It seems in many cases that she intentionally avoided the smoother and more unusual rhymes."[81]

This we know: together Todd and Higginson changed enough to persuade influential readers that a new style of American women's poetry did exist—terse, compressed, audacious, vigorous, powerfully engaged with the very mysteries of life and death and offering a glimpse of experiences "too intense to be more plainly intimated."[82] Given the commercial success of the 1890 volume and its warm reception in influential critical corners, Higginson wrote to Todd in April 1891, "Let us alter as little as possible, now that the public ear is opened." He added, "One poem only I dread a little to print—that wonderful 'Wild Nights,'—lest the malignant read into it more than that virgin recluse ever dreamed of putting there. Has Miss Lavinia any shrinking about it? You will understand & pardon my solicitude."[83] Miss Lavinia did not shrink and "Wild Nights" was included among the love poems of the new volume. It was quoted in full by the *Springfield Republican* reviewer, Charles Goodrich Whiting, who despite Todd's assurance that Dickinson "'was not an invalid and lived in seclusion from no love disappointment'" did not shrink from asserting that the love poems could "never could have been written without experience; the deepest feeling must have inspired them, and no one can read them without the conviction that Emily Dickinson knew what she was writing about, whether or not her seclusion was due thereto."[84] As to Mabel, she understood the power of erotic fantasy and was not about to object to Dickinson's dream-life, which she understood as richly traumatic, like her own. Perhaps, too, she understood Higginson's comment as a harmless form of minor flirtation, which it was.

Although in the 1890 "Preface," Higginson did not acknowledge that he and Todd were engaged in creative editing, in the 1891 "Preface," which she alone signed, Todd was more candid. I have already quoted the passage in which she refers to Dickinson's "rather perplexing foot-notes, affording large choice of words and phrases." She also stated that Dickinson capitalized almost every important word and that in her later years she had abandoned almost all punctuation except dashes. Anyone looking carefully at the book would know that the texts had been altered. The footnotes were gone, there were not that many unusual capitals, and there were very few dashes. Justifying these changes and others which were not mentioned, Todd wondered aloud, "To what further rigorous pruning her verses would have been subjected had she published them herself, we cannot know. They should be regarded in many cases as merely the first strong and suggestive sketches of an artist, intended to be embodied at some time in the finished picture." She noted too that "in the copies which she sent to friends, sometimes one form, sometimes another, is found to have been used."[85]

The Artificiality of Modern Life

Praising Dickinson's directness and simplicity in the "Preface" to the 1891 *Poems*, Todd presented her as an alternative to "modern artificiality." She was less than candid in stating that "without important exception, her friends have generously placed at the disposal of the Editors any poems they had received from her; and these have given the obvious advantage of comparison among several renderings of the same word."[86] Surely Susan did not place any of the poems she had received from Emily at Todd's disposal or, for that matter, at Higginson's. She was outraged by Todd's poaching and longed to expose her rival's double life. With Higginson, she took the high road, writing him that " 'The Poems' will ever be to me marvellous whether in manuscript or type." Her graciousness notwithstanding, she does blame him for telling her that the poems were "un-presentable" and discouraging her efforts.[87] Probably they discussed publication when Higginson visited her at The Evergreens in late July 1888—he was in town for a meeting of the American Philological Association and mentions the visit in his diary. Susan's "unpresentable" comment underscores the crucial role that Todd played in the fall of 1889 when she visited Higginson in Boston and read aloud to him, embodying possibilities he had not previously seen.

After Susan read his *Christian Union* article, she stopped speaking to Lavinia and hoped to find a publisher for at least some of the poems in her possession, but when Lavinia asserted her legal rights, she backed down. It goes without saying that Austin was not supporting Susan in the parallel project, since nobody imagined that there would be sufficient demand for two books. He may also have taken a perverse pleasure in thwarting her. She therefore explained to William Hayes Ward, editor of the New York *Independent*, "Mr. Dickinson thinks as Col. Higginson and Niles are to bring out another vol. of the poems, it is not best, or fair to them to print many. I do not feel in any way bound to them, but will of course defer to his wish in the matter."[88]

It was not until after Austin's death in August 1895 that Mabel, too, ran into serious trouble with Lavinia, although there had been provocations before. For example, Lavinia made the outrageous suggestion that Higginson leave his coworker's name off *Poems: First Series*, writing him that Mabel was to be "*sub rosa*, for reasons you will understand." Part of her letter is missing, so we don't know what she told him after that, but he was surely discovering that "it is hard to steer safely among Dickinsons!"[89] Then in 1894 there were problems with the book of letters that Mabel was gathering with Lavinia's help. When Lavinia wanted the contract to be issued in her name alone, Austin came down hard on her. "Vinnie is an awful snake," Mabel wrote in her diary, "but all the same it hurts me very much."[90] Lavinia had spent most of her life with no money of her own and reveled in the prospect of royalties. She was also offended by Mabel's preface, which minimized her importance as a collaborator. These conflicts were compounded by her fear of Susan, who was not one to be easily thwarted.

In more ways than one, the trouble went back to Austin. Years earlier, he had drafted a will and extracted a secret promise from Lavinia. Writing to Mabel, he explained that the will was "not quite as [he] wanted it, but best for now."

> I have left all my share of my father's estate to Vin with the request that she shall turn it over to you. She has promised to do this, so you are protected in any case.
> I will see you tomorrow.
> W. A. Dickinson[91]

Mabel kept the document, but the ruse did not work because Lavinia was human. Not only was she entranced by the romance of dollars, but she also did not want to risk further alienating Sue. For his part, Austin must have felt that he could trust Lavinia, despite that fact that his half of the patrimonial package included her home. He chose the easy way out, asking her to do something he was afraid to do himself.

The strategy backfired. Lavinia stalled, thus making it clear that she had no intention of turning over Austin's half of his inheritance to Mabel, which included a meadow of seven or eight acres and certain stocks and bonds, as well as his share of the Homestead. Yet Lavinia was depending on Mabel to finish editing *Poems: Third Series* and did not want to risk alienating her further. Understandably, Mabel was distraught. She had lost the lover who wrote to her shortly before his death, "All the old things and real things are solid—never more so—adamantive. You must understand—and believe."[92] Without Austin, her substitute father, Mabel's world was an unreal place, but as we have seen she was not one to fold under the pressure of events and unarticulated feelings. Instead, she interpreted her pain as "signet royal of my closeness to my dear master."[93] The suicide she was anticipating would have to wait, and she began to discipline herself to stop thinking about it.

Two days before Mabel submitted the manuscript of *Poems: Third Series* to Roberts Brothers, she recorded in her diary that Vinnie was "going to do one lovely thing."[94] On February 7, 1896, Lavinia did indeed transfer to the Todds a strip of land fifty-four feet wide adjoining their house to the east, which rounded off their property nicely. It was part of the meadow and both Todds believed that Austin had intended them to have it; he had already started planting it, landscape gardening being one of his passions. The deed was signed in the presence of Mabel's attorney in the evening at the Homestead. Apparently neither Mabel nor Lavinia wanted it recorded immediately: Mabel hoped to be out of the country before Susan found out what had happened, and Lavinia was no doubt conflicted about transferring land to Mabel and David that would otherwise have gone to her heirs, Mattie and Ned. In any event, she seems to have deluded herself into thinking that she could keep her "one lovely thing" from her financial adviser Dwight Hills, who did not want her signing away land without his knowledge. Gordon explains,

> Lavinia had a business adviser in place of Austin, another rather volatile gentleman, Dwight Hills, for twenty-four years President of the First National Bank of Amherst. Aware of the pressure on Lavinia to hand over land, he had warned her not to sign any paper without his knowledge. Hills spoke as a protector and Lavinia, rumour said, warmed to this attention from a mature bachelor who lived with his mother. In her youth Lavinia had been a demonstrative young woman with long black hair tinged with red. It was still long and luxurious, and sometimes she shook it out and aired it, combing it with her fingers to the tips. She would rather not annoy Mr Hills with the 'lovely thing' she would do for Mabel Todd.[95]

For these and more obscure reasons, when a "Record of conveyance was made in the Registry of Deeds at Northampton on April 1, 1896," the Todds were unaware of it.[96] They left for Japan several days later, where David would again attempt to photograph the corona of a total solar eclipse, and they were still in Japan at the end of August when Sue saw a nasty critical notice in the *New York Tribune*.

It began, "Mrs. Mabel Loomis Todd has a heavy responsibility to answer for," and without having seen the new book, seized the opportunity to dismiss what had come before:

> There is no injustice in . . . anticipating the character of the "third series." The first contained much inferior matter, the second was even more disappointing, and it is incredible, we repeat, that Mrs. Todd could have brought together enough good verse to make a new collection. What she has really done, we suspect, has been to collect fragments or even complete poems which belong, as nine-tenths of Emily Dickinson's verses belong, to the sphere of casual, moody writing, to a class of verse which most poets, whether they have genius or not, regard as mere trifles or experiments. Sometimes the genius, the great genius, can afford to print these trifles, once he has made his position secure; but a poet like Emily Dickinson could never safely do any such thing. Her vogue has passed—it was a temporary affair in its highest estate—and now such reputation as she has among minor lyrists is imperilled by the indiscretion of her executors. Poor misunderstood authorship! How it must hunger in its grave to be protected from its friends![97]

Angrier than usual, Susan communicated her fury to Lavinia through her son Ned, who was used to being caught in the crossfire of his parents' battles. "It makes me shudder to think of having the family name dragged before an unwilling public," he wrote, "and by a woman who has brought nothing but a sword into the family."[98]

The *Tribune* aside, reviews of the 1896 volume were generally respectful, and even Higginson was touting Dickinson as a woman of genius.[99] This was the first poem volume that Todd had edited on her own, and without Higginson to restrain her, she was engaging in even more "creative" editing than before. Todd had submitted the manuscript of *Poems: Third Series* while she was in Japan and must have taken copies of the originals with her, but as

Caroline C. Maun tells us, roughly a third of the published poems contain omitted stanzas.[100] That same month, the *Outlook* published her article on Oahu College, in which she quoted a truncated version of "The reticent volcano keeps / His never slumbering plan" (*Fr* 1776). Although the poem has three stanzas, the *Outlook* version she submitted has two.[101] Granted that if one had to omit a stanza, Todd picked the right one; it is apparent that the omitted middle is part of the poem's plan. Why, the speaker asks, do human beings need an audience when both nature and God are so adept at keeping secrets? Growing bolder, Todd was shortening texts that she published in *Poems: Third Series* in more intact forms.

RETICENCE.
The reticent volcano keeps
    His never slumbering plan;
Confided are his projects pink
    To no precarious man.

If nature will not tell the tale
    Jehovah told to her,
Can human nature not survive
    Without a listener?

Admonished by her buckled lips
    Let every babbler be.
The only secret people keep
    Is Immortality.[102]

Several weeks after their return on October 22, 1896, Mabel was horrified to discover that she and David were being sued for misrepresentation and fraud, not by Sue but by Lavinia. She immediately consulted a high-powered Boston attorney, Everett C. Bumpus. They flirted and he assured her that Lavinia had no case. Lavinia entered suit on November 17, 1896, claiming that she had been tricked into signing the deed and had misunderstood its intent. Bumpus helped Mabel to file a Defendants' Answer in mid-December. Under these circumstances, she set aside work on the fourth volume of poems she had begun editing and concentrated on writing and speaking about Japan. She also concentrated on salvaging her reputation and David's.

After various legal maneuvers, including an attempt to settle out of court and a delay because of Lavinia's weak heart, on October 4, 1897, the Todds countersued for slander. There were postponements, an important witness (housekeeper Maggie Maher) was privately cross-examined by both counsels, and there were conflicts about which trial should be held first. The court opting to give the slander trial precedence, it began on February 28, 1898, in the Superior Court of Hampshire County, Northampton, with Justice John Hopkins of Millbury presiding. Mabel did not appear in court, perhaps on the advice of her attorney, although David was there, as was Lavinia, backed by Ned and Mattie. The case was dismissed.

The next day, with the same judge presiding, Lavinia's suit was heard and widely reported in the local press. It quickly emerged that public opinion was siding with a supposedly naive member of the old Connecticut Valley elite versus a sophisticated woman of the world; adultery was in the interstices of the record. For example, Mabel claimed that Austin wanted her to have the disputed fifty-four-foot-wide strip of land to compensate her and David for their work on the 1890 *Poems*. That may have been plausible, but people wondered why he had given the Todds the land on which their present home stood, a gift made in June 1886, well before Mabel commenced her (or their) editorial labors. Then, too, there were Maggie's detailed accounts of the trysts between Mabel and Austin. For example:

> "Did you observe any act of intimacy between Mr Dickinson and Mrs Todd?" [Lavinia's attorney asked.]
>   "I remember at one time when Mr Dickinson brought some laurel to trim Mrs Todd's front hall stairs, and he placed the laurel there for her in a large vase, and she put her arms around him and kissed him and said, 'You dear old man'."[103]

Finding for the plaintiff, Judge Hopkins delivered his verdict on April 3, declaring the land deed which she had signed to be null and void. Although Mabel was required to return the part of the meadow that she had annexed— the fifty-four feet that Vinnie had inspected by moonlight and that the Todds believed Austin had intended them to have—she was not forced to return the poems and letters in her keeping, even after the failure of the appeal she and David made to the Massachusetts Supreme Court, Justice Oliver Wendell Holmes presiding. Whatever the law, Mabel felt strongly about her rights as Austin's heir, continuing to believe for the rest of her life that she was the true wife and Susan the interloper. It was *she* who had loved Austin and who had saved him from despair.

Justifying Despair

There was only so far that Mabel wanted to go in exploring the roots of her own despair, but she was certainly committed to containing it. Justifiably, she was proud of the intellectual and emotional efforts she had made to launch Dickinson for an 1890s public, even if (due to circumstances beyond her control) they could not be sustained. Mabel's Dickinson helped her to "justify – Despair," to normalize her own despair and to contain it (*Fr* 355). As "The Wife – without the Sign," the unofficial wife who suffered for her love but whose authentic "Title" was "divine" (*Fr* 194), Mabel's Dickinson reinforced a myth of self-blamelessness which exonerated her from the gender anxieties that might otherwise have been overwhelming.

For a larger public, Mabel Todd explained that Emily Dickinson exemplified the lighter side of woman thinking—she had not suffered a love disappointment and was not bitter. In introducing the *Letters*, which she almost preferred to the poems, Todd reflected on Dickinson's sense of humor, "the frolicsome gayety, which continually bubbled over in her daily life": "The sombre and even weird outlook upon this world and the next, characteristic of many of the poems, was by no means a prevailing condition of mind; for, while fully apprehending all the tragic elements of life, enthusiasm and bright joyousness were yet her normal qualities, and stimulating moral heights her native dwelling-place."[104] Mythologizing Dickinson in these terms, she could continue to view herself as a superior being, even if she had suffered a love disappointment and was bitter about it. It is not my purpose to subject Todd's achievement to harsh psychological scrutiny or to probe the oedipal roots of her dependence on Austin. Rather, I would note that in constructing Dickinsonian subjectivity, Todd and Susan joined hands. Susan too was intent on blocking psychological readings of her brilliant friend. In the obituary she published in the *Springfield Republican* the day before the poet's funeral, she established a biographical narrative that contained no hint of thwarted ambition, of sexual despair, or even of simple bereavement. Susan's Dickinson was a relic of an earlier time. She wrote,

The death of Miss Emily Dickinson, daughter of the late Edward Dickinson, at Amherst on Saturday, makes another sad inroad on

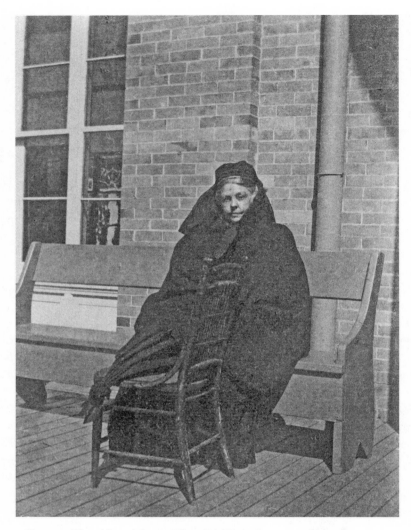

Figure 12. The widowed Susan Gilbert Dickinson in 1897, perhaps taken during her travels in France. Courtesy Todd-Bingham Picture Collection, Yale University. MS 496E, Series I, Box 16, Folder 170.

the small circle so long occupying the old family mansion. It was for a long generation overlooked by death, and one passing in and out there thought of old-fashioned times, when parents and children grew up and passed maturity together, in lives of singular uneventfulness unmarked by sad or joyous crises. Very few in the village, except among the older inhabitants, knew Miss Emily personally, although the facts of her seclusion and intellectual brilliancy were familiar Amherst traditions. There are many houses among all classes into which treasures of fruit and flowers and ambrosial dishes for the sick and well were constantly sent, that will forever miss those evidences of her unselfish consideration, and mourn afresh that she screened herself from close acquaintance. As she passed on in life, her sensitive nature shrank from much personal contact with the world, and more and more turned to her own large wealth of individual resources of companionship, sitting thenceforth, as some one said of her, "in the light of her own fire." Not disappointed with the world, not an invalid until within the past two years, not from any lack of sympathy, not because she was insufficient for any mental work or social career—her endowments being so exceptional—but the "mesh of her soul," as Browning calls the body, was too rare, and the sacred quiet of her own home proved the fit atmosphere for her worth and work. All that must be inviolate.[105]

This beautifully composed biography is deeply self-revealing. It represents Dickinson as having a "social career" such as Susan had, and it mythologizes woman's place as the home, which is ironic in the light of the ways in which Susan's own "hearthstone shrine" had been desecrated. Mourning Dickinson, Susan takes a nostalgic look back at the golden days before Austin and Mabel began to conspire against her and to shut her out of their imaginary kingdom. For Susan too, "The Things that never can come back, are several – / Childhood – some forms of Hope – the Dead" (*Fr* 1564). One can only hope that in these later years, she took pleasure in knowing that she had performed many social duties unselfishly, weathering and to some extent relishing the "joyous crises" to which her social embeddedness exposed her.

Be that as it may, Susan and Austin were together on one point: there was to be no publicity about a love disappointment. Yet when she wrote to Higginson in 1890, she explained more candidly, "I trust there may be no more personal detail in the newspaper articles. She hated her peculiarities and shrank from any notice of them as a nerve from the knife. I sometimes shudder when I think of the world reading her thoughts minted in deep heartbroken convictions."[106] This point of view can be reconciled with Susan's significantly more guarded public statement. She did not believe in a love disappointment *and* recognized her brilliant friend's peculiarities. Mabel came close to saying the same thing. But since most reviewers assumed that the poetry was inspired by deep feeling, authors' lives were fair game. Both Susan and Mabel leave us with a psychological void. If Dickinson had not suffered a love disappointment and was not bitter, what were her peculiarities?

Certainly it was not the psychologically intact Dickinson who captured the attention of William Dean Howells, the esteemed literary critic whom Mabel (re)met in the summer of 1890 in Lynn, Massachusetts, where—with her mother, Grandma Wilder, and Millicent—she was staying in a seaside boarding house. When Mabel showed him some of Dickinson's poems, he was immediately struck by their intense sincerity and their acquaintance with grief. He was in deep mourning for his daughter Winifred, an aspiring poet who had died after a long and futile struggle with a disease that was diagnosed and misdiagnosed but was probably anorexia nervosa. Over the years, the strain on Howells and his wife, Elinor Mead Howells, was almost unbearable. Toward the end, Winnie had seemed to be improving, and then they lost her. From this vantage point, Howells praised "the utterance of this most singular and authentic spirit," Dickinson, for being "true as the grave and certain as mortality."[107]

Howells wrote what was probably the single most influential review of Dickinson in the 1890s, but the wound of his daughter's death never fully healed. Years later, after he and Elinor stopped at Winnie's grave on their way through Boston, he wrote to his close friend Mark Twain, explaining that the gravesite visit was "an indescribable experience" but that it seemed as if Dickinson could voice his despair. "I thought I could tell you about it, but I can't," he explained, "Do you know those awful lines of Emily Dickenson [*sic*]? 'The sweeping up the heart, / And putting love away / We shall not want to use again / Until eternity.' They express the awful despair of it."[108] In coming years, Dickinson's poetry was often associated with sweeping up the heart and putting love away, and it is ironic that Susan and Austin's daughter Martha Dickinson Bianchi was one of the most aggressive proponents of a failed romance theory.[109]

And what of Mabel? Despite the trauma of Austin's death in 1895 and of the public trials by which she was humiliated in 1898, she continued to thrive, in her fashion. A passionate, intellectual woman, from girlhood she was driven to make a name for herself. Her youthful journal, the second of three, is in the Sterling Library, Yale University. It is labeled, "To be on no account opened or read—at least during the writer's life." At twenty-one, Mabel Loomis writes, "I am in such a mixed up state of mind tonight that I scarcely know which end I am standing on. I should like to know for what reason God gives women talent. It seems absurd for them to have it, because, in order to make anything of it, to amount to any definite total, they must remain unmarried, and that is certainly not right for all."[110] Not long thereafter she also wrote, "When the man comes whose mind & soul are large enough not to cramp me,—that is the principal thing I look for—& who can love me with a grip like Death, then, I will love him so well as to go to the stake for him, & until then I am oh! God anhungered & You [give] me no food. I wish I believed in prayer, but I do have a dim sort of feeling that my great far away father in heaven will satisfy me in this."[111]

In marrying David, Mabel Loomis chose sex over suffering and suffered for her choice. He supported her in her ambitions but proved not to be the steadying influence for which she longed. Moving to Amherst with some reluctance as a faculty wife, she was determined not to let herself be cramped by "family cares" or by confining gender ideologies that made it absurd for God to give women talents. Because of her connection to the poet's brother Austin, she began to communicate with Emily, with whom she also began to identify. Eventually, she found her talents stretched to the limit as Dickinson's advocate and editor. Like Dickinson, she was not religious in any conventional sense of the word, but she had an innate faith that God would not have given married women talents unless they were meant to use them and was resolute in her determination to transform Dickinson from a coterie poet into a major literary figure.

The only poem she cites in full in her "Introductory" to the 1894 *Letters* may serve as well to bring this chapter to a close:

> We never know how high we are,
>   Till we are called to rise;
> And then, if we are true to plan,
>   Our statures touch the skies.

Figure 13. Mabel Loomis Todd and David Peck Todd, at their elaborately
decorated home in 1907. Courtesy Todd-Bingham Picture Collection, Yale
University. MS 496E, Series I, Box 4, Folder 56.

The heroism we recite
  Would be a daily thing
Did not ourselves the cubits warp,
  For fear to be a king.

She then asked, "Must not one who wrote that have had her ever-open shrine, her reverenced tribunal?"[112] This gloss on the poet's inner life is an exquisite act of self-fashioning. Like the troubled and gender-troubling Mabel Loomis Todd who made it possible for contemporary readers to appreciate the pleasures of Dickinson's texts, the question is at once sincere and sly, self-deluded and shrewd. If the romance of real estate was not lost on her, who better than she to testify to the romance of romance?

Chapter 3

"The Wholesomeness of the Life": Marianne Moore's Unartificial Dickinson

In a poem written decades before she became famous as a baseball-loving, oddball literary aunt, Marianne Moore expresses her admiration for emblematic creatures who succeed in defeating "the gaping multitude." This early syllabic experiment has a distinctly odd title, "Polyphonic Craftsman, Coated Like a Zebra, Fleeing Like the Wild Ass, Mourning Like a Dove," and it has a magnificent last line: "I shall not cavil at you for being perverse." If we take Moore's title as an invitation to dwell in possibility, "Polyphonic Craftsman" can shed light on her version of veracity and of Dickinson circa 1914:

> You are not a candle but the light that is yourself—
>   Unseizable as moon and inescapable as sun;
>   You are the transcendentalized criterion
>   Of forthright action in a stolid universe.
>
> Dissonance is in the air: you are the orchestra.
>   Amusing animal, too bent upon your body's good
>   To make the gaping multitude your picnic food—
>   I shall not cavil at you for being perverse.[1]

To set out on a journey through literary history with Moore, though, is to skip lightly over some of the omissions which, as she later noted, "are not accidents."[2] For example, a poem such as "Polyphonic Craftsman" goes out of its way to degender the "You" whom it addresses, and it frustrates our desire to understand what kind of forthright action the speaker has in mind. Under what circumstances is fleeing itself a forthright action, and why does she consider the universe stolid? To what extent is Dickinson her companion in dissonance, as her playful combination of full and off rhymes might seem to suggest? In what follows, I will locate Mooresque perversity in a complex family romance organized by a powerful mother. Because of her mother's influence on her poetry, and for its exemplary oddness, their unusually intimate lifelong bond warrants careful attention.

By all accounts, Mary Warner Moore was an intensely "watchful" parent, and Marianne later suggested that she had been spoiled for the world's rough and tumble by a mother who supervised every aspect of her life, including her writing.[3] We will never know whether Mary Warner Moore's over-attention to her daughter's development would have been less constant had circumstances been different. What happened was this. In 1887, while she was pregnant with Marianne, this ambitious mother watched with fear, courage, and revulsion as her husband collapsed into an agitated and delusional depression. To protect herself, her little son John Warner, and her unborn daughter, she returned to Kirkwood, Missouri, where her father, John Riddle Warner, was the socially prominent minister of the First Presbyterian Church. Hers was both a forthright action, and a flight.

After her father died unexpectedly in 1894, Mary published an edition of his sermons, prefaced by a memorial tribute which gives us some sense of her strategic rhetoric and emotional enthusiasms. The book is dedicated "To the Presbyterian Church of Kirkwood, Missouri, between whom and their beloved pastor the ties of affection increased and strengthened with twenty-seven years of faithful service."[4] Idealizing her lost protector, she perpetuates his words not only to honor him but also to strengthen the bonds of affection between herself and her children. These were halcyon times, according to Mary, when they all lived together in an idyllic setting, in a small white parsonage "amid the green, with its peaked roof and porches covered by coral honeysuckle." In the "Wren's Nest," the "praise-notes of two little grandchildren" became part of a melody of "songs in the night, from those who could in sorrow 'make melody in their hearts unto God.'"[5] The smallness is part of her endangered intimacy project. Photographs, however, show an ample dwelling, and biographer Linda Leavell observes that there were four servants: a Danish cook, a white country "girl," an Irish-Catholic nurse-maid, and a black manservant ("who had charge of, among other things, the fastidious reverend's clothes").[6] As both Leavell and Mary record, for much

of this period (1887–1894), there was also a widowed surrogate mother, maternal aunt Mary Eyster whom Mary addressed as Mother and whom the children called Grandma.[7] In early childhood, then, young Marianne was not
only carefully watched but watchful, and one of the people she enjoyed
watching the most was her handsome and popular brother, whom she
admired for his high spirits and boldness.

Mary herself had a deprived and unsettled youth following the early loss
of her mother, who was a civilian casualty of the battle of Gettysburg. After
opening her home to strangers who had arrived to help tend the wounded,
Mary Craig Warner died tragically of typhoid fever. She was already in frail
health, and as Moore later explained, "Conditions in Gettysburg were very
unwholesome."[8] Eventually, little Mary was sent to live out a lonely childhood near Pittsburgh with her father's devoutly religious Presbyterian parents. On Sundays, Mary entertained herself by playing with her shadow on
the wall. Well-meaning family and friends urged the grieving widower to
remarry, but he never found another like his beloved "Jennie Craig." Mary
emphasizes his mournful fidelity to his one true love in her memoir.

After the Reverend Warner moved to Kirkwood, leaving four-year-old
Mary in Pennsylvania, his strong "home-longings" were attenuated when
"love for Christ's sake to his people soon became love for their own sakes."[9]
He visited her twice a year, in December and in August, and their regular
correspondence was a light of Mary's youth. In 1879, following the deaths of
her grandparents, she was reunited with her father and took her rightful place
as dutiful daughter. At fourteen, she was attractive, articulate, and poised;
she made friends easily and began to attend the Mary Institute in St. Louis.
It was an elite private school for girls founded by T. S. Eliot's grandfather,
and she took the train daily. Whenever possible, she visited with her mother's
Pennsylvania family, being especially fond of her mother's sister Mary Craig
Eyster, who loved her dearly. Mary Warner was an avid reader of British
literature, she played the piano, and she liked to paint. After graduating from
the Institute, she enrolled briefly in the Washington University School of
Fine Arts either as a full- or part-time student, in 1884 to 1885.[10] By this time,
though, she had met lively and extravagant John Milton Moore, and he was
determined to marry her. As for herself, she was less in love. As Mary explains
in a brief, unfinished memoir, she struck up a strong friendship with his
sister, who was related to a prosperous elder in her father's church. The sister
lived in Portsmouth, Ohio, on the Ohio River, where the Moore family
owned an iron foundry. Mary took the train from St. Louis to Cincinnati,

where she was met by her future mother-in-law. Together, they took the boat to Portsmouth—and there the memoir breaks off. Even toward the end of her long life, Mary could not bear to continue.[11]

What happened was this. John Milton Moore was a mainly self-taught engineer who spent a year at the Stevens Institute of Technology, and there are various accounts of his professional ambitions—at Stevens he liked acting—but while the young couple was living in Newton, Massachusetts, he collapsed under some combination of internal and external pressures—the latter intensified by his inability to support his growing family. When her father, who was supporting them, urged Mary to return to Kirkwood, she complied. This disastrous marriage was Mary's life-sorrow, as she called it, and she sought spiritual comfort in the idea that God was the father of her young son and her only true husband.[12] Although John Moore, who had begun to recover, begged her to return to him after Marianne's birth, she would have none of it, even to the point of refusing the financial support of his relatives.

Given the anxiety-producing events of Mary's infancy and childhood, followed by the dashed hopes and turmoil of her once-hopeful marriage, we should not be surprised that an intense need to control both herself and others emerges from her writings. Thus in the self-revealing "Biographical Sketch" which prefaces her edition of her father's *Sermons*, her rhetoric reinforces the lesson of filial obedience. She explains, of her own father's childhood and youth, "They were uneventful years, yet marked by the strong characteristic of affection for, and companionship with, his mother. No feature of his character stood forth more prominently than his devotion to her." "As a boy, he was full of fun and youthful pranks. Yet no play could detain him when he felt his mother listened for his coming; nor was any sport attractive that lacked the endorsement of this best friend of his childhood; while to serve her, in any way, was his chosen pleasure. Thus friendship with one who was devout, wise, and strong formed a wide foundation upon which was builded the character of after-years."[13] Mary tried to build this kind of intimate and controlling relationship with both of her children.[14] There is more. Her father's mind was meditative and poetical. After the death of his wife,

The effervescence of youth was changed; but no bitterness was seen in that fair face; the beautiful light of patience shone from those trustful eyes; blue like heaven above, and the emblem of truth. The

firm chin, whose lines softened so easily when his heart was touched
for others' woe, and the high, white forehead, was the Master's
framework: "Pictures of silver" indeed; while "apples of gold" were
the words that fell from the lips.[15]

No bitterness and no self-absorbed selfishness. These are the emotional and
behavioral ideals Mary hoped to actualize in her own life and in the lives of
her children. Further, this ornate passage emphasizes the importance of language and of apt quotation. Citing Proverbs 25:11, "A word fitly spoken is
like apples of gold in pictures of silver," Mary suggests that judicious quotation may be a sign of inner grace. In her youth and under her mother's
regime, Marianne began to learn the art of select citation.[16]

   Sermons marks Marianne's first appearance in print. On page 18 of her
"Biographical Sketch," Mary Warner Moore introduces her daughter's
prayerful voice to the public: "'Dear Lord, make our grandpa thy dearest
angel. Do not let him stay sorry for us, but let him behold thy face, so that
he shall be satisfied with thy likeness; and make him to go up and down from
heaven to earth, like those angels that Jacob saw upon the ladder.'"[17] We
next hear Marianne's filtered voice in a letter in which her mother quotes
several rhymes. Writing to her cousin Mary Craig Shoemaker on March 12,
1895, Mary explains that Marianne has "compose[d] odes and sonnets for
your benefit; one of which I copy as follows: 'The shadows now they slowly
fall: making the earth a great dark ball.' 'Pussy in the cradle lies—and sweetly
dreams of gnats and flies.'"[18] Animals, we see, have already made their
appearance. Before long there was a charmingly illustrated letter-poem to
"St. Nicklus," asking him to bring Warner a horn "And me a doll / That is
all."[19] And then, in late December 1896, again to cousin Mary Shoemaker,
who had sent a gift: "You would have laughed surely, could you have heard
my daughter's lament that the *poetry* was for Warner, rather than her. She
dotes on poetry to a perfectly horrible degree. I know we shall yet have a
poetess in the family, and finish our day languishing in an attic (prior to the
ages when posterity & future generations will be singing our praises)."[20] Mary
has no doubt that the world will be singing their joint praises and that they
will continue to share a joint living space. They will finish their days in the
same attic. Dwelling in possibility, we can imagine Mary revising Dickinson's
"Publication – is the Auction / Of the Mind of Man." Both Dickinson and
Mary dream about inhabiting a "garret" (*Fr* 788), but Mary's is the more
companionable.

Figure 14. Mary Warner Moore and her two children, about 1891.
Courtesy Rosenbach Museum & Library.

In fact, Mary was not sure where to live after her father's death, and several months later, she and the children moved to Ben Avon, near Pittsburgh, to be near her Uncle Henry Warner, who was a successful investor. Mary had no experience in managing money, and the prospect of remaining in Kirkwood posed practical problems, to say nothing of the difficulty of raising her young children in the absence of family. Uncle Henry was recently widowed and offering her emotional and financial support. Although her standard of living declined, she feared that if she stayed in Kirkwood, her in-laws would try to contact her.[21] "These were not," Leavell explains, "happy years," but Mary was "devastated" when her uncle died.[22] After a period of indecision which included thoughts of moving back to Kirkwood and opening a boarding house, she settled on Carlisle, which had excellent schools for the children and was close to her maternal Craig relatives, though not oppressively so. In Ben Avon, they had been living with her Warner cousins.[23] In Carlisle, for the first time, they had a home of their own.

Mary did not move to Carlisle for her job. Rather, as Leavell explains in her richly textured biography, the Moores arrived there in late 1896, and it was not until the fall of 1899 that she began teaching English at the Metzger College, formerly Metzger Institute, the private school for girls from which Marianne graduated in 1905.[24] Conveniently, it was across the street from their house, and they lived there for several months while 343 North Hanover Street was being repaired and they awaited the arrival of their furniture from Kirkwood. Although she was still grieving her various losses, Mary quickly formed a strong friendship with the family of George Norcross, the pastor of the Second Presbyterian Church. The Norcrosses had four daughters, three of whom graduated from Bryn Mawr and one of whom, Mary Jackson, became her intimate friend in 1900. In *Holding on Upside Down*, Leavell offers a detailed, sensitive account of their romantic attachment and of its likely effect on Marianne. In the winter of 1903, she resigned her position as assistant bursar at Bryn Mawr because of nervous prostration, and when she returned to Carlisle, the psychological and physical intimacy between the Marys deepened. When the occasion permitted, the two Marys traveled together, slept together, and were hoping to build a house together, either on Monhegan Island, Maine, or in the mountains close to Carlisle. In brief, Mary Norcross helped to prepare Marianne for college and Marianne admired her deeply. She was also somewhat jealous of her mother's lover.[25]

Aided by Mary Norcross, who was an Arts and Crafts enthusiast and a high-strung New Woman, Marianne successfully passed her college entrance exams, but the transition to Bryn Mawr was more than bumpy, and she was panicked at being away from home. Her college years have been amply discussed: the extreme homesickness at the beginning; the Bryn Mawr system of crushes and smashes—women formalizing their eroticized affection for each other; and comments from teachers asking her to be clearer in her writing. Of these, my favorite is from January 17, 1907, during sophomore year, when she complained to her mother and brother, "History is discouraging. We had 3 questions in our quiz. I got merit, passed & failed, that is, on the average passed. I think I worked too hard before hand. Dr. Andrews wrote at the end, 'Try to express yourself more clearly and accurately.' "[26] Moore did, in her poem " 'He Wrote the History Book,' " which she published in 1916 and then again in 1921, with a note of explanation:

> There! You shed a ray
>   of whimsicality on a mask of profundity so
>   terrific, that I have been dumbfounded by
> it oftener than I care to say.
>   *The* book? Titles are chaff.
>
> Authentically
>   brief and full of energy, you contribute to your father's
>   legibility and are sufficiently
> synthetic. Thank you for showing me
>   your father's autograph. (*P* 89)[27]

The note reads, "At the age of five or six, John Andrews, son of Dr. C. M. Andrews, said when asked his name, 'My name is John Andrews; my father wrote the history book' " (*Pr* 276). Moore does not tell us that Andrews was the history professor at Bryn Mawr who criticized her writing, but her point is crystal clear.[28] Hegemonic history is just one version of events, and to believe otherwise is foolish. That's why titles are chaff, as they are in Moore's poem "Marriage," which I will discuss shortly.

   If John Andrews lacks imagination, his pride in his father is not unappealing. Currently his "father's autograph," he has time to grow. The speaker is not too impatient with him, but rather with people, men in particular, who never achieve emotional, intellectual, or cultural maturity.[29] Little John Andrews is a direct descendant of Randolph Miller, the outspoken *enfant terrible* brought to life by Henry James in *Daisy Miller*. "This old Europe," he exclaims, finding nothing to his liking, and "I'm an American boy."[30] For Moore, James took on a local habitation and a name because of her college crush on his niece Peggy. Moore admired her "fearfully intellectual appearance" and "perfect lack of artifice and experience."[31]

"'He Wrote the History Book'" is unusual for Moore in that it is anchored by the figure of a child. It is both clear and complex, moving easily from a seemingly trivial exchange to a larger problem of meaning. It satirizes limited communities of knowledge, those communities most of us inhabit while we are young. And then, if we are lucky, we read Henry James and learn to appreciate the liberating power of American sincerity which, as Moore constructs it, is both a form of social affection and of self-knowledge. She writes, in her wonderfully titled essay "Henry James as a Characteristic American," "Underlying any variant of Americanism in Henry James' work is the doctrine, embodied as advice to Christopher Newman, 'Don't try to be anyone else'; if you triumph, 'let it then be all you'" (*Pr* 316).[32]

Mooresque sincerity begins at home, depends on knowing oneself, and demonstrates that there is emotionally gratifying life and work available to single women who, like James, are "probably so susceptible to emotion as to be obliged to seem unemotional" (*Pr* 401). The "probably," a characteristically Mooresque caution, reminds us that for her, sincerity is not an all-out struggle against convention; rather, Mooresque sincerity accommodates formal modes, and perhaps shockingly, "expediency determines the form" ("The Past is the Present," *P* 88).

Expediency Determines the Form

While "'He Wrote the History Book'" links legibility and patriarchal authority and mocks the latter as synthetic, at first glance "Marriage" seems to claim the synthetic as its genre but also to abandon the synthesizing power of a unifying perspective. Moore herself described this puzzling work as "a little anthology of statements that took my fancy." A little anthology it may be, but it is also her longest poem. We may never know what prompted her speculations on the subject in 1922—whether, for example, she was driven into poetry by the marriage of convenience between her lesbian friend Bryher and the louche writer Robert McAlmon, whom both she and her mother disliked, or whether her well-heeled friend Scofield Thayer's seductive behavior toward her offended her into verse.[33] Fascinating as are the particulars of her reaction to Bryher and "Piggy" McAlmon (to say nothing of her reaction to Bryher's companion and lover the poet "H. D."), and of her tense and skillful social moves when dining alone with Thayer in his luxurious apartment shortly before the volatile Thayer left for Europe and his analysis with Freud, the poem itself aggressively resists narrativizing. Its adamant refusal to settle for a single point of view is reinforced by an elaborate web of references, many of them in the form of seemingly random quotations. Writing about this "prodigality of allusion" in 1961, Moore explained, evasively, "The thing (I would hardly call it a poem) is no philosophic precipitate; nor does it veil anything personal in the ways of triumphs, entrapments, or dangerous colloquies. It is a little anthology of statements that took my fancy."[34]

But if there is no philosophic precipitate, there is a concern announced in the opening lines that provides a sort of a theme:

> This institution,
> perhaps one should say enterprise
> out of respect for which
> one says one need not change one's mind
> about a thing one has believed in,
> requiring public promises
> of one's intention
> to fulfill a private obligation. (*P* 62)

The word "one" resonates, and it serves several functions. Although Moore's speaker is preserving the right to change her mind and her affections, she likes the theory of marriage and its promise of permanence. Although the institution of marriage freezes, fixes, and renders static what should remain liquid, fluid, and moving, her speaker distrusts the volatility of passion. If she were forced to choose between self-expression and self-repression—but the poem is designed to evade that choice. In this abstracted version of the history of romantic love, "dialogue allows Moore to remove herself from the context of the poem so that the critique of marriage implicit in the poem does not reflect on the poet."[35]

The word "one" has a further function. Not only does it offer an alternative to a melodramatic marriage plot, in which marriage "is universally associated with the fear of loss," as Moore suggested in one of her working drafts, but it is gender-neutral.[36] Here we need to remember that Moore was frequently addressed by her mother and brother as "Rat" or "Ratty," and that in their extensive correspondence, the Moores engaged in word play which degendered Marianne. As a staged family—as Biter (Warner) and Fangs (Marianne) and the Fawn (Mary), for example—the Moores played against fixed social roles, but within carefully proscribed bounds. As soon as Warner left "The Nest" to attend Yale in 1904, if not before, the Moores performed fantasy roles they found liberating and which had the effect of excluding outsiders. "Marriage" is also an exercise in liberation and containment.

The poem's most conventional voice is contained graphically by quotation marks but liberated spatially from the tyranny of the left-hand margin. Set apart by its simple diction as well, this voice dramatically interrupts Moore's cool-toned, polysyllabic analysis of the history of coupled love:

> "I am such a cow,
> if I had a sorrow
> I should feel it a long time;
> I am not one of those
> who have a great sorrow
> in the morning
> and a great joy at noon." (*P* 69)

Here Moore is updating and parodying the poetess, or nightingale tradition as defined by Cheryl Walker in *The Nightingale's Burden: Women Poets and American Culture Before 1900*. Walker explains that "until the second world war what was understood to be 'women's poetry' was still essentially poetry belonging to this tradition: ambivalent, personal, passionate lyrics claiming some special wisdom derived from female experience."[37] As redefined by Moore in "Marriage," the nightingale's burden is emotional constancy. This emotionally candid voice is hard to forget, but Moore immediately slips into another voice and another role. Thus the poem leaves us with an ironized image of an "archaic Daniel Webster," proclaiming "'Liberty and union / now and forever'." That is "the essence of the matter," and so too are "the Book on the writing-table; / the hand in the breast-pocket" (*P* 69–70). This hand, or handwriting, is both on display and self-involved. Without offering a full reading either of the poem's network of references or of its deliberately inconclusive ending, I will suggest that to refer to the poem's author as "Moore" at this point seems itself an archaic gesture. So insistent is her desire to escape from the gender vulnerability of a secret sorrow that one wants to refer to the disappearance of the authoritative author function. Hence, "a little anthology of statements that took my fancy."[38]

Earlier, I suggested that one Mooresque version of sincerity, as it emerged from "'He Wrote the History Book,'" depended on self-knowledge. One might reasonably ask whether the personae in "Marriage" are self-aware, and in response to this question, I would say no. For example, Adam and Eve, who are introduced in lines 9 and 10 ("I wonder what Adam and Eve / think of it by this time"), are rhetorically adept but not introspective. They dominate the poem's opening scene, and Moore's Eve is the more vivid of the two:

> Psychology which explains everything
> explains nothing,
> and we are still in doubt.
> Eve: beautiful woman—
> I have seen her
> when she was so handsome
> she gave me a start,
> able to write simultaneously
> in three languages—
> English, German and French—
> and talk in the meantime;
> equally positive in demanding a commotion
> and in stipulating quiet:
> "*I* should like to be alone";
> to which the visitor replies,
> "I should like to be alone;
> why not be alone together?" (*P* 62–63, lines 18–34)

Since this is the most erotically charged of the poem's various scenes, we may want to conclude that Moore is consciously or unconsciously voicing lesbian desire.[39] Laurence Stapleton, though, observes that one of the drafts reverses genders: "Adam / I have seen him when he was so handsome that he gave me a start." In Moore's draft, Adam disappears after revealing his true colors: "then he went off / appearing in his true colours / the transition fr. Apollo to Apollyon / being swift like Jack before and after the beanstalk." Whether Apollo or Apollyon, Moore's inconstant Adam troubles the speaker's equanimity. He participates in what queer theorist Heather Love refers to as "eros's relentless narrative logic of pursuit, consummation, and exhaustion."[40] Finally, the abandoned notebook passage reiterates the poem's clearest theme, which is social rather than psychological or introspective: "this division into masculine and feminine compartments of achievement will not do . . . one feels oneself to be an integer."[41]

By implication, Moore's female artist has an androgynous imagination, and I want to compare her edited manuscript to an unlikely source, Walt Whitman's "Once I Pass'd through a Populous City." Early biographers mistakenly attributed this personal-sounding poem to a New Orleans romance, perhaps with a proud Creole beauty, by whom Whitman is mistakenly thought to have fathered six children. A year before Moore composed "Marriage," however, Emory Holloway published the poem's manuscript version, which reveals that the beloved "she" was a manuscript "he." Whitman, he suggests, "deliberately attempted to mystify the reader."[42] Although Moore probably was not aware of Holloway's discovery, her notebook demonstrates that she was experimenting with Whitman-like gender crossings, even if Whitman's "flamboyant male homoerotic (and heteroerotic) poetry and persona" was problematic for her and not easily placed in her "history of politeness" (P 63).[43]

Before she composed "Marriage" under some combination of internal and external pressures, Moore justified her gender deviance in the boldly titled early poem "'And Shall Life Pass an Old Maid By?'" which concludes with a warning against pathologizing the celibate woman, a cultural type she mockingly describes as unreadable:

> How diagnose felicity?
> It is an abstract thing, distributed impartially
>   Between good, bad, all sorts—and is renounceable.
> Who knows where it may be, or may not be?[44]

Yet "'And Shall Life Pass an Old Maid By?'" remained unpublished until 2003, and Moore's celibacy aroused curiosity in her own time. Her sexually adventuresome friend Bryher, for example, who had traveled with Havelock Ellis and was a Freud enthusiast, attempted a diagnosis of Moore's apparent flight from sexuality in the first year of their mainly epistolary friendship. Moore, she quickly concluded, was ascetic, flirtatious, boyish, and the victim of some strange repression.[45] Moore used Freud, or her version of Freud, to suggest that human nature was more varied than Bryher was willing to allow. Moore's letter is tactful but firm:

> What you say is true; the physical is important as well as the spiritual and I don't doubt that a thousand derangements are the result of our misunderstanding of the physical. Freud says his object is to substitute a conscious for an unconscious—a normal for a pathogenic conflict and we must do this if we can. A knowledge of abnormal conditions is a help in understanding normal conditions but as Freud says, our capacity for transferring energy from one field to another is almost infinite and the adjustments of one need to another, involve so many things that it is no easy matter to be absolute as to what course of action we are compelled to adopt for our all round best good.[46]

In contemporary critique, Kathryn Kent, among others, links Moore's gender deviance to a self-confident queer identity. Picking up on the pivotal phrase "criminal ingenuity" in "Marriage" ("requiring all one's criminal ingenuity / to avoid!" [*P* 62]), she explains, "The word 'criminal' echoes the medical and legal prohibitions of the turn of the century and the present, which classify any kind of existence outside of marriage as a crime: crimes against nature are sexual acts, the purpose of which is not heterosexual reproduction. Furthermore, 'deviant' sexualities have been, for at least the last two centuries, consistently identified with criminality. Moore identifies herself as a 'criminal,' as someone who does not fit into the heterosexual social order."[47] Further, Kent suggests that Moore's later career exemplifies "the spinster figure of the nineteenth century remade into an empowering and perhaps (auto)erotic public identity."[48] Building on this model, queer theorist Benjamin Kahan explores some of the ways in which Moore's celibacy and celebrity validated the condition of the socially useful and psychologically satisfied spinster.[49] Kahan's argument is most persuasive in his analysis of Moore's last book, *Tell Me, Tell Me: Granite, Steel, and Other Topics*, which was published in 1966, when, as Kahan notes, Moore had achieved crossover fame between elite and middle-class consumers of culture. She was throwing out baseballs at Yankees games, hobnobbing with George Plimpton, conversing with Mohammed Ali. For both Kent and Kahan, autoerotic pleasure is a Mooresque subtext, and while neither of them cites chapter and verse, "the hand in the breast-pocket" with which "Marriage" concludes can be read as a displaced, autoerotic trope.

Although both Kent and Kahan focus on Moore's later career, I have been describing some of the ways she justified her gender deviance with considerable humor almost from the beginning and nowhere more brilliantly than in "Marriage," her most ambitious poem. Fuller attention to Mooresque sexuality and affectional choice would need to account for the sadomasochistic fantasies reflected in such excessively gorgeous passages as the following, again, from "Marriage":

> Below the incandescent stars
> below the incandescent fruit,
> the strange experience of beauty;
> its existence is too much;
> it tears one to pieces
> and each fresh wave of consciousness
> is poison. (*P* 63)

On the one hand, we might say that Moore is speaking of heterosexuality; on the other, we might note that the lines suggest a less emphatically contextualized evocation of beauty, as in Dickinson's "Beauty crowds me till I die" (*Fr* 1687). Neither poet specifies what kind of beauty she has in mind, but in both, intense aesthetic experiences can arouse fantasies of fulfillment that both poets are at pains to indulge and to control:

> Beauty crowds me till I die
> Beauty mercy have on me
> But if I expire today
> Let it be in sight of thee – (*Fr* 1687)

In disrupting identity, aesthetic experiences can become inseparable from what Moore calls "love undying" (*P* 148).[50] The aesthetic experience of love is diversified and in that sense "expedient." In Moore, diversification is a form of erotic sublimation. It is a way of escaping the bonds of womanhood and of lyric tradition. It is also a way around the "fear of loss" to which the poetry notebook Moore was keeping in 1922 testifies. That fear subtends the poem's satire and to some extent Moore's life. Mary, she knew, would never leave her, at least not voluntarily.

So while it is true that, in "Marriage," "men have power / and sometimes one is made to feel it" (*P* 67), women have power too, and Moore follows the thought with a line from a parody on Alexander Pope's "The Rape of the Lock" which she and a college friend wrote after Moore had cut off her own trademark locks: "What monarch would not blush / to have a wife / with hair like a shaving brush" (67).[51] Is hair like a shaving brush attractive? Perhaps not, and who knows whether it is nice and soft and tickly or prickly instead, but isn't a shaving brush usually an article of a man's rather than a woman's toilette? Does the blush symbolize shameful pleasure—a tantalizing mixture of propriety and indecency?[52] The Dickinsonian blush lasts longer:

> Rearrange a "Wife's" Affection!
> When they dislocate my Brain!
> Amputate my freckled Bosom!
> Make me bearded like a man!
>
> Blush, my spirit, in thy Fastness –
> Blush, my unacknowledged clay –
> Seven years of troth have taught thee
> More than Wifehood ever may!
>
> Love that never leaped it's socket –
> Trust intrenched in narrow pain –
> Constancy thro' fire – awarded –
> Anguish – bare of anodyne!
>
> Burden – borne so far triumphant –
> None suspect me of the crown,
> For I wear the "Thorns" till *Sunset* –
> Then – my Diadem put on.
>
> Big my Secret but it's *bandaged* –
> It will never get away
> Till the Day it's Weary Keeper
> Leads it through the Grave to thee. (*Fr* 267)

Whereas Dickinson chooses Christ as her role model, Moore fancies herself more in the statesman role. She takes pleasure in performing like a distinguished orator, "the Book on the writing-table; / the hand in the breast-pocket" (*P* 70).

"Marriage" seems to offer the promise of wholeness, or as the mock-heroic conclusion states, of "'Liberty and union / now and forever'" (*P 70*). This promise is unfulfilled in conventional aesthetic terms. Rather, "Marriage" participates in a larger and more fragmented discursive field, and while its wholeness has been variously defined, the mythic structure seems to fizzle out, the authorial voice that got us going having lost interest in our first parents—unless the ghost of a common language lingers in the image of "the Book," if we take "the Book" to be the Bible. But is this the book that "He" wrote? If so, where does that leave the revisionary woman poet? Has she tabled the Book?

Just as Dickinson inhabits "Wife" fantasies and enacts seduction scenes in which a "Thee" is emotionally present, she tests out the role of mother, especially in relation to her "flowers," which she compares to her poems. Moore resists both seduction scenes and the role of the mother, and in theorizing Moore's queer nonidentity, John Emil Vincent suggests that her poems do not sound as though she is oppressed by a burden which she must "'bring to birth in order to obtain relief.'"[53] Vincent's analysis highlights the extent to which Modernist lyric conventions extend gender-and-biologically-conscious Romantic tropes of inspiration, yet "Marriage" is noteworthy for its resistance to parenting metaphors, especially for Eve—unless one rereads "she gave me a start" to mean she was the inspiration for the poem. Eve then becomes Marianne Moore's maternal muse, even if her Adam is strangely "unfathered."

In place of the father, Moore had her self-confident brother and powerful, nurturing mother, as well as friends and teachers whose specific languages she translated into her own idiom. One such source was the distinguished president of Bryn Mawr, M. Carey Thomas, whom Moore knew personally and to whom "Marriage" acknowledges its indebtedness. Here is Moore's note as it appears in the last edition published during her lifetime, the 1967 *Complete Poems*:

Lines 200–204: *"Men are monopolists. . ."* Miss M. Carey Thomas, Founder's address, Mount Holyoke, 1921: "Men practically reserve for themselves stately funerals, splendid monuments, memorial statues, membership in academies, medals, titles, honorary degrees, stars, garters, ribbons, buttons and other shining baubles, so valueless in themselves and yet so infinitely desirable because they are symbols of recognition by their fellow-craftsmen of difficult work well done." (*P* 272n)

And here are the relevant lines of "Marriage":

> She says, "Men are monopolists
> of 'stars, garters, buttons
> and other shining baubles'—
> unfit to be the guardians
> of another person's happiness." (*P* 67)

The quotation is from Carey's speech on "Present Day Problems in Teaching," published in the *Mount Holyoke Alumnae Quarterly* in January 1922, in which she reflects on changes in the status of women over the past decade. Moore picks a lively passage in an exceptionally long sentence and condenses it down to a few lines.[54] If we compare Moore's note to her own text, however, it is apparent that in addition to editing Carey, she is also editing herself. For example, there are no line numbers in the text, and Moore's line numbers do not compute on their own terms. She quotes two lines of Carey (the quote within the quote) and keys her note to five lines of text rather than four. Unless we stop the quotation after line 204 on the word "of," there is an unaccounted extra line, "another person's happiness."

To sum up. The quote within a quote ("'stars, garters, buttons / and other shining baubles'") occupies part but not all of lines 202–3, with the word "of" emphasized by its odd placement at the start of the line. Given that Eve herself is a quoter leaping across centuries from prehistory to 1921 or 1922 or 1923, and that Moore's note doesn't exactly square with her text—a text whose lineation she rearranged in the poem's various editions—the textual evidence encourages us to disbelieve that there is a single voice we can trust.[55] In its multiple editions and polyvocality, the "final" version of "Marriage" suggests that the gulf between the odd man and odd woman out cannot be resolved by a single myth, quotation, or convention, but the take-home point ("unfit to be the guardians of / another person's happiness") can lead to a larger view: men have demonstrated their incapacity for governance in the public as well as the private spheres. Moore, however, does not overinsist; her tone is light, and her Eve is severely flawed.

While the poem offers no easy solution to the problems of governing either the self or others, Bryn Mawr College perhaps approached Moore's

ideal of an elegantly appointed and civil state, and after an initial bout of
intense homesickness, she quickly became part of a community of writers
centered around the college literary magazine, *Tipyn o'Bob* (Welsh for "a little
bit for everyone"). Although she was not a consistently outstanding student,
Moore's association with *Tip* made her a campus celebrity.[56] In the fall of her
senior year, she wrote home that in one of her Chapel talks, Carey Thomas
criticized her story "Philip the Sober" for its affectation but praised "two
excellent poems in the paper [*Tip*] by the same author" and read one of them
("To My Cup-Bearer") aloud. Based on her letter, Moore did not take Carey
Thomas's charge of affectation too seriously. She commented, "And anon I
intend to try what may be done in the world of letters minus 'affectation' in
a bald form."[57] That is, Moore was not going to give up "affectation," artifice, or insincerity; she was going for affect in a subtler form. Kipling, Oscar
Wilde, and Swinburne were running through her head, but while imitating
their styles in both her poetry and prose, Moore had the self-confidence to
compete on her own terms. Here is the early Moore's sentimentalist, à la
Kipling:

> The Sentimentalist
> Sometimes in a rough beam sea,
> When the waves are running high,
> I gaze about for a sight of the land,
> Then sing, glancing up at the sky,
> "Here's to the girl I love,
> And I wish that she were nigh,
> If drinking beer would bring her here
> I'd drink the ship's hold dry."

And here is her Swinburnean sybarite:

> To My Cup-Bearer
> A lady or a tiger lily,
> Can you tell me which,
> I see her when I wake at night,
> Incanting, like a witch.
> Her eye is dark, her vestment rich,
> Embroidered with a silver stitch,
> A lady or a tiger lily,
> Slave, come tell me which?

Finally, her Wildean Phillip, a handsome prince in love with a hard-to-get, New Womanish countess:

> "You cannot think me so frivolous, Isabella, as not to think I intend that you shall marry me, if you wish to, when I ask you to." Philip fixed his eyes on the ceiling, and Isabella, having walked the length of the room away from him, watched him for a long time, unobserved, her head slightly drawn back, her impassive, delicate features expressing a severity and sensitiveness contradicted by the look in her eyes. She felt that Philip possessed an underlying defect; that somehow he needed to be brought to his senses. She felt vaguely that his offer to marry her was, in a way which she could not detect, insincere. (*Pr* 23)

Although she was not permitted to major in English because the faculty did not appreciate her critical writing—grades depended mainly on written essays—in the spring of her senior year, she was able to take an elective course offered by Georgiana Goddard King, a determined free spirit who was a friend of Gertrude Stein's.[58] The course, "Imitative Writing," was a study of seventeenth-century British prose writers which included, expediently, Emily Dickinson.

The E Multiplying

So far as we know, then, Moore first read Dickinson in her senior year at Bryn Mawr, when the ambitious young woman from Carlisle was introduced to such essayists as Bacon, Hooker, Fulke Greville, Raleigh, Jeremy Taylor, Burton, and John Milton. Emily Dickinson, Swinburne, and Henry James, though not part of the official curriculum, were discussed as "observers of civility and decency of order." Nevertheless, according to Moore's notes, they had all been accused of being "carnnally minded and earthly minded" [*sic*]. Dickinson was praised as an ironist and Moore noted that "in Irony the pt is to keep your temper don't fall into invective."[59] In contemporary discourse, we tend to take it for granted that Dickinson was an ironist, but in 1909 this was an unusual insight, and in Moore's class notes, we catch a glimpse of an avant-garde discourse imported by King from bohemian and lesbian New York. In published reviews, Dickinson

Figure 15. Marianne Moore as a senior at Bryn Mawr College, 1909.
Courtesy Rosenbach Museum & Library.

was often described as arch, whimsical, and humorous, but "irony" lifts
her out of a fast-fading past and locates her in the modern era.[60] Moore's
language is arresting: "carnnally minded and earthly minded." In what
follows, I take a closer look at how those tropes played out in Moore's
career and in her emerging thoughts about yet another American Eve, this
time the E multiplying into Emily. Emily and erotics. Emily and erudition.

Emily and eager energy. Emily engaged—but to what and to whom? Where would it lead?

After college, Moore moved back home. She trained as a secretary, taught at the Carlisle Indian School for three and a half years, was unemployed, tried to get a job as a journalist, published poems, and moved to New Jersey with her mother in 1916. Her brother was already there. Then it was on to New York and Greenwich Village, where she worked as a part-time librarian before editing the *Dial*, a well-funded arts magazine in which she had published a lot of prose but not about the woman from Amherst. After the *Dial* folded in 1929, she and her mother moved to Brooklyn, where Moore was again working as a part-time librarian. (Her mother had not worked since quitting her job in Carlisle in 1913, although she assisted Marianne in her editing and writing.) Fortunately, there was some family money, and Warner had married a woman of some wealth. They provided Mole and Rat with a stipend, and Mole and Rat were good at economizing.

Her public silence on the subject of Dickinson notwithstanding, in private Moore had been carefully tracking Dickinson's rising reputation. For example, in 1912, she jotted down the title of an article in the *Forum*, "Three Forgotten Poetesses" (Dickinson was one of them), and in 1915, she noted Elizabeth Shepley Sergeant's *New Republic* review of *The Single Hound*, which described Dickinson as "An Early Imagist." From the review, Moore copied this verse into her reading diary:

> A little Madness in the Spring
> Is wholesome even for the King,
> But God be with the Clown –
> Who ponders this tremendous scene –
> This whole Experiment of Green –
> As if it were his own![61]

There are other indications of Moore's private recognition of Dickinson's fame, with a 1924 letter to three friends connected with the *Dial* (discussed below) occupying the middle ground.

Throughout her editorial career, however, Moore was publicly silent on the question of Dickinson's significance to Modernist culture, and as editor of the *Dial*, she rejected Hart Crane's sonnet "To Emily Dickinson," which she subjected to "the shadow of underappreciation."[62] Meanwhile, during the 1920s, Moore's rising reputation was strategically coupled with Dickinson's by people such as Scofield Thayer, the wealthy young aesthete who was Moore's predecessor as editor at the *Dial* and one of the magazine's co-owners. In January 1925, when the *Dial* named Marianne Moore as the recipient of its prestigious and lucrative annual award, Thayer chose Dickinson's line "Ring, for the scant salvation!" as his epigraph.[63] Thayer underscored the Dickinson connection in the announcement's second sentence, when he praised Moore as "incomparably, since the death of Emily Dickinson, America's most distinguished poetess." Responding in the 1924 letter addressed jointly to the magazine's managing editor Alyse Gregory, to Thayer, and to his partner James Sibley Watson Jr., Moore wrote that "to be associated with Emily Dickinson's rigorous splendor is rare and trembling praise." "Trembling praise" suggests the precariousness of Moore's identification with Dickinson at this time. She continued, "Mr. Thayer's brilliant antitheses and criticism will cause me to be read about even if I am not read."[64] As for herself, although schooled to rebound after disappointment, Moore passionately wanted to be read, and in her eyes Dickinson's intellectual isolation was a problem, as was Thayer's choice of the word "poetess." The circumscribed role of the poetess was not one that Moore wished to claim for herself, especially since she was so often characterized as a minor rather than a major voice in American poetry and in Transatlantic modernism. To the extent, then, that Dickinson was minoritized, Moore was dubious about the value of the association, although her gratitude for the prestigious award was genuine. Previous winners were Sherwood Anderson, T. S. Eliot, and Van Wyck Brooks; after Moore, the winners were E. E. Cummings, William Carlos Williams, Ezra Pound, and Kenneth Burke. And the $2,000 cash gift was nice too.

Unlike Williams, who could deliver a baby in the morning and write a poem at night, Moore was fully absorbed by her day job as editor of the *Dial* and published no poems after the Dial Press reissued *Observations* in 1925 (with some emendations). Therefore, when Moore agreed to review the 1931 *Letters of Emily Dickinson*, edited by Mabel Loomis Todd, she was reemerging as a publishing poet after a long silence. Times had changed since the days when she had trouble placing her reviews, and the editor of *Poetry*, Morton Zabel, asked her to do it. Thus, in the summer of 1932, she was developing a context in which to understand this new and enlarged edition of Dickinson's letters and, to that end, reading widely.[65] Reviewing Dickinson's letters helped to reaffirm Moore's commitment to her own verse. In coming to terms with an ampler version of Dickinson than she

Figure 16. Marianne Moore in 1924. Photograph by Sarony Studio. Courtesy Rosenbach Museum & Library.

had known before, Moore satisfied her personal "expressionary need" and moved toward greater self-integration (*Pr* 14).[66] "If we care about the poems," she wrote, "we value the connection in which certain poems and sayings originated. The chief importance of the letters for us, however, is in their establishing the wholesomeness of the life." Of most interest to me, Moore denied that Dickinson was a recluse, as in effect does much contemporary

critique, which is eager to represent "our" Emily Dickinson as socially
engaged and savvy, engaged not to a person but to the immediacy of her
culture. In Mole's terms, much contemporary criticism is interested in Emily
and the ephemeral.

Yet images of Dickinson as unwholesome originated in her own time and
were fueled by her legendary solitude. Even her friend Thomas Wentworth
Higginson commented publicly on an "excess of tension, and . . . an abnormal life."[67] He was drawing on recollections of an 1870 visit. In the biocritical
narratives that proliferated during the early twentieth century, Dickinson's
supposed unworldliness was variously described. Almost everyone agreed,
however, that some explanation for her reclusion was needed. If she didn't
have a broken heart, what was going on?

Protectively, niece Martha Dickinson Bianchi asserted that those
"behind the hedge" understood Dickinson as "outsiders" could not. Given
that she herself controlled access to so many of Dickinson's manuscripts,
there was power in her claim. But Bianchi's introduction to *The Single Hound*
demonstrates that even those *behind* the hedge were mystified by an unheart-
broken being who was of "fairy lineage." Her genius, the niece explained,
was "peculiar," and when intruders threatened, she flitted as no one else
could, "like a shadow upon the hillside, a motion known to no other mortal."
"She was averse to surveillance of every description," Bianchi wrote, "and
took pains to elude it." Although she could be delightfully catty about other
women—"Listen! Hear them kiss, the traitors!"—Dickinson basked in the
radiant atmosphere of Bianchi's mother whom she addressed as "Only
Woman in the World" and "Avalanche of Sun." These dear dead women saw
each other with some regularity, and with some irregularity, "for though they
lived side by side with only a wide green lawn between, days and even weeks
slipped by sometimes without their actual meeting." Was this because Sister
Sue was so "blessedly busy" in her home, with her "three children growing
up about her?" If, as Bianchi stated, "the romantic friendship of my Aunt
Emily and her 'Sister Sue' extended from girlhood until death," why were
there not more actual meetings? And, more to the point, why did Dickinson
refuse to cross her father's ground to any house or town? Sue lived next door;
why avoid that space until her beloved eight-year-old nephew Gilbert was
dying? Why avoid that space, as the neighbors gossiped, for fifteen years?[68]
In short, what was Emily Dickinson's secret?

In *The Single Hound*, Bianchi describes her aunt as an unfathomable
being. She was somewhat devious. She was witty and willful. She had an

ample fund of indignation when others were in danger. She was not only tremendously fond of children, she was childlike herself. This contradictory being proffered dangerous treats: "There was an unreal abandon about it all, such as thrills the prodigality of dreaming." Yet if Bianchi scoffed at the Dickinson being taught in colleges as a rare strange being, "a weird recluse, eating her heart out in morbid and unhappy longing, or a victim of unsatisfied passion," she describes "at least one passionate attachment whose tragedy was due to the integrity of the Lovers, who scrupled to take their bliss at another's cost." While insisting on her aunt's probity, Bianchi nevertheless produced a Dickinson who was something of a femme fatale. "The list of those whom she bewitched . . . included college boys, tutors, law students, the brothers of her girl friends,—several times their affianced bridegrooms even; and then the maturer friendships,—literary, Platonic, Plutonic; passages varying in intensity." She was wicked, but not too wicked. Mainly, however, Bianchi's beloved and baffling aunt was

> not daily-bread. She was star-dust. Her solitude made her and was part of her. Taken from her distant sky she must have become a creature as different as fallen meteor from pulsing star. One may ask of the Sphinx, if life would not have been dearer to her, lived as other women lived it? To have been, in essence, more as other women were? Or if, in so doing and so being, she would have missed that inordinate compulsion, that inquisitive comprehension that made her Emily Dickinson? It is to ask again the old riddle of genius against every-day happiness. Had life or love been able to dissuade her from that "eternal preoccupation with death" which thralled her if she could have chosen—you urge, still unconvinced? But I feel that she could and did, and that nothing could have compensated her for the forfeit of that "single hound," her "own Identity."

In this seminal account, Emily Dickinson emerges as the agent of her own peculiar destiny. Without denigrating the more conventional life-choices of her mother Susan Gilbert Dickinson, to whom *The Single Hound* was dedicated, Bianchi sought to produce Dickinson as a special case of genius knowing its own mind. There was the suggestion that Dickinson's mother was anxious, overly solicitous, prosaic. There was the suggestion that Dickinson feared her father. And there was the suggestion that Dickinson, although physically timid, would not compromise. Bianchi, however, did little to explain Dickinson's aversion to surveillance of every kind, or the "inordinate compulsion" that "thralled her."[69]

How, then, to justify Dickinson's various resistances to gendered social norms without trivializing other women's choices? Before Bianchi's intervention, James Warwick Price, writing in the *Forum* in 1912, had suggested that "one must study Emily Dickinson not merely mainly, but almost wholly, through her verse; the outward facts of her life were the fewest and, in a way, the least characteristic." Dickinson's intimates were "the sunsets and breezes," her companions the birds, a few friends, and her thoughts. She was a recluse by habit and by temperament. She had an intuitive knowledge of Mother Nature, and "she looked through Nature up to Nature's God with a very Emersonian self-possession." Comparing Dickinson to another forgotten poetess whose life was also "slight in incident" (Amy Levy) and then to Emma Lazarus of Statue of Liberty fame ("Here again was a life hidden, a personality withdrawn"), Price drew on Higginson's influential account to position this almost forgotten poetess not in the "glorious company" of literature's immortals but in the more modest field of "secondary literature." Price thus attempted to confine Dickinson to the place in literary history he reserved for Levy and Lazarus, the former erroneously described as an English factory girl, the latter correctly described as a New Yorker and a child of privilege. Yet for both Levy and Lazarus, there was "the heritage of Hebraic destiny, the fate of a nation seemingly born to suffer." Ironically, then, in this company, Dickinson emerges as a comparatively blithe spirit and as more of a survivor. Whereas Amy Levy committed suicide in her late twenties and Lazarus died painfully in her late thirties, Dickinson lived into her fifties "and there was not an hour in the day but was eloquent to her." True, there were occasional notes of complaint, but in Price's child-of-nature (biographically ignorant) reading, "The poetess voiced her differings with this world not often enough for them to be fairly spoken of as characteristic."[70]

As if in response to this unduly apologetic argument, in the following year Martha Hale Shackford published an article in the *Atlantic Monthly* praising Dickinson for her resistances to history and to lyric traditions of gender. Shackford, who taught English at Wellesley College, had a professional interest in the lives of saints, and she admired Dickinson for taking a "keen, shrewd delight in challenging convention" and for overthrowing the reader's spiritual ease. It was Dickinson's "sharp stabbing quality" that she admired, and readers needed to recognize that "it is essentially in the world of spiritual forces that her depth of poetic originality is shown." Mentioning Dickinson in the same breath as Shakespeare, Wordsworth, and Keats, Shackford praised the poet's personal courage while mystifying Dickinson's nontextual relationships with anyone other than herself. True, Dickinson was writing out of personal experience, some of it unmistakably grim, but Shackford expressed no interest in particularizing or pathologizing the poet's disappointments. Instead, she focused on Dickinson's stylistic achievements rather than her supposed personal failures, and she affirmed that "Emily Dickinson is one of our most original writers, a force destined to endure in American letters." This adult Dickinson would have appealed to Moore, as would Shackford's determination to shift talk of secrets from the life to the work. Shackford stated, "The secret of Emily Dickinson's wayward power seems to lie in three special characteristics, the first of which is her intensity of spiritual experience." It was less clear what the other two secrets were, although she "isolated herself from the petty demands of social amenity" and her "capacity for feeling was profound."[71]

By the summer of 1918, then, when Moore and her mother were moving from a spacious parsonage in Chatham, New Jersey, to a cluttered apartment in Greenwich Village with greater " 'accessibility to experience,' " there were a number of provocatively different Dickinsons available, although much of her work still remained unpublished (*P* 54). For example, there was the unworldly saint and imp described by the artist Marsden Hartley in an essay in the *Dial* which Moore is likely to have read.[72] Hartley's Dickinson was forever young, a "remarkable girl" who exemplified "poetry in its most delightful and playful mood." Hartley asked, "What must have been the irresistible charm of this girl who gave so charming a portrait of herself to the stranger friend who inquired for a photograph: 'I have no portrait now, but am small like the wren, and my hair is bold like the chestnut bur, and my eyes like the sherry in the glass that the guest leaves!' " "The amplitude of garden . . . was her universe," Hartley explained. "Ordinary she never was; common she never could have been. For she was first and last aristocratic in sensibility, rare and untouchable, often vague and mystical, sometimes distinctly aloof. Those with a fondness for intimacy will find her, like all recluses, forbidding and difficult." Hartley's "sky child" finds everything "wondrous, sublimely magical, awesomely inspiring and thrilling." Pert and impertinent, she was not heavy going. She sent the heavenly ministerial tendencies flying. "What a child she was, child impertinent, with a heavenly rippling in her brain!"[73]

Thus, there were comic, pathetic, and tragic narratives of Dickinson's life in place and available to Moore in the teens and twenties, and women reviewers, including poets, were at least as disturbed as their male peers by the conflict between Dickinson's genius and her—but that's the question. What was it? Inaccessibility to experience? Homecenteredness? Neurosis? What motivated the "process of 'interiorization'" Moore describes in her well-informed and carefully researched essay (*Pr* 291)? Amy Lowell, for example, described Dickinson as victimized by cultural prudery. Lowell's Dickinson starved herself: she hung her womanhood upon a bough and played ball with the stars too long. She "hoarded—hoarded—only giving / Herself to cold, white paper." She was a "Frail little elf, / The lonely brain-child of a gaunt maturity. . . . The garment of herself hung on a tree / Until at last she lost even the desire / To take it down." Lowell asked, "Whose fault?" and answered provisionally, Queen Victoria's. Or Martin Luther's. "And behind him the long line of Church Fathers / Who draped their prurience like a dirty cloth / About the naked majesty of God."[74] And Lowell had lectured and written, "I wonder what made Emily Dickinson as she was. She cannot be accounted for by any trick of ancestry or early influence." Lowell was certain, however, that Dickinson was the victim of some undiagnosed nervous disorder.

> As the years went on, she could scarcely be induced to leave her own threshold; what she saw from her window, what she read in her books, were her only external *stimuli*. Those few people whom she admitted to her friendship were loved with the terrible and morbid exaggeration of the profoundly lonely. In this isolation, all resilience to the blows of illness and death was atrophied. She could not take up her life again because there was no life to take. Her thoughts came to be more and more preoccupied with the grave. Her letters were painful reading indeed to the normal-minded. Here was a woman with a nice wit, a sparkling sense of humour, sinking under the weight of an introverted imagination to a state bordering upon neurasthenia; for her horror of publicity would now certainly be classed as a "phobia." The ignorance and unwisdom of her friends confused illness with genius, and reversing the usual experience in such cases, they saw in the morbidness of hysteria, the sensitiveness of a peculiarly artistic nature. . . . All her friends were in the conspiracy of silence.[75]

Lowell dreamed of breaking through this conspiracy by writing a Dickinson biography, but as she predicted in a letter to Mabel Loomis Todd, it never materialized.[76]

In her carefully crafted review, Moore granted that Dickinson was "not usual" (*Pr* 292). She "understood the sudden experience of unvaluable leisure by which death is able to make one 'homeless at home'" (*Pr* 291). While Moore acknowledged that Dickinson's life was perhaps dominated by a "notable secret," she insisted that Dickinson was "not a recluse, nor was her work, in her thought of it, something eternally sealed" (*Pr* 290, 291). The statement that Dickinson was not a recluse is surprising in the light of so much evidence to the contrary, but Moore insisted, "One resents the cavil that makes idiosyncrasy out of individuality, asking why Emily Dickinson should sit in the dim hall to listen to Mrs. Todd's music. Music coming from under a window has many times been enhanced by its separateness; and though to converse athwart a door is not usual, it seems more un-useful to discuss such a preference than it would be to analyze the beam of light that brings personality, even in death, out of seclusion" (*Pr* 291). Normalizing Dickinson in a variety of ways—after all, what's *wrong* with listening to music or conversing while hidden behind a door?—Moore concluded by saying that "in studying the letters one seems to feel an anxiety lifted" (*Pr* 293).

According to Moore and some of the critics she had been reading, Dickinson's poetry emerged out of New England traditions of "'exciting realness,'" a quality which Moore also praised in the letters.[77] Why, then, did Dickinson acquiesce in "deferred publication?" The answer: because "she valued her work too much to hurt it if greater stature for it could be ensured by delay." Moore implies that Dickinson, "a truly unartificial spirit," refused to compromise, "flashing like an animal—with strength or dismay" (*Pr* 291). Though it is unclear how publication would have hurt Dickinson's poems, Moore anticipates contemporary critique in suggesting that Dickinson was engaged in "deferred publication." Her prescient logic returns us to the larger question about the woman poet and love that was at the heart of Dickinson's secret, however construed. As those in the know knew, Moore was extraordinarily attached to her mother. Was there a secret that motivated this attachment? Was individuality idiosyncrasy? Was idiosyncrasy neurosis? "Love can make one / bestial or make a beast a man," Moore wrote after her mother's death, a death that was also one of the defining turning points of the late stage of her career:

Thus wholeness—

wholesomeness? say efforts of affection—
attain integration too tough for infraction. (*P* 147)

Integration may be the goal, yet the Dickinson review is from time to
time fractured by commentary that seems either narcissistic or just plain
odd. For example, Moore ranked Dickinson before Emerson, Hawthorne,
Thoreau, and Bryant, while linking her to John Greenleaf Whittier, whom
she apparently considered Dickinson's equal for refinement and originality.
Indulging in her penchant for word painting, Moore attributed to Dickinson
her own values, projecting onto her "an element of the Chinese taste . . . in
its daring associations of the prismatically true; the gamboge and pink and
cochineal of the poems; the oleander blossom tied with black ribbon; the
dandelion with scarlet; the rowan spray with white" (*Pr* 292).[78] Despite these
sensuous associations, which reach their apogee when Moore discusses "the
behavior of an ear that lives on sound"—and here Dickinson "gives one
a start"—Moore remained conscious of the larger problem: how to attain
integration for herself while coming to terms with the dejection that she also
recognized as part of Dickinson's experience. Dickinson was a "person of
power and could have overcome had she wished to any less than satisfactory
feature of her lines," Moore asserted (*Pr* 292). While writing her review,
however, she copied out "After great pain, a formal feeling comes" and penciled in the word "repressed," followed by a question mark.[79] If repression
was an issue in Dickinson's life, how did it function in her own?

While still in college, Moore began her extensive reviewing career, and
in 1920, she became a regular reviewer for the *Dial*. From July 1925 to July
1929, she also wrote a monthly "Comment" page in her capacity as editor.
In none of these prose pieces does Dickinson's name appear.[80] When she
needed a reviewer for Bianchi's *Life and Letters*, Moore turned to Charles K.
Trueblood, who, writing for the *Dial* in April 1926, seemed to accept the
thwarted romance theory that was at the heart of Bianchi's narrative without,
however, dwelling on it. Instead, Trueblood credited Dickinson with a "brilliant understanding of the heart and its suffering," described her as a visionary who could inspire others, and praised her as a practitioner of "lyric
asceticism." Trueblood's review thus underscored "the comfort that so many
have found in her, so many of the stricken." Nevertheless, he felt compelled
to defend Dickinson against her detractors and, in language partially quoted

Figure 17. Marianne Moore and her mother Mary Warner Moore in 1932, when Marianne was working on a review of *Emily Dickinson's Letters* for *Poetry*. Photograph by Morton D. Zabel, who commissioned the review. Courtesy Rosenbach Museum & Library.

by Moore, he explained that "her utterance shows so little of the morbidness which often accompanies the growth inward of mental being."[81] In her review, Moore takes a swipe at the arrogance of twentieth-century male critics, but she also quoted Trueblood, whose views on biography she respected, to the effect that "the process of 'interiorization' was not a dark one" (*Pr* 290). This focus informed her assertion that Dickinson was a "magnificent entity" and that her letters were "full of enthusiasm" (*Pr* 290).

"Comparing omissions with inclusions," Moore now wrote, "one notes reticence: a determination to cover from the voracity of the wolfish, a seclusive, wholly non-notorious personality; an absence of legend; and care lest philistine interest in what is fine be injudiciously taxed" (*Pr* 290). Moore herself, for all her highbrow enthusiasms, was also a philistine, in that she was genuinely interested in writers' lives. "My favorite reading is almost any form of biography," she stated (*Pr* 648). Moore's research included biographies by Josephine Pollitt and Genevieve Taggard that advanced the thwarted romance theory; she knew that there was no absence of legend when it came to Dickinson.[82] What she means is that there is no basis for legend, gossip, or scandal. Dickinson does not deserve her press.

Moore fastens on Dickinson's vulnerability to her antagonists—the "wolfish" philistines—but she occludes the specific circumstances of Dickinson's fantasized disgrace. The "wolfish" philistines are sniffing out scandal where none exists. Mabel Loomis Todd is a "more than usual editor," and the fate of her early twentieth-century reprint of the 1894 *Letters* in "'one volume, and sold for twenty-five cents a copy,'" is "a circumstance that rivals in irony the stealing of a Bible from a church pew" (*Pr* 290). This is an odd comparison, but Dickinson's "innocence," like the Bible's, is "invulnerable to betrayal or curiosity" (*Pr* 290).[83] Dickinson's *reputation*, however, is vulnerable, and as Moore herself had written in her Bryn Mawr notebook, she was accused of being "carnnally minded and earthly minded." What makes Dickinson (and Moore) so vulnerable is precisely the absence of verifiable fact. It encourages speculation, and legends proliferate even when confronted with a wholly nonnotorious personality, such as Dickinson or Moore. And if it is to be regretted that Dickinson is the subject of salacious speculation (she has done nothing to inspire it), it is also infuriating.

Moore is not willing to let it go at that, though. Her Emily Dickinson does have an erotic secret. "A significant group of the letters as first issued is here significantly augmented—that to Mr. C. H. Clark and his brother concerned the Reverend Charles Wadsworth. Though innocence is invulnerable to betrayal or curiosity, one objects to sharing emotion that was intended only for another, and we are glad that if Emily Dickinson's notable secret has not perfectly the aspect of a secret, it is revealed by herself rather than by 'so enabled a man' as the twentieth-century critic" (*Pr* 290). Thus, in the very first paragraph of her review, Moore couples Dickinson's name with Wadsworth's, whom Bianchi had claimed was Dickinson's one passionate attachment, the married Philadelphia preacher to whom she lost her heart and whom she renounced, with her lover's assent, for the greater good. So even innocent, reclusive persons with wholly nonnotorious personalities can have secrets that may be misunderstood. Is it proper for twentieth-century critics to reveal those secrets? Apparently not, but female editors such as Todd may be in a different category. "In search and research, in divining dates and scripts, by consultation with persons, that she might somewhat perpetuate the magnificent entity Emily Dickinson was; in sensibility that has not suppressed, and in candor that has not victimized, Mrs. Todd has been more than the usual editor" (*Pr* 290).

In writing about Dickinson, Moore sought to lay to rest questions about gender identity and erotic normality that were also raised about her, as she must have known. Regarding Dickinson's poem "The Spirit lasts – but in what mode" (*Fr* 1627), she affirmed that "in these days of composite intellect and mock-modest impersonalism, this nakedness is striking. If our capacity for suffering is the necessary antithesis of our capacity for joy, we would—with Emily Dickinson—not wish to have it less. 'Though I think I bend,' she said, 'something straightens me'" (*Pr* 293). In writing about Dickinson, Moore was defending not only the wholesomeness of Dickinson's life but also choices she herself had made. She disagreed with Amy Lowell's reading of Dickinsonian eroticism, which she is likely to have known. We recall that Lowell described a phobic aversion to publicity and an imagination introverted to a state bordering upon neurasthenia. Moore would have none of it, yet we may wonder how she understood the detailed connections that compose her personal and professional narrative. When she explained her aesthetic to Williams, she professed to despise "connectives."[84] As understood by Moore, what *is* the relationship between wholesomeness and connection? These are large questions, which hint that "in this morose part of the earth" it may not be a privilege to see so much confusion. Confusion may be responsible for "ferocity" and for "complicated starkness" (*P* 80), qualities which comport oddly with the refinement she also values.[85]

Be that as it may, after satisfying herself that Dickinson might be a model for a spiritually uplifting New Woman, Moore felt no further need to write about her. There are sporadic mentions of Dickinson in her subsequent prose, such as a footnote to Louise Bogan's "masterly critique" of the 1955 Johnson *Variorum*, which Moore praises as "summarizing Emily Dickinson" (*Pr* 487).[86] But Moore could not deny the power of expediency and the appeal of expedient forms. She herself had adapted to circumstances far from ideal, and Dickinson, she came to understand, had done the same. Although Moore's Dickinson has a thorn in her side, she is resilient and something strengthens her: "Though I think I bend, something straightens me" (*Pr* 293). That something was mysterious and here we reach the limits of rational argument. What makes one person able to transcend suffering while another sinks beneath the tide was a subject that Moore, wisely, did not attempt to address. Better to do what she could, and in the next chapter we will see where some of her attempts to counsel a younger writer led.

Chapter 4

Moore, Plath, Hughes, and "The Literary Life"

We climbed Marianne Moore's narrow stair
To her bower-bird bric-à-brac nest, in Brooklyn.
Daintiest curio relic of Americana.
Her talk, a needle
Unresting—
. . . .
(Whoever has her letter has her exact words.)
                    —Ted Hughes, "The Literary Life"

Marianne Moore and Sylvia Plath? An odd couple. Marianne Moore and Ted Hughes? An odder couple still. But in the 1950s, Moore's literary life was remarkably public and social. She was an important friend to Plath, then to Hughes, and then, to Plath's dismay, not to the two of them together. This much of the Moore-Plath-Hughes story has been available at least since the publication of Plath's abridged journals in 1982, but now there is more to consider because of the poem sequence, *Birthday Letters*, in which Hughes violated his need to distance himself from Plath and her admirers; time was drawing short and he wanted to set the record straight.[1]

Published in 1998, *Birthday Letters* has already garnered a great deal of attention, but the attack on Moore in "The Literary Life" has gone largely unnoticed.[2] This thirty-third poem in the sequence is not obviously part of the failed family romance narrative that organizes the volume, and to date, journalist Erica Wagner's has been the only substantial commentary. She finds Hughes's narrative of a spoiled friendship unremittingly bitter. Yet the

sardonically titled memory-poem reveals more than bitterness "undis-
guised."[3] "The Literary Life" imagines a reader willing to look harder for the
missing letter described in the poem, and by extension, Hughes complicates
previous accounts of the fate of Plath's famously missing journals.[4] I have
located this letter from Moore to Plath, which, together with several other
previously unpublished letters by Moore, reveal some of the fault lines in
Hughes's account and in the gendered politics of mid-twentieth-century
Anglo-American poetry.

  Birthday Letters opens with the question "Where was it?," a question
that reverberates poignantly throughout the sequence as the poet shapes his
tale of perversely missing years.[5] Lamenting the fate of his literary life/wife,
Hughes writes, to Plath, "The dream you hunted for, the life you begged /
To be given again, you would never recover, ever. / Your journal told me the
story of your torture" (*BL* 21). As represented by Hughes, Moore emerges as
one of Plath's torturers and, to a lesser degree, as one of his own. Initially,
however, Moore was not "spiteful" as Plath concluded, or as Plath's poem
"The Rival" would have it, "Spiteful as a woman."[6] Rather, Moore liked
Sylvia Plath personally, wanted to help her, and admired her talent. She
nevertheless came to find Plath lacking in "spiritual resilience," then called
her "bitter," "burnt out." Eventually, Moore attacked her for being a
mother. Historicizing Moore's growing estrangement from Plath provides a
more thickly textured account of Hughes's role in this personal and social
drama than has been available—a role minimized, not to say virtually eclipsed
in his poem. In the end, Moore was even more deeply resistant to Plath's
project than has been previously supposed and for somewhat different
reasons.

The Contest for Spiritual Resilience

In a personal letter written on July 13 and 14, 1958, Marianne Moore agreed
to recommend Sylvia Plath for a grant, but she also called her "too unrelenting." In this chapter, I explore both the public and private significance of
Moore's criticism of Plath and of Plath's response to that criticism, which
she interpreted as "spiteful" (*Unabridged* 406). The relationship between the
two poets began auspiciously enough, when Moore helped Plath to win a
prize while she was still a senior at Smith College, but the future was bleaker.
Early on, Plath was eager to establish herself as "The Poetess of America"

Figure 18. Marianne Moore and Sylvia Plath at Mount Holyoke College, April 1955. The photograph appeared in the *Christian Science Monitor* on April 18 and is mentioned in a letter Plath wrote to her mother that week. Courtesy Rosenbach Museum & Library.

(*Unabridged* 360) or, if that goal proved impossible, to establish herself as a representative woman poet of her time. It was natural that she should turn to Moore for help. By the mid-1950s, Moore had emerged as an icon of popular culture without losing her place in the Modernist hierarchy of greats.[7] As is well known, popular and intellectual success were tremendously important to Plath, and she was delighted to meet Moore in person in April 1955, when Moore was one of the judges for the Glascock Poetry Contest sponsored by Mount Holyoke College. Her desire to ingratiate herself with the older poet is apparent in the Mount Holyoke photograph, in which a demurely dressed Plath listens attentively to Moore, over whom she seems to tower. Although this towering effect may be partly based on contingencies—a higher chair, a lower sofa, Plath's extra inches in her own person, the photographer's angle—it also captures Plath's ambition not just to equal Moore but to surpass her.

Surpass her how? Well, for one thing, Moore did not extol the virtues of the "blazing" sexual love that Plath was coming to view as an essential component of female poetic identity, nor did she celebrate "Male virility," as Plath understood herself to be doing (*Unabridged* 209, 594). Influenced in part by neo-Freudian psychological discourses legitimating sexual pleasure, Plath was determined to claim the sensual freedom that she believed she had earned as a New Englander transcending her supposedly puritanical roots.[8] Bringing her own obsessions to bear on this depuritanizing project, she was dubious about autoerotic alternatives to heteronormativity, about lesbians, and about spinsters such as Moore, who, in her reading of the tradition, were too self-absorbed to attend to the cry of a child, anybody's child, in the street ("Female Author," *Collected* 301). The Lady of Shalott, sacrificing experience for art, she would not be. Notwithstanding, Plath admired Moore's self-confidence and her freedom to be herself. She also hoped that Moore's poetics would help to steady her. As she later explained in a letter dated June 11, 1958, to her brother Warren describing her own poem "Mussel-Hunter at Rock Harbor," "This is written in what's known as 'syllabic verse,' measuring lines not by heavy and light stresses, but by the *number* of syllables, which here is 7. I find this form satisfactorily strict (a pattern varying the number of syllables in each line can be set up, as M. Moore does it) and yet it has a speaking illusion of freedom."[9]

To amplify further. Plath met Moore in April 1955, when Moore was judging an undergraduate poetry contest at Mount Holyoke College. Plath, a Smith College senior, was cowinner of this contest, along with William Whitman, a Wesleyan junior who eventually published a chapbook called *The Dancing Galactic Bear* but whose career as a poet did not get very far. In suggesting that the prize be split between Whitman and Plath, this is what Moore had to say: "Sylvia Plath is my choice for the prize—*unless* Mount Holyoke is willing to divide it between Sylvia and William Key Whitman. The balance is even, I think. I wish—wish very much—you may feel you can divide it."[10]

In the light of later events, it is curious that Moore went on to praise Plath's poetry not only for its technical proficiency but also for its patience with life. Although she considered Whitman's "To a Fox Girl on Her Birthday" the single best poem in the contest, she found the spirit of his work inflexible and spiritually less alert than Plath's—indeed willfully static spiritually, compared with Plath's. Plath, she explained to the committee head, professor of English Joseph Bottkol, "has a reserve of strength and is more patient with life" (Holyoke Ms.).

For her part, Plath was thrilled with the opportunity to interact with Moore and wrote to her mother, enthusiastically to say the least,

> Well, all things come to those who wait, and my waiting seems to be extended for two weeks until the judges decide, after reading our poems over in the quiet of their boudoirs, which of the six of us deserves the coveted prize. . . . Suffice it to say that I don't know when I've had such a lovely time in my life. I took to Marianne Moore immediately and was so glad to have bought her book and read up about her, for I could honestly discuss my favorite poems. She must be in her late seventies [Moore was a decade younger] and is as vital and humorous as someone's fairy godmother incognito. Interestingly enough, she asked about you and said she hopes to meet you some day, and also said you should be proud of me, which I thought I'd tell you in case you didn't already know! (*Letters* 168)

Later that weekend, "Marianne Moore signed a dear autograph in [Plath's] book of her poems," but one of the other judges, John Ciardi, drank scotch with her for hours over the kitchen sink at someone's party, and when she received a letter from him calling her a real discovery and offering to help advance her career by introducing her around, he instantly became her favorite of the three judges—Wallace Fowlie, who did not care for her poetry, was the third (*Letters* 169, 171). Still, Moore was a kindly presence waiting in the wings and she asked Bottkol "not [to] darken the horizon of any contestant by letting him or her see my notes verbatim. Could you quote what surely might be helpful and nothing else?" (Holyoke Ms.). Plath was therefore informed that Moore admired her "spirit, patience, craftsmanship, and strong individuality" and that "her main adverse criticism is of a too adjectival manner at times bordering on formula."[11] Plath found this formalist criticism easy to take, as it did not attack her character or temperament. Plath also had Moore's blessing for "a true ear—an independent ear" and "talented compactness." "Each poem has corroborating individualities," Moore observed, "and No pains are spared" (Holyoke Ms.). In a brief opening speech, Moore had counseled *all* the young poets—there were six finalists—to "write what you are impelled to write" and to respond resiliently to "rebuffs and unfavorable comments."[12] This was to the well and good, but unfortunately, Plath was already overly sensitive to criticism and too determined to please.

The Husband, the Marriage, and the Visit

Moore praised Plath's poems for their independence and individuality, but Plath also looked to others, including Moore, for self-definition.[13] In her evolving struggle to weave "chaos and despair—and all the wasteful accident of life—into a rich and meaningful pattern" (*Unabridged* 342), she found that her moods were so disjunctive that she could not count on herself for steadiness. In some measure, Plath's emotional volatility accounts for the inordinate influence on her of Hughes, whom she married in June 1956, while studying English literature at Cambridge University. (Their whirlwind four-month courtship, with its bites and rippings and sexual heat, is well documented.) Plath influenced Hughes's poetry as well, and from the beginning was invested in advancing his career. Thus, following up on a lead she had gotten at a party, in the fall of their first year of marriage she typed up the manuscript of her husband's *The Hawk in the Rain*, may have made some decisions about the volume's contents, and sent it out.[14] Both she and Ted were tremendously elated when on February 23, a telegram arrived announcing that he had won the contest sponsored by the 92nd Street Y, which guaranteed publication. There were 256 entrants, and Hughes was the unanimous choice of the three judges: Moore, W. H. Auden, and Stephen Spender. Plath confided to her journal, "Even as I write this, I am incredulous. The little scared people reject. The big unscared practising poets accept. I knew there would be something like this to welcome us [back] to New York! We will publish a bookshelf of books between us before we perish! And a batch of brilliant healthy children! I can hardly wait to see the letter of award (which has not yet come) & learn details of publication. To smell the print off the pages!" (*Unabridged* 270). Next, a problem developed. In judging *The Hawk in the Rain*, Moore wrote that "the work has focus, is aglow with feeling, with conscience; sensibility is awake, embodied in appropriate diction."[15] In addition to the title poem, she particularly admired "The Thought-Fox," "Griefs for Dead Soldiers," and "The Martyrdom of Bishop Farrar." But she wanted Hughes to eliminate three of the forty or so poems altogether. As Plath explained to her poet friend Lynne Lawner, who also participated in the Holyoke contest, "Dear familiar Marianne Moore . . . objected to 3 'bawdy' poems which weren't really."[16] Ted first refused to withdraw the poems, then thought better of it and capitulated to Moore's demand. Consequently, *The Hawk in the Rain* was published by Harper in the United States and by Faber in England without "The Little Boys and the Seasons," "The Drowned Woman," or "Bawdry Embraced."[17]

These poems had all been published elsewhere by the time the book was reviewed in the *New York Times* in October 1957, and as Plath repeatedly observed, the prize genuinely transformed Hughes's career. Yet while she took pleasure in being identified as a famous poet's wife, she was edgy about her own book-in-progress. Hers came slower than his, especially after she took the job teaching English at Smith College she had worked so hard to get. Teaching stopped her writing, and Plath's journals recount the personal reasons: fevers, fears about Ted's sexual restlessness, paranoia about colleagues, most of whom she despised, and so forth. At a deeper level, Plath had difficulty believing in herself as an intellectual, even though her father had been a professor at Boston University and her mother, Aurelia Schober Plath, taught there as well. Aurelia took up this career to support the family after her husband's death, and although Otto Plath had been a professor of German and biology and part of the regular Arts and Sciences faculty, Aurelia was relegated to the practical arts division, where she developed courses in typing and shorthand for medical secretaries. Plath looked down on her mother's career, but when she returned to her own college as an instructor, Plath could not tolerate the uncertainties of classroom performance.

At this time in her life—she had been married for only a year and a half—Plath felt the need to differentiate herself more sharply from her mother, with whom she was strongly bonded. But if taking up and trying to redefine her mother's occupation was a step in the wrong direction, public narratives also undermined Plath's confidence in her teaching life. At her own Smith graduation in 1955, former and future presidential candidate Adlai Stevenson had issued a "call to greatness," urging her class to influence society from the home and to cultivate the nurturing qualities unique to their gender. This separate spheres rhetoric was so pervasive in the Cold War 1950s that it is not surprising that Stevenson should have exploited it. What is of particular interest is that Sylvia liked the speech. She wrote to her friend Lynne Lawner at the time, "Adlai Stevenson, operating on the hypothesis that every woman's highest vocation is a creative marriage, was most witty and magnificent."[18] Plath's sense of humor stood her in good stead on this occasion, and a creative marriage was exactly what Plath sought and thought she found in her union with Hughes. The graduation ceremony itself, where Moore received an honorary degree, was complicated by the fact that Plath's mother was seriously ill and had been released from a hospital to attend.

As Plath remarked to her brother in November 1957, "There is nothing worse than going back to a place where you were a success and being miserable" (*Letters* 329). She *was* miserably unhappy as an instructor at Smith, but fortunately vacations brought some relief, and Plath was especially pleased by her rapid-fire production of eight poems in eight days during the spring break. Reflecting on her fortunes on a Saturday in late March 1958, her ambition resurfaced. She called herself "Arrogant," but continued,

> I think I have written lines which qualify me to be the Poetess of America (as Ted will be The Poet of England and her dominions). Who rivals? Well, in history—Sappho, Elizabeth Barrett Browning, Christina Rossetti, Amy Lowell, Emily Dickinson, Edna St. Vincent Millay—all dead. Now: Edith Sitwell & Marianne Moore, the ageing giantesses & poetic godmothers. Phillis McGinley is out—light verse: she's sold herself. Rather: May Swenson, Isabella Gardner, & most close, Adrienne Cecile Rich—who will soon be eclipsed by these eight poems: I am eager, chafing, sure of my gift, wanting only to train & teach it—I'll count the magazines & money I break open by these best eight poems from now on. We'll see. (*Unabridged* 360)

Preferring to train and teach her gift rather than to instruct her students, Plath felt that she had given birth to her true self and was "breaking open my real experience of life." Previously, she had been "shut up, untouchable, in a rococo crystal cage, not to be touched" (*Unabridged* 356). The opening up metaphor, loosely linked to childbirth, establishes a form of successful modern American womanhood: authoring poems, she deferred birthing babies, and the deferral was justified metaphorically, as one form of self-expression mutated figuratively into another.

In *The Feminine Mystique* (1963), Betty Friedan famously taught us that American postwar culture discounted the importance of individual achievement for women and tried to contain female energies within the middle-class home. Recently, however, revisionist feminist historians have described a much more complicated set of pressures and opportunities to which highly educated women such as Plath were responding.[19] In *The Bell Jar*, published in the same year as Friedan's *Feminine Mystique*, Plath described a fig tree scenario corresponding to a multiplicity of choices facing her semiautobiographical heroine, Esther Greenwood. Esther imagines that in order to be a "famous poet," she would have to reject other enticing options: especially "a husband and a happy home and children."[20] Unlike Esther, however, Plath intended to combine a life of individual achievement, sexual pleasure bordering on the violent, and socially useful work. Plath intended to have it all and, in her optimistic moods, believed that having it all was possible, especially if financial pressures abated. Unlike the caricatured and fragmented "female author" of her poem of the same name, she wanted to exemplify personal ambition, personal pleasure, social usefulness, and the institution of bourgeois motherhood. Seemingly none of her colleagues at Smith had succeeded in this project, but Plath was convinced that the personal could be the political. What she feared was the "just personal" she understood as neurosis (*Unabridged* 311). Her self-castigating psychoanalytic vocabulary was highly developed.

At Smith, Plath both exhibited gender anxieties and reflected on them, yet teaching turned her into a nervous wreck. By Thanksgiving break, she decided to abandon the profession. In December, she was physically ill and returned to her mother's house in Wellesley, canceling the last week of classes to do so. The Christmas holiday provided some respite, but, returning to Northampton in January, she felt cut off from the world and from the world of poetry—although not from its careerist and highly personalized (as she understood them) politics. There still remained women and men on the Smith faculty whom she admired, but these exceptions (such as Elizabeth Drew and Daniel Aaron) were few and far between. Mainly, she was disenchanted by professors such as Newton Arvin, who had been so fascinating to her as a student. She felt that spiteful people were waiting for her to fail. She was waiting to fail herself. Ted remained her lifeline to the wide world of poetic genius, but he was advising her to "'Get hold of a thing & shove your head into it'" (*Unabridged* 328). Plath, however, fearing the limitations of an autobiographical point of view, aimed to write poetry that was not "just personal" and would let the "external world in" (*Unabridged* 311). Ted believed then and continued to believe that Plath's true subject was her "painful subjectivity."[21]

Plath's creativity was unblocked during spring vacation, but she could barely tolerate the end of the term. These tensions were in the background of the visit that Plath and Hughes paid to Moore after the semester ended.

Nor did Moore disappoint them, although Plath confided to her mother that "she talked a blue streak." Nicely fed on strawberries and sesame seed biscuits and milk, she came away persuaded that Moore was "lovely . . . and admires Ted very much" (*Letters* 340). Possibly she ignored signs that Moore admired Ted more than herself, and on her return to Northampton, she wrote to Moore, asking her to be a recommender for a Saxton grant.[22] Moore, the patron of both Plath and Hughes, had seemed happy, her genius untormented. And Moore's poetry, with its swerve away from the "shove your head into it" brutality of the merely personal, let in some of the external world without sacrificing her inimitable style—though as Steven Gould Axelrod and others have observed, Plath had tried to imitate it.[23] If not a sexual role model, Moore nevertheless exemplified personal autonomy, and Plath emerged from this rejuvenating New York visit believing that the "ageing giantess" would sponsor her for a "Saxton," enabling her to complete the book of poems, variously titled, on which she was then working. As we have seen, this was not to be.

Moore's Letters

As recounted by Hughes in "The Literary Life," Plath became hysterical when she received Moore's letter, dated July 13 and 14. Plath vented in her journal,

> Marianne Moore sent a queerly ambiguous spiteful letter in answer to my poems & request that she be a reference for my Saxton. So spiteful it is hard to believe it: comments of absolutely no clear meaning or help, resonant only with great unpleasantness: "don't be so grisly", "I only brush away the flies" (this for my graveyard poem), "you are too unrelenting" (in "Mussel-Hunter"). And certain pointed remarks about "typing being a bugbear", so she sends back the poems we sent. I cannot believe she got so tart & acidy simply because I sent her carbon copies ("clear," she remarks). This, I realize, must be my great & stupid error—sending carbons to the American Lady of Letters. (*Unabridged* 406)

In poems such as "Moonrise," with its graveyard setting, and "Mussel Hunter at Rock Harbor," with its claim to a particular type of reclusive or suicidal realism, its "soaring beyond the pleasure principle into the numinous pursuit of death," Plath exhibited the intransigence that characterized her mature style.[24] Interestingly, though, the poem that made Moore happy not to be on a boat—the implication being that she would lose her lunch—was "Sow," about which Plath says nothing in her journal entry. The poem takes a "tour" through a barnyard, where the speaker and her lover encounter not a nursing mother—though this figure is vividly evoked—but a sow old enough to be a great-grandmother, whose opportunities for satisfactory sex are unfortunately diminished. In some respects a humorous poem, Plath's "Sow" violated Moore's sense of decorum. This was one "tour," with a stop for a swig at the "pink teats," that she did not care to take.[25]

Despite her reservations about all three poems, however, the actual letter that Moore wrote conveys a much more mixed message. For example, Moore softens the tone of her typed commentary with more intimate, handwritten additions and interpolations which personalize the aesthetic judgments, especially since Moore writes of sympathizing with Plath in her struggles, difficult, she notes, when one is so talented. Functionally speaking, Moore agrees to write the letter of recommendation Plath requested and apologizes for the delay in getting back to her—Moore had been out of town and her teeth were bothering her. Plath, too, was having health problems in July: her depression had again taken hold. But her focus on Moore's concern with propriety—the carbon copies rather than the originals—deflects the more obvious criticism of her choice of subject matter.[26] The whole interaction was complicated by the fact that while Plath was waiting for a response, someone—either Plath or Hughes, or Plath acting for Hughes—had sent Moore an original, not a carbon, of Hughes's poem "Pike." In her praise of the poem, Moore referred to the "largess of a first copy," so Plath's reading has at least this much to be said for it. Moore compares valuable clear carbons, valuable that is, to the sender, to the generosity of an original, an original valuable to both sender and receiver. Moore wrote that "typing is a bugbear and clear copies, valuable, so here are the pages, you scrupled to supply me." "Scrupled" seems to mean "troubled," as in "You took the trouble." And then, not caring to be indebted to either Hughes, Ted or Sylvia, Moore returned everything.[27]

As we have seen, in her initial response of July 13, Moore is not criticizing Plath for sending carbons of her own work, and she ends the July 13 version of the two-part letter, "Yours warmly," adding a further and very understandable apology for having made Plath "wait and wait." A self-critical parenthesis "(I know what it's like to need something and never hear because the

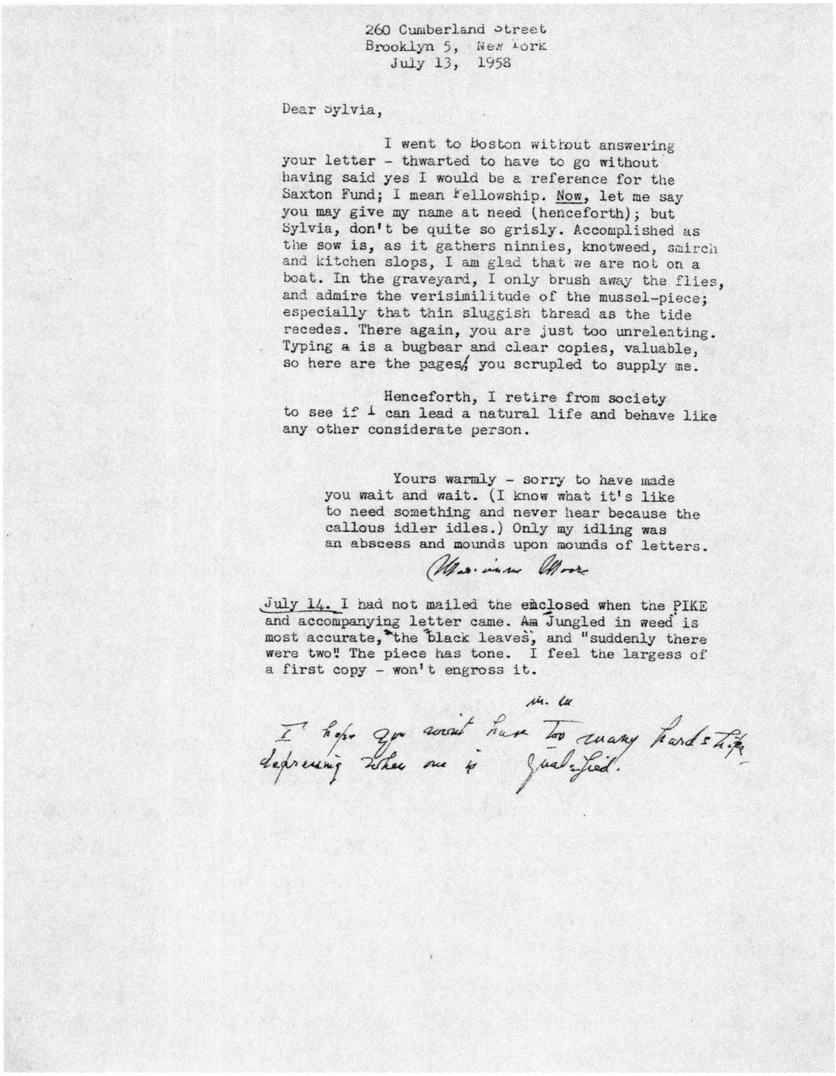

260 Cumberland Street
Brooklyn 5, New York
July 13, 1958

Dear Sylvia,

        I went to Boston without answering
your letter - thwarted to have to go without
having said yes I would be a reference for the
Saxton Fund; I mean Fellowship. <u>Now</u>, let me say
you may give my name at need (henceforth); but
Sylvia, don't be quite so grisly. Accomplished as
the sow is, as it gathers ninnies, knotweed, smirch
and kitchen slops, I am glad that we are not on a
boat. In the graveyard, I only brush away the flies,
and admire the verisimilitude of the mussel-piece;
especially that thin sluggish thread as the tide
recedes. There again, you are just too unrelenting.
Typing a is a bugbear and clear copies, valuable,
so here are the pages you scrupled to supply me.

        Henceforth, I retire from society
to see if I can lead a natural life and behave like
any other considerate person.

        Yours warmly - sorry to have made
you wait and wait. (I know what it's like
to need something and never hear because the
callous idler idles.) Only my idling was
an abscess and mounds upon mounds of letters.

<u>July 14.</u> I had not mailed the enclosed when the PIKE
and accompanying letter came. Am Jungled in weed is
most accurate, "the black leaves", and "suddenly there
were two". The piece has tone. I feel the largess of
a first copy - won't engross it.

Figure 19. Letter from Marianne Moore to Sylvia Plath, July 13 and 14, 1958.
Photograph courtesy of Mortimer Rare Book Room, Smith College Library.
Permission for the book and electronic use of the letter is granted by Literary
Estate of Marianne C. Moore, David M. Moore, Successor Executor of the
Literary Estate of Marianne Moore. All rights reserved.

callous idler idles)" is especially gracious.[28] But the contrast between Moore's enthusiasm for "Pike" and her criticism of Plath's poems is instructive and not commented upon by Plath in her *Journal*, perhaps because she was unwilling to accept the fact that Moore viewed the two of them differently. Whereas Plath's "Sow," her "monument / Prodigious in gluttonies . . . stomaching no constraint" (*Collected* 61) aroused Moore's instinct to regurgitate, Hughes's "Pike," despite its ominous undertones, struck her as "accurate." When Hughes described pike, and by extension people, eating each other, Moore was not revolted. And yet, these perfect fish, "Killers from the egg," with their "malevolent aged grin,"

> spare nobody.
> Two, six pounds each, over two feet long,
> High and dry and dead in the willow-herb—
>
> One jammed past its gills down the other's gullet:
> The outside eye stared: as a vice locks—
> The same iron in this eye
> Though its film shrank in death.[29]

Strong stuff but not, from Moore's perspective, alarming. In reading his work, she did not fear for Hughes, whereas Moore seems genuinely concerned about Plath's "many hardships, depressing when one is qualified." And so she tries to let her down as gently as possible, without holding back the criticism and the advice she feels compelled to offer. One of the imponderables here is how much Moore knew about Plath's breakdown and attempted suicide in college. Her maternal protectiveness—not inconsistent with tough love—probably owes something to this knowledge.

Despite Moore's reservations, by the end of July, "Mussel Hunter at Rock Harbor," "Moonrise," and "Sow" were accepted for publication, but Plath had a discouraging fall. She did not get the grant she wanted and, suffering from writer's block, took a typing job in the psychiatry clinic of Massachusetts General Hospital, both to ward off the "Panic Bird" that possessed her and to expand her knowledge of troubled human nature. Hoping to become more objective about herself (*Unabridged* 141), in December 1958 she began weekly sessions with her former psychiatrist Ruth Beuscher, who famously encouraged her to acknowledge her hatred for her mother. Beuscher wanted Plath to unrepress, rehearse, and interpret the childhood traumas organized by her father's death—a death that Hughes too, in *Birthday Letters*, understands as the root of her difficulties. Moore also had a missing father, but her poetry suggests that self-repression can be a good thing and that some strategic forgettings are necessary; strategic forgettings, even for survivors of catastrophic events, can enable those "efforts of affection" to which Moore was committed in both her public and private lives.[30]

For his part, and despite his growing reputation, Hughes was homesick in the United States, and after a second year spent freelancing in Boston and writing at Yaddo, he insisted on returning to England. Plath acquiesced. Their first child was born in London, in April 1960, and William Heinemann issued *The Colossus and Other Poems* in October. At least one review accused Plath of imitating established poets, giving John Crowe Ransom and Moore as examples.[31] Following a miscarriage in February 1961, a pregnant Plath sought a grant to support her writing, again turning to Moore for assistance. Since by this time Moore strongly preferred Hughes's poetry to hers, the Hughes connection was problematic for Plath in more ways than one, and now history repeated itself, with a vengeance.

Moore had helped Hughes to win a Guggenheim in 1958, and Plath continued to hope that this enthusiasm for Hughes would be beneficial to her own career. By November 1961, however, Moore was out of patience, writing to Henry Allen Moe, head of the foundation, that Sylvia Plath was not living up to her original promise, whereas Hughes's "moral fervor" was unmistakable. And since "her husband" had twice as much talent, why not give the grant to him? It is highly unlikely that Plath ever saw this letter, in which Moore remarked, "You are not subsidized for having a baby." Moore also took Plath to task for contributing to the world's overpopulation! Let people think about their social responsibilities before bringing more children into the world, Moore counseled. Although *The Population Bomb* (1968) had not yet been published, overpopulation *was* a concern at the time, and perhaps Moore had been reading Richard Martin Fagley's *Christian Responsibility and the Population Explosion* (1960), which, in exploring the attitude of various religions to birth control, concluded that birth control was indeed compatible with Christianity. Something more intimate is at stake here, however, and Plath seems to have touched a raw nerve. Although we do not have Plath's 1961 cover letter to Moore, it appears that she unwisely asserted the value of her experience as a mother in putting herself forward.[32] Plath felt that she was reaching to deeper levels in her "real" self; Moore felt insulted. Asked at about this time about her own "inordinate interest in animals and

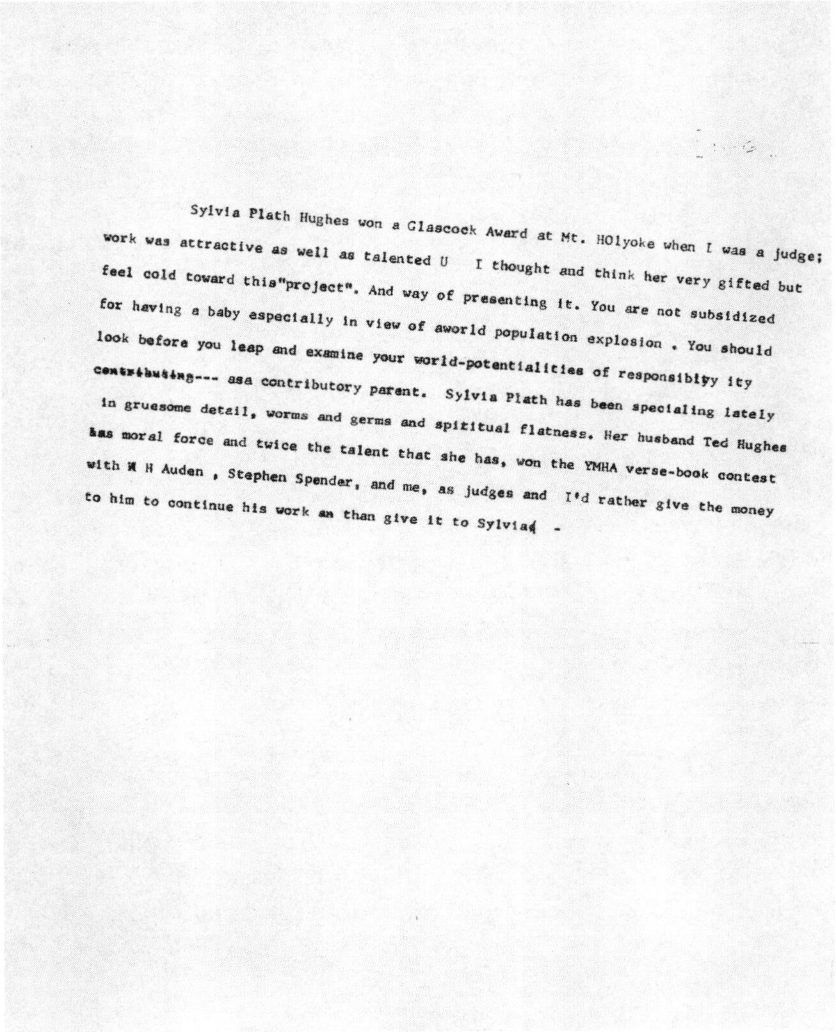

Sylvia Plath Hughes won a Glascock Award at Mt. HOlyoke when I was a judge;
work was attractive as well as talented U   I thought and think her very gifted but
feel cold toward this"project". And way of presenting it. You are not subsidized
for having a baby especially in view of aworld population explosion . You should
look before you leap and examine your world-potentialities of responsibiﬂy ity
contrﬁbuﬁﬁng--- asa contributory parent. Sylvia Plath has been specialing lately
in gruesome detail, worms and germs and spiﬁitual flatness. Her husband Ted Hughes
has moral force and twice the talent that she has, won the YMHA verse-book contest
with H H Auden , Stephen Spender, and me, as judges and I'd rather give the money
to him to continue his work an than give it to Sylviaﬁ -

Figure 20. Letter from Moore to Henry Allen Moe, dated November 1961.
She refuses to sponsor Plath for a Guggenheim award and indicates her strong
preference for Hughes. Moore also criticizes Plath for contributing to the
population explosion. Photograph courtesy of Rosenbach Museum & Library.
Permission for the book and electronic use of the letter is granted by Literary
Estate of Marianne C. Moore, David M. Moore, Successor Executor of the
Literary Estate of Marianne Moore. All rights reserved.

athletes," Moore replied, "They are subjects for art and exemplars of it, are they not? minding their own business. Pangolins, hornbills, pitchers, catchers, do not pry or prey—or prolong the conversation; do not make us selfconscious."[33] The intimate revelations in which Plath was coming to specialize made Moore feel self-conscious. Notwithstanding, the social logic of Moore's letter does not show her at her best, especially since Hughes is not faulted for fathering children.

Plath's Revenge

Normative literary histories have taught us that "American poetry in the middle decades of the twentieth century center[ed] on the lives of the poets themselves" which were "peculiarly difficult, even impossible to live."[34] Anne Sexton and Plath, W. D. Snodgrass, Theodore Roethke, Robert Lowell, Randall Jarrell, and John Berryman—these "confessional" poets are seen, collectively, as composing a school of intimate revealers.[35] Moore, on the other hand, as a member of the first generation of women modernists, rebelled against essentializing, autobiographical constructions of lyric subjectivity that tended to perpetuate the association of woman and victim. For example, here is Moore's poetry as characterized by May Swenson in 1964:

> Marianne Moore's poetry is uniquely unself-conscious and unself-centered. Who of us is able to be such an acute instrument for the objectification of sensual perceptions and states of mind as she, without emphasizing *self* as a subject. There is neither self-pity nor self-aggrandizement in her poems. Where a capital *I* begins an observation, it is never to say, using the excuse of being a poet: "See how *I* have loved, or suffered. . . . See what *I* have discovered." It is rather to present, often in the plainest terms, a wisdom, a conviction, a piece of advice that has a general application. She dares to do this in the midst of language often as incredibly opulent—and this to a purpose—as the peacock's tail.[36]

The intellectually challenging poetry for which Moore is best known is suspicious of anything resembling unmediated self-revelation, although, especially in her early and late poems, Moore does express emotions—bitterness, for example, and nostalgia—which we may reasonably attribute to her biographical self.

Yet exposing potentially embarrassing secrets was clearly not her mode, as for many years it was not the mode of her long-term protégée Elizabeth Bishop, who told her student and friend Wesley Wehr, "I *hate* confessional poetry, and so many people are writing it these days [in the 1960s]. Besides, they seldom have anything interesting to 'confess' anyway. Mostly they write about a lot of things which I should think were best left unsaid."[37]

Just as Bishop's attitude toward confessional poetry was more complex than her 1966 statement to Wehr suggests, so too Moore's version of modernist anticonfessionalism was impure. At its best, her poetry is energized by the tension between her desires to tell and not to, a tension that she often reconciles, to the extent that she does, through wit. For example, in "Silence," when Moore writes about "her" father, she dupes the unsuspecting reader and then confesses to the trick by providing a footnote attributing the role of daughter to one "Miss A. M. Homans." It is Miss Homans, we are informed, who seems to accept the advice proffered by "her" genteel father, that " 'The deepest feeling always shows itself in silence; / not in silence, but restraint.' "[38] Moore ironizes the words of the father without revealing shameful secrets that readers are encouraged to understand as her own. Some readers, rendered curious by the heightened intensity of the poem's indirection, will feel impelled to move beyond the text, back toward a baffling but also clarifying point of origin: the writer's life.[39]

Moore's public life was singularly free of scandal, but in examining her letter to the Guggenheim Foundation, we have stepped into her semipublic life, in which the deepest feelings were not always restrained. Moore's letter of disrecommendation to the Guggenheim Foundation criticizes Plath for being a mother and not taking seriously enough her "world potentialities of responsibility as a contributory parent." Charles Molesworth observes that "because Moore chose to remain single all her life, she was perhaps disposed to be more than tolerant of those who had not started a family of their own."[40] Her swipe at Plath shows the violent, antinatalist side of that tolerance, and Moore is " '[un]characteristically intemperate' " ("Blessed Is the Man").[41]

It seems that Plath unwittingly stepped into a debate that Moore was having with herself about personal and social responsibilities and, a year and a half later, Moore was distinctly uncomfortable when she was unable to respond positively to *The Colossus*, explaining to Judith Jones, Plath's American editor, "I need commiseration. I do like to like a book, especially anything by Sylvia Plath."[42] But she called Plath "bitter," "frostbitten," "burnt out," "averse." Plath was stung by the criticism, which Jones shared with her, and sought revenge in "The Tour," when she was in full *Ariel* bloom. The poem is dated October 25, 1962, and Moore is a prototype for the generic and censorious maiden aunt who visits the speaker and finds her too messy. "I am bitter? I am averse?" Plath writes, flinging Moore's words back at her. There was plenty of oral aggression to go around, and, picking up on the language of Moore's anti-*Colossus* letter, she warns her not to stick her finger in a "frost box" that represents the speaker's anger, her poems, and something vaginally obscene: "O I shouldn't put my finger in *that* / Auntie, it might bite! / That's my frost box, no cat, / Though it *looks* like a cat, with its fluffy stuff, pure white. . . . Toddle on home to tea."

In high dudgeon, Plath demonstrates her verbal poise, evoking Moore's penchant for exotic flora and fauna, her trademark hat, her interest in machines—all her glittering surfaces: "And I in slippers and housedress with no lipstick." And, recalling the visit to Moore's apartment, when Moore served the Hugheses sesame seed biscuits and strawberries and milk, Plath offers to feed her unwanted guest "Millions of needly glass cakes," "Lemon tea and earwig biscuits—creepy-creepy." Plath's sense of humor had not deserted her, although "The Tour" went through seventeen worksheet drafts—further evidence of Plath's unresolved relationship to Moore who, in her maiden aunt guise, enters the poem accompanied by "a gecko, the little flick!" There is also a weirdly unexplained third figure, introduced in the last two stanzas and identified as "the nurse!" I speculate that this wiggly fingered, imperfectly sexualized figure ("bald . . . no eyes") represents Hughes, who, in Plath's imagination of him/her, "can bring the dead to life." Perhaps he is the gecko reborn. Plath, however, did not include this poem in her *Ariel* manuscript, and the nurse figure is denied the faculty of vision. Perhaps too, the nurse represents Plath herself in embryo, the Plath who needs to cure herself. "I must be my own doctor," she had reminded herself (*Unabridged* 401). Perhaps good advice, but could she take it?[43]

The Final Tour

As "The Literary Life" attests, Moore had unwittingly been scripted into the Hughes's erotic tragedy, and when Moore met Hughes at a party in London in 1964, she was seeking closure. The poem describes a Moore intent on placating not only him but also Plath's ghost:

> She wanted me to know, she insisted
> (It was all she wanted to say)
> With that Missouri needle, drawing each stitch
> Tight in my ear,
> That your little near-posthumous memoir
> 'OCEAN 1212'
> Was 'so wonderful, so lit, so wonderful'—(*BL* 76)

Representing himself as the inconsolable mourner, Hughes refuses to accept her tribute, and one hears him invoking the words of Emily Dickinson, some of whose work he edited during the 1960s, "Endow the Living – with the Tears – / You squander on the Dead" (*Fr* 657).[44] For tears, we can read "praise."

Hughes's chronology, however, is mistaken. Whatever happened could not have occurred "a decade later," that is, in 1968, since Moore made her third and last trip to England in 1964.[45] The party narrative sounds plausible: after Plath's death, why *not* try to say something consoling, and given Moore's reservations about the poetry, why not praise the childhood memoir in which innocence disappears like a "fine, white flying myth?" ("Ocean 1212-W").[46] Suffice it to say that the Smith College library contains Plath's copy of Moore's *Collected Poems* (1951), bearing Moore's inscription, "Sylvia Plath's turned down corners and underlinings make me feel that there was some reason for the collecting of these poems. I am grateful, to have a reader." The date was April 16, 1955, while Moore was a judge in the Mount Holyoke contest that meant so much to Plath. And reading Moore's signature poem "Marriage," the first passage Plath underlined is the following: "Psychology which explains everything / explains nothing, / and we are still in doubt." For much of her married life, Plath tried unsuccessfully to hide her anxieties from Hughes. All the more poignant then is her underlining from "Silence": "The deepest feeling always shows itself in silence; / not in silence, but restraint."[47]

Hughes considered this important advice—bad in some situations, good in others.[48] However self-justifying his appropriation of Moore—he too could be unrelenting, lacking in patience and spiritual strength—Moore continued to remind him of the time when he and Plath were so intimately identified with each other that he experienced her criticism of Plath as a rejection of himself. Several years after Plath's death, Hughes was quoted in the *Manchester Guardian* as saying, "There was no rivalry between us as poets or in any other way. It sounds trite but you completely influence one another if you live together. You begin to write out of one brain. . . . It was all we were interested in, all we ever did. We were like two feet, each one using everything the other did. It was a working partnership and was all-absorbing. We lived it. There was an unspoken unanimity in every criticism or judgment we made. It all fitted in very well."[49] As recorded in Plath's 1958 journal entry, "we" sent her typescript to Moore, and Hughes presumably encouraged her to do so. As recorded in "The Literary Life," Plath and Hughes found common cause in their mutual turning away from Moore, but his was the heroic part. He picked Plath up, when, under pressure from Moore, she threatened to hurl herself down. Moore thus functions as scapegoat while justifying Hughes's panicked flight from Plath: he too gasps for oxygen and cheer. In the historical time excised from the poem, however, Plath could not afford to give up on Moore, and the promise of professional help she represented, without a further fight.

Less than two weeks before her suicide, Plath wrote a poem to a child, in which she explained, "Your clear eye is the one absolutely beautiful thing" (*Collected* 265). That seems a fitting note on which to end a public and a private story robbed of its unifying ending: the fantasy ending in which Plath and Moore meet in the London hotel where Moore is staying during her 1964 visit to England. In this reassuring setting, over a late afternoon cup of tea, Plath describes the new poems she wrote after the breakup of her marriage. Moore, impressed by Plath's spiritual resilience, compliments her on the successes of her personal and professional life. Together, they discuss the future of Anglo-American poetry. Marianne then quotes from one of her own, something about "everlasting vigor, / power to grow," and something about a sun, "that comes into and steadies my soul" ("The Pangolin").[50] It is raining and while she, Marianne, "talk[s] a blue streak" (*Letters* 233), Plath, unperturbed, is textualizing the conversation: it has the makings of a good story.

Chapter 5

Plath's Dickinson: On Not Stopping for Death

We first hear Sylvia Plath's voice in the Boston Sunday *Herald*, on August 10, 1941, saying, "Dear Editor: I have written a short poem about what I see and hear on hot summer nights." It was less than a year after the death of her father, and this is what she sent: "Hear the crickets chirping / In the dewy grass. / Bright little fireflies / Twinkle as they pass." Identified in the caption as an "8-YEAR-OLD POET," and then described in an endnote as an eight-and-a-half-year-old from Winthrop, this already complicated young girl was proud to be a member of the *Herald*'s Good Sport Club for Children. It had a motto: "A good heart wins fairly and loses gamely." "Are you a good sport?" the paper asked its young readers.[1]

Sad to say, our officially certified Good Sport had already begun to lose faith in winning fairly and losing gamely. Indeed, her mother describes the specific moment when Sylvia turned her face to the wall, or more literally hid under a blanket to block out the news of her father's death. It was early in the morning, and Sylvia was reading in bed. Aurelia Plath explains, "She looked at me sternly for a moment, then said woodenly, 'I'll never speak to God again!'"[2] Some months later, with Aurelia's encouragement, Plath composed her little meditation on the sights and sounds of a passing summer evening. Titled simply "Poem," it evokes a magical time when she was still on speaking terms with God, a time before pathos. Picking up that strain of Dickinson's religious imagination in which "Beauty – is Nature's Fact," the little girl's fifteen words rhyme "Hear" with "Here." Only in retrospect do these words seem determined to validate her right to be heard and to have a continuing life of her own. "The Earth has many keys," Dickinson wrote, in a multiversioned elegy she called "My Cricket." Plath, too, had many keys, and for all of them, Dickinson's phrase "Enlarging Loneliness" proved prophetic (*Fr* 895A).

Plath's New England childhood, with its further-in-summer weathers, was meticulously edited and documented not only by her mother but also by the equally ambitious Sylvia, who, as Paul Alexander notes, became "adamant about saving her poems, copying them into one of three books—a scrapbook, a diary, or a document she labeled *Life Poem Book*."[3] Saving and moving on as we would expect her to do, in junior high school Plath expanded her archive of comparatively untroubled nature poems, writing on such subjects as "The Spring Parade," "March," "The Rain," and "My Garden." In the normal course of events, Dickinson was one of her models. Her diary entry for June 7, 1945, indicates that she recited "I'll tell you how the Sun rose" in class. She was frightened, but the words came pouring out of her:

> I'll tell you how the Sun rose –
> A Ribbon at a time –
> The Steeples swam in Amethyst –
> The news, like Squirrels, ran –
> The Hills untied their Bonnets –
> The Bobolinks – begun –
> Then I said softly to myself –
> "That must have been the Sun"!
> But how he set – I know not –
> There seemed a purple stile
> That little Yellow boys and girls
> Were climbing all the while –
> Till when they reached the other side –
> A Dominie in Gray –
> Put gently up the evening Bars –
> And led the flock away – (*Fr* 204)[4]

Even at twelve, she liked being part of a tradition of women poets speaking to themselves and to others about important subjects such as the mysteries of life and death. "A Dominie in Gray": the schoolteacher's gentleness was reassuring.

Starting high school in tenth grade, she was influenced by an inspiring teacher, Wilbury Crockett, who praised her "lyric gift beyond the ordinary." She was overjoyed, noting in her diary, "He liked 'I Thought That I Could

Not Be Hurt' above the rest." But she was concerned about the effect of poetry on "the little strategy of 'popularity'" she was developing.[5] Poetry notwithstanding, she *did* develop popularity, had many friends, and Crockett, among others, testified to the fact that she was not only creative but also "exceptionally well-adjusted."[6] Then it was the summer of 1950, and she had graduated from Bradford (later Wellesley) High School. In the journal she began keeping in July, we can hear her delving deeper into that most fascinating of subjects, herself and her mood swings. The following entry is set somewhere between the library of an actual house in which she was babysitting and the sumptuous mansion of her luxury-ridden dreams.

> Here I sit in the deep cushioned armchair, the crickets rasping, buzzing, chirring outside. It's the library, my favorite room, with the floor a medieval mosaic of flat square stones the color of old book-bindings . . . rust, copper, tawny orange, pepper-brown, maroon. And there are deep comfortable maroon leather chairs with the leather peeling off, revealing a marbled pattern of ridiculous pink. The books, all that you would fill your rainy days with, line the shelves; friendly, fingered volumes. So I sit here, smiling as I think in my fragmentary way: "Woman is but an engine of ecstasy, a mimic of the earth from the ends of her curled hair to her red-lacquered nails."[7]

In this portrait of a ladylike scene, the participant-observer is attracted to the fragmentary odd detail, the sight that won't quite fit. The text moves from crickets, their sound now rougher, to something showing that shouldn't be (the ridiculous pink underlay), to books and luxury, to ecstasy, to mimicry, and to gender as performance. Dragged down by lust and hating the boys who can "dispel sexual hunger freely," the writerly Plath is also curiously detached from a sense of herself as a real and honest person in search of sexual pleasure. She enjoys watching herself watching, almost to the point of dissolving the psychological boundary between herself and those, the boys, who do not suffer as she does, "in soggy desire, always unfulfilled." The prize-winning Plath was soon to depart for college, where she would continue to engage in bouts of self-worship and self-loathing, yet a depressive tide was pulling her back and down, and in the journal entry cited above, she describes herself as "drowning." She could resist this tide and its accompanying gender confusions up to a point. What would that point be?

The Perennial Emily

Multitalented, her drawings published as well as her writings, Plath in effect chose authorship early, and despite some nervous crises, she excelled in her first two years at Smith. At twenty, she was about to finish her junior year and thought that she would be attending Harvard during the summer—studying short story writing with Frank O'Connor, who had risen from the slums of Cork, Ireland, to distinguish himself at home. Yeats compared his short stories to Chekhov's, and now in the United States, his readership was larger still. Plath wondered what to submit to the workshop competition. To be on the safe side, she chose "Sunday at the Mintons'," which had already been published in *Mademoiselle* magazine, earning her a prize and five hundred huge dollars. In "The Mintons'," Plath impulsively inhabits a fantasy-ridden female imagination liberated from male authority and voice. The focalizer is a librarian, a deceptively bland heroine who finds herself circumscribed by her "domestic duties." In fantasy, she deftly extinguishes her fastidious older brother Henry (James?). Transfigured, he becomes "a colossus astride the roaring sea, an expression of unusual and pained surprise growing on his white, uplifted face." She drowns him (out), as "her high-pitched, triumphant, feminine giggle mingled with the deep, gurgling chuckle of Henry, borne along beneath her on the outgoing tide." O'Connor found the "Mintons'" disturbing, thought she would be disruptive, and did not admit her to the class.[8]

This disappointment was still to come when Plath wrote to her mother on April 22, 1953, enclosing three clever poems consciously modeled after Emily Dickinson as a birthday present for Aurelia, who was about to turn forty-seven. Readers will hear different Dickinsons in these imitative poems, as well as different Plaths. For example, there is the risk-taking Plath/Dickinson of "Verbal Calisthenics," who compares the ingenuity of her love to the ingenuity of her language (the "daring adjective," the "adroit conjunction," the "athletic" verb). Of course there is the danger of a fracture, a fall, a plunge, and a swoon, as Plath/Dickinson, the acrobat poet, treads "circus tightropes / Of each syllable." In this show-offy capacity, Plath/Dickinson is figured as a brazen He. Then there is the more recognizably gendered, more cautious lyric actor of "Parallax" (which links "mortal lack" to "minor love"). While "Parallax" wants to announce that love is the power that rules the world, these are poems whose erotic emotions don't bear looking into too deeply—except for "Admonition," the shortest and most coherent of the

group. It probes the relationship between love and torture, which is camou-
flaged as science:

> If you dissect a bird
>   to diagram the tongue,
> you'll cut the chord
>   articulating song.
>
> If you flay a beast
>   to marvel at the mane,
> you'll wreck the rest
>   from which the fur began.
>
> If you assault a fish
>   to analyse the fin,
> your hands will crush
>   the generating bone.
>
> If you pluck out my heart
>   to find what makes it move,
> you'll halt the clock
>   that syncopates our love.[9]

In "Admonition," a tight form restrains feeling which threatens to spin
out of control. Using aggressive verbs such as "dissect," "cut," "flay,"
"wreck," "assault," "crush," "pluck out," and "halt," Plath seeks to disman-
tle her dutiful daughter persona. Paradoxically, she mimics Dickinson's quatrains, her short lines, and her subtle use of assonance and consonance. But
far from being a reaffirmation of straight, white, middle-class American girlhood, "Admonition" wants to lure us into a dubiously gendered, sadomasochistic emotional zone set in no particular time or place which Dickinson's
"Master" letters also inhabit. Thus, while all of Plath's birthday poems pay
lip service to something called love, "Admonition" more boldly flaunts its
warning against intimacy.[10]

In a fit of rage, Plath later burned her mother's letters, and we do not
know how Aurelia responded at the time to the gift of the three poems,
which was accompanied by a request for criticism. In *Letters Home*, however,
a gathering of her deceased daughter's letters mainly to her, there is implied

criticism of "Admonition." As editor, Aurelia Plath dropped stanza 3 and changed "my heart" to "the heart" in line 1 of stanza 4. These changes make "Admonition" less violent and less personal. She prefaced all three poems with the boast attributed to Sylvia, "Any resemblance to Emily Dickinson is purely intentional" (*Letters* 110).[11] Because Dickinson was Aurelia's favorite poet, this intertext tightens the chord that links them, but it also makes Dickinson the tie that binds.

Plath's deliberate allusion to Dickinson has been widely quoted and/or absorbed as fact by scholars such as Marjorie Perloff, Margaret Dickie Uroff, Linda Wagner-Martin, Steven Gould Axelrod, Gayle Wurst, and Christina Britzolakis, but it is no longer part of Aurelia's typescript of *Letters Home* preserved by the Lilly Library at Indiana University. Instead, there is a short page which has been cut at the top, reading, "Tell me what you think about the poems. XXX Sivvy . . . P. S. If you ever have a while with nothing to do (ho ho!) you could type up these poems, centered, singlespaced, on good paper (without name or anything) & send 'em to me! XX S."[12] Someone, presumably Aurelia, cut the top inch and a half of the sheet of paper on which Plath invokes Dickinson. That is, she literally cut the paper on which this reference to Dickinson appears; she "cut the chord" that produced the song, an action against which "Admonition" warns. As Aurelia explains in the "Introduction" to *Letters Home* and elsewhere, Dickinson was early on her own "new Bible" and she and Sylvia read Dickinson together during Sylvia's precollege years. Admiring, even worshipping Dickinson, she wanted Sylvia to admire and perhaps to worship her too, and not just for her own sake but for the gendered tradition she represented.

Of course the possibility exists that Aurelia engaged in even more intrusive editing, herself inserting the allusion to Dickinson, but I think that unlikely. Plath liked doing imitations and later determined to "imitate" O'Connor's stories, wanting to use what he could teach (*Unabridged* 452–53). This blunt invocation of her precursor is nevertheless unique, and my analysis of "Admonition" as intertext linking mother and daughter assumes that just before her *Bell Jar* summer, Sylvia, having "found her God in Auden" ("He is Wonderful and / Very Brilliant, and / Very Lyric and Most / Extremely Witty") (*Letters* 108), was polytheistic and looking for other gods as well. A faithjumper like her mother (Aurelia was a lapsed Catholic who became a Methodist and then a Unitarian), Sylvia Plath was hoping to be saved by female deities too, even if the tradition seemed thin. As she later wrote to her poet-friend Lynne Lawner, with whom she was constructing an emotional sisterhood "on the other side of the moon," "Except for M. Moore & Elizabeth Bishop what women are there to look to? A few eccentrics like Edith Sitwell, Amy Lowell. And the perennial Emily, I suppose."[13]

Did Sylvia write something embarrassing to Aurelia on the missing part page? That seems unlikely. Rather, I speculate that as the mother of a famous suicide, Aurelia was trying to cut her losses. Perhaps impulsively, she defaced the typescript, while printing its original message. Note that the most immediately personal lines, those asking Aurelia to retype her gift when she gets a chance and to send the poems back to Plath, do not appear in *Letters Home*. Here, too, Aurelia was attempting to disengage, and given the glare of publicity in which she was then living, it is understandable that she would want to withhold something for herself, some relic of a happier time. In her younger days, she had wanted to write family fiction, but the text of her daughter's life belonged to so many other people that she felt violated by a literary history in which her life-drama was being grotesquely distorted.[14]

When Aurelia was editing *Letters Home*, literary historians were producing the bereaved mother (was this the good mother?), the resentful mother (was this the bad mother?), and the dead daughter famous for her wrath: the poetic genius whose life, like Emily Dickinson's, "had stood – a Loaded Gun" (*Fr* 764). Considered as historical persons and as cultural productions, these three (the good mother, the bad mother, and the dead daughter who contained elements of both) already had a deeply sedimented history between them when Plath produced her ambivalent remark about "the perennial Emily, I suppose." Let me briefly amplify the earliest phase of their relations.

Dickinson's tense probings of patriarchal power made her an almost inevitable part of the self-education of ambitious young women in the twentieth century, especially women with clearly defined or even vague literary leanings. For someone such as Aurelia Schober, who grew up in Massachusetts in the early twentieth century, reading Dickinson was part of a quest for full citizenship in an alien context. Aurelia, the daughter of Austrian immigrants, vividly recalled being punished by her father for bringing schoolyard English home with her. "Shut up," she told him. Although her parents were "ardent converts to American democracy" (*Letters* 4), Aurelia recalled being physically and verbally harassed by her schoolmates during World War I for her "spy-face" and German-sounding surname. Partly in response to these pressures, Aurelia herself became an ardent convert to an American civil religion organized by educational institutions and literary culture. In the early 1920s, when she was a junior in high school, as she explains,

I had the good fortune to have an inspirational English teacher who improved my taste. From then on Emily Dickinson's poetry became my new bible; the novels of Scott, Dickens, Thackeray, Eliot, the Brontës, Jane Austen, Thomas Hardy, Galsworthy, Cooper, Hawthorne, Melville, and Henry James—in fact, the world of American and English prose and poetry burst upon me, filling me with the urgency to read, read. I lived in a dream world . . . and the family's stock answer to "What's RiRi [my nickname] doing?" was "Oh, she's reading *again*." (*Letters* 5)

Graduating from Winthrop High in 1924 as the salutatorian of her class, RiRi dutifully enrolled in a two-year program at Boston University's College of Practical Arts and Letters, pleasing the charming and vulnerable father who wanted her to be a "business woman." According to biographer Paul Alexander, to whom she granted numerous interviews, Aurelia "held down odd jobs to supplement the partial scholarships the school had awarded her," while participating in such extracurricular activities as "the English Club, the Writers' Club, the Student Government Board, the German Club (for which she served as both president and vice-president) and her college's junior yearbook, on which she served as editor-in-chief." Alexander quotes the following intriguing description of her editorial aura: "The staff will never forget those board meetings, those would-be 'scoldings,' and those cherished words of approval and praise." It seems that Aurelia was inspirational, wielding the right combination of carrot and stick, and something of a gender bender: "The German Club nearly lost its sensational 'young man,' when *Sivad* [the yearbook] won an efficient editor-in-chief," the editors wrote under her picture, "but Aurelia played both roles admirably."[15] In response to his versatile daughter's successes, Frank Schober relented, and Aurelia was able to enroll for another two years and to study modern languages. In 1928, she graduated from the College of Practical Arts and Letters at the top of her class.

Degree in hand, Aurelia taught English and German at Melrose (Massachusetts) High School for a year, and by living at home, she saved enough money to return to Boston University the following year for a master's degree in English and German in the College of Liberal Arts. As she notes in *Letters Home*, her own father spoke four languages (presumably German, English, Italian, and French), and she further observes that her husband (né Platt) was "a gifted linguist." They started dating after she completed his class in Middle High German in the spring of 1930. Otto Plath was twenty-one years her senior and she was attracted, as Marjorie Perloff observes, by his "learning . . . and virile good looks."[16] Although personally reticent, he could be dramatic, especially in his science classes: "To demonstrate man's illogic, the professor would skin a dead rat, slice meat from its bones, sauté the meat in a pan, and, as his students gazed on in horror, proceed to eat the fried meat piece by piece. 'Rat meat might be thought of as disgusting and inedible,' he would declare, munching heartily, 'but it is really no different from rabbit meat, which people have eaten as a delicacy for centuries.' "[17]

Apparently some niceties of taste eluded Otto, and Aurelia was taken aback when he invited her to join him at a colleague's home for a country weekend at the end of the spring semester. She accepted the invitation because he was handsome, professionally successful, and a link to her Germanic heritage. Otto, she writes, "grew up in the country town of Grabow, Germany (Polish Corridor territory), speaking German and Polish, and learning French in school. His citizenship papers indicate his nationality was uncertain. He told me his parents were German but that one grandmother was Polish" (*Letters* 8). "From the fall of 1930 on," she continues, "our friendship developed and deepened": "Weekends found us hiking through the Blue Hills, the Arnold Arboretum, or the Fells Reservation. The worlds of ornithology and entomology were opening for me, and we dreamed of projects, jointly shared, involving nature study, travel, and writing. . . . I succeeded in interesting Otto at that time in the fine productions then given at the Boston Repertory Theater—Ibsen, Shaw, and modern plays of that era—as well as sharing my enthusiasm for literature" (*Letters* 10). As it turned out, Otto was still legally married to a woman in Wisconsin with whom he had lived briefly in his youth.[18] But a divorce was easily arranged, and Otto, Aurelia, and her mother drove to Nevada together, where the couple were married in early January 1932. Although Aurelia had "enjoyed teaching German and English in Brookline High School," after the marriage, she "yielded" to his wish and became "a full-time homemaker" (*Letters* 10). They wanted children right away, and Sylvia was born at the end of October. A son, Warren, followed two and a half years later. Aurelia explains, "While Otto did not take an active part in tending to or playing with his children, he loved them dearly and took great pride in their attractiveness and progress. Once, as we looked in upon our sleeping two, he remarked softly, 'All parents *think* their children are wonderful. *We* know!' " (*Letters* 16).

Dutifully if not zestfully, Aurelia supported Otto's career. She helped to transcribe his lecture notes, served as his research assistant, and edited his

Figure 21. Otto Plath at the blackboard, 1930. This image is immortalized in "Daddy." Note the cleft in his chin.

Figure 22. A happy day in the park in 1933, with Otto, Aurelia, and Sylvia as a toddler. Helle Collection of Plath Family Photographs. Courtesy Mortimer Rare Book Room, Smith College Library. © The Estate of Aurelia S. Plath.

manuscripts. But they had few friends in common and "social life was almost nil for us as a married couple" (*Letters* 12). Moreover, Otto was determined to have his own way and was unused to "the free flow of communication, and talking things out and reasoning together just didn't operate." To keep the peace, she learned to "become more submissive, although it was not [her] nature to be so" (*Letters* 13). Life was circumscribed, especially after Otto developed a mysterious illness for which he refused medical treatment— believing, tragically, that he had an inoperable cancer. As Aurelia took on more and more responsibility for the children, his condition worsened and by 1940, he was gravely ill. When he died of complications following surgery, Sylvia said, as we have seen, "I'll never speak to God again!" She also made the beleaguered Aurelia promise "NEVER TO MARRY AGAIN" (*Letters* 25). Which she never did. In the coming years, needing to support herself and her children, Aurelia combined households with her own parents and returned to teaching English and German for the better part of two years. Then, in 1942, she accepted an opportunity at Boston University to develop a course in shorthand and typing for medical secretaries. Her ulcers and repressed rage notwithstanding, Aurelia demonstrated, as Langdon Hammer remarks, that "professional identity . . . was not simply coded as masculine." Yet if, during the coming years, she made Dickinson "a constant" in Sylvia's education, she also demonstrated that a mother's professional identity could intensify the daughter's ambition to define the terms of her own success.[19] Biography, then, teaches us that Aurelia's professional ambitions were magnified in the career of her covertly rivalrous daughter who, in poems such as "The Disquieting Muses," also blames her mother for insensitivity to the long Dickinsonian shadows by which she, the daughter, is beset.

Fast forward. Harvard Summer School has rejected Sylvia, she has spent six traumatic weeks in New York, and in suburban Wellesley is on the verge of a major nervous breakdown. In late August, she tries to commit suicide by swallowing sleeping pills and nearly dies but is rescued by her grandmother and her brother. Aurelia arranges for Sylvia to have the best of care, paid for by her mentor Olive Higgins Prouty, and she enters McLean Hospital in September. In January 1954, she returns to Smith as a special student and publishes two of her Dickinson imitations in the *Smith Review*.[20] For "Admonition," she has not adopted Aurelia's big change: she keeps the third stanza to which Aurelia objected, although the last stanza reads "*the* heart" rather than "*my* heart" (italics mine). Plath considers various careers before taking up a Fulbright Scholarship to study English literature at Cambridge University, primarily literature by men. There, she meets "that big dark, hunky boy, the only one there huge enough for me," and "the biggest seducer in Cambridge," that Ted Hughes. At a party triumphantly described in Plath's *Journals*, he rips off her "lovely red hairband scarf which has weathered the sun and much love," kissing her on the neck. For her part, she bites him "long and hard on the cheek," and blood runs down his face (*Unabridged* 211, 213, 212). "I can see how women lie down for artists," she concludes (*Unabridged* 212).

Figure 23. Aurelia with Sylvia and her brother Warren, in the rear of their home in Wellesley, Massachusetts, September 1949. She comments on the verso, "Sylvia—almost 17 / Warren—14 1/2. This does not do either Sylvia or Warren justice, but is excellent of me." Helle Collection of Plath Family Photographs. Courtesy Mortimer Rare Book Room, Smith College Library. © The Estate of Aurelia S. Plath.

Fast forward again. Stunned by Plath's death, Hughes needs to communicate with Aurelia. At first he can't, but in mid-March he writes to her, suggesting that "Sylvia was one of the greatest truest spirits alive, and in her last months she became a great poet, and no other woman poet except Emily Dickinson can begin to be compared with her, and certainly no living American."[21] Plath had heard a version of this comparison before. After separating from Ted, she wrote to her brother and sister-in-law, "The critic of the *Observer* is giving me an afternoon at his home to hear me read all my new poems! He is *the* opinion-maker in poetry over here, A. Alvarez, and says I'm the first woman poet he's taken seriously since Emily Dickinson! Needless to say, I'm delighted." In her role as a loyal family member, she added, "Now can you possibly get mother to stop worrying so much?" (*Letters* 476). Ted's version is slightly different. Whereas Alvarez compares Plath to Dickinson, Ted compares Dickinson to Plath.

The literary history Aurelia was constructing had more modest goals. As we have seen, she introduced the future "poetess of America" to Dickinson during her childhood, and through Sylvia she continued her own education. Moreover, Aurelia Plath had many literary enthusiasms, including Edna St. Vincent Millay, from whose "Renascence" she quotes in *Letters Home*. She remembers, "Sylvia was particularly moved by the lines 'A man was starving in Capri; / He moved his eyes and looked at me; / I felt his gaze, I heard his moan, / And knew his hunger as my own'" (*Letters* 32). Sylvia, too, was hungry for inspiration from many sources, and although she included three Dickinson poems in an anthology she made for her high school English class, when she published a story in *Seventeen* magazine the summer after she graduated, she turned not to Dickinson but to Sara Teasdale for a title ("And Summer Will Not Come Again"). And she quoted the second stanza of Teasdale's short lyric "An End" in the story itself:

> On the long wind I hear the
>   winter coming,
> The window panes are cold and
>   blind with rain;
> With my own will I turned the
>   summer from me
> And summer will not come to
>   me again.[22]

In locating Teasdale as a role model, Plath was acknowledging the problem of love loss for women, a problem intensified by her unusually close bond with her mother.[23] Feeling the need to distinguish her voice from the voice of the mother who had so deeply influenced her, "They can't shut me up," she wrote after her breakdown, describing a professional rejection she could handle (*Letters* 157). It was harder to deal with her mother's neediness. Later still, she wrote, in "Poem for a Birthday," "Mother, you are the one mouth / I would be a tongue to. Mother of otherness / Eat me" (*Collected* 132).

"Summer" features an unresilient heroine who unwittingly drives her life's only true beau away. Unfortunately, the story has prophetic power, in that it anticipates one of the narratives we can tell about Plath's breakup with Ted Hughes. When the hero dallies, and with a blonde, Celia cannot stop her mean, cutting, sarcastic "flood of words." ("If he thought she would just take him back meekly," and "Too late she stopped the flood of words, frightened at the silence hanging between them," and then, "There was something so final in the way he left, not looking back.") The heroine's (perhaps) unwarranted jealousy destroys a romance that, had she been able to see beyond the moment, might have flourished.

In the short run, however, Plath's story attracted an admirer in Eddie Cohen, a college student from Chicago who wrote her a fan letter, her first. They corresponded for the next several years, discussing sex and neuroses and, among other topics, Emily Dickinson. When Plath mentioned Dickinson, Cohen, a self-styled "semi-bohemian" and "cynical idealist," answered, "Yes, I've heard of [her]," warning "Syl" that it would be almost impossible for her to have a full-powered career and a "normal" family life. She liked the fact that he was "slightly soiled," calling him a "lovely, immoral, radical" outsider, but when he came to visit her at Smith, they both froze up. There was a silent, three-hour drive to Wellesley, and when they reached 26 Elmwood Road, "she thanked him for driving her home, introduced him to her mother, who had come to the door, and dashed upstairs." Eddie was "confused and insulted." "Strangely enough," Cohen was to comment, "none of this seemed to effect [*sic*] the tremendous rapport Syl and I had on paper, and we very shortly had the Post Office working overtime. We made plans to meet again, and did, the following spring. I came with a friend, and we double-dated with Syl and a friend. This time there was no trauma—nor anything else. Our relationship seemed as sterile in person as it was fertile via the mails."[24]

While Cohen and Plath bonded as slightly soiled misfits, Plath continued to resist the idea that she could not have an impressive career and a "normal" family life. Her mother encouraged her aspirations along those lines, and as Lynda Bundtzen points out, another boyfriend, Dick Norton, approximated the man of Aurelia's dreams.[25] Norton's parents were her friends, and Norton himself was (here I quote Eddie, quoting Plath) "handsome, brilliant, personable, athletic, and generally simply wonderful." This boy next door was also (according to Sylvia, writing to Aurelia) "the foremost-doctor-to-be-in the next-decades": "He knows everything. . . . He has an amazing mind and a remarkable group of highly developed skills—dancing, skating, swimming, & so on. . . . He's the most stimulating boy I've ever known. . . . I adore him and worship his intellect and keen perceptions in almost every field."[26] Readers of *The Bell Jar* will remember that Esther Greenwood's conflicts are intensified when she can no longer sustain her "Buddy" romance. As a consequence, she breaks her leg skiing. Plath, too, had a skiing accident and Eddie Cohen was ready with a diagnosis: "Incidentally, you are going to be a mighty maimed sort of person if you make a habit of substituting broken legs and other forms of violence for the colds which have been your psychological catharsis in the past." Picking up on Plath's anxious need to overidealize men, to build them up and tear them down, and on her relationship with Dick Norton as "vicious, biting, and competitive," Cohen urged her to seek psychiatric help. Writing as a concerned older brother (he had been unsuccessful in his attempt to seduce her), he stated,

> I am not striving to be an alarmist, although such may be my effect. I am merely taking cognizance of the fact that all the danger signals which I have noted in you from time to time have suddenly all popped up at once. . . . From time to time you have related to me stories of incidents in which a handsome stranger has popped up and you have established an immediate and miraculous rapport with him [as Plath was to do with Hughes]. Then, after a rapturous few days, he fades out of your life, temp. or perm. There have been at least a half dozen such occurances [*sic*]. . . . You attach tremendous significance to these meetings, and what their real meaning may be, I haven't the foggiest notion.[27]

Cohen's bewilderment is understandable.

In any event, the first phase of Plath's charade of "normalcy" ended abruptly with her attempted suicide, but like her immortal Lady Lazarus, she

still had many lives to live, one of which involved Richard Sassoon, an aspiring writer to whom she sent "Verbal Calisthenics" (he liked it).[28] She met
him in April 1954, when the *Smith Review* published this version of "Verbal
Calisthenics," in which a risk-taking speaker is aiming for the stars:

> My love for you is more
>   athletic than a verb,
> agile as a star
>   the tents of sun absorb.
>
> Treading circus tightropes
>   of each syllable,
> the brazen jackanapes
>   would fracture if he fell.
>
> Acrobat of space,
>   the daring adjective
> plunges for a phrase
>   describing arcs of love.
>
> Nimble as a noun,
>   he catapults in air;
> a planetary swoon
>   could climax his career,
>
> but adroit conjunction
>   eloquently shall
> link to his lyric action
>   a periodic goal. (*Collected* 314)

Plath liked almost everything about Sassoon except his small stature. He was
not quite her size (she was 5′9″), and she usually dated men who were taller.
But his very name evoked poetry (his father was a cousin of British World
War I poet Siegfried Sassoon) and as she explained to her mother, he was not
only a senior at Yale but also a British citizen and a "Parisian fellow" whose
talk delighted her (*Letters* 136). Sassoon, she believed, had a lot to teach her
about "lyric action" and other actions as well. "Darling, darling," he wrote,
"I dare not let you grow up without me . . . I tell you I am the best educator

in your country."[29] They played spanking games and encouraged each other in perverse, antibourgeois fantasies. Poetry, he lectured her, is not only a tortuous discipline but also a perverse art. It appears that Sassoon was a daring lover, as was Plath with him.

Neither Sassoon nor Plath was ready to settle down, and he warned her about his divided self, his impulsivity, and his depressions. "I am always two and must always be," he wrote, "I have tried to hide it, but you must know this of me—I see strange visions in my depressions and I am impetuous and I wish my will done immediately, because there is a constant fear of an end in me."[30] Sassoon's cautious streak won out when Plath showed up in Paris several years later, hoping to rekindle their romance. As described in his story "The Diagram," it may have happened like this:

> It was one of those mad holiday times of which you remember everything in a jumbled fashion, and particularly you mix up what happened and what might have happened because you never had time for clarifying these things when they were going on. . . . I was trying to make up my mind about a girl [Plath] I most genuinely loved who was coming to Paris to see me [he was studying at the Sorbonne], where I wouldn't be because of having gone away to try to make up my mind, and from whose letters I understood was going to start having an affair with a certain fellow [Ted Hughes] so as to make me jealous and give me a mind to marry her, which I was unwilling to do just because of this imminent unfaithfulness— all very complicated; I kept writing her telegrams and not sending them.[31]

And so, having just started an affair with Hughes, Plath tried to run back to Sassoon, who had left the country to avoid meeting her (it was spring break for both of them). They never saw each other again, and Plath had other erotic lives to live. One included Amherst College graduate Gordon Lameyer, with whom she took a grim trip through Germany after Sassoon dumped her, and one included Ted.[32]

As we have seen, in periods of heightened stress, of which there were all too many, Plath developed intense romantic attachments to men who, as Eddie Cohen remarked, she eventually demonized. Returned to Cambridge in mid-April after traveling with Gordon, Sylvia announced to her mother that the trip had been "a mistake." She also announced that she had "fallen terribly in love, which can only lead to great hurt." Enjoying the drama of the emotional risks she was taking, she added, "Forgive my own talk of hurt and sorrow. I love you so and only wish I could be home to help you in yours" (*Letters* 233). Writing to Aurelia the next day, she names her dark Romantic hero: "this man, this poet, this Ted Hughes" (*Letters* 234).

"This is Eden here, and the people are all shining," Sylvia wrote (*Letters* 239), sounding both like a young Emily Dickinson and very *unlike* her, for she added, "I know that within a year I shall publish a book of 33 poems which will hit the critics violently in some way or another. My voice is taking shape, coming strong. Ted says he never read poems by a woman like mine; they are strong and full and rich—not quailing and whining like Teasdale or simple lyrics like Millay; they are working, sweating, heaving poems born out of the way words should be said. . . . Oh, mother, rejoice with me and fear not" (*Letters* 244).[33] Drunk on Ted, she enclosed three poems: "Firesong," a tribute to the "brave love" she implores to "burn on, burn on" (*Collected* 30); "Strumpet Song," in which she identifies sardonically with a "foul slut, [her] seamed face / Askew with blotch, dint, scar" (*Collected* 33–34); and "The Queen's Complaint," which is particularly interesting for its Gothic association of love-madness and death (*Collected* 28–29). Featuring a giant "With hands like derricks, / Looks fierce and black as rooks," this model destroyer is patterned after Hughes, who later observed that Sylvia enjoyed casting him in a fantasy-ridden, superman role. Or, as the poem has it, "Her dainty acres he ramped through / And used her gentle doves with manners rude" (*Collected* 28). "Ramped." The closest Dickinson comes is "rampant" in "Nature – the Gentlest Mother is," where Nature, "Impatient of no Child – / The feeblest – or the Waywardest – . . . . Restrain[s] Rampant Squirrel – / Or too impetuous Bird" (*Fr* 741). Dickinson's poem also contains the word "Admonition," which we can reread in light of Plath's warnings about the power of female rage. Ramped. Rammed. Jammed. Raped. "Ramped": the word has a venerable lineage and is perhaps one of those Plath retrieved from the thesaurus that she enjoyed rampaging through. The love-crazed queen is one of Plath's comedic alter egos, she who wanders the world (tramping and vamping) looking for her demon lover.

> So she is come to this rare pass
> Whereby she treks in blood through sun and squall
> And sings you thus:

'How sad, alas, it is
To see my people shrunk so small, so small.' (*Collected* 29)

Influenced by Keats and Dickinson, by popular culture and other sources, Plath articulates a structure of erotic submission that anticipates desertion and shrunken identity for herself. "Poetry is the most ingrown and intense of the creative arts," she later wrote, and while "the modern woman . . . demands as much experience as the modern man," she felt a strong urge to submit herself to Ted's force. "It would require a long discipleship" (*Unabridged* 450, 452, 451). In June 1956, with Aurelia standing up somewhat reluctantly—she had wanted a big wedding and was the sole attendant—Plath married a poet who encouraged her to think of herself as a powerful originator. She believed that he was her best critic, as she was his (*Letters* 243).[34]

After Plath and Hughes returned to *her* country, they settled into an apartment on tranquil Elm Street in Northampton, where sometime between September 1957 and September 1958, Plath retyped "Admonition," changed several words, and retitled it "Warning." It was the unpublished orphan of her Dickinson trio. She also retyped "Verbal Calisthenics," perhaps because she wanted to recapture its Sassoon-aura.[35] There was already trouble in the marriage and Plath, who was ill at ease in the classroom, feared that her deep life in poetry was over. During spring vacation, however, she was "taken by a frenzy" and completed eight new poems in eight days (*Unabridged* 356). In one of them, "The Disquieting Muses," the speaker reflects on the pedagogy of her childhood and attempts to come to terms with her mother's legacy:

Mother, mother, what illbred aunt
Or what disfigured and unsightly
Cousin did you so unwisely keep
Unasked to my christening, that she
Sent these ladies in her stead
With heads like darning-eggs to nod
And nod and nod at foot and head
And at the left side of my crib?

Mother, who made to order stories
Of Mixie Blackshort the heroic bear,
Mother, whose witches always, always

Got baked into gingerbread, I wonder
Whether you saw them, whether you said
Words to rid me of those three ladies
Nodding by night around my bed,
Mouthless, eyeless, with stitched bald head.

In the hurricane, when father's twelve
Study windows bellied in
Like bubbles about to break, you fed
My brother and me cookies and Ovaltine
And helped the two of us to choir:
'Thor is angry: boom boom boom!
Thor is angry: we don't care!'
But those ladies broke the panes.
. . . .
Day now, night now, at head, side, feet,
They stand their vigil in gowns of stone,
Faces blank as the day I was born,
Their shadows long in the setting sun
That never brightens or goes down.
And this is the kingdom you bore me to,
Mother, mother. But no frown of mine
Will betray the company I keep. (*Collected* 74–76)

As represented in this fateful family romance, it is easy to see what is wrong with Aurelia. Escaping into sentimental fantasy, she overestimates her own power and underestimates the power of her enemies, which is the power of pure negativity. While seeming to say yes ("to nod, / And nod, and nod"), they maintain an appalling silence. Even as Aurelia (the symbolic mother) makes up stories about heroic bears, these uninvited guests maintain the power of speechlessness, which is figured as the adamant of death.

Plath had been working out the emotional logic of this artfully staged monodrama for a long time. In the early 1950s, the "Thor is angry" mantra pops up in a short story, "Among the Bumblebees," which chronicles the death of an adored father from the perspective of Alice Denway, a deceitful daughter who imitates his powerful voice: "Alice learned to sing the thunder song with her father: 'Thor is angry. Thor is angry. Boom, boom, boom! Boom, boom, boom! We don't care. We don't care. Boom, boom, boom!'

And above the resonant resounding baritone of her father's voice, the thunder rumbled harmless as a tame lion."[36] Yes, Thor is angry, but so too is Alice, who resents the attention her saintly mother devotes to the family's men. For in addition to her demanding father, she has an adorable little brother who can do no wrong. He is "blond and gentle and always sickly." Rather than allying herself with Warren, whom she enjoys tormenting, Alice bonds with her father and dismisses the "made-to-order" stories told by her mother, whose face is "tender and soft like the madonna pictures in school." This distracted mother is dangerously out of touch with her daughter's emotional realities, and at the story's end, Alice feels "lost and betrayed."[37]

Although "The Disquieting Muses" emerged on the page in March 1958, when Plath blithely explained to Aurelia that she had discovered her "deepest source of inspiration, which is art: the art of primitives like Henri Rousseau, Gauguin, Paul Klee, and De Chirico" (*Letters* 336), the poem conducts an extended dialogue with Plath's richly evolved need to free herself from Aurelia's sphere of influence.[38] It is ironic that at this point, she seems to have remembered Aurelia's favorite poet, Dickinson, the Dickinson who also disliked "Soft – Cherubic Creatures" and who, like Plath, attacked the supposedly civilizing rule of "Gentlewomen":

> One would as soon assault a Plush –
> Or violate a Star –
>
> Such Dimity Convictions –
> A Horror so refined
> Of freckled Human Nature –
> Of Deity – Ashamed –
>
> It's such a common – Glory –
> A Fisherman's – Degree –
> Redemption – Brittle Lady –
> Be so – ashamed of Thee – (*Fr* 675)

Turning the tables on her critics, Dickinson engages in reverse shaming without attacking the pedagogical practices of her own mother, as she did in some of her letters. Instead, she appoints herself spokesperson for "freckled Human Nature," and it is Christ who authorizes her social transgressions, whatever they may be. Plath's bad teacher is more depressingly personal.[39]

Yet Plath's purported unteachability was complex, and by March 1958 she was attending further to Dickinsonian confessions of failure. Plath knew that Dickinson had anticipated her dilemma—her tone deafness, her woodenness, her disfigurement:

> I cannot dance opon my Toes –
> No Man instructed me –
> But oftentimes, among my mind,
> A Glee possesseth me,
>
> That had I Ballet Knowledge –
> Would put itself abroad
> In Pirouette to blanch a Troupe –
> Or lay a Prima, mad,
>
> And though I had no Gown of Gauze –
> No Ringlet, to my Hair,
> Nor hopped for Audiences – like Birds –
> One Claw opon the air –
>
> Nor tossed my shape in Eider Balls,
> Nor rolled on wheels of snow
> Till I was out of sight, in sound,
> The House encore me so –
>
> Nor any know I know the Art
> I mention – easy – Here –
> Nor any Placard boast me –
> It's full as Opera – (*Fr* 381)

For both poets, the ballet serves as a model of the artificial performance of gender, but Dickinson whirls away the shame of gender nonconformity in a dazzling fantasy of public acclaim. For her part, Plath exposes her precursor's fantasy of self-sufficiency, which is out of the realm of possibility for most women. Women, Plath insists, need their publics and pay a heavy emotional price for their social failures.

Although as a schoolgirl Plath had admired Dickinson's poetry of the rising sun, in "Because I could not stop for Death," she accesses the Dickinson whose ominous setting sun predominates and whose life-drama turns, as does Plath's, on unbidden traveling companions.

> Because I could not stop for Death –
> He kindly stopped for me –
> The Carriage held but just Ourselves –
> And Immortality.
>
> We slowly drove – He knew no haste
> And I had put away
> My labor and my leisure too,
> For His Civility –
>
> We passed the School, where Children strove
> At Recess – in the Ring –
> We passed the Fields of Gazing Grain –
> We passed the Setting Sun –
>
> Or rather – He passed Us –
> The Dews drew quivering and Chill –
> For only Gossamer, my Gown –
> My Tippet – only Tulle –
>
> We paused before a House that seemed
> A Swelling of the Ground –
> The Roof was scarcely visible –
> The Cornice – in the Ground –
>
> Since then – 'tis Centuries – and yet
> Feels shorter than the Day
> I first surmised the Horses' Heads
> Were toward Eternity – (*Fr* 479)

Writing her own obituary, Dickinson's speaker permits herself to be transported to worlds unknown. The first step is easy. The gentleman-caller she calls Death is kindly, civil. He does what she cannot do, and the journey is a leisured one. Accompanied by Immortality, she thinks she has all the time in the world and in other worlds beside.

Time was on Plath's mind when, having just written eight poems in eight days, she commented on what she hoped would be her place in history:

> Arrogant, I think I have written lines which qualify me to be The Poetess of America (as Ted will be The Poet of England and her dominions). Who rivals? Well, in history—Sappho, Elizabeth Barrett Browning, Christina Rossetti, Amy Lowell, Emily Dickinson, Edna St. Vincent Millay—all dead. Now: Edith Sitwell & Marianne Moore, the ageing giantesses & poetic godmothers. Phillis McGinley is out—light verse: she's sold herself. Rather: May Swenson, Isabella Gardner, & most close, Adrienne Cecile Rich—who will soon be eclipsed by these eight poems. (*Unabridged* 360)

Although Dickinson figures as part of a tradition, Plath accords her no special emphasis. What stands out is the antagonism that shapes Plath's feminism and her correspondingly thin sense of time.

For his part, Ted was feeling out of place in a country whose poetry he viewed as suffused with national faults. Americans lacked individuality. Except for their families, they were rootless. Their bread was tasteless, their cars too big, their cellophane obscene. The culture was antipoetic and so too were the people, whose lack of inwardness was terrifying. Sylvia put it more simply. "Ted is very homesick," she wrote to Lynne Lawner in March 1959, by which time the Hugheses were deciding to make their base in England, perhaps after a year in Rome.[40] "What am I afraid of?" Sylvia asked herself, "Growing old and dying without being Somebody?" (*Unabridged* 470). To encourage herself, she remarked, "I look queerly forward to living in England: hope I can work for some weekly in London, publish in the women's magazines, maybe. England seems so small and digestible from here" (*Unabridged* 470).

Despite their quarrels and their glooms, Sylvia continued to work tirelessly toward her goal of being a "Somebody," and that fall, while she and Ted were at Yaddo, the artists' colony in New York State, she heard from an editor at the British publisher William Heinemann, asking about her book manuscript. By then, she was authentically pregnant—there had been a false pregnancy earlier—and she recorded a dream about a "blond baby boy named Dennis riding, facing me, my hips, a heavy sweet-smelling child. The

Figure 24. Sylvia Plath and Ted Hughes, December 1959, shortly before they returned to England for the birth of their first child. The photograph was taken by Plath's college roommate Marcia Brown Stern. Courtesy Mortimer Rare Book Room, Smith College Library.

double amazement: that he was so beautiful and healthy and so little trouble" (*Unabridged* 521).[41] During their remaining time in the United States, Plath continued to track the ups and downs of her panics, her literary productivity, and her life with Ted. The categories fused. "Dangerous to be so close to Ted day in and day out," she wrote, "I have no life separate from his, am likely to become a mere accessory" (*Unabridged* 524). After an Atlantic crossing on the S.S. *United States* and a brief stay in London, Sylvia and Ted spent the Christmas holiday with his parents and sister in Yorkshire, found a small flat in a pleasant neighborhood in North London, settled into it, and awaited the birth of their baby. On April 1, Sylvia placed a call to her mother, who asked anxiously, "Is it Nicholas or Frieda Rebecca?" To which she responded ecstatically, "Oh, Frieda Rebecca, of course! Ein Wunderkind, Mummy. Ein Wunderkind!" (*Letters* 373).

Meanwhile, Ted was being lionized and that summer he began to reconfigure his relationship to Emily Dickinson. Writing to his sister Olwyn to share his excitement, he asked, "Have you ever read Emily Dickinson's poetry? I've just rediscovered her. She wrote hundreds & hundreds of these small incredible poems—lived a more or less isolated spinsterish life in the small churchy town of Amherst, in Mass.—contemp of the Brontes, save that she lived to 56 [55]. I've just known small selections of her poems before—but now I've got hold of a volume [edited by Johnson]. The most unself-conscious poetry ever, the most intensely occupied with her thought,— Shakespearean language & genuine."[42] It was a lovely time in the marriage, and Sylvia and Ted both adored the baby.

Thinking ahead, in late August, Ted wanted to order a three-volume edition of the works of "America's greatest poet, without a doubt." Sylvia would be twenty-eight on October 27, and the Johnson *Variorum* would be a perfect birthday present. He wanted to surprise her and wasn't sure of the price, so he wrote to Sylvia's mother and brother, asking them to mention it casually in their next letter. "We have both, with a great shock," he explained, "discovered Emily Dickinson."[43]

In May 1962, he wrote again, this time to Aurelia alone, asking her to send the one-volume edition and referring to Dickinson, somewhat sardoni-cally, as part of Sylvia's "Holy Trinity."[44] By then, there was trouble in Para-dise. The marriage was coming apart, and Plath was coming into her own.

Stairways of Surprise

Less than a year after Plath's terrifying suicide, Ted Hughes published a review in the British magazine the *Listener*, describing Dickinson as a mystic. He wrote,

> Like Whitman and Emerson, her contemporaries, she has been enlightened by an ecstatic vision, a basic poetic experience that recurs almost like a physical state, and, with her, at an abnormal intensity. In this mystical moment she encounters either her own soul, or the soul within the Creation and within its creatures. But she is more interesting than Whitman or Emerson, and more up-to-date, in that she is not sure she likes the looks of this soul-thing. Her ecstasy—"ecstasy" is one of her favoured words—is also terror, convincingly. She wants to believe that the great Creation-sustainer

is God's love but it affects her often enough as if it were the final
revelation of horrible Nothingness:

> Most, like Chaos—Stopless—cool,
> Without a Chance, or Spar,
> Or even a Report of Land
> To justify—Despair.[45]

Hughes was reviewing Charles R. Anderson's *Stairway of Surprise*, which
purports to free Dickinson from biographical critique. Taking its title from
Emerson's poem "Merlin," *Stairway* removes Dickinson from a gender-
specific context and identifies her with a "kingly bard." Anderson believed
that Dickinson's concern was not "merger with God through intuition or
ritual, but discovery of the inner paradise of art through the language of
surprise." As a belated New Critic, he was inspired by the recently published
Johnson *Variorum*, which he hailed as "a complete scholarly edition . . . that
resolves the problem of a definitive text as well as can be hoped for, though
it still leaves some difficult questions unanswered." Anderson promised to
give Dickinson's poems the attention they deserve as coherent art objects and
to tell a success story. His Dickinson, like Emerson's Merlin, was to "mount
to paradise / By the stairway of surprise," though her mounting was more of
a descent into the polar privacy that constituted "a soul admitted to itself—/
Finite infinity."[46]

Even Anderson, however, was intermittently seduced by the logics of
biographical critique, and in explaining Dickinsonian ecstasy, he revealed
that he had been reading her letters. "From the evidence of the letters,"
Anderson writes,

> Emily Dickinson found her personal pleasure like other mortals in
> home and friends, nature and books. But the ecstasy of her lyric
> poems springs from a more compulsive source. "Sang from the
> Heart, Sire," one begins, "Dipped my Beak in it." In another avow-
> ing "Bind me—I still can sing," she says that banished or slain she
> will remain "Still thine." Some deep personal experience of love
> seems behind these poems, and some emotional crisis related to it
> may have precipitated her poetic career, shortly before the age of
> thirty. It was in later life, presumably, that she summed up more
> calmly:

That Love is all there is,
Is all we know of Love.[47]

Ecstasy and compulsion. Here Anderson picks up on the lack-of-control theme so marked in Dickinson's posthumous reception, but it turns out to be a good thing because it is disciplined and integrated into a larger developmental arc and life story. In the end, there was wisdom, and "the tensions that had created the great poems had been relaxed." Blurbing the book, Millicent Todd Bingham proclaimed, "Here, at last, is a scholar worthy to present Emily Dickinson to posterity . . . Here is the whole sweep of her genius from the 'acrobatics of composition' to the ever-mounting climax of her mighty poems on death and immortality."[48]

Hughes's Dickinson is less well balanced, and while love was not the flood subject of his review, he could not avoid it altogether. He explains that her "curious marriage poems instate her as a nun, as priestess of the Beautiful, of the Absolute, or as a corpse, for they are usually also funeral poems." Hughes's language is itself at its most beautifully uncanny when he pivots around a letter, one quoted by Anderson but reappropriated by Hughes, to describe a poet-detective who investigates herself into her own death. Just as Plath had warned in "Admonition," Hughes concluded that some things do not bear looking into too deeply:

The solidest, and perhaps the most characteristic, pieces belong to the after-phase of doubt and ironic query. ". . . we both believe, and disbelieve, a hundred times in an Hour, which keeps believing nimble," she wrote in a letter. But the more she needed to believe, in immortality, in the eternal orders of bliss, and the longer she lived with only hints and no evidence but frequent intimations to the contrary, the more agonisingly she doubted. Accordingly, the image of the final investigator, the same throughout her work, becomes more and more obsessive: and it is a person piercing the facade with the act of death. This is also a plain, self-descriptive image, of herself at the greatest moment of her life, during the poetic vision, where the whole problem keeps on renewing itself: her frozen, deep-sleep posture of communion with the mystery.[49]

For Hughes there was no progress, no development. Rather, the image of the final investigator is "the same throughout her work."

Although he was somewhat dissatisfied with Anderson's choice of poems, Hughes's homage to the "spacious inner drama and inner geography, behind all her words" concluded that Anderson's study should encourage "the full-scale adoption of a poet who stands easily and not outlandishly with our two or three greatest." Note that "our" bridges Anglo-American tradition and that Dickinson was not just a great woman poet but a "witty philological genius" whose discovery in words of "utterly new meanings that are pressing to be uncovered . . . invites comparison with Shakespeare." This was high praise indeed. Shakespeare's cultural capital can be taken for granted; then too, Hughes strongly identified not only with Shakespeare's genius but also with his supposed sexual desperation, which he understood as the fable on which the entire oeuvre depended.[50] In 1963, Hughes's Dickinson confronted love and death with abnormal intensity and was an obsessive seeker after immortality, but despite "her disappointed love for certain men," she did not suffer from depression and lived to tell the tale. "Her metaphors do not finalise a likeness," he explained, "they open relationships of unexplored possibility, so that instead of a procession of models she produces teeming vistas of world-life. This quality of her thought, using a mystery of language to engage a mystery of the world, is her strongest charm."

Five years later, introducing and editing *A Choice of Emily Dickinson's Verse*, Hughes extended some of the themes of the earlier review. The selection of 101 poems roughly equaled the number discussed in full by Anderson, but Hughes had criticized Anderson's anthology as not as "exciting" as it could be, and many of the choices (roughly three quarters) were new. Whereas Anderson had opted for thematic groupings, Hughes organized his anthology chronologically. The first poem, however, was an exception, and he now quoted "That Love is all there is, / Is all we know of Love" in its entirety.[51] Again Hughes included the four poems mentioned in his *Listener* review ("It was not Death," "A Wind that rose," "Exultation is the going / Of an inland soul to sea," and "Could mortal lip divine"), but he excluded "Sang from the Heart, Sire," and "Bind me – I still can sing," the Master-construct poems which Anderson had mentioned in his biographical digression. Of the poems in Sylvia Plath's high school anthology ("Presentiment," "The Sky is low," and "He ate and drank the precious Words)," Hughes preserved "Presentiment—is that long shadow—on the Lawn—/ Indicative that Suns go down—/ / The Notice to the startled Grass / That Darkness—is about to pass." His "Introduction" states that his choice of poems is idiosyncratic, because Dickinson's "unique and inspired pieces are very many, and very varied." Disclaiming the desire to choose representative selections, he concluded, "Finally, I chose the pieces I liked best at the time of choosing, well aware that among so many poems of such strong charm this choice must be far from final, for me or for any reader."[52]

Despite its local enthusiasms, the tone of this "Introduction" is flat. As Maria Stuart notes, Hughes's analysis grounds Dickinson's religious struggles "in an iconic narrative of American nationhood," but to the extent that he projected himself imaginatively into Dickinson's dilemma, he was also writing about himself as a tragic hero.[53] Between 1963 and 1968, a great deal had happened to Hughes, and these were the darkest years of his life. Believing that post-Puritan civilization was designed to kill the necessary animal/devil in man, he justified actions that were also encouraged by the sexually permissive atmosphere of the London circles in which he traveled at the time. His infidelity to Plath was followed by infidelity to Assia, the woman he describes in *Birthday Letters* as "Slightly filthy with erotic mystery – / A German / Russian Israeli with the gaze of a demon / Between curtains of black Mongolian hair." So who was she? The "Lilith of abortions," or his idolized Goddess of Complete Being, or both? And who was he, a Puritan or a libertine, a favored son or a secret daughter? Although Hughes's compulsive promiscuity was rooted in psychic depths he barely understood himself, Assia herself was initially ambivalent in her commitment to Hughes and reluctant to leave her husband, to whom she in fact returned after Plath's death. The psychoerotic circumstances, coupled with Hughes's responsibilities for his children and eventually his parents, were threatening to spin out of control.[54]

Yet Hughes was a survivor, and when *Ariel* was published in England in 1965, he was engaged in a carefully calibrated balancing act, in "Verbal Calisthenics." As he told Plath's mother, he "wanted to set just enough factual notes to the more obscure pieces to make the strong close link evident between her poems and her real world," a real world of which he was evidently a crucial and perhaps terrorizing part. "At the same time," he explained to her,

> I wanted to set in the forefront, at as early a stage in the great
> inevitable exegesis as possible, the claim that Sylvia was not a poet
> of the Lowell/Sexton self-therapy, or even national therapy, school,
> but a mystical poet of an alltogether higher—in fact of the very
> highest—tradition. I didn't want to press this claim too hard,
> though I think I have a right to say what I think about it, and I

think my claim, even if it raises some temporary would be debunk-
ers, will eventually stand. There is simply nobody like her. I've just
finished re-reading all Emily Dickinson for a small selection, and
my final feeling is that she comes quite a way behind Sylvia. As for
Lowell etc, if he is a fine doctor, she is a miracle healer. There is no
comparison. But I want to avoid seeming to set myself up as the
high priest of her mysteries—and so I've limited myself in these
notes to the lowest order of editor's facts.[55]

Telling not all the truth but telling it slant, Hughes surely was influenced by
Plath in writing about Dickinson, and he tells Aurelia as much in this letter.
Could it be that both Dickinson and Sylvia were mystics of the highest
order? If so, what was the relationship between himself and his dead wife's
mysticism? Hughes, fancying himself a devout antinomian, enlisted Dickinson in a transatlantic drama of healing. Writing about her allowed him to
communicate indirectly with his dead wife and her tormented mother, whom
he described to Anne Sexton as "really . . . an extraordinary woman. Every
time I meet her I'm more impressed."[56] Writing about Dickinson potentially
buffered him against his American critics, most of whom were women who
sided with Plath in the polarized drama of their lives. And writing about her
allowed him to bridge the gap between English and American poetics—she
became one of "ours" in a transatlantic merger, displacing Elizabeth Barrett
Browning and Christina Rossetti in the process. If, as Hughes explains in the
birthday letter "Life after Death," "We were comforted by wolves," describing his pitifully shrunken family, his version of Dickinson consoled him
too.[57] Dickinson's sexual drama did not bear looking into too deeply, neither
did Plath's, neither did his. No one was a guilty poet of the national self-
therapy school. Confession was out, mysticism in. Both Dickinson and Plath
were mystics, and mystics of the highest order.

    Eventually, this line of thinking justified Hughes's belief that Plath's
suicide was fated from the first; he was only a bystander in a tragedy that had
been preordained from the start. In his words, "Your father / Was your God
and there was no other," a proposition he was revising to include "a gilded
theatre suddenly empty / Of all but the faces / The faces faces faces faces //
Of Mummy Daddy Mummy Daddy – / Daddy Daddy Daddy Daddy /
Mummy Mummy" (*BL* 153, 169). In absolving himself of guilt, he absolves
Plath as well. Only Assia, it seems, had agency, for all the good it did her.

In sum, after Plath's death, Ted kept the faith, after his fashion. His rearrangement of the *Ariel* sequence has been widely criticized, but in important respects, he was a brilliant editor. Turning a twosome into a threesome, with Dickinson in the middle, was a literary plan that worked—unlike the other material plans mutually hatched by Plath and Hughes that so tragically failed. The impact of *A Choice of Emily Dickinson's Verse* on Dickinson's British reputation is difficult to gauge, although there is no reason to doubt that its impact was positive.[58] Clearly, the book played its part in advancing Hughes's reputation, and as I have been suggesting, the project was effectively grounded in his version of psychological realism. Hughes's Dickinson was a diversion from and a defense against the tragic particulars of personal history, for even at that terrible moment, "Crow had to start searching for something to eat."[59]

Her black moods notwithstanding, before the apocalypse, Plath too was searching for something to eat, and at her most inspired, in poems such as "Black Rook in Rainy Weather," she dared to hope for miracles "To set the sight on fire / In [her] eye" (*Collected* 57). Unfortunately, she knew too much about short-lived miracles. One of them was Ted.

This chapter has traced the development of Plath's relationship to an evolving Dickinson, arguing that theirs was an uneasy bond. One last example may suffice. At some point in her literary apprenticeship, Plath took notes on the development of a normal personality à la Arnold Gesell, the founder of the Gesell Institute for Child Development at Yale. Remarks such as "Growth a concept to conjure with" appear in an undated notebook which has the word "Manzi" on the cover. After "Growth a concept to conjure with" (underlined), Plath wrote, "E. Dickinson—'can you teach me how to grow, or is it unconveyed like melody & witchcraft?' 'Growth of man like growth of nature gravitates within . . . it stirs alone.' "[60] Plath seems to be free associating. From memory, she quotes a letter from Dickinson to Thomas Wentworth Higginson (*L* 261) and follows it up with a poem which, parsing the relationship between the poet and her audience, idealizes "the solitary prowess / Of a Silent Life" (*Fr* 790). Plath aimed to achieve "solitary prowess" without being silenced as Dickinson had been by cultural constraints on female voice. In her struggle to grow, she recognized the need for self-mastery, even as she found her precursor's insights into the gendered psychology of victimhood inspiring.[61] In the last phase and in the last phrases of her very public career, Plath extended Dickinson's project too far, literalizing the death wish Dickinson was able to control. It then became her husband's task

ok

to pick up the pieces, and in his extremity, he produced a depoliticized, aestheticized Dickinson whose "mysticism" he associated with Plath's. In the following pages, we will see Plath imagining alternatives to mysticism and to a faltering family romance. We will see her imagining what it would be like to be, to be encouraged by, and to compete with the "lesbian & fanciful & jeweled" Elizabeth Bishop (*Unabridged* 322). Perhaps Bishop, even more than Dickinson, had learned how to "dwell in Possibility – / A fairer House than Prose" (*Fr* 466). Perhaps Bishop could teach her how to deflect "that White Sustenance – / Despair" (*Fr* 706).

A Queer Interlude

At that moment in February 1958 when Sylvia Plath was trying to nerve herself up for teaching her winter classes in snowbound Northampton, she thought about her rivalry with Elizabeth Bishop—of which the Pulitzer Prize–winning Bishop in faraway Brazil was sublimely unaware. And Plath being Plath, she wrote about it. "Six weeks more of snow & sleet. O keep healthy. I breathe among dry coughs & clotted noses. I must, on the morning coffee-surge of exultation & omnipotence, begin my novel this summer & sweat it out like a school-year—rough draft done by Christmas. And poems. No reason why I shouldn't surpass at least the facile Isabella Gardner & even the lesbian & fanciful & jeweled Elizabeth Bishop in America. If I sweat the summer out" (*Unabridged* 322). This journal entry is the first appearance of the word "lesbian" in Plath's writings, and it is surely a very early allusion to Bishop as a lesbian. Lorrie Goldensohn notes, "During her lifetime her homosexuality surfaced nowhere in print."[62] How, then, should we interpret Plath's tone?

A few months later, lesbians and gay men were those "queer people" with whom she could not identify, whereas in the February entry, "fanciful" is ambiguous, as is "jeweled" (*Unabridged* 363). "Fanciful" could be an asset or could signify a lack of realism, while "jeweled" loops Bishop back into an earlier tradition associated with the ornamental poetess. It too has its pluses and minuses and sounds archaically beautiful. (Moore had called Bishop "Archaically New" in an early review.[63]) "Fanciful" and "jeweled" to some extent neutralize the negativity that Plath associated with nonnormative sexual practices. That said, the "lesbian" inscribes Bishop in an eccentric, minoritized position, and Plath was eager, at least consciously, for ever more normative gender identification and experience. Thus we move on to journal entries in which Plath reminds herself to "work on femininity" and, after many bumps in the road, to a vehement critique of the erotics of male psychological and political power (*Unabridged* 467).

Although a contemporary language of bisexuality was not part of her vocabulary, as Jacqueline Rose has noted, there is some unrepressing of same-sex desire in a late poem such as "The Rabbit Catcher," which describes "a place of force," where desire is malignant and formless and indistinguishable from the desire to assault an ambiguously gendered other (*Collected* 193).[64] Earlier, when Plath discussed the erotics of lesbian desire with her psychiatrist, she asked, "What does a woman see in another woman that she doesn't see in a man?" To which the psychiatrist, Ruth Beuscher, responded, "Tenderness" (*Unabridged* 460). Plath emphasized this exchange in *The Bell Jar*, which manipulates the trope of the tragic lesbian. Readers will recall that Joan Gilling hangs herself after being rejected by the Plath-identified heroine. "You make me puke, Joan," says Esther.[65]

The virulence of Plath's campaign against homo-identification in *The Bell Jar* raises as many questions as it answers, but the text does suggest that by the spring of 1961 when she began drafting the novel, she was edging toward a less rigid view of same-sex desire. Although Esther is repelled by Joan and Joan's erotic partner Dee Dee, she begins to fall in love with her psychiatrist, Dr. Nolan, a stylish character who combines the features of a perfect wife, the movie star Myrna Loy, and a mother. Plath's history with psychiatrists has been amply documented, but it is worth noting several overlooked facts about Dr. Nolan's original, Ruth Beuscher, and about the cultural climate in which their relationship flourished.

First, Plath was predisposed toward worshipping psychiatrists and their regimen of talk therapy. In 1952, when she was a sophomore at Smith and before her suicide attempt of the following summer, she noted in her journal, "A psychiatrist is the god of our age" (*Unabridged* 151). Second, Beuscher believed that same-sex desire was the result of parental failure but that psychologically damaged homosexuals were to be treated sympathetically by society, as well as by the medical profession. Third, after Plath's death, which affected her deeply, Beuscher divorced her second husband, resumed the name Ruth Tiffany Barnhouse, and eased up on the practice of psychiatry to become an Episcopal priest—in her later years, she was a professor of theology at Southern Methodist University with a specialty in pastoral care. In 1998, Karen Maroda interviewed her at her home in Nantucket. Barnhouse was witty and outgoing but visibly upset by erotic interpretations of Plath's poem "Lesbos." Asked by Maroda how she felt about Sylvia, she admitted reluctantly that she loved her.[66]

This therapeutic context helps to explain an odd entry in Plath's 1958 *Journal*, in which she frames the question of same-sex love as a diversion from what she views as her real problem, the inability to separate from her mother. In psychoanalytic therapy, Plath was intended to transfer her conflicted feelings about her mother onto Beuscher; with Beuscher's help, she was to work them through and to achieve the psychological integration, stability, and maturity that had hitherto eluded her. She feels ashamed, however, of her intense attachment to Beuscher and labels her desire to please her psychiatrist as "extra-professional" (*Unabridged* 484). Although unspecified "immediate jealousies" are inhibiting her therapy, she feels reluctant to tell Beuscher what they are. She frames her problem as her "extra-professional fondness" for her psychiatrist, whom she had previously described as "one of my best friends, only 9 years older than I . . . tall, Bohemian, coruscatingly brilliant." We know that Plath feared being stigmatized as damaged.[67] Yet given Beuscher's widely shared theory about the origins of homosexual desire in parental failure, the inhibition was a symptom of the problem. By this therapeutic logic, Plath's "extra-professional fondness" for Beuscher was grounded in her excessive attachment to her mother. For all these reasons, then, Plath continued to experience herself as needing to work on her "femininity." That meant she needed to work on feeling heterosexual and worthy of loving Ted, who often greeted her with "hostile silences" (*Unabridged* 484).

Working on femininity also meant working on becoming a mother, as was her having-it-all heroine "Ruth B."[68] As a mother, Plath hoped to free herself from her role as a damaged, covertly man-hating daughter. Yet in October 1959, a pregnant Plath complained of feeling "oddly barren." She wrote, "The physical world refuses to be ordered, created, arranged and selected. I am a victim of it . . . not a master" (*Unabridged* 516). Not being pregnant evidently had some appeal at a time when she was feeling unattractive and fantasizing about Marilyn Monroe as her beauty consultant. She was feeling uncreative (*Unabridged* 513–14).[69] In this self-hating moment, Plath moved to an enthusiastic response to Bishop: "Am reading Elizabeth Bishop with great admiration. Her fine originality, always surprising, never rigid, flowing, juicier than Marianne Moore, who is her godmother" (*Unabridged* 516). Plath's journal juxtaposes these entries: first barren, then Bishop, first victim, then nature's "master" (the word "mistress" would not have had the same autonomous valence). Where to go from here? Could her own muse be a woman?

Although Plath and Bishop never met face to face, several weeks after commenting on Bishop's juiciness, she did meet Bishop's friend, the poet May Swenson. Plath noted, "M. S. Independent, self-possessed. Ageless. Bird-watching before breakfast. What does she find for herself? Chess games. My old admiration for the strong, if Lesbian, woman. The relief of limitation as a price for balance and surety" (*Unabridged* 525).[70] There follows a sad little journal entry in which Plath describes Ted as the one person she loves or *could* love, a crucial distinction. "Take hold. Study German today. The [type-writer] ribbon is terrible. So am I. I have the one person I could ever love in this world. Now I must work to be a person worthy of that" (*Unabridged* 525). Plath is saying two things: that she loves Ted and that if she were a better person she *could* love him. At this pregnant moment, she does not feel worthy or, in conventional terms, womanly.

As a mother, Plath continued to work on her femininity and on combining motherhood with professional success. In February 1962, for example, she and Ted were among the poets featured by *London Magazine*, all of whom were asked, "What living poets continue to influence you, English or American?" Neither named the other, and Plath responded, "The poets I delight in are possessed by their poems as if by the rhythms of their own breathing. Their finest poems seem born all-of-a-piece, not put together by hand; certain poems in Robert Lowell's *Life Studies*, for instance; Theodore Roethke's greenhouse poems; some of Elizabeth Bishop and a very great deal of Stevie Smith. ('Art is wild as a cat and quite separate from civilization.')"[71] Which parts of Bishop's oeuvre moved her most deeply? The overtly feminist "Roosters" is a candidate, though I suspect that Plath liked Bishop's cool tone in works such as "The Map," her emotional poise in "Invitation to Miss Marianne Moore," and her formal dexterity in "Sestina." But did "Argument" strike her as too tame, "Insomnia" too civilized? Or did "Filling Station" seem too feminine and crocheted—was it too put together by hand ("Somebody loves us all")?

> Oh, but it is dirty!
> —this little filling station,
> oil-soaked, oil-permeated
> to a disturbing, over-all
> black translucency.
> Be careful with that match![72]

In one of the many books Plath did not live to read, the social anthropol-
ogist Mary Douglas links dirt to social disorder and to concepts of pollution
and taboo. Douglas asserts, "There is no such thing as absolute dirt: it exists
in the eye of the beholder." She adds, "I am personally rather tolerant of
disorder."[73] *Tolerant* is not a word that comes to mind when we think of
Sylvia Plath. Had she lived longer, would her kitchen have been less spotless
and would the confused combination of tones that define her poem "Lesbos"
have been less intense? The humor, the arrogance, the viciousness, the
wistfulness—what would have happened to them?

> I should sit on a rock off Cornwall and comb my hair.
> I should wear tiger pants, I should have an affair.
> We should meet in another life, we should meet in air,
> Me and you. (*Collected* 228)

Chapter 6

Elizabeth Bishop
and the U.S.A. Schools of Writing

Without exception the letters I received were from people
suffering from terrible loneliness in all its better-known forms,
and in some I had never even dreamed of. Writing . . . was a
way of being less alone.
                    —Bishop, "The U.S.A. School of Writing"

When Sylvia Plath died of terrible loneliness in her chilly London flat in
winter, Elizabeth Bishop was in Brazil, where a "confused migration" had
brought her.[1] She stayed because of love and social circumstances that facilitated her writing. Yet news blackouts disturbed her, and she welcomed gos-
sipy letters from Robert Lowell, who kept her abreast of U.S. politics and the
contentious national and international literary scene. On October 27, 1963,
he wrote asking if she had read Plath's "terrifying and stunning" poems in
the latest issue of *Encounter*. Lowell, who had been Plath's teacher, connected
their power to "whatever wrecked her life." He added, "They seem as good
to me as Emily Dickinson at the moment."[2] Bishop did not reply until
November 26, when John F. Kennedy's assassination preoccupied her. "The
last days have been like a bad dream, of course," she noted, saying nothing
about either Dickinson or Plath. Some years later, in response to a compliment Lowell paid her in a published interview, she insisted, "I'd rather be
called '*the 16th poet*' with no reference to my sex, than one of 4 women—even
if the other three are pretty good."[3] Using that insistence as a guide, this

chapter seeks to place Bishop's aversion to gender criticism and sex stereotyping in a larger frame of personal and cultural reference. I will concentrate on connecting Bishop's poetry and prose to writings to and about her, on her intimacies with women, and on her deeply conflicted response to the emergence of a public discourse of queerness in her time. My title is taken from Bishop's story, "The U.S.A. School of Writing," which describes the workings of a correspondence school and reflects on literary symbols of the dominant cultural order. In this posthumously published satire, Bishop situates herself in relation to other American writers—among them Emily Dickinson, Walt Whitman, Marianne Moore, and one Jimmy O'Shea, of Fall River, Massachusetts, an imaginary character whose bad teeth are a sign of his general fecklessness. I will say more about Jimmy and his fellow students later on.

No Reference to My Sex

In Brazil, Bishop settled into a committed lesbian relationship with Lota de Macedo Soares, a powerful woman with many friends. Lota, whom she described to Lowell as "the friend I'm living with here," was able to introduce her to "the literary lights" and to keep her from feeling "'out of touch' or 'expatriated' or . . . suffer[ing] from lack of intellectual life." Further, as Bishop explained, the Brazilians were "frank, startlingly so," but she said nothing to Lowell or to her other friends about the intimate, sexual dimension of this frankness, rather characterizing the people she was meeting as "extremely affectionate [in] an atmosphere that I just lap up."[4] Some months after settling in, when her relationship with Lota began to look and feel like an unofficial marriage, she wrote a love poem for Lota that she eventually sent to May Swenson, the "little poet" ("not bad, & a nice girl") whom she had met at Yaddo before her departure.[5] In her reply, Swenson, a lesbian, commented on Bishop's aesthetic and emotional reticence, claiming to understand the feeling but not the occasion, at least not in the kind of detail that would satisfy her curiosity: "THE SHAMPOO I like *very* much . . . but would have a deuce of a time saying why . . . that is, it feels like something has been left out—but this makes it better, in a way . . . a mysteriousness, although the expression is perfectly straightforward." She amplified, "I remember a poem of yours about his 'green gay eyes' that seemed even more mysterious in the same kind of way. I felt the emotion or the impression being expressed, but couldn't seize an outline of what was behind it."[6] The "even more mysterious" poem Swenson cites is a sonnet on the theme of erotic waste, in which a heartsick speaker longs to be liberated by "some relaxed, uncondescending stranger."[7] This briefly glimpsed "gay" muse is gendered male, while the poem's occasion seems to have been a quarrel between two women, one of whom humiliates the other. I want to read the "relaxed, uncondescending stranger" as someone who affirms the speaker's worth and who has the power to rescue her from the humiliating life she knows.[8]

Probably from the beginning of their relationship, Bishop realized that Lota, despite her high spirits, was not relaxed.[9] As Victoria Harrison notes in a sensitive analysis of "The Shampoo," a draft describes her as "so voluble, so volatile / by night, by day," a producer of "explosions."[10] For a time, Lota's explosions were not directed against Elizabeth, and as Harrison further notes, the poem closes "in a very daily sort of intimacy."[11]

The shooting stars in your black hair
in bright formation
are flocking where,
so straight, so soon?
—Come, let me wash it in this big tin basin,
battered and shiny like the moon. (*Poems* 66)

When "The Shampoo" was turned down by the *New Yorker* and *Poetry*, Bishop wondered why. "It seems perfectly clear to me," she wrote to Swenson, "and rather pretty."[12] Several years later, after the poem appeared in the *New Republic*, Bishop commented on the silence with which it was received even by her friends, including Marianne Moore. Was there something mysteriously "indecent" about it she had overlooked, she wondered, somewhat disingenuously. In fact, this was not a conversation about facing "the tender passion" she was eager to pursue.[13]

Thinking Back Through Our Mothers

Lota could be hard on herself and on others, had many talents, and was used to having her own way. The political appointment she accepted in 1961 made that close to impossible. "Painful distances" grew in the relationship, and in

1967, she joined Bishop in New York City, only to end her own life with an overdose of valium.[14] Bishop, who told Lowell she was "just naturally born guilty," never fully recovered from this tragedy.[15]

Eight years later, she attempted to write a review of Plath's *Letters Home*, which she was forced to abandon because of the memories of wrecked lives it reanimated. She began by joking about the U.S. government's attempt to promote personal letter writing and the telephone company's attempt to promote itself, thus discouraging the more old-fashioned practice. Noting that "one can't really 'review' letters, or criticise them," because they are always in such "close relation to the character and life of their writers," Bishop hoped to discriminate between letters written by ordinary people such as her Aunt Grace, her favorite aunt, and letters written by professional authors such as herself. But the distinction she was trying to draw did not hold. Discussing the relative talents of male and female letter-writers, she suggested that "at the domestic end" women letter-writers "usually come off best." That thought led to the concept of duty letters to one's family and to one's mother. Duty to one's mother was a subject she could not handle. At the top of the two-page typescript, an exasperated Bishop conceded in pen, with another, larger exclamation point, "Gave up on this!"[16] One of her friends (Anne Hussey) remembers, "The project put her in [Harvard's] Stillman Infirmary, she was so upset by it. She got out of the contract medically. She had her doctor call Harper and Row to say that she was physically unable to meet the commitment."[17]

The subject matter of *Letters Home* was traumatic for Bishop for several reasons. As Hussey, a poet who had been Bishop's student recalls, "Elizabeth found appalling the girlishness, immaturity, and naiveté that Sylvia Plath's letters to her mother indicated and continued to indicate through her life."[18] Even as Bishop had worked to distance herself from her mentally ill mother, she feared that she herself was incapable of deep love. Engaging *Letters Home* thus intensified her battle with depression. Panicked, Bishop phoned Hussey, who drove in from the suburbs to listen to a distraught account of personal and professional paralysis. Bishop, however, was not interested in connecting the subject matter of *Letters Home* to her own struggles with her mother; or if she did, she did not voice the connection to Hussey, whom she described as "so beautiful, and so nice, that everyone loves her."[19] Instead, she dismissed Plath's letters as "stupid."[20]

I am suggesting, then, that Bishop's terror as a blocked critic of Plath's letters emerged from a life-defining struggle. During the years when she could distance herself physically and psychologically from her chronic loneliness and nervous despair, the strong-willed Lota acted as a surrogate mother. She provided the elegant house in the country, the apartment in Rio, and many other comforts of home. She delighted in Bishop's accomplishments, obsessed about her drinking, and called her "Cookie." As their relationship disintegrated, Bishop could not bear to be alone, and her drinking threatened to spin out of control. She turned to other lovers for support, and Lota's psychiatrist urged her to leave the country, which she did. Throughout what proved to be the ordeal of her last years with Lota, Bishop's response to wrecked lives was framed by her identification with and resistance to the mentally unstable mother she scarcely knew. Emily Dickinson would have understood her dilemma. "I never had a mother," she said poignantly. "I suppose a mother is one to whom you hurry when you are troubled" (L 342b). For Bishop, a mother can also be someone to whom you turn for professional advice, and during her senior year at Vassar, she met Moore, who not only helped her to gain a national readership but also seemed to transport her into an exotic world in which idiosyncrasy was the norm.[21] Because a crucial turning point in their friendship has been so well described by others, I will note only, quoting Lynn Keller, that "Moore's rewriting of 'Roosters' . . . mark[ed] a decisive shift in their literary relationship. From then on [1940] Bishop rarely sent [her] unpublished work."[22] Moore, however, did not claim to have rewritten "Roosters" on her own. As she explained to Bishop, she rewrote it with her mother.[23]

Just as Bishop never finished her review of *Letters Home*, she never published "Efforts of Affection," the Moore-themed memoir on which she worked intermittently for many years. Although it is the richest autobiographical account of her indebtedness to Moore and of Moore's to her, Bishop didn't consider it finished. A key moment occurs when she identifies with a "very well known and polished writer, who had known Marianne since he was a young man and felt great admiration for her," and who was never invited to the Moores', "although his friends were." "Once," Bishop explains, "I asked innocently why I never saw him there and Marianne gave me her serious, severe look and said, 'He *contradicted* Mother.'"[24] To what extent, then, did female alliances and by extension female poetic tradition depend on not contradicting mother, or as I will suggest, was contradiction its core element?

In Bishop's literary history, Mary Warner Moore does not get the last word about Ezra Pound or anything else: "Once, as I was leaving and waiting for the slow elevator, I noticed a deep burn in the railing of the staircase and commented on it. Mrs. Moore gave a melancholy sigh and said, '*Ezra* did that. He came to call on Marianne and left his cigar burning out here because he knows I *don't like cigars. . . .*' Many years later, in St. Elizabeths Hospital, I repeated this to Ezra Pound. He laughed loudly and said, 'I haven't smoked a cigar since I was eighteen!' "[25] Although Bishop strongly suggests that Mary Warner Moore was not a dependable narrator and that Marianne was sexually neurotic, as a team the Moores were inspiring, and she never left their apartment at 260 Cumberland Street in Brooklyn without feeling strangely uplifted by their staunch commitment to each other and to the writing life.

Yet "Efforts of Affection" was posthumously published, it seems, because Bishop was never quite sure how much she wanted to mock, contradict, and humiliate the woman poet who functioned as her literary mother. If the rhythms of Bishop's response to Moore's behavior are complex, they are positively irresolute in her descriptions of Moore and her mother at home. For example:

> Mrs. Moore was in her seventies when I first knew her, very serious—solemn, rather—although capable of irony, and very devout. Her face was pale and somewhat heavy, her eyes large and a pale gray, and her dark hair had almost no white in it. Her manner toward Marianne was that of a kindly, self-controlled parent who felt that she had to take a firm line, that her daughter might be given to flightiness or—an equal sin, in her eyes—mistakes in grammar. She had taught English at a girls' school and her sentences were Johnsonian in weight and balance. She spoke more slowly than I have ever heard anyone speak in my life. One example of her conversational style has stayed with me for over forty years. Marianne was in the kitchen making tea and I was alone with Mrs. Moore. I said that I had just seen a new poem of Marianne's, "Nine Nectarines & Other Porcelain," and admired it very much. Mrs. Moore replied, "Yes. I am so *glad* that Marianne has *decided* to give the inhabitants of the *zoo* . . . a *rest.*" Waiting for the conclusion of her longer statements, I grew rather nervous; nevertheless, I found her extreme precision enviable and thought I could detect echoes of Marianne's own style in it: the use of double or triple negatives, the lighter and wittier ironies—Mrs. Moore had provided a sort of ground bass for them.[26]

Leaning now toward acceptance of Mrs. Moore's constant pressure on Marianne and now toward censure, Bishop remains puzzled by their conspiratorial silences. Within this obsessive, other-worldly family context, she wonders at "the rarity of true originality, and also the sort of alienation it might involve."[27] Although she defends Moore against attacks by contemporary feminists, "I do not remember her [Marianne] ever referring to Emily Dickinson," Bishop records. And as for the erotic Whitman: "E*liz*abeth, don't speak to me about that man!" Later in this chapter, we will see that this pairing opens a space for Bishop's intervention into the politics of the American literary canon. For the moment, however, she holds her tongue. Following Moore's imperious "don't speak," she confides to the reader, "So I never did again."[28] The explanation leaves Dickinson dangling. If in "Efforts of Affection," Bishop speaks both for and against Moore's experience, voice, and values, she nevertheless identified with Moore's struggle to perfect her poetry and to conquer the "element of mortal panic and fear underlying all works of art."[29] Her poetics was based on coming to terms with this element, as was Dickinson's.

Life had nevertheless taught Bishop that *"the choice is never wide and never free." "Is it lack of imagination that makes us come / to imagined places,"* she asks, *"not just stay at home?"* (*Poems* 75).

> *Continent, city, country, society:*
> *the choice is never wide and never free.*
> *And here, or there . . . No. Should we have stayed at home,*
> *wherever that may be?* ("Questions of Travel")

According to one of Bishop's many friends, just after Lota's traumatic death, "she talked more about her terribly unhappy childhood than anything. She talked mostly about how awful it was not to have a mother [because she ended up] just not knowing how to make relationships with people. Elizabeth said that not having a mother to turn to [forced her to] go into [herself] much more."[30] The danger was that she would go into herself and not return. She feared her mother's fate.

Bishop's creativity, like Dickinson's, exposed her to danger, and there is a curious moment in the pre-Brazil correspondence when Bishop writes to her artist friend Loren MacIver, after a drunken telephone call, "I'm sorry if I sounded rather goofy last night—terribly sorry. So many things seem to have been happening all at once to me and my friends—and on top of it I

Figure 25. Elizabeth Bishop and her mother, Gertrude Bulmer
Bishop. Courtesy Archives and Special Collections, Vassar
College Libraries. Ref. #6.323. Folder 100.1.

simply can't stop writing. It's the strangest thing and I think I'm just worn
out." She was at Yaddo where it *was* her job to write. But Bishop is describing
compulsion.[31] One thinks of her sandpiper, a figure for the poet, who struggles hard and futilely: "Poor bird, he is obsessed!" (*Poems* 126). The poise
and calm and self-assurance for which Bishop was praised by official and
unofficial reviewers was a triumph of form over fear, and we now know quite
a remarkable lot about the lack of self-composure that produced the panics

that produced the alcoholism. We also know a lot about Bishop's sexual conflicts and the Cold War context that exacerbated her need to camouflage her sexual orientation and desires. We know that Bishop's tranquility effect on the poetic page was achieved at the cost of considerable self-suppression. She reacted strongly against confessional poets who (in her view) had not sufficiently silenced themselves, and she reacted strongly against the emotional neediness of Dickinson's letters to a slightly older friend, to which we will now turn. They reminded her of the outrageous claims women could make on each other, a subject with which she was all too deeply and intimately familiar.

Love from Emily

On August 27, 1951, the *New Republic* published Bishop's pointed and poignant review of an edition somewhat misrepresented by the title *Emily Dickinson's Letters to Doctor and Mrs. Josiah Gilbert Holland.*[32] A handful were mutually addressed, but most were written to Elizabeth, who opened her mail one day not long after her husband's death to find the hauntingly beautiful condolence poem, "The Things that never can come back, are several." The first thought is almost too harsh to bear, and one can feel Dickinson straining to make it tolerable. In the context of her friend's companionate marriage, Dickinson seems to argue both that a spirit such as Elizabeth's is self-sufficient and that, like Josiah, she carries her happiness with her. From this perspective, and because of the emotional unity by which the couple had been defined, it is possible for Dickinson to imagine that Josiah Gilbert Holland is both dead, alive, and always at home: "Himself – at whatsoever Fathom / His Native Land." In our time, the poem is rarely discussed, but when Muriel Rukeyser read it on her radio program "Sunday at Nine" in 1949, she grouped it with others by Dickinson, which seemed to her "a chart of the strengths of the spirit." "The things that never can come back are several," she said, is "one of the great poems of our language . . . that speaks for the profundities of loss, and the places of the spirit in the spirit's own right, and of the enlargement which is joy, even joy gone."[33]

> The Things that never can come back, are several –
> Childhood – some forms of Hope – the Dead –
> Though Joys – like Men – may sometimes make a Journey –

And still abide –
We do not mourn for Traveler, or Sailor,
Their Routes are fair –
But think enlarged of all that they will tell us
Returning here –
"Here"! There are typic "Heres"—
Foretold Locations –
The Spirit does not stand –
Himself – at whatsoever Fathom
His Native Land – (*Fr* 1564)

Dickinson knew Josiah Gilbert Holland at least by reputation when he came to Amherst on a hot, dusty day in June 1853 to celebrate the opening of the railroad. (She observed the public ceremony from a secluded spot in a neighbor's woods [*L* 127].) A month later, both Hollands dropped in unexpectedly at the Dickinsons' spacious house on West Street, had "Champagne for dinner, and a very fine time" (*L* 132). In September, Emily and her sister Lavinia visited them, and as Alfred Habegger states, this visit when "the sisters spent a night at their Springfield home . . . [was] Emily's only known trip to a new friend who wasn't a relative. That she and Vinnie returned a year later for a longer stay tells us a major new stimulus had entered the poet's life, initiating one of her closest, longest-lasting, and least understood friendships."[34] After Dickinson "lost the run of the roads," as she phrased it (*L* 410), it was mainly through letters that she and Elizabeth kept in touch. Here is what she wrote in about August 1856:

Don't tell, dear Mrs. Holland, but wicked as I am, I read my Bible sometimes, and in it as I read today, I found a verse like this, where friends should "go no more out"; and there were "no tears," and I wished as I sat down to-night that we were *there* – not *here* – and that wonderful world had commenced, which makes such promises, and rather than to write you, I were by your side, and the "hundred and forty and four thousand" were chatting pleasantly, yet not disturbing us. And I'm half tempted to take my seat in that Paradise of which the good man writes, and begin forever and ever *now*, so wondrous does it seem. My only sketch, profile, of Heaven is a large, blue sky, bluer and larger than the *biggest* I have seen in June, and in it are my friends – all of them – every one of them – those who are with me now, and those who were "parted" as we walked, and "snatched up to Heaven". . . .

I'm so glad you are not a blossom, for those in my garden fade, and then a "reaper whose name is Death" has come to get a few to help him make a bouquet for himself, so I'm glad you are not a rose – and I'm glad you are not a bee, for where they go when summer's done, only the thyme knows, and even were you a robin, when the west winds came, you would coolly wink at me, and away, some morning!

As "little Mrs. Holland," then, I think I love you most, and trust that tiny lady will dwell below while we dwell, and when with many a wonder we seek the new Land, *her* wistful face, *with* ours, shall look the last upon the hills, and first upon – well, *Home!*

Pardon my sanity, Mrs. Holland, in a world *in*sane, and love me if you will, for I had rather *be* loved than to be called a king in earth, or a lord in Heaven. (*L* 185)[35]

This is a provocative letter. It personalizes religious rhetoric, makes Elizabeth Holland the center of a sentimental sisterhood, and raises questions about insanity on a global scale. It asks for love (but from whom?) and apologizes mock-seriously for needing too much of it. It looks to the afterlife for erotic fulfillment and rejects that future, opting instead for the secret satisfactions of the present. Other than in nature, where are those satisfactions to be found?

The Holland letters are heavily edited, and most of the reviews commented favorably on Ward's intervention. In the *New York Times*, for example, Thomas H. Johnson stated enthusiastically, "The new letters have been edited, the old restudied and set in chronological arrangement, and the whole held together with running commentary. The presentation is handled in the tradition of fine scholarship."[36] In the *New York Herald Tribune Book Review*, George Whicher agreed and went further: "It is not too much to say that this is the truest book of Emily Dickinson's writing and the truest book about her and her circle that has yet been put in print."[37]

Because of the care Ward had evidently taken with historical and textual research, her commentary about Dickinson's love life was influential. In *American Literature*, Grace B. Sherrer wrote, "The long debated supposition that the Reverend Charles Wadsworth was the symbol of earthly love in

Figure 26. Elizabeth Chapin and Josiah Gilbert Holland, in *Emily Dickinson's Letters to Dr. and Mrs. Josiah Gilbert Holland.* In an early letter to Elizabeth, Dickinson asserted, "I would rather *be* loved than to be called a king in earth, or a lord on Heaven."

Emily's life is confirmed by references in the letters."[38] (In fact, these references are slight.) Whicher agreed with the Wadsworth thesis, while the *New Yorker* summarized more cautiously: "Some new light is cast on Miss Dickinson's attachment to the Reverend Charles Wadsworth; it appears that Mrs. Holland occasionally forwarded the poet's letters to him."[39] Exceptionally, Richard Chase was downright skeptical:

> Mrs. Ward's collection of letters offers no striking biographical revelations. There is nothing here to encourage speculation about the "love affair" of Emily Dickinson and the Reverend Mr. Charles Wadsworth. The poet was accustomed, indeed, to inclose unaddressed notes to Wadsworth in her letters to the Hollands, to be addressed by Dr. Holland [*sic*] and forwarded to Philadelphia. She expressed her fear of imposing upon the Hollands in this matter by such fanciful language as "I once more come, with my little Load—Is it too heavy?" Though the atmosphere of intrigue lends a

touch of romance to the relation of Emily Dickinson with her "Philadelphia friend," Mrs. Ward is certainly correct in deciding that the moral—she finds it hard to say the sanctimonious—Dr. Holland would have participated in none but the most spotless conspiracies.[40]

In the *Saturday Review of Literature*, Henry W. Wells comments on Wadsworth too, calling him "Emily's friend of the spirit."[41] Among reviewers, Bishop was exceptional (perhaps unique) in her sensitivity to Dickinson's friendship with Elizabeth, coupled with her failure (if it was a failure) to mention Wadsworth.[42]

So who *was* Elizabeth Holland, and what else do we know of her? She was high-spirited and witty, seven years older than Dickinson, better armored socially, and she appreciated Dickinson's literary allusions (to Dickens, the Brontës, George Eliot, the Bible, Shakespeare, Longfellow, Elizabeth Barrett Browning, Henry James, and many others). She was "a good and thrifty housekeeper" who helped her husband in his career.[43] She was not easily disconcerted, and it was to Elizabeth that Dickinson wrote, "Had we the first intimation of the Definition of Life, the calmest of us would be Lunatics" (*L* 492). She laughed a lot. I think of her as the kind of strong-hearted person described in Dickinson's poem "A Shady friend" who could lift her up when she was down.

> A Shady friend – for Torrid days –
> Is easier to find –
> Than one of higher temperature
> For Frigid – hour of mind –
>
> The Vane a little to the East –
> Scares Muslin souls – away –
> If Broadcloth Hearts are firmer
> Than those of Organdy –
>
> Who is to blame? The Weaver?
> Ah, the bewildering thread!
> The Tapestries of Paradise
> So notelessly – are made! (*Fr* 306)

While Dickinson was copying this poem somewhat notelessly into Fascicle 14, Elizabeth, so far as we know, was not urging her toward publication.

In an 1893 letter to Mabel Loomis Todd, however, she states, "I regret I had so few of the many letters dear Emily wrote me to send you. As I remember them, there were many more interesting and quaint than these I have."[44] Some of the missing letters were later recovered and printed in Ward's edition. "My tiny friend," Dickinson called her (*L* 269); "my little Sanctuary" (*L* 521), "dear Sister" (*L* 354), "my sweet elder sister" (*L* 202), "Little Sister" (*L* 399), "God's little Blond Blessing" (*L* 589), "Sister Golconda" (*L* 685), and "the Angel Wife" (*L* 687).

Dickinson's metaphoric language exerts a high degree of control over the friendship, but it is difficult to know what to make of her obsession with Elizabeth's size. In some way, miniaturizing Elizabeth authorizes Dickinson to own her. Miniaturizing herself can also intensify their bond. "Smaller than David you clothe me with extreme Goliath," she wrote (*L* 318). We know that Elizabeth had an ample life of her own and, according to one of her husband's biographers, that she was "of medium height." As a young woman, her eyes were "frank and fearless":

> A miniature of Mrs. Holland . . . shows her with a fair complexion, a rosy bloom, a pair of remarkably frank and fearless bluish-gray eyes, and a wealth of soft brown hair. She was of medium height, but looked fairly petite beside the tall and stalwart figure of her husband. His dark-olive complexion and black eyes and hair gave him a Spanish look, but when illuminated in talking or in lecturing, his face had a remarkable brilliancy of expression, and the two presented that happy contrast which some philosophers deem essential to perfect mutual admiration in husband and wife.[45]

In 1872, when she was close to fifty, Elizabeth's life of her own included serious eye problems that necessitated surgery. It was then that Dickinson wrote, "To have lost an Enemy is an Event with all of us, almost more memorable perhaps than to find a friend."[46] Although Dickinson had severe eye problems in 1864–65, she does not mention the noisy particulars of her experience. Rather, she converts particularity into abstraction, even as she tempers the sententiousness of her pronouncement with an "almost" and a "perhaps." "We are proud of her safety," she writes, addressing Elizabeth in the third person, "Ashamed of our dismay for her who knew no consternation." She remains "our little Sister," and her bravery is legendary (*L* 377).

Elizabeth Luna Chapin Holland's life of her own included many broth-ers and sisters, a close relationship with her mother, and the loss of her father when she was ten. She began to live with a well-to-do businessman-uncle in Albany, New York, where she bonded with her vivacious cousins and attended the prestigious Albany Female Academy. According to Ward, who is identified on the title page of *Emily Dickinson's Letters to Dr. and Mrs. Josiah Gilbert Holland* as the Hollands' granddaughter, Elizabeth came to enjoy the liberality of Albany society but returned to Springfield to help her hard-pressed mother when her schooling was over. She was the eldest daugh-ter.[47] Several years later, "frank and fearless" Elizabeth Chapin married "Gil-bert" Holland, an ambitious young man whose parents were poverty stricken. He couldn't afford the training to become a minister, did not aspire to the law, and turned to doctoring instead, an occupation that didn't really suit him, although the "Doctor" title clung to him for the rest of his life. (In the family, he was known as "Gilbert.") To be sure, literature was Holland's first love, and while still practicing medicine, he founded the *Bay State Weekly Courier*, a newspaper that failed after six months. Next he tried schoolmaster-ing for a semester at a commercial college in Richmond, Virginia, but he was homesick for "Lizzie," his friends, and New England ways. In January 1848, both Hollands travelled to frontierlike Vicksburg, Mississippi, where Josiah supervised public education and began to publish sentimental poems such as "Fleta Gray" in Nathaniel Parker Willis's *Home Journal*.[48] Elizabeth taught school, became pregnant, and criticized Southerners for their impracticality in her letters home.[49]

After their return to Springfield in the summer of 1849, Holland's career flourished. Samuel Bowles invited him to join the *Springfield Republican* as Associate Editor, having already been favorably impressed with what he knew of his writing, which included a series of prose sketches of plantation life.[50] At first a local and then a national celebrity, Holland was a popular lyceum lecturer who sought to elevate "the standard of Christian manhood and womanhood" in such best-selling books as *Titcomb's Letters to Young People, Single and Married*, which Dickinson knew, as did other members of her circle such as Thomas Wentworth Higginson. Explaining his goals in a dedi-cation to the Reverend Henry Ward Beecher, Holland (using the pen name Timothy Titcomb, Esq.) refers to gender as a distinct social class and justifies the inclusion of advice to both men and women in a single volume: "You will notice that I address my letters to the young men, young women, and young married people, as classes, with distinctness of aim and application, while I inclose all in a single volume. I have intended the whole book for each class. I believe that each should know what I have to say to the other. I have written nothing to one class which it would not be well for the other to know."[51]

Although from many perspectives Dickinson was in a class of her own, she responded consistently and enthusiastically to reports of Holland's success and to the success of their companionate marriage. In March 1859, for example, she wrote to Elizabeth, memorably employing a bachelor persona, "I gather from 'Republican' that you are about to doff your [widow's] weeds for a Bride's Attire. Vive le fireside! Am told that fasting gives to food marvellous Aroma, but by birth a Bachelor, disavow Cuisine" (*L* 204).[52] Apparently fasting *did* give to "food" marvelous aroma, and some nine months later, while Josiah was away on another lecture tour, the Hollands' daughters Annie and Kate were joined by their baby brother, Ted. Dickinson wrote that she was praying for them all (*L* 210). In 1860, when baby Ted needed an operation on his foot, she seized the opportunity to speculate about the relationship between feet, the phallus, gender transgression, and genius: "How is your little Byron? Hope he gains his foot without losing his genius. Have heard it ably argued that the poet's genius lay in his foot – as the bee's prong and his song are concomitant" (*L* 227). Dickinson wrote again, complaining politely of neglect and wondering about her friend's health. She suggested that little Annie send her a "picture of an erect flower" if Elizabeth was well and if not, "she can hang the flower a little on one side!" Then she fantasized about a spectral audience that could hear her letters and songs and poems, even if the Hollands, and Elizabeth in particular, were laughing at her, along with the whole United States (*L* 269).[53]

For whatever reason, there is a gap in the extant exchange of letters from at least 1862 to 1865, although four poems sent to the Hollands have been attributed to these years.[54] When the correspondence picks up again in November 1865, Dickinson had just returned from a six-month stay in Cambridge where she was being treated for eye trouble and depression. She writes about her sister-in-law Susan; about craving news of her journalist friend Samuel Bowles; about love, death, fraud, and the truth; and about the departure of the Irish servant Margaret O'Brien on whom the household work depended: "I winced at her loss, because I was in the habit of her, and even a new rolling-pin has an embarrassing element, but to all except anguish, the mind soon adjusts" (*L* 311). Dickinson was also embarrassed when Elizabeth visited her in May 1866. Apologizing for her social awkwardness she wrote,

"When you had gone the love came. I supposed it would. The supper of the heart is when the guest has gone. Shame is so intrinsic in a strong affection we must all experience Adam's reticence" (*L* 318). We know that shame did not prevent Dickinson from issuing commands. "Send no union letters," she wrote after Elizabeth had made the mistake of addressing a letter to both Emily and Lavinia: "A mutual plum is not a plum. I was too respectful to take the pulp and do not like a stone" (*L* 321).

Meanwhile, Holland published his timely *Life of Lincoln*, and the pace of his lecturing accelerated. Scholar Allen C. Guelzo summarizes:

> Abraham Lincoln's coffin had lain in the receiving vault in Springfield's Oak Ridge Cemetery for less than three weeks when a dapper, walrus-mustachioed New Englander stepped off the train and checked into Springfield's St. Nicholas Hotel. He was Josiah Gilbert Holland, one-time editor (and still part owner) of the Springfield, Massachusetts, *Republican*, a nationally popular writer of advice books, and (what would turn out to be most memorably) part of a small circle of admirers and encouragers of an unknown Amherst poet named Emily Dickinson. None of those attributes, however, provided the slightest qualification for the task that brought him to the Illinois namesake of his hometown, which was the writing of a biography of Abraham Lincoln. Holland had not known Lincoln personally—had never even met him casually. Notwithstanding these deficits, Holland produced a landmark Lincoln biography, the first of any substantial length as a biography, the first with any aspirations to comprehensiveness, and a best-seller of 100,000 copies that was published in several languages.[55]

Although the book's success enabled the couple to build a splendid new home, Springfield could not hold him or them for long. Following a grand tour of Europe in 1868–70, Josiah moved to New York City to become the founding editor of *Scribner's Monthly*, the big-circulation "Illustrated Magazine for the People" that published women writers and attempted to discipline their unfeminine professional ambition. Given his innate conservatism, it may seem strange to us that Dickinson was proud of his success, and it may seem strange that at some level, Dickinson viewed Holland as one of her supporters.[56] I have no doubt that she did, perhaps more as a person than as a poet (if we can make that distinction). Vicariously, she participated in his

travels (and Elizabeth's) and told Higginson that "Timothy Titcomb" had
brought her a picture of "Mrs. Browning's tomb" as a souvenir (*L* 342b).
(She already had several others and gave Holland's gift to Higginson for his
wife.)

Because Lavinia eventually burned Elizabeth's letters, as she did other
correspondences, the edition Bishop reviewed is a one-sided affair. We learn
a great deal about Dickinson's dream-life and very little about Elizabeth's, in
part because Elizabeth, unlike Dickinson, seems to be inhabiting her dream-
life in the present. Dickinson's letters are ardent and orphic, passionate and
profound. "Only Love can wound," she wrote, "Only Love assist the Wound.
. . . If my Crescent fail you, try me in the Moon" (*L* 370). "Perhaps you
thought dear Sister, I wanted to elope with you and feared a vicious Father.
It was not quite that."

> Life is the finest secret.
> So long as that remains, we must all whisper.
> With that sublime exception I had no clandestineness.
> It was lovely to see you and I hope it may happen again.
> These beloved accidents must become more frequent. . . .
> To shut our eyes is Travel.
> The Seasons understand this.
> How lonesome to be an Article! I mean – to have no soul. (*L* 354)

"Our unfinished interview like the Cloth of Dreams, cheapens other fabrics,"
Dickinson wrote (*L* 359). And, wistfully, after another of Elizabeth's infre-
quent visits,

> I miss your childlike Voice –
> I miss your Heroism.
> I feel that I lose combinedly a Soldier and a Bird.
> I trust that you experience a trifling destitution.
> Thank you for having been.
> These timid Elixirs are obtained too seldom. . . .
> Parting is one of the exactions of a Mortal Life. It is
> bleak – like Dying, but occurs more times. (*L* 399)

And she enclosed the following poem, a fair copy in ink, signed "Emily,"
which appears in this form in the Ward edition:

Longing is like the Seed
That wrestles in the Ground,
Believing if it intercede
It shall at length be found.

The Hour and the Clime—
Each Circumstance unknown,
What Constancy must be achieved
Before it see the Sun![57]

Elizabeth Holland is not likely to have known that Dickinson sent the poem (with three different line breaks) to Thomas Wentworth Higginson, and she may not have known that Dickinson often sent versions of the same poem to different correspondents with personalized introductions, as though the poem were suited to a single epistolary occasion. Certainly, she did not know that Brenda Wineapple would read "Longing" as an instrument of flirtation with Higginson.[58]

For Sharon Cameron, the poem exemplifies "a powerful discrepancy between what was 'inner than the bone' . . . and what could be acknowledged." She suggests that "the opening . . . has an exactitude the conclusion lacks."[59] Cameron's line of thinking inspires a further question. If longing is found, if it cuts through polite surfaces, by whom is it discovered? While the poem may figure the finder as "the Sun," we can also read "the Sun" not as the proximate object of desire but rather as an emblematic figure shedding light on what Henry James called "one of those friendships between women which are so common in New England." "The Sun" may represent self-knowledge or the externalization of that knowledge to the unnamed beloved. While composing *The Bostonians*, which was serialized in the *Century* in 1885–86 (J. G. Holland died while editing its first number), Henry James asked himself "what was the most salient and peculiar point in our social life. The answer was: the situation of women, the decline of the sentiment of sex, the agitation on their behalf." In this famous *Notebook* entry, with its problematic reference to "the sentiment of sex," James further explained, "The subject is strong and good, with a large rich interest. The relation of the two girls should be a study of one of those friendships between women which are so common in New England. The whole thing as local, as American, as possible, and as full of Boston: an attempt to show I *can* write an American story." And, James remarked, there had to be a newspaperman, an energetic reporter: "I should like to *bafouer* [ridicule] the vulgarity and hideousness of this—the impudent invasion of privacy—the extinction of all conception of privacy."[60]

We know that "relationships between single women in late nineteenth-century New England were common enough to have been called 'Boston marriages', and James's clever but unstable sister, Alice, of whom he was very fond, had formed one in the latter part of her life with a woman named Katharine Peabody Loring."[61] If we are willing to use "Boston marriage" to describe a powerful erotic relationship between women who do not live together, one of whom is happily married, the term helps us to understand Dickinson's flirtation with Elizabeth and to embed her writings within a larger sex/gender project. I find elements of a Boston marriage in the metaphoric structure of the Holland letters, when Dickinson's language suggests a long-term union, an erotic sisterhood; moreover, her obsession with Elizabeth's size can be read as a symptom of the partly repressed fantasy of bodily contact in which she is the dominant partner.

The reviewer of this interesting volume of letters—*poems* and letters, really—was identified as "Elizabeth Bishop, author of *North & South*, winner of the Houghton Mifflin Poetry Award in 1945 and a Guggenheim Fellow in 1947." Readers were further informed that she had just been given "the first Lucy Martin Donnelly Fellowship by Bryn Mawr College," a grant with no residency requirement for which she had been recommended by Moore.[62] Bishop's *New Republic* review had taken her nearly a year to write and was headlined "LOVE FROM EMILY." Picking up on Theodora Ward's statement that Dickinson was an emotionally demanding friend, Bishop explained,

> In a sense, all of Emily Dickinson's letters are "love-letters." To her, little besides love, human and divine, was worth writing about, and often the two seemed to fuse. That abundance of detail—descriptions of daily life, clothes, food, travels, etc.—that is found in what are usually considered "good letters" plays very little part in hers. Instead, there is a constant insistence on the strength of her affections, an almost childish daring and repetitiveness about them that must sometimes have been very hard to take. Is it a tribute to her choice of friends, and to the friends themselves, that they *could* take it and frequently appreciate her as a poet as well? Or is it occasionally only a tribute to the bad taste and extreme sentimentality of the times?

At any rate, a letter containing such, to us at present, embarrassing remarks as, "I'd love to be a bird or a bee, that whether hum or sing, still might be near you," is rescued in the nick of time by a sentence like, "If it wasn't for broad daylight, and cooking stoves, and roosters, I'm afraid you would have occasion to smile at my letters often, but so sure as 'this mortal' essays immortality, a crow from a neighboring farmyard dissipates the illusion, and I am here again." In modern correspondence expressions of feeling have gone underground: but if we are sometimes embarrassed by Emily Dickinson's letters we are spared the contemporary letter-writer's cynicism and "humor."[63]

Bishop interpreted her task strictly, saying nothing about the twenty-nine poems the volume offered, though she softened her tone as the short essay developed by comparing some of Dickinson's "homely" images in their "solidity" to George Herbert's. She also said something nice about Ward's editing and liked the illustrations, among them "a charming photograph of Lavinia Dickinson, laughing, and holding one of her innumerable cats."

If Bishop's sense of Dickinson as an overly demanding friend is the essay's dominant motif, "Love from Emily" further suggests that Bishop was responding to Dickinson's emotional intensity as a narrowing of perspective. On the one hand, "It is curious to think of the Dickinson family reading the Springfield *Republican* as religiously as they must have from the many glancing references to it; but except for generalizations usually turned into metaphors, current events rarely appear in these letters." On the other, "In modern correspondence expressions of feeling have gone underground."[64] Reading Bishop's review, we might conclude that Dickinson's letters of "gratitude and devotion" were directed equally toward Elizabeth and Josiah. In this regard, the review itself goes underground.

If Bishop is most deeply touched (or stung) by letters from the early years, she is wonderfully sensitive to Dickinson's development. When praising Dickinson's use of solid, homely images, she notes that "as the letters grow more terse and epigrammatic, one is reminded not only of Herbert's poetry but of whole sections of his 'Outlandish Proverbs.' And one is grateful for the sketchiness: it is nice for a change to know a poet who never felt the need for apologies and essays, long paragraphs, or even for long sentences. . . . It is the sketchiness of the waterspider, tenaciously holding to its upstream position by means of the faintest ripples, while making one aware of the

Figure 27. Lavinia Dickinson with one of her many cats, reprinted in *Emily Dickinson's Letters to Dr. and Mrs. Josiah Gilbert Holland.* Courtesy of the Jones Library, Inc., Amherst, Massachusetts.

current of death and the darkness below."[65] Yet here Bishop quotes nothing and does not permit Dickinson to speak in her own voice. The effect is to suggest that while Dickinson's uncensored expressions of feeling may seem childish to modern ears, and while we may be grateful for her sketchy tenacity, there is something frightening in the example of her "faintest ripples." At the moment when she inhabits the review most fully, Bishop leaves us with a vision of insect or instinctual life, "making one aware of the current of death and the darkness below." Then she pulls herself back to end on a more cheerful note, reminding readers that in time further letters "may yet come to light."

That Infuriating Book

A few months after "Love from Emily" was published in the *New Republic*, Bishop was on a freighter that landed her in Brazil. During the trip, she met "Miss Breen," the retired six-foot-tall policewoman with the bright blue eyes who sidesteps danger in "Arrival at Santos" (*Poems* 65–66).[66] She also completed a review of *The Riddle of Emily Dickinson*, which appeared in the *New Republic* in August 1952. Bishop believed that the review, headlined "Unseemly Deductions," was never published, and she told her friend Cal Lowell as much.[67] For many years, this myth persisted in the Vassar Archive and other sources, underscoring our sense that while attracted to dangerous subject matter, Bishop was conflicted about her critical intervention. Did she want to silence speculation about Dickinson's sexual identity or to make sure that this delicate conversation was properly conducted? As she explained to Lowell, she hoped that she had written a "withering" review but was not sure that she had succeeded.

In *The Riddle of Emily Dickinson*, Rebecca Patterson argued that Dickinson and a young widow, Kate Scott Turner, had fallen in love with each other, that they had a two-year romance which was erotically unconsummated, and that Kate broke off the friendship when it became too threateningly passionate. According to Patterson, the solution to the riddle of Emily Dickinson was quite simple: she suffered from a broken heart. Less simple was the fact that Dickinson's disappointing lover was a woman. *Riddle* was a groundbreaking book, the first to describe Dickinson as a (thwarted) lesbian and to link her to a clearly eroticized Sappho. There were honorific comparisons of Dickinson to Sappho in the 1890s, and Dickinson herself had mentioned Sappho in a poem about old books and "precious – mouldering pleasure[s]" (*Fr* 569). Dickinson, though, participates in a nineteenth-century American tradition in which Sappho is admired as an intellectual woman and a passionate lyricist, but in which her "wild love" for "fair girls and young men" is not a necessary component of the myth.[68] To the extent that Dickinson was connected to Sappho in the first half of the twentieth century, the same-sex lover dimension was usually ignored. Amy Lowell, for example, linked Dickinson, Elizabeth Barrett Browning, and Sappho in "The Sisters" in 1922, but as Betsy Erkkila suggests, while "Sappho represents the freedom, mobility, and sexual desire associated with the New Woman in early twentieth-century discourse. . . . Dickinson [figures] as a sterile and fragile Victorian anorexic who gave up 'womanhood' for poetry and metaphysics."[69]

Patterson's melodramatic style turned the conversation in a distinctly different direction, with geography being a dominant metaphor and one that was close to Bishop's heart:

> Like many other poets of northern climes Emily Dickinson was in love with the South. She also valued the cool discipline and the austerity that she associated with the North, and these two sides of her nature warred in her perpetually. The South symbolized escape and sensuous freedom. Just as one stripped off heavy layers of clothing on a tropic island (the poet dreamed of the "spicy isles"), so one stripped off the stifling Puritan taboos against pleasure and lived in the sun of enjoyment. Emily was far from being the cool New England nun of popular fancy; she was a sensuous, passionate woman. In her love of the sun and of the South she could have written with Sappho: "For me richness and beauty belong to the desire of the sunlight." Emily undoubtedly read the fragments of Sapphic verse published by her friend Higginson in 1871, and she herself may have noticed resemblances of temperament. In the driving passion and intensity of her poems she was a Sappho without the informed sensuality.[70]

Patterson amplifies the lovelorn Sappho connection by describing Higginson's essay, explaining that unlike the native of Lesbos, the Amherst Dickinson does not have the social or cultural support to achieve success in same-sex love. Even Dickinson's reading of Sapphic verse occurred too late, a decade after the crisis involving Kate Scott Turner that Patterson details.

In *Riddle*, the word "lesbian" is never used, but it turns out that Kate was not Dickinson's first love:

> In her first youth Emily identified Susan Gilbert with the South— "the love South." Sue was "Egypt," and had a "torrid spirit" and "depths of Domingo." Then Kate appeared on the scene, and in a

poem ("As the starved maelstrom laps the navies") Emily wrote of hungering for "a berry of Domingo and a torrid eye." With her dark hair and brilliant dark eyes, Kate looked somewhat like Sue, but she had a warmth and a passion of which Sue gave little evidence. So pronounced was Kate's longing for the South and sunlight that a friend of later years made a particular reference to her passion for "brighter climes." She spent as much of her life as possible on the French and Italian Rivieras and in other sunny spots of Italy. The transfer of the southern symbolism to Kate was appropriate, indeed well-nigh inescapable.[71]

Patterson went on to develop her interpretations of geographical symbolism in later works, but the florid personalism of her style is at its full in *Riddle*, which, the jacket copy suggests, "raises a baffling problem in human behavior, a mystery profounder than the one it solves."[72]

Bishop was enraged by the argument. She made it clear that she had no use for literary detective work, at least not in this instance, and in reacting so strongly to Patterson's thesis, which grants one woman's homoerotic desire cultural presence, she was undoubtedly imagining what it would be like were she herself to encounter a critical biographer lacking what she saw as even the rudiments of tact. "Why do so many books of literary detective-work," she wrote, "even when they are better authenticated, better written and more useful in their conclusions than Mrs. Patterson's, seem finally just unpleasant? Perhaps it is because, in order to reach a single reason for anything as singular and yet manifold as literary creation, it is necessary to limit the human personality's capacity for growth and redirection to the point of mutilation. It could not very well be a pleasant process to observe." And the review concluded, "These 400 pages are still many sizes too small for Emily Dickinson's work. Whether one likes her poetry or not, whether it wrings one's heart or sets one's teeth on edge, nevertheless it exists, and in a world far removed from the defenseless people and events described in this infuriating book." Rhetorically, Bishop's tone seems calculated to discourage even careful studies of same-sex desire; the most obvious reading of her review is that it is homophobic, that a self-protective Bishop has internalized the homophobia of her time and place.

With the advantage of hindsight, we can distinguish between the effect of Bishop's strategic rhetoric and her more intimate ambivalence about reading queer community through Dickinson's story. For Bishop does grant that part of Patterson's account could be true, the part that has to do with Emily Dickinson being in love with a woman and it not working out well. Claiming objectivity for herself, Bishop remarks, "That her thesis is partially true might have occurred to any reader of Emily Dickinson's poetry—occurred on one page to be contradicted on the next, that is—but even so, why is it necessary for us to learn every detail of Kate Scott's subsequent life for fifty-seven years after she dealt Emily Dickinson this supposedly deadly blow?" A good question, but again, Bishop's language does not encourage curious readers to inquire further.

In trying to contextualize both Patterson's achievement and Bishop's "withering" review of "this infuriating book," I began to search out contemporary reviews. I had assumed they would be few in number and published in relatively obscure places. But it turns out that *Riddle* was reviewed not only by the *New Republic* but also by the *Nation*, the *New York Herald Tribune*, the *New York Times*, the *San Francisco Chronicle*, the *Saturday Review of Literature*, and the *New Yorker*, to say nothing of such journals as *American Literature*, the *Kenyon Review*, *Southwest Review*, *New Mexico Quarterly*, *Poetry* magazine, the *New England Quarterly*, and so on. Without making this hunt a life-project, I rather easily retrieved some fifteen reviews, and taking them all in all, Bishop's was the most obviously emotional (i.e., no one else called it an infuriating book).[73] The *New Yorker* review was far from sympathetic, but it was comparatively dispassionate, and because it is mercifully short, I cite it in full:

> Mrs. Patterson's thesis—that Emily Dickinson's progressive eccentricity, as well as the inspiration of very nearly all her poetry, sprang from her short and baffled friendship (1859–1861) with one Kate Scott Turner (later Anthon)—is elaborated at length and with the aid of much unsupported conjecture. That Emily Dickinson was attracted to this rather worldly visitor to Amherst seems to be a fact, but since it is on record that the poet's affections were widely diffused among friends of both sexes, and that she was not too crushed by grief in 1862 to reach out for a new friendship by writing to Thomas Wentworth Higginson, it is improbable that she celebrated this one encounter throughout her life, sometimes under the cover of masculine pronouns. The picture of Mrs. Anthon as an American "cultured" expatriate and emotional drifter, from the seventies to the First World War, has a period interest, however.

Like Bishop, the *New Yorker* writer objects to Patterson's presentation of the argument, and like Bishop, the anonymous *New Yorker* writer assumes that creativity is overdetermined: however important, no single biographical event can account for anyone's genius. The *New Yorker* writer is more explicit than Bishop permitted herself to be in suggesting that "the poet's affections were widely diffused among friends of both sexes."

On the other hand, Bishop gestures toward a more explicitly erotic affection, when she writes that "for 400 pages Mrs. Patterson tracks down the until now unknown person (she believes it to have been a person, not persons) for whom Emily Dickinson is supposed to have cherished a hopeless passion and to whom she is supposed to have written every one of her love poems. . . . The two young women met and fell in love; about a year later Kate Scott broke it off in some way, and Emily Dickinson had been christened and launched on her life of increasing sorrow and seclusion. It was all as simple as that." Bishop accuses Patterson of restricting "the human personality's capacity for growth and redirection" and of mutilating the defenseless dead. While granting that Patterson's thesis may be partially true, she insists that "a poet may write from sources other than autobiographical" and that Emily Dickinson must have felt satisfaction in her work. Overall, then, Bishop concentrates on demolishing Patterson's critical authority. She was but one of many to take this tack.

Thomas Johnson, for example, writing in the *New York Times*, describes an 1865 letter from Emily to Kate that Patterson did not know about and whose cheerful emotional tone Johnson uses to contradict Patterson's thesis. Further, he draws on his superior knowledge of the dating of Dickinson's poetry to demolish Patterson's credibility. "Emily Dickinson's poems and letters," he writes, "have always shown an unusual dependence on other people, both men and women. To say, as the author does, that 'women alone had the power to wound her,' or that 'there is no man—no real man—anywhere in the poems' seems perverse." Other major reviews, for example by George Whicher and Richard Chase and John Ciardi, have somewhat different emphases. Almost all reviewers were willing to grant that there might be some credible elements to Patterson's argument but that, as Johnson suggested, it was so poorly deployed that "there was no way of telling."

As previously noted, Bishop's review was written at a very difficult time of her life. Her alcoholism was out of control, and she needed to get away from the tumultuous New York literary scene, where, despite extensive psychotherapy, she felt ill-used and out of place.[74] On the freighter she was

Figure 28. Elizabeth Bishop with Tobias in 1954, fulfilling her dream of being part of a family with pets. Taken on the patio at Samambaia, the elaborate country estate she shared with her Brazilian friend and lover Lota de Macedo Soares. Courtesy Archives and Special Collections, Vassar College Libraries. Ref. #3.454. Folder 100.25.

taking around the world which landed her in Brazil, she did not know she was to find a physical, emotional, and intellectual haven with Lota. What she did know was that Dickinson, despite her reclusion and limited social life, had been almost childishly daring in her self-revelations. Bishop did not want to repeat Dickinson's mistakes. As she was to explain from Brazil in "The U.S.A. School of Writing," although expressing oneself was a way of being less alone, discovering the "mysterious, awful power of writing" involved social and psychological risks she wanted to spare herself and her readers. Like Dickinson, Bishop was alert to the destructive potential of the printed word for a writer's "admirers, friends, lovers, suitors, etc."[75] What did that "etc." include?

Bishop's desire not to offend the sensibilities of her audience can be better understood in the homophobic context of the postwar era when her vehement critique of Patterson was written. In *Odd Girls and Twilight Lovers:*

A History of Lesbian Life in Twentieth-Century America, Lillian Faderman explains, "The public image of the lesbian as sick in the years after the war confirmed the need for secrecy. A lesbian understood that if her affectional preference became known outside of her circle of lesbian friends she would be judged . . . by that preference and found mentally unhealthy."[76] Camille Roman, too, helps us to understand Bishop's response to the climate of her times. In *Elizabeth Bishop's World War II—Cold War View*, she observes, "Bishop's understated but keen sense of marketplace politics also enabled her survival as a woman and lesbian during a troubled and turbulent time. She strategically withdrew into the culturally sanctioned role of the private woman hidden from public view. Then, with her protective circle of inti- mates, friends, and literary peers, she continued to promote this image of herself."[77] To the extent though, that Bishop's strategic withdrawal was less radical than Dickinson's, Bishop could not hide herself from public view. To the extent that she was a publishing poet, she was no longer, strictly speaking, a private woman.

If Bishop's stance was anxious, it was also principled. Even when Second Wave feminism began to normalize public displays of lesbian desire, Bishop preferred to render the idiosyncratic social and emotional texture of her erotic relationships rather than to identify herself as a lesbian. On this subject, Valerie Traub is useful. In *The Renaissance of Lesbianism in Early Modern England*, she contends, "Notwithstanding its enabling, even life-affirming utility to countless individuals and collectivities, lesbian is a rather coarse and confining category of erotic identity. Lesbian not only implies a coherent and stable erotic orientation, but the achievement of this orientation through a developmental process of increasing self-awareness and self-expression— hence, the centrality of the metaphors of the closet and coming out." Traub further notes, "Identity categories such as lesbian represent erotic orientation as much for the benefit of others as for the benefit of the self. . . . Nor does the category of bisexuality lay to rest the conflicting identifications, investments, comforts, and satisfactions that together can comprise the erotic self."[78] Early and late, Bishop zealously guarded her power to name herself and felt personally diminished by rigid sexual classifications. Like Dickinson, she was an "I," and an "I" could not be confined to a predictable erotic satisfaction.[79] Along these lines, Bishop's suggestion that Dickinson may have been in love with a *number* of women is of particular interest. In a parenthesis quoted above, she writes that Patterson believes Dickinson's beloved to have been a woman rather than women. This parenthetical amplification, multi-plication, and diversification corresponds to Bishop's experience. One of her strategies for dealing with real or perceived erotic defeat was to move on by forming alternative attachments, as she did in her childhood and, eventually, from Lota. Moving on, though, was a compromise with desire. It was the first attachment that was the most intense.

Bishop's erotic reticence, then, marked the convergence of politics, pride, and the ineluctable, or temperament, which is why she never fully came out of the closet. Although, as we saw in an earlier chapter, Sylvia Plath refers to Bishop as a "lesbian" in her 1958 journal, Bishop was not identified publicly as a lesbian until after her death.[80] In response to the sexual revolution of the sixties, she remained wary, famously telling Frank Bidart that she believed in "Closets, closets, and more closets."[81] Homophobia being what it is, her reaction is understandable. But the point I want to make now is that Bishop emerged from her once idyllic life in Brazil feeling she was no good at love; her pathos-driven history seemed to preclude continuing erotic success. Thus when her student Wesley Wehr asked her for advice about his love life—this was in Seattle in 1966—Bishop said, "You want to ask me a question about W-h-a-t? Did you say it was about *love*? What would *ever possibly* give you the idea that *I of all* people would know *anything* about a thing like *that*?" Later that afternoon, when they had finished some shopping and were walk-ing down University Way, she turned to him saying, "Wes, I'm awfully sorry that I dodged your question the way I did. It took me by surprise, and I just didn't know how I should answer it. But I've been thinking about it, since you did ask me. And I will say *this* much: if any happiness ever comes your way, *GRAB IT!*"[82] This advice sounds very much like the aging Lambert Strether on the "live all you can" theme, and I would like to turn now to Bishop's receptivity to an ambassador-in-the-rough who stayed home, who offered her another model of American authorship, and of (possibly) erotic success.

Whitman and the U.S.A. School of Writing

The year is 1956. In California, Allen Ginsberg publishes the little book *Howl*, with its grocery-laden homage to Walt Whitman, "A Supermarket in Califor-nia." Obscenity charges follow. In Brazil, Bishop, who is enjoying a self-chosen exile from the competitive pressures of North America, tries unsuc-cessfully to publish a fictionalized account of a job she held for less than a week when she was just out of college. "The U.S.A. School of Writing" is almost as food obsessed as Ginsberg's "Supermarket," but Bishop's Whitman is tucked away discretely in a single sentence in the story's ninth paragraph. This Whitman figures obliquely and is easily overlooked. Whereas Ginsberg's "lonely old grubber" eying the supermarket clerks is a "dear father" and faithful companion for the outsetting Beat bard, Bishop's Whitman writes "big books, with lots of ego and emotion in them" and she treats him with disdain.[83] Yet Whitman, I will suggest, productively troubles the Vassar graduate famous for her reticence as she attends both to the crude outlines of his (perceived) claims and their nuances. In 1956, when Bishop won the Pulitzer Prize for her recently published *Poems: North & South—A Cold Spring*, "Whitman" offers Bishop a point of departure for a multifaceted satire on the sexual politics of the male-dominated American public sphere. This story opens up larger questions of influence which are relevant to Bishop's reading practices and choices of (North) American traditions.

"The U.S.A. School of Writing" deftly theorizes an American idiom. Published posthumously (*New Yorker*, 1983), it begins,

> When I was graduated from Vassar in 1934, during the Great Depression, jobs were still hard to find and very badly paid. Perhaps for those very reasons it seemed incumbent on me and many of my classmates to find them, whether we had to or not. The spirit of the times and, of course, of my college class was radical; we were puritanically pink. Perhaps there seemed to be something virtuous in working for much less a year than our educations had been costing our families. It was a combination of this motive, real need for a little more money than I had, idle curiosity, and, I'm afraid, pure masochism that led me to answer an advertisement in the Sunday *Times* and take a job. It was with a correspondence school, the U.S.A. School of Writing.

What follows is a shrewd and hilarious account of the commercialization of the American spirit. In the tawdry, fourth-floor, walk-up offices "of an old tumble-down building near Columbus Circle," the idealistic Vassar graduate, a young woman of slender but independent means, memorably encounters Mr. Black, the school's president, who explains that "the U.S.A. School of Writing stood for 'The United States of America School of Writing.'" With her impeccable credentials, she is hired on the spot, and in addition to the typists, there is only one other employee, "Mr. Hearn," who turns out to be "a tall, very heavy, handsome woman, about thirty years old, named Rachel, with black horn-rimmed glasses, and a black mole on one cheek." Sharing an office with the chain-smoking "Hearn"/Rachel turns out be an *experience*, in part because of her aggressive efforts to get the reluctant Bishop to join the Communist Party.

Eating lunch with Rachel in a cafeteria where she orders three sandwiches ("lox and cream cheese on a bun, corned beef and pickle relish on rye, pastrami and mustard on something-or-other") turns out to be an "experience" too: "She *shouted* her order. It didn't matter much, I found, after a few days of trying to state my three terms loudly and clearly; the sandwiches all tasted alike. I began settling for large, quite unreal baked apples and coffee. Rachel, with her three sandwiches and three cups of black coffee simultaneously, and I would seat ourselves in our wet raincoats and galoshes, our lunches overlapping between us, and she would harangue me about literature." So the scene is now set. Rachel is a sincere, affable, exploited, somewhat manic woman. Her private life is minimal, her love life apparently nonexistent. Marginalized herself, she sympathizes with outcasts, including such outcasts as Bishop, the disdainful observer who forms part of the lonely hearts crowd. Rachel has predictably meretricious, left-wing literary tastes, and all the authors she admires are men, but she has her unpredictable human side too. "She never attempted politics at lunch," Bishop explains, "I don't know why." And then: "She had read a lot and had what I, the English major, condescendingly considered rather pathetic taste. She liked big books, with lots of ego and emotion in them, and Whitman was her favorite poet."[84]

In version one of at least four drafts, Rachel "had a sort of half-baked taste, she had read quite a lot and tried rather pathetically to be high-brow—she liked 'big' books, with lots of emotion—Whitman was of course her favorite poet." In version two, emotion is more closely associated with ego, and this is the version that stuck. Now it would be easy to suggest that as a woman poet, Bishop is mocking Whitman as the author of big and sexist books. The antiheroine Rachel can be read as a cartoon Communist who admires Whitman, himself a cartoon poet associated with "dated and unpleasant" things. Yet both the drafts and the published version of the story implicate Whitman in an oblique and unfinished conversation about gender performativity and its relationship to "Modern Love." Fulfilling her duties under the name of her predecessor "Mr. Margolies," the crossdressing Bishop persona engages in a covert flirtation with the aggressively leftist "Mr.

Hearn." While both female employees (Bishop and Rachel) adopt male pseudonyms for the sake of literary authority, the narrator's true politics, including her true gender politics, remain elusive.[85]

The figure of Whitman is thus ambiguously deployed. On the one hand, he is associated with a crude social realism that effectively mystifies power relations in the literary marketplace. On the other, he is associated with a woman who is "the entire brains of the place."[86] Although the so-called students specialize in "True Confessions," Bishop's confession never comes. Rachel is an object of desire, while the figure of Whitman serves to link women and to ensure that never the twain shall meet. Official and unofficial literary networks impede same-sex love. As represented by Bishop, sometimes Rachel is handsome, poignant, and touchingly earnest. Other times she is unbearable.

When Bishop submitted the story to the *New Yorker* in 1956, she stated tentatively, "I don't know whether you'll be able to use this true, but awfully simple, autobiographical sketch or not . . . Perhaps it should be called '*Rachel & The U.S.A. School of Writing*' since it is divided evenly between the two" (Bishop's ellipses). Rejecting the piece, *New Yorker* editor Katharine White explained,

I'm terribly sorry to have to report that the decision went against "The U.S.A. School of Writing." The vote was mixed, and the piece seemed to arouse two quite opposite sets of opinions among the four editors who read it. The deciding one was [William] Shawn's, of course, and he felt that both this kind of correspondence writing school and the character of Rachel were familiar as subject matter. Another point made against the piece was that, in a way, it broke in two between the school and Rachel, about half the piece being devoted to each. One trouble I myself found, although I was entertained throughout, was that from the way you wrote the piece, one could not be quite sure how much was fact and how much fiction, but this I felt you could clarify. Perhaps you intend it as a short story, but if it is all true, as you said in your letter, I think you could make this plain to your reader, and that the piece would gain by it. Indeed, what I had hoped was that, if treated as fact, the story might make an "Onward and Upward with the Arts" piece for us, but Bill Shawn didn't agree. He felt it needed more humor for that and less

familiar material. Anyway, none of us thinks it works as fiction, so
the answer has to be a regretful no. I'm terribly sorry.

Bishop responded graciously, "Please don't feel badly about the U. S. School
of Writing!—I had a feeling it wouldn't do, but it was something I wanted
to get down. Maybe sometime I'll do it over again, at greater length, I think,
and 'make something of it.'" Sometime never came.[87]

In "The U.S.A. School" Whitman is associated with male tradition and
with problematic sexual, ethnic, ethical, and class signifiers. As described in
this pseudo-memoir, he impedes the formation of same-sex bonds between
women, as does the narrator's self-effacing irony. In the same year that
Bishop tried to publish this generically indeterminate work—was it fact or
fiction or both?—an interviewer recorded that "just as Gide preferred Victor
Hugo, Elizabeth Bishop singles out Walt Whitman among contemporary
poets." And when interviewed in Brazil in 1970, Bishop identified Walt
Whitman as the greatest North American poet, but she added, à la Gide on
Victor Hugo, "alas."[88] Given her anxieties about herself as a public person,
together with her deep suspicion of abstractions, Bishop produced no essay,
no review, no seasoned meditation on American literary politics and poetics.
She tried but couldn't bring it off. Absent such works, "The U.S.A. School
of Writing" helps us to understand her mid-career attitudes toward the
U. S.'s most thoroughly canonical poet, while the generic instability to which
the New Yorker objected now seems, in the wake of poststructuralist critique,
a particular strength.

As is well known, Bishop's early childhood was disrupted by her father's
untimely death, by her mother's nervous breakdown, and by the loss of Great
Village, the Nova Scotia home of her mother's family. Displaced to Massachusetts, first to Worcester and then to Revere, a working-class suburb of
Boston, she emerged as a dreamy, moody, and anxious child, fearful of making mistakes and overeager to please. This virtual orphan was not without
either material or emotional resources, and at eight, she began writing poetry;
at twelve, she won an American Legion prize for an essay anticipating her
subsequent fascination with geography and travel. Beginning with a line like
"From the icy regions of the frozen north to the waving palm trees of the
burning south," this lost essay on Americanness apparently had vista, and
Bishop returned to the subject of Americanness, American poetics, and love
American style intermittently throughout her career.[89] If Whitman offered
one point of entry to this large theme and Dickinson another, Whitman

seems to have been the more constant influence, if for no other reason than that he could displace Dickinson as a precursor. Likening influence to friendship, Gertrude Stein once observed, "Friendship goes by favour. There is always danger of a break or of a stronger power coming in between. Influence can only be a steady march when one can surely never break away."[90] For Bishop, there was no steady march with Dickinson.

Bishop probably owned a copy of Dickinson in her youth, but archives are incomplete and that copy has disappeared. Her 1926 "Variorum" of *Leaves of Grass* has been carefully preserved in the Elizabeth Bishop Collection of Houghton Library, Harvard University. This *Leaves of Grass*, whose flyleaf contains a girlish signature, was probably acquired when she was fifteen and unashamedly loving Whitman. It has many red pencil markings. (Other books by Bishop in the Houghton collection are marked very lightly if at all, and I don't believe she had the nerve to mark up in her teens.) "1934" is written in the margin of Whitman's 1855 prose "Preface," in a paragraph beginning "The Americans of all nations at any time upon the earth have probably the fullest poetical nature." Thus the red pencil markings probably date from 1934, for Bishop a pivotal and empowering year in more ways than one.[91] Not only did she graduate from Vassar but she also met Marianne Moore, who encouraged her to try to establish a full-fledged writerly career. Having edited her college yearbook and published poems, stories, reviews, and essays mainly in high school or college venues, Bishop was trying to reach a broader audience. Engaging more deeply with Whitman in 1934 was part of this project. In trying to break out of her limited, elite circle, Bishop was responding obliquely to his expansive (and yet egocentric) call to poets to come. "Arouse!" he wrote in one of the epigraphs to his big book, "for you must justify me."[92]

Bishop's deeply sedimented imagination of Whitman was full of odd twists and turns and creative ambivalences that were never fully resolved, corresponding in that regard to her love life, which she famously identified with "the art of losing." As we know from biographers Brett C. Millier, Gary Fountain, and Peter Brazeau, Bishop had at least eight significant relationships with women lovers, among them Louise Crane, Marjorie Carr Stevens, Lota de Macedo Soares, Lilli Correia de Araújo, "Suzanne Bowen," Linda Nemer, and Alice Methfessel, whose potential loss inspired the villanelle "One Art." Although she considered herself a feminist, Bishop was not overtly political, distrusted sexual exhibitionism whether homo or hetero, and took Whitman to task for it. Thus in writing to her friends Frani Blough

Muser and Margaret Miller in 1938—Bishop had been in love with Margaret and perhaps still was—she used Whitman as a whipping boy along the following lines: "I'm reading Emma Goldman . . . and have just about decided to sign up with the Anarchists—or jump in with them, I think, is a nicer way of putting it. Why not join me? It's marvelous—all you have to do, apparently, is read Emerson's *Essays*, Whitman, and other equally dated and unpleasant works, and advocate 'free love.' "[93] This anti-Whitman rhetoric persists in "The U.S.A. School of Writing," but as a teenager, the books in which Bishop immersed herself included *Leaves of Grass*. "When I was thirteen," she explained, "I discovered Whitman, and that was important to me at the time."[94] Or the recollected chronology could be altered. "I've never studied 'Imagism' or 'Transcendentalism' or any isms consciously," she wrote to her first biographer Anne Stevenson, "I just read all the poetry that came my way, old, new. At fifteen I loved Whitman."[95] Over the course of years and in her poems, notebooks, and marginalia, a series of Whitmans emerge, but her copy of *Leaves of Grass* has no markings in the *Calamus* sequence or in *Children of Adam* or even in "Song of Myself." In fact, among poems, she waited until page 211 before marking a line in "Out of the Cradle Endlessly Rocking," her pencil underlining *Translating*, as in "Cautiously peering, absorbing, *translating*."

Contrary to what we might expect, she pays particular attention to the 1855 prose "Preface," her pencil coming alive when she reads that "the Americans of all nations at any time upon the earth have probably the fullest poetical nature." And she liked "Here is not merely a nation but a teeming nation of nations. Here is action untied from strings necessarily blind to particulars and details magnificently moving in vast masses." She was excited by paragraph 20's reference to the "precise object" that "exhibits a beauty." Bishop's 1934 Whitman is an imagist and a theorist of poetic value, but he is not the poet of the body extolling himself or one who reconfigures lyric to accommodate same-sex love.[96] It's hard to believe that with her interest in water, Bishop's pencil skipped over "Crossing Brooklyn Ferry" but it did, marking instead "As I Ebb'd with the Ocean of Life," in which the speaker recovers from a life-threatening depression issuing from his failures as a poet. (He has unfinished business with his father and mother too.)

Further, in 1934 Bishop liked Whitman's vaguely symbolic flags and tried for many years to write a poem sequence called "Flags and Banners," which seems unlikely for her. A cryptic entry in one of her early notebooks reveals that she associates flags and banners not only with "American themes" but also with motion and dreams, and it seems that Bishop found in flags and banners a potential erotic code. "FLAGS AND BANNERS," "FLAGS AND BANNERS," "FLAGS AND BANNERS," she writes in emphatic capital letters, and then, after several lines appears, clearly, the word "Whitman," followed by these quotations: "Running up out of the night, bringing your cluster of stars, (ever-enlarging stars,)" and "Delicate cluster! flag of teeming life! / Covering all my lands—all my seashores lining!" The first is from "Song of the Banner at Daybreak," one of the poems that Bishop singled out in the Holloway edition. It's an unusual poem for Whitman, a verse drama in which five speaking roles are assigned, to "Poet," "Pennant," "Child," "Father," "Banner and Pennant." The second poem, "Delicate Cluster," is only eight lines long:

> Delicate cluster! flag of teeming life!
> Covering all my lands—all my seashores lining!
> Flag of death! (how I watch'd you through the smoke of battle pressing!
> How I heard you flap and rustle, cloth defiant!)
> Flag cerulean—sunny flag, with the orbs of night dappled!
> Ah my silvery beauty—ah my woolly white and crimson!
> Ah to sing the song of you, my matron mighty!
> My sacred one, my mother.[97]

Ironically, the vaguely symbolic Whitmanian flag can become an emblem of disguise. It is a thoroughly public object, which the visionary (or demonic) poet can transform into a secret and private possession. It has a history both sacred and obscene, and resembles a person, "woolly white and crimson," venerable and embarrassed. Like Edgar Allan Poe's purloined letter, it hides in public, covering—and that's the question. What song of love and death does it defiantly cover? In 1934, the year in which Bishop's mother died, she seems to have been looking for images of family and nation with which to refresh her soul; poems such as these provided some comfort. In defining herself against a male-dominated contemporary landscape of writing, Bishop could locate in Whitman's undertones a sexually indeterminate or androgynous mother.

In addressing poets to come, Whitman described himself as a man who "sauntering along without fully stopping, / turns a casual look upon you and then averts his face, / Leaving it to you to prove and define it, / Expecting the main things from you." The "averts his face" part turns out to be important.[98] Bishop's reconstructed "Whitman" provided her with a lesson in erotic coding, while her annotations in *Leaves of Grass*, together with her early notebooks, underscore her genius for binding disparate images together. Objects, she knew, can seem to embody both ideas (such as the idea of patriotism) and feelings (such as the feeling of being stifled). Bishop reads flags as "things, folded—to be flung and breathing—the fish's gills."[99] And in "Faces," she checked the lines "This face is a haze more chill than the arctic sea, / Its sleeping and wobbling icebergs crunch as they go." Given her own fascination with chilly climes and "breathing plain[s] of snow," it is not surprising that Bishop found in Whitman's iceberg[s] an arresting image. Less predictably, she underscored "Out of this face emerge banners and horses," finding in Whitman's exuberance an effective South to her North but passing up the more obvious image: "This face is flavor'd fruit ready for eating."[100] Like Dickinson's bachelor who disavows cuisine, Bishop encountered surprising resistances in herself to unabashed "eating."

Dreams were her forte. In dreams, she could loaf and invite her soul. Inloop'd desires deferred by day could flower at night, as flags took on uncanny, polyvocal, symbolic significance. Flags and sweet flags: although there is not a single mark in the "Calamus" section of Bishop's *Leaves*, the connection between flag and sweet flag (the latter Whitman's phallic symbol) may not have been lost on her. George Washington, Susan Warner, Edgar Allan Poe: these are some of the people who figure in her projected, polysexual sequence on American themes, in which Whitman is the "parent leaf." "Name it 'friendship if you want to," she writes, in an almost illegible scrawl, "like names of cities printed on maps the word is much too big, it . . . tells nothing of the actual *place* it means to name." Extending these ideas, Bishop drafted "The Map," in which the sea is "unperturbed" (a Whitmanian word), the theme of friendship is approached obliquely, and "emotion too far exceeds its cause." As if to conclude this subtle colloquy with herself, in which so much is lightly touched on and yet inaccessible, her speaker asks, "Are they assigned, or can the countries pick their colors?"[101] Bishop continued to debate this issue of representation and self-representation in all of her subsequent books, while Whitman helped her to translate a language of patriotic and "manly love" into a more cosmopolitan mode. Flags, flowers, water, and dreams—they ran together like countries in her mind.

In the "U.S.A. School of Writing," Whitman is associated with a problematic male tradition, while in poems, notebooks, and marginalia, another

Figure 29. Lota de Macedo Soares, who called Bishop "Cookie" and provided all the comforts of home. Courtesy Archives and Special Collections, Vassar College Libraries. Ref. #6.281. Folder 100.6.

Whitman emerges: someone whose intense interest in the "precise object" matches her own: "Name it 'friendship' if you want to." "Under a sky of gorgeous, under-lit clouds," Bishop writes in "Santarém," the lovely pastoral sights an oblique homage to "Crossing Brooklyn Ferry," "everything [was] gilded, burnished along one side, / and everything bright, cheerful, casual—or so it looked." When these fleeting impressions suffice, the speaker's memories are suspended and her self-doubts dissolved. Bishop's poem wards off disaster on a golden evening but concludes ironically with a line attributed to a fellow passenger on her river voyage, a Dutch businessman who asks, after seeing an exquisite wasps' nest, "What's that ugly thing?" Revaluing the overlooked, Bishop's feminism resists such shorebound judgments.

Using One's Life as Material

As we have seen, Bishop's friendships were strained by competing claims. For example, when Robert Lowell included desperate letters from his ex-wife Elizabeth Hardwick in his sonnet sequence *The Dolphin*, Bishop wrote him a ten-page letter in which she protested, "One can use one's life as material—one does, anyway—but these letters—aren't you violating a trust? IF you were given permission—IF you hadn't changed them . . . etc. But *art just isn't worth that much.*" The issue for Bishop is not whether or not to use one's life as material but how to do it, and her friendship with Lowell heightened her awareness of the danger of his method. Reading Lowell with her deep knowledge of his personal situation, Bishop found herself needing to confront him, which was not her usual mode, especially with him. The letter was "hell to write," and after an interval she went on to ask his advice about her Harvard salary, concluding, "Forgive my sordidness (as Marianne would call it)."[102] Lowell responded by thanking her for her very specific, line-by-line comments, before justifying his use of Hardwick's letters—he knew that Hardwick would be upset, but he thought that the sequence showed her in a good light.[103]

This episode raises the more general problem not only of writing about one's life but of reading to recuperate a "real" self. Reading Whitman, Bishop does not comment on his life as she does on Dickinson's, nor does her extant library suggest an interest in his letters. One looks in vain for Gay Wilson Allen's *The Solitary Singer: A Critical Biography of Walt Whitman*, which was published in 1955 when Bishop was thinking seriously about national identity and which quickly emerged as a classic of its kind. Reading Dickinson, Bishop turned to letters and biographies for context and to Richard Sewall's *The Life of Emily Dickinson*, which she may have considered for review. Inside the front cover of volume 1, she wrote, "Elizabeth Bishop Boston, 1974 (asked from F., S., & G) [Farrar, Straus, and Giroux]." Bishop's marks show that

Figure 30. Elizabeth Bishop and Robert Lowell on the beach at Rio, July 1962. Courtesy Archives and Special Colleges, Vassar College Libraries. Ref. #6.61. Folder 100.11.

she was interested in something the poet's brother said about old fogies and religion; in David Todd and Austin and Mabel; in the "specifics" of "Austin's wretched domestic life"; in the "specifics" behind Dickinson's poems of loss and rejection; in the "specifics" of Dickinson's disappointment in Sue, "a youthful affinity that came to nothing"; and so on. But reading biographically for a "real" self did not assuage Bishop's doubts about the poet's insularity. Sewall, who demonstrated that Emily Dickinson did not "write in total isolation, shut off from the world, meditating among her flowers," explained, "Of few poets could the claim be made more confidently that her life was her work."[104] That was not enough for Bishop, who never believed that Dickinson wrote in total isolation but who continued to believe that Dickinson was a self-caged bird, like Gerard Manley Hopkins, who succeeded in surviving on little but whose muse was "a rusty nail dropped in the cup or saucer," which apparently contained "stale green(?) water." Evidently this is not an appealing diet. The sinker is Bishop's exclamation, "How they complained!" It is as if she had looked into the bottom of Dickinson's deep wells of thought and found nothing but debris.

From Bishop's perspective, Dickinson, however sincere and self-sustaining, proved troublesome for her lack of "common experience." In 1978, after an evening reading at Bennington College, Bishop got together for breakfast with a student reporter who quoted an interview in which she said, "Sometimes I think if I had been born a man I probably would have written more. Dared more." Responding to the reporter's follow-up question, "Do you feel that there is something in a woman's perception of life as an observer that makes her poetry different from a man's?" Bishop stated,

> Women's experiences are much more limited, but that does not
> really matter—there is Emily Dickinson, as one always says. You just
> have to make do with what you have after all.
>
> It depends on one's temperament I suppose. Some women cer-
> tainly can write like Emily Dickinson, the kind of poetry with no
> common experience to speak of at all.[105]

Bishop went on to describe some women as needing to get out and climb Mt. Everest, which is hardly an example of the ordinary, daily life Bishop had hoped to find more of in Dickinson's letters and in her poetry.

It appears, then, that Dickinson offered no example of the usual hero-isms with which most of us who are not Mt. Everest climbers have to content ourselves, and I have been suggesting that Bishop's Whitmans begin to fill that gap. To be more precise, Bishop's Whitmans fill it more than Dickinson does, even if a fairer assessment of Dickinson would show her as an Everest climber on what Adrienne Rich describes as "her own premises." To take but a single example, in which Dickinson leads another woman on a metaphoric climbing expedition:

> I showed her Hights she never saw —
> "Would'st Climb," I said?
> She said — "Not so" —
> "With *me* —" I said — With *me*?
> I showed her Secrets — Morning's Nest —
> The Rope the Nights were put across —

And *now* — "Would'st have me for a Guest?"
She could not find her Yes —
And then, I brake my life — And Lo,
A Light, for her, did solemn glow,
The larger, as her face withdrew —
And *could* she, further, "No"?[106]

Reading Dickinson in that "good new edition" which made her more palatable, Bishop would have discovered that the poem was written in about 1862, as was its mate, that Dickinson sent the "She" version to her friend Sue, and that she placed a "He" copy in a packet.

Despite an obvious point of contact between Bishop and Dickinson on the subject of gender subversion and lesbian desire, at Bennington, Bishop reinvoked the grating "teeth on edge" phrase of her pre-Brazil, "Love from Emily" review. Although Dickinson's stock had soared since that time, and Sewall's biography had demystified some issues and presented the "specifics" of others, Bishop's identificatory anxieties prevailed. What if Dickinson's "premises," to quote Rich again, were too idiosyncratic? Surely Whitman was not Everyman, yet there is a wonderful moment in Bishop's correspondence with Frank Bidart in which she writes, "Think young. . . . It's our only hope!!", signing herself "Walt Whitman."[107] Bidart was in his thirties, Bishop in her sixties, and Whitman was known to favor young men. When I repeated this anecdote to a gay friend, he asked, "Does this mean that if she were Walt Whitman she would be in love with him [Bidart]?" It's a good question.

Although Bishop was consistently committed to her belief that Dickinson lacked "common experience" and survived on a meager diet, after the publication of the Johnson edition, she tried to soften her condescending attitude and does so in a 1956 letter to Lowell that ranges from seriousness to humor: "Did I really make snide remarks about Emily Dickinson? I like, or at least admire, her a great deal more now—probably because of that good new edition, really. I spent another stretch absorbed in that, and think (along with Randall) [Jarrell] that she's about the best we have. However—she does set one's teeth on edge a lot of the time, don't you think? 'Woman' poet—no, what I like to be called now is *poetress* . . . I think it's a nice mixture of poet and mistress."[108] Bishop's "We" is a community of knowledge grounded both in common experience and in its ability to revalue the previously overlooked. But is she referring to Americans, women poets, herself and Lowell and their circle, or to a more visionary company of kindred spirits? And what if the best "We" have is none too good?

By aligning herself with Randall Jarrell, Bishop was siding with one of the most widely respected critics of the mid-twentieth century. He was a close friend of Lowell's, and Jarrell's community of greats included Bishop, whose poetry he praised for being "quiet, truthful, sad, funny, [and] most marvelously individual." Dickinson was more extreme: "Her poetry is the diary or autobiography—though few diaries or autobiographies compare with it for intentional and, especially, unintentional truth—of an acute psychologist, a wonderful rhetorician, and one of the most individual writers who ever lived, one of those best able to express experience at its most nearly absolute."[109] Unlike Jarrell, Bishop was not interested in learning "all there is to know about one woman." She was not really drawn to Dickinson the acute psychologist. Her marks in Johnson replicate her reading history: it takes her a long time to warm up, to the extent that she ever does, and there are no check marks in volume 1, while the first poem marked in volume 2, the off-key elegy "If you were coming in the Fall," is hardly a poem of psychological extremism.

Considering Bishop's objections to Dickinson's awful-but-not-cheerful mode, we can read "If you were coming" through her eyes as comparatively good humored, even lighthearted:

> If you were coming in the Fall,
> I'd brush the Summer by
> With half a smile, and half a spurn,
> As Housewives do, A Fly.
>
> If I could see you in a year,
> I'd wind the months in balls —
> And put them each in separate Drawers,
> For fear the numbers fuse —
>
> If only Centuries, delayed,
> I'd count them on my Hand,
> Subtracting, till my fingers dropped
> Into Van Dieman's Land.
>
> If certain, when this life was out —
> That yours and mine, should be

I'd toss it yonder, like a Rind,
And take Eternity —

But, now, uncertain of the length
Of this, that is between,
It goads me, like the Goblin Bee —
That will not state — its sting.[110]

Reading Dickinson through Bishop, we find a speaker who teases us (as life teases her) with the idea that she can master disaster (the loss of You) by representing her frustration as finite. She leaves us by calling such faith into question when an irrational X factor—the Goblin Bee, or nature, which won't cooperate or yield to literary language—intrudes on her fantasy. Because nature or the nature of the beloved will not speak to her, the poem ends with a barb that reduces her to silence. "It" will not state its sting and she has nothing more to say.

"Now I knew I lost her," the last poem Bishop marked in her copy of Johnson's volume 2, also plays on the theme of the beloved's inaccessibility. The situation is graver:

Now I knew I lost her —
Not that she was gone —
But Remoteness travelled
On her Face and Tongue.

Alien, though adjoining
As a Foreign Race —
Traversed she though pausing
Latitudeless Place.

Elements Unaltered —
Universe the same
But Love's transmigration —
Somehow this had come —

Henceforth to remember
Nature took the Day
I had paid so much for —

> His is Penury
> Not who toils for Freedom
> Or for Family
> But [for] the Restitution
> Of Idolatry.[111]

Robbed by "Nature" and unable to explain "Love's transmigration" to herself, Dickinson attempts to achieve a broader perspective on any worthless sacrifice. The poem opens strongly by contrasting physical presence and emotional remoteness, but the speaker is unable to account for the neglect she suffers, and her "I" is virtually extinguished after the confession, "Somehow this had come." Read through Bishop, the poem arouses our suspicion that Dickinson was an overdemanding friend, though she portrays herself as a constant woman in an inconstant world. Read through Dickinson, the poem anticipates Bishop's love of travel and ability to withdraw into herself in social situations she finds threatening. For both poets, writing becomes a solution to the problem of love's migration—it makes them feel less alone—and both suggest that under the wrong circumstances, writing it will not right it. Dickinson explains that working for personal or collective freedom or to support a family may pay off, whereas love, which she compares to idolatry, can never be recovered. With this conclusion, Dickinson almost admits that she no longer wants to recapture a past in which she had unrealistic expectations of her all-too-human friend.

Other Dickinson poems and letters organized by female friendships and the hope and fears and regrets they generate anticipate elements both of Bishop's life story and of her oeuvre. For example, "The last Night that She lived" creates a context for thinking about Lota, Bishop's beloved and funny companion, who ended up a mere shadow of her former self and unable to go on. Her death changed Bishop's life and poetry forever, as Dickinson's poem might have predicted. Like Bishop, Dickinson notices smallest things:

> The last Night that She lived
> It was a Common Night
> Except the Dying — this to Us
> Made Nature different
>
> We noticed smallest things —
> Things overlooked before

By this great light upon our Minds
Italicized — as 'twere.

As We went out and in
Between Her final Room
And Rooms where Those to be alive
Tomorrow were, a Blame

That Others could exist
While She must finish quite
A Jealousy for Her arose
So nearly infinite —

We waited while She passed —
It was a narrow time —
Too jostled were Our Souls to speak
At length the notice came.

She mentioned, and forgot —
Then lightly as a Reed
Bent to the Water, struggled scarce —
Consented, and was dead —

And We — We placed the Hair —
And drew the Head erect —
And then an awful leisure was
Belief to regulate —[112]

"The last Night that She lived" also creates a context for memorializing
Bishop's mother Gertrude, whose death in 1934 was barely mentioned by
Bishop at the time. Yet in a notebook Bishop kept that summer, when she
was vacationing on Cuttyhunk Island off the Massachusetts coast, she
observed, "A poem should be made about making things in a pinch—& how
it looks sad when the emergency is over." "The idea of making things do—of
using things in unthought of ways because it's necessary—has a lot more to
it. It is an island feeling certainly." And then from Dickinson, slightly mis-
quoted, "We play with paste till qualified for pearl—." Bishop continued, by
way of illustrating her concern with island feelings, "The awful tears a man

must shed when he carves his house with a jackknife. Using oleomargarine during the War. Doing it deliberately [is] different from accepting it is *all* that way. (You aren't really denying yourself much—no matter what you deny yourself)."[113]

Bishop doesn't sound fully convinced that self-denial is a worthy artistic goal, and her comment seems to endorse self-mutilation as an act of minor heroism. Recollected in comparative tranquillity, to carve one's body (house) with a knife is sad. Yet during the emergency, self-mutilation is better than being carved up by someone else or by a nameless fate. Or experiencing oneself as a castrated man. As she explains in "Crusoe in England,"

> The knife there on the shelf—
> it reeked of meaning, like a crucifix.
> It lived. How many years did I
> beg it, implore it, not to break?
> I knew each nick and scratch by heart,
> the bluish blade, the broken tip,
> the lines of wood-grain on the handle . . .
> Now it won't look at me at all.
> The living soul has dribbled away.
> My eyes rest on it and pass on. (*Poems* 156)

Understandably, Bishop's most consistent desire is to take command of herself as a person and as a poet, to qualify in both roles for "pearl," or excellence. Playing with "paste," with unreal things and feelings, is fine during one's youth, but who would be a girlish "fool" forever?

> We play at Paste —
> Till qualified, for Pearl —
> Then, drop the Paste —
> And deem ourself a fool —
>
> The Shapes — though — were similar —
> And our new Hands
> Learned *Gem*-Tactics —
> Practicing *Sands* —[114]

The specter of foolishness continued to haunt Bishop, who never fully exorcised the condescending stranger within. Summing up her response to the communal energies of Second Wave feminism, she explained in 1974, "Now people think I'm being an elitist. But I like my anthologies, all the arts, mixed: sexes, colors and races. Art is art and should have nothing to do with gender." Further: "It takes probably hundreds of things coming together at the right moment to make a poem and no one can ever really separate them out and say this did this, that did that." And: "Most of my writing life I've been lucky about reviews. But at the very end they often say 'The best poetry by a woman in this decade, or year, or month.' Well, what's the worth?"[115]

Even during the period of her fullest "heart's release," the comparatively relaxed flourish years of her romance with Lota, Bishop's anxieties about gender sorting persisted. One sees this in her poem "Exchanging Hats," which satirizes queerness. It appeared in the April issue of *New World Writing*, the literary magazine described as "ugly" in Frank O'Hara's elegy, "The Day Lady Died."[116] In Bishop's send-up of traditional gender roles, the men are feminized and the women masculinized.

> Unfunny uncles who insist
> in trying on a lady's hat,
> —oh, even if the joke falls flat,
> we share your slight transvestite twist
>
> in spite of our embarrassment.
> Costume and custom are complex.
> The headgear of the other sex
> inspires us to experiment.
>
> Anandrous aunts, who, at the beach
> with paper plates upon your laps,
> keep putting on the yachtsmen's caps
> with exhibitionistic screech,
>
> the visors hanging o'er the ear
> so that the golden anchors drag,
> —the tides of fashion never lag.
> Such caps may not be worn next year. (*Poems* 198–99)

While "Exchanging Hats" opens a space to subvert the socialized real ("custom and costume"), its arch tone (a "slight transvestite twist") is threatened by "exhibitionistic screech." Wanting to suggest that gender fashions, like hats, can be donned and doffed at will, the poet finds herself "drag[ged]" down by the "perversities" of the new.

> Or you who don the paper plate
> itself, and put some grapes upon it,
> or sport the Indian's feather bonnet,
> —perversities may aggravate
>
> the natural madness of the hatter.
> And if the opera hats collapse
> and crowns grow draughty, then, perhaps,
> he thinks what might a miter matter?

Changing fashions "may not be worn next year"; they can be discarded as easily as yachtsmen's caps, or paper plates, or an Indian's feathered bonnet. "Exchanging" evokes a selfish scenario in which people, too, can be discarded at will. Bishop never reprinted it, and in that sense the poem itself becomes a disposable text or object. It takes pleasure in sounds, such as "Anandrous aunts" and "what might a miter matter." As the sounds begin to talk to each other, and as the speed of this self-talking intensifies, the dream of a common context collapses. Miters, symbols of clerical authority, no longer prevail, and unless I am growing antic, Bishop is punning on her family name, which no longer either joins her to a larger community or restrains her. To wear a hat or not to wear a hat: that is the question.

As a child, Bishop herself had been treated as a disposable object when she was abruptly taken from Canada to the United States by her wealthy paternal relatives. Having been forced to exchange one family for another, she tended to idealize the security and simplicity of Great Village, her first home. "Exchanging Hats," however, alludes obliquely to a destructive battle of the sexes which threatened to rip her home apart. It draws on hostile memories of "Aunt Hat," the wife of her infinitely more appealing and pathetic uncle Neddy. In real life, "Neddy" was her mother's brother Arthur Boomer, a tinsmith who loved children, whose passion was fly fishing and whose drunken dissipation represented "the devil of weakness." As described by Bishop in a late prose memoir, he and "Hat," his chronically enraged wife, are a hellish couple: "If Uncle Neddy was a 'devil,' a feeble, smokey-black one, Aunt Hat was a red, real one—redheaded, freckled, red-knuckled, strong, all fierce fire and flame. There *was* something of the Old Nick about her. They complemented each other; they were devils together." It follows that "Aunt Hat had 'no luck' with plants; in fact, nothing would grow for her at all." Similarly, the "avernal" or hellish aunt in "Exchanging Hats" is "anandrous" and unmaternal.[117] She is nevertheless privy to a mysterious, occluded vision the poem's "I" is eager to share. As her poem seeks an ending, Bishop turns the joke to advantage, writing, "Aunt exemplary and slim, / with avernal eyes, we wonder / what slow changes they see under / their vast, shady, turned-down brim." This shady lady is not unalluring.

Liking her anthologies, sexes, and races mixed, Bishop also insisted defensively that "art is art, and should have nothing to do with gender." Gender, as she understood it, was all too often an isolating category of analysis that overemphasized the difference between people. Even while writing to feel less alone, she could not ignore that difference. Like Dickinson's, her project was shaped in part by conflicts between personal and cultural narratives of gender and by other conflicts as well. At the end of her posthumously published memoir "The Country Mouse," a child narrator poses the question, "*Why* was I a human being?"[118] This question generalizes the gender anxiety she voices in signature works such as "In the Waiting Room," in which she reminds herself, "you are an *I*, / you are an *Elizabeth*, / you are one of *them*. / *Why* should you be one, too?" (*Poems* 150). It remains suspended in her poetry, in her prose, and in her life project, as in Dickinson's, with whom she had more in common than she cared to acknowledge. Apologizing for her neediness, Dickinson once wrote, "My friends are my 'estate.' Forgive me then the avarice to hoard them!" (*L* 193). Dispossessed of family, Bishop understood the urgency of the plea.

To the extent that the U.S.A. Schools of Writing represent gendered social compulsion, Bishop flees. To the extent that they represent cross-gender compassion, she longs for a space in which she can breathe freely, drink modestly, and write encouraging letters to hapless students such as Jimmy O'Shea—a brilliantly conceived character whom she recycles from an earlier story. In "The U.S.A. School of Writing," the semiliterate Jimmy functions as a sentimental object. It is fitting that an abject letter from him "which expressed the common feeling of time passing and wasted, of wonder and envy" causes her to quit her job. In the utopian future I imagine for the Bishop who is no longer herself an object of compassion, she sets up a small printing press and Mr. Jimmy O'Shea—after how many years?—finds that there is life after seventy. After seventy, he becomes an author! As he wrote so many years earlier in his pathetically inept way, "I know there is a big field in this art."[119] Little does poor Jimmy know that the press has a double mission. Part of it, the money-making part, is devoted to the publication of boring books. Mr. James O'Shea of Fall River, retired, forms part of their list. Enriched by the profits from Jimmy's "long stories of 60,000 or 100,000 words," Bishop & Company also publishes poets speaking from what Dickinson called "many and reportless places" (*Fr* 1404). In this imaginary U.S.A. School of Writing, theoretical antagonisms such as "life/death, right/wrong, male/female" no longer signify. In this utopian community of sorrow and love, Elizabeth Bishop reclaims her mother's watch, reads Dickinson less anxiously, and finds her lucky voice.

Dickinson and the Demands of Difference

Who was Emily Dickinson? In the preceding pages, I have described how some of her most deeply inventive readers interpreted the demands of a poetry that arouses curiosities it refuses to satisfy. Who was Emily Dickinson? She, too, wondered. In this book, I describe attempts to normalize a poet who refuses to be normalized. My opening chapters show that her nineteenth-century reception was organized by a strongly gendered debate about the seeming irregularity of her prosodic forms and the seeming illogic of her life. We know that Dickinson anticipated this debate and to some degree shaped it before history escaped her control, opening the texts she left in varying degrees of completion to public view. Such is the irony of her reclusion, a subject that inspired gossip in her lifetime. Her contemporaries did not think of her as normal.

Perhaps because of her vivid imagination of competing models of authorship, Dickinson uses the word "normal" exactly once, to tell a story of heroism thwarted.[1] In lines written in pencil when she was about forty, she was reflecting on the gap between her ambition and her achievement. Taking up the very American theme of the unlived life, she feared that her most productive working days were over. The manuscript has an alternative word for "normal." It is "daily":

> We never know how high we are
> Till we are asked to rise
> And then if we are true to plan
> Our statures touch the skies –

> The Heroism we recite
> Would be a normal thing
> Did not ourselves the Cubits warp
> For fear to be a King – (*Fr* 1197)

So far as we know, Dickinson never showed these lines to anyone else, nor did she recite them for a friend. "Normal" (like "daily") appears on the back of a bill for milk from a Mrs. Kingman, and it is possible that Kingman's name inspired this reflection on self-defined, self-acknowledged power and how a woman poet might achieve it (*Fr* 1197). Here is the paradox: whatever its personal origin, "We never know how high we are" is a publicly oriented poem; it challenges us to undertake heroic reading—to amplify our usual limits and to gratify curiosities we did not know we possessed. The poem's compressed argument puts pressure on the word "Cubits," which was somewhat abstruse in 1871 and which is even rarer today. With this word, Dickinson begins to explain what warps us. And then she stops. The reading I find most powerful is this: although a biblical cubit takes the male body as its norm (according to her *Webster's*, a cubit is "the length of a man's arm from the elbow to the extremity of the middle finger"), the female speaker's normal, however generalized and disguised, must take a different measure. Dickinson's *Webster's* further notes that the word "cubit" is derived from the Latin *cubitus* and "probably allied to the Latin *cubo* . . . signifying a turn or corner."[2] Fair enough. As we see, Dickinson's poem puts pressure on the idea of turning a corner; she considered the word "growth" as a variant for "plan," speculating as she does about who or what asks us to rise. A question remains, though. Why is the syntax of the poem's penultimate line so contorted? Is it because Dickinson is unsure about how much blame to assign to herself, worrying as she does about the intimate relationship between warping (or turning corners) and being warped (or being cornered)? In her mind, is she warping lyric space and by extension progressive human history, or is lyric space and by extension regressive human history warping her?

This is a study of the gendered anxieties organized by one fearfully courageous woman's literary work. I argue that Dickinson's ambivalence toward remembered, actual, and potential intimates opened a space for poets to come. My analysis is based on the assumption that reading closely is an intimate act. To return to a point I made in the Introduction, in Dickinson's imagination, intimacy and shame are often intertwined. Applying a version of this idea to lyric, Gillian White has recently remarked, "Shame involves thinking about what others think about you."[3] My project is predicated on the assumption that few poets have thought more deeply about this aesthetically and psychologically demanding subject than the Dickinson who declared, " 'If I read a book [and] it makes my whole body so cold no fire ever can warm me I know *that* is poetry. If I feel physically as if the top of my head were taken off, I know *that* is poetry. These are the only way I know it. Is there any other way' " (*L* 342a). Certainly there are less violent ways of thinking about the relationship between poems, poets, and their readers. For example, Dickinson's 1844 *Webster's* defines "intimacy" as "Close familiarity or fellowship; nearness in friendship," adding that an intimate is "a familiar friend or associate; one to whom the thoughts of another are intrusted without reserve."[4] Let us attend closely, then, to the poet who wondered quite shamelessly what it would be like to stun, electrify, and electrocute her readers "With Bolts – of Melody!" (*Fr* 348). Let us attend closely to the paradoxical power of our Emily Dickinsons. To describe how Dickinson became ours is to put pressure on the collective pronoun. What, then, constitutes an enduring reading public for Dickinson and for American women's poetry? By what gendered loyalties is it defined?

The word "Our" in my title points to some common imagination of a poet whose appeal depends not only on her self-proclaimed outsider status but also on her taken-for-granted insider status. Granted that Dickinson cannot be owned—that her multifaceted achievement exceeds any critic's ability to define it—in this book I am interested in clarifying Dickinson's legacy for women poets who, I argue, in writing about Dickinson are writing about themselves as well. They use Dickinson to test the validity of their own emotional and intellectual needs. Thus *my* Emily Dickinson is both singular and representative, a person and a symbol. This methodological assumption is pushed to its limit in my fourth chapter, where I describe how Sylvia Plath attempted to project Dickinsonian authority onto Marianne Moore, while the specific figure of Dickinson disappears from view.

If, then, this book began with a desire to see how and why women poets recovered a Dickinson hidden from history, it led to a more nuanced understanding of how literary women who were not primarily poets affected the tradition: women such as Dickinson's pioneering editor Mabel Loomis Todd, the subject of my second chapter, who prided herself not only on her intellectual abilities but on her fleshly arts of seduction.[5] It also led to a closer look at women such as Helen Hunt Jackson, the subject of my first chapter, whose contemporary reputation as a strong poet has not, as a rule, stood the test of time. As we move further into the twenty-first century, Dickinson's ability to provoke controversy continues to enhance the power of her appeal. To modify the question I posed earlier, in interpreting Emily Dickinson's complex legacy, what can we find out about the individual and collective reading practices that have shaped us? It is my contention that Dickinson represents the intimacies of difference: the sociability that draws us together and the profound self-absorption that keeps us apart. Her paradoxical self-awareness encourages us to draw close and to keep our distance. What she provokes in sociable and self-absorbed others is the heart of my study of American women poets choosing traditions.

Notes

INTRODUCTION

1. See Sianne Ngai, *Ugly Feelings* (Cambridge, MA: Harvard University Press, 2005).

2. "Group culture": quoted from Muriel Rukeyser, *The Life of Poetry* (Ashfield, MA: Paris Press, 1996), p. 109. Citations are to this edition.

3. Rukeyser, *The Life of Poetry*, p. 78.

4. Muriel Rukeyser, *Willard Gibbs* (Garden City, NY: Doubleday, Doran, 1942), p. 100.

5. Rukeyser, *The Life of Poetry*, p. 76.

6. Rukeyser, "Easter Eve 1945," in *The Collected Poems of Muriel Rukeyser*, ed. Janet E. Kaufman and Anne F. Herzog (Pittsburgh: University of Pittsburgh Press, 2005), p. 277.

7. Richard Rorty, *Achieving Our Country: Leftist Thought in Twentieth-Century America* (Cambridge, MA: Harvard University Press, 1998).

8. Unpublished journal, Library of Congress, Muriel Rukeyser Papers, Part I, Box 1, Diaries and Appointment Books. Quoted from September 30, 1945.

9. Rukeyser, *Willard Gibbs*, p. 175.

10. Rukeyser, *Willard Gibbs*, pp. 175, 174.

11. Rukeyser, *The Life of Poetry*, p. x.

12. Rukeyser, "Josiah Willard Gibbs," *Physics Today* 2.2 (February 1949): 6–7.

13. Rukeyser, "Poem Out of Childhood," in *The Collected Poems*, p. 3.

14. See Edward Brunner, *Cold War Poetry* (Urbana: University of Illinois Press, 2001), p. 51. See also John Ciardi, *Mid-Century American Poets* (New York: Twayne, 1950).

15. See Rukeyser, *The Life of Poetry*, p. 95.

16. Rukeyser, *The Life of Poetry*, p. 90.

17. Rukeyser, *The Life of Poetry*, p. 95.

18. Rukeyser, *Willard Gibbs*, p. 175.

19. *A Historical Guide to Emily Dickinson*, ed. Vivian R. Pollak (New York: Oxford University Press, 2004).

20. *The Letters of Emily Dickinson*, ed. Thomas H. Johnson and Theodora Ward, 3 vols. (Cambridge, MA: Harvard University Press, 1958), 1: 264. The manuscript is missing, but there is a facsimile of the first paragraph in *Letters of Emily Dickinson*, ed. Mabel Loomis Todd, 2 vols. (Boston: Roberts Brothers, 1894), 1: 158.

21. Rukeyser, *Willard Gibbs*, p. 175.

22. "How happy is the little Stone," *Variorum* 3: 1372–75.

23. The Dickinson six: "A triumph may be of several kinds," "Their height in heaven comforts not," "The soul selects her own society," "My life closed twice before its close," "I

never saw a moor," "Because I could not stop for Death." The Rukeyser four: "Eyes of Night-Time," "Easter Eve, 1945," "Song" ("A voice flew out of the river as morning flew"), and "To Enter That Rhythm Where the Self Is Lost." The other poets on the Library of Congress recording are Edwin Honig, George Barker, and (briefly) Oscar Williams, who organized the session.

24. For example, the poem we index as "Triumph may be of several kinds" (*Fr* 680) appears as "A triumph may be of several kinds" in *The Complete Poems of Emily Dickinson*, ed. Martha Dickinson Bianchi (Boston: Little, Brown, 1924), pp. 210–11. The same text is reproduced in *The Poems of Emily Dickinson*, ed. Martha Dickinson Bianchi and Alfred Leete Hampson (Boston: Little, Brown, 1930) and in *The Poems of Emily Dickinson*, ed. Martha Dickinson Bianchi and Alfred Leete Hampson (Boston: Little, Brown, 1937). The other five poems are also identical in the three Bianchi-sponsored editions. Thus, Rukeyser reads "Because I could not stop for Death" (*Fr* 479) with its famously missing fourth stanza. In an e-mail to me, September 6, 2012, William L. Rukeyser states that his mother owned the three-volume Johnson edition, but he does not know when she acquired it.

25. Rukeyser, review of Marianne Moore's *O to Be a Dragon*, *Saturday Review* 42 (September 19, 1959): 18.

26. Rukeyser papers, review of *O to Be a Dragon*, Library of Congress, Part I, Box 9, Folder 6. See also Moore's response denying the inaccuracy of the note to "In the Public Garden," "Psalm 23—traditional Southern tune, arranged by Virgil Thomson." Moore claimed to have it on good authority (her pastor and his organist), but Rukeyser disputed her claim.

27. Lawrence B. Rukeyser died in 1958 and left his estate to his second wife, Flora Lyons Rosenmeyer. She was Muriel Rukeyser's maternal aunt. Both she and her sister, Frances Steloff, objected strenuously to Lawrence's 1953 remarriage, and Muriel was bitter about being disinherited. The Library of Congress has pathetic letters from Flora written after Lawrence's death pleading with Muriel not to cut off contact with her. In earlier years, they had been very close, and Muriel seems to have preferred her to her mother Myra.

28. Theodora Van Wagenen Ward was the granddaughter of Elizabeth Holland, to whom Dickinson sent "The Things that never can come back, are several" (*Fr* 1564), signing it "Emily, in love." On Dickinson's friendship with Elizabeth and Josiah Gilbert Holland, see Chapter 6. See also *The Poems of Emily Dickinson: Variorum Edition*, ed. R. W. Franklin (Cambridge, MA: Harvard University Press, 1998), 3: 1367–68. On Dickinson and gift exchange, see Paul Crumbley, *Winds of Will: Emily Dickinson and the Sovereignty of Democratic Thought* (Tuscaloosa: University of Alabama Press, 2010), chap. 4. For a resistant reading of "The Things that never can come back, are several," see Alexandra Socarides, *Dickinson Unbound: Paper, Process, Poetics* (New York: Oxford University Press, 2012), p. 149. As an elegy for J. G. Holland, who died in 1881, she finds it far from consoling.

29. Perry Miller, review of *Emily Dickinson: An Interpretive Biography*, by Thomas H. Johnson, *New England Quarterly* 29.1 (March 1956): 102.

30. Adrienne Rich, "'I Am in Danger—Sir—,'" *Necessities of Life: Poems 1962–1965* (New York: Norton, 1966), p. 33.

31. Rich, "'Vesuvius at Home': The Power of Emily Dickinson," *On Lies, Secrets, and Silence: Selected Prose 1966–1978* (New York: Norton, 1979), pp. 157–83. The "whole biographies" quotation is from the title poem of *Necessities of Life*, p. 9.

32. Rich first wrote about Dickinson in 1963, in *Snapshots of a Daughter-in-Law*, in which "A thinking woman sleeps with monsters. / The beak that grips her, she becomes." Quoting the line "*My Life had stood—a Loaded Gun*," Rich describes a double figure, two women,

really, who morph into each other: the first reading patiently in an Amherst pantry while the iron is heating and the jellies cooking on the stove; the second, dehumanized, "iron-eyed and beaked and purposed as a bird / dusting everything on the whatnot every day of life" (p. 10). "I Am in Danger" was first published in 1964, and quotes Higginson on "my partially cracked poetess at Amherst." For this letter to his sister Anna, see Chapter 1. Cited in Jay Leyda, *The Years and Hours of Emily Dickinson*, 2 vols. (New Haven: Yale University Press, 1960), 1: 263.

33. Henry David Thoreau, *Journal*, ed. John D. Broderick (Princeton: Princeton University Press, 1981), 4: 307.

34. "This curious man": Rukeyser, "Thoreau and Poetry," in *Henry David Thoreau: Studies and Commentaries*, ed. Walter Harding, George Brenner, and Paul A. Doyle (Rutherford, NJ: Fairleigh Dickinson University Press, 1972), pp. 103–17. Rukeyser spoke at a Thoreau Festival at Nassau Community College in Garden City, Long Island, on May 11, 1967. The essay is based on the talk.

35. Helen Hunt Jackson, *Mercy Philbrick's Choice* (Boston: Roberts Brothers, 1876). I discuss the novel in Chapter 2.

36. See Barbara Antonina Clarke Mossberg, *When a Writer Is a Daughter* (Bloomington: Indiana University Press, 1982).

37. In *The Diary of Alice James*, January 6, 1892, she writes, "It is reassuring to hear the British pronouncement that Emily Dickinson is fifth-rate—they have such a capacity for missing quality; the robust evades them equally with the subtle. Her being sicklied o'er with T. W. Higginson makes one wonder lest there be a patent flaw which escapes one's vision." Quoted in Klaus Lubbers, *Emily Dickinson: The Critical Revolution* (Ann Arbor: University of Michigan Press, 1968), p. 42.

38. See Rebecca Patterson, *The Riddle of Emily Dickinson* (Boston: Houghton Mifflin, 1951). For Bishop's review, see "Unseemly Deductions," *New Republic* 127.7 (August 18, 1952): 20. For Bishop's review of *Emily Dickinson's Letters to Dr. and Mrs. Josiah Gilbert Holland*, ed. Theodora Van Wagenen Ward (Cambridge, MA: Harvard University Press, 1951), see "Love from Emily," *New Republic* 125.9 (August 27, 1951): 20–21.

39. See Sandra M. Gilbert and Susan Gubar, *No Man's Land: The Place of the Woman Writer in the Twentieth Century*, 3 vols. (New Haven, CT: Yale University Press, 1988–94).

40. See Betsy Erkkila, *The Wicked Sisters: Women Poets, Literary History, and Discord* (New York: Oxford University Press, 1992).

41. See Virginia Jackson, *Dickinson's Misery: A Theory of Lyric Reading* (Princeton, NJ: Princeton University Press, 2005).

42. On Dickinson and confusion, see Sharon Cameron, *Choosing Not Choosing: Dickinson's Fascicles* (Chicago: University of Chicago Press, 1992). On Dickinson's "scraps," see Marta L. Werner, ed. *Emily Dickinson's Open Folios: Scenes of Reading, Surfaces of Writing* (Ann Arbor: University of Michigan Press, 1995); *Radical Scatters: Emily Dickinson's Fragments and Related Texts, 1870–1886* (Ann Arbor: University of Michigan Press, 1999); and *The Gorgeous Nothings*, ed. Marta L. Werner and Jen Bervin, with a Preface by Susan Howe (New York: New Directions, 2013).

43. Thomas Gardner, *A Door Ajar: Contemporary Women Writers and Emily Dickinson* (New York: Oxford University Press, 2006), p. 6.

44. Zofia Burr, *Of Women, Poetry, and Power: Strategies of Address in Dickinson, Miles, Brooks, Lorde, and Angelou* (Urbana: University of Illinois Press, 2002), jacket copy.

45. Gwendolyn Brooks, *Report from Part One* (Detroit: Broadside, 1972), p. 56.

46. Lesley Wheeler, *The Poetics of Enclosure: American Women Poets from Dickinson to Dove* (Knoxville: University of Tennessee Press, 2002). On page 92, she comments on a photograph of Brooks at Emily Dickinson's home included in *Report from Part One*, which is captioned, "'I think Emily, after the first shock at my intrusion, would have approved of my natural.'"

47. See, for example, D. H. Melhem, "Gwendolyn Brooks and Emily Dickinson," *Emily Dickinson International Society Bulletin* 7.1 (May/June 1995). For theoretical background, see also Vivian R. Pollak, "Dickinson and the Poetics of Whiteness," *Emily Dickinson Journal* 9.2 (2000): 84–95, and Erkkila, "Race, Black Women Writing, and Gwendolyn Brooks," in *The Wicked Sister*, pp. 185–234.

48. For Sylvia Plath's citation of Dickinson's witchcraft letter, see Chapter 5.

49. See Ella Gilbert Ives, "Emily Dickinson: Her Poetry, Prose and Personality," *Boston Evening Transcript* (October 5, 1907): 3. The essay is reprinted in *The Recognition of Emily Dickinson*, ed. Caesar R. Blake and Carlton F. Wells (Ann Arbor: University of Michigan, 1964), pp. 71–78.

CHAPTER I

1. Helen Hunt Jackson's *Bathmendi: A Persian Tale* (Boston: Loring, 1867) was based on a widely imitated novella by the French nobleman Jean-Pierre Claris de Florian (1755–94). It was the first of her many books for children and several months before her death she published a revised version, which she had cast into rhymed couplets. See Helen Hunt Jackson ["H. H."], "Bathmendi," *St. Nicholas: An Illustrated Magazine for Young Folks* 12.7 (May 1885): 508–12. The Persian origins of this tale are questionable and it more likely reflects French orientalism. On the disciplinary function of children's literature, see Karen Sánchez-Eppler, *Dependent States: The Child's Part in Nineteenth-Century American Culture* (Chicago: University of Chicago Press, 2005).

2. See Helen Hunt Jackson, "Coronation," *Atlantic Monthly* 23.136 (February 1869): 241–42. This issue also included Whitman's "Proud Music of the Sea-Storm," an essay by Harriet Beecher Stowe, and an installment of Higginson's Newport novel *Malbone*.

3. Helen Hunt Jackson, "Tribute," *Verses* (Boston: Fields, Osgood, 1870), pp. 58–59. Whatever Jackson's desire to claim Emerson as her muse, the rhythms of her poem are halting and the iterated negations—"no king," "no man," "No white dove," "no wine"—hint at a subversive subtext in which male artists are ineffective guides. Meanwhile, the "full ear" carried by the speaker, like a phallus full of "true seed," works toward gender equality by sexualizing the exchange. On "Days," Dickinson, and inspiration, see Lawrence Buell, *Emerson* (Cambridge, MA: Harvard University Press, 2003), pp. 138–39.

4. Unsigned review of *Verses* (Boston: Roberts Brothers, 1873), *Springfield Republican*.

5. Unsigned review of *Verses*, *Nation* 12.298 (March 16, 1871): 184. On Jackson's rebuttal, see Kate Phillips, *Helen Hunt Jackson: A Literary Life* (Berkeley: University of California Press, 2003), p. 301n68.

6. Thomas Wentworth Higginson, "A New Poetess," in *Woman's Journal* 51 (December 24, 1870): 405.

7. Helen Hunt Jackson, "The Abbot Paphnutius," in *Scribner's Monthly* 1.2 (December 1870): 170–72.

8. For a classic but controversial study of alliances between liberal ministers and women writers, see Ann Douglas, *The Feminization of American Culture* (New York: Alfred A. Knopf, 1977).

9. Higginson, quoted in Tilden G. Edelstein, *Strange Enthusiasm: A Life of Thomas Wentworth Higginson* (New Haven: Yale University Press, 1968), p. 89.

10. Henry David Thoreau, quoted in Edward J. Renehan Jr., *The Secret Six: The True Tale of the Men Who Conspired with John Brown* (New York: Crown, 1995), pp. 64–65.

11. The Worcester Disunion Convention circular is quoted in Brenda Wineapple, *White Heat: The Friendship of Emily Dickinson & Thomas Wentworth Higginson* (New York: Alfred A. Knopf, 2008), p. 89.

12. Higginson, "Helen Jackson ('H. H.')," in *Contemporaries* (Boston: Houghton, Mifflin, 1899), pp. 157–58. Higginson may have been familiar with an essay published by Edward Bissell Hunt, in which he argued that "Our country is not a natural home for the negro, and he is only here on compulsion. He belongs within the tropics, whence he came." See Capt. E. B. Hunt, *Union Foundations: A Study of American Nationality as a Fact of Science* (New York: D. Van Nostrand, 1863), p. 49.

13. "Decoration Day," in *Verses* 1870, pp. 79–80, laments the "Graves of the precious 'missing,' where no sound / Of tender weeping will be heard, where goes / No loving step of kindred." "Freedom" defends the freedmen against contemporary charges of lawlessness and was published in *Scribner's Monthly* in 1875. More impassioned is "Too Much Wheat," which appeared on the front page of the New York *Independent* on November 6, 1884. The poem describes "a tale of shame," given that "Brothers of ours, though their skins are red . . . starve like beasts in pens and fold, / While we hoard wheat to sell for gold." See also "The Indian's Cross and Star," New York *Independent* 35.1802 (June 1883): 1.

14. Virginia Jackson, "'The Story of Boon'; or, The Poetess," *ESQ* 54.1–4 (2008): 245. "H. H." met Anna Leonowens, author of *The English Governess at the Siamese Court*, at the home of Anne Lynch Botta in New York City. On the role of the salon in developing personal publics, see Julia Ward Howe, "The Salon in America," in *Is Society Polite? and Other Essays* (New York: Lamson, Wolfe, 1895). See also Eliza Richards, *Gender and the Poetics of Reception in Poe's Circle* (Cambridge: Cambridge University Press, 2004), pp. 7–11, 32–35, 72–75, 76, 126.

15. Edwin P. Whipple, "Some Recent Women Poets," *Scribner's Monthly* 10.1 (May 1875): 100–6. On "Joy," see Helen Hunt Jackson, *Verses* (Boston: Roberts Brothers, 1873), pp. 33–34.

16. "Nebulae," *Galaxy* 17.2 (February 1874): 282.

17. Signed X. Y. Z., review of *Verses* (1873). Source unidentified. Helen Hunt Jackson Papers, Part 2, Ms 0156, Box 2, Folder 23j, Special Collections, Tutt Library, Colorado College, Colorado Springs, Colorado.

18. "Dedication" is identical in *Verses* (Boston: Fields, Osgood, 1870) and in *Verses* (Boston: Roberts Brothers, 1873).

19. Higginson, review of 1870 *Verses*, *Atlantic Monthly* 27.161 (March 1871): 400.

20. "Truest flavor of manhood": "H. H." to journalist Kate Field, March 7, 1866, Boston Public Library. See also Gary Scharnhorst, *Kate Field: The Many Lives of a Nineteenth-Century American Journalist* (New York: Syracuse University Press, 2008).

21. See Phillips, p. 103. See also Anna Mary Wells, *Dear Preceptor: The Life and Times of Thomas Wentworth Higginson* (Boston: Houghton Mifflin, 1963), pp. 198–212.

22. Higginson, "Helen Jackson ('H. H.')," *Contemporaries*, p. 164.

23. Higginson, "To the Memory of H. H.," *Century Illustrated Magazine* 32.1 (May 1886): 47.

24. Higginson, "Helen Jackson ('H. H.')," *Contemporaries*, p. 162.

25. Deborah Vinal Fiske, quoted in Richard B. Sewall, *The Life of Emily Dickinson*, 2 vols. (New York: Farrar, Straus, Giroux, 1974), 2: 325.

26. Deborah Vinal Fiske, quoted in Phillips, p. 46.

27. Nathan Welby Fiske and Deborah Vinal Fiske, in Phillips, p. 12.

28. Phillips, p. 61. For Emily Norcross Dickinson's letters, see *A Poet's Parents: The Courtship Letters of Emily Norcross and Edward Dickinson*, ed. Vivian R. Pollak (Chapel Hill: University of North Carolina Press, 1988).

29. Jackson, quoted in Ruth Odell, *Helen Hunt Jackson [H. H.]* (New York: D. Appleton-Century, 1939), pp. 31, 24.

30. Helen Jackson, quoted in Phillips, p. 55.

31. Nathan Welby Fiske, quoted in Phillips, p. 54.

32. Jackson, quoted in Phillips, p. 55.

33. Odell, p. 34.

34. Helen Jackson, quoted in Phillips, p. 55.

35. Edward Dickinson owned John S. C. Abbott's *The Mother at Home; or the Principles of Maternal Duty* (1833). In John Cody's *After Great Pain: The Inner Life of Emily Dickinson* (Cambridge: Harvard University Press, 1971), the conduct book is demonized for contributing to the Dickinsons' supposedly dysfunctional family life. See also Alfred Habegger, *"My Wars Are Laid Away in Books": The Life of Emily Dickinson* (New York: Random House, 2001), pp. 91–92. Jacob Abbott taught briefly at Amherst College and coauthored a Sunday school pamphlet with Helen's father. The novelist Elizabeth Stuart Phelps was one of his pupils at the Mount Vernon School in Boston. Later, Jacob Abbott wrote the popular Rollo stories for children, but it was the more empathic John who encouraged Helen. More generally, for the importance of academies, seminaries, and collegiate institutes in women's higher education at the time, see Mary Kelley, *Learning to Stand and Speak: Women, Education, and Public Life in America's Republic* (Chapel Hill: University of North Carolina Press, 2006).

36. Helen Hunt Jackson, "October's Bright Blue Weather," *Poems* (Boston: Roberts Brothers, 1892), p. 254. For an allusion to "ghastly poems extolling October's bright blue weather," see Sylvia Plath, "America! America!" in *Johnny Panic and the Bible of Dreams: Short Stories, Prose, and Diary Excerpts* (New York: Harper & Row, 1979), p. 54. See also Elizabeth Bishop, "Travelling, A Love Poem (or just Love Poem?)" in *Edgar Allan Poe & The Juke-Box: Uncollected Poems, Drafts, and Fragments*, ed. Alice Quinn (New York: Farrar, Straus and Giroux, 2006), p. 162.

37. When the Hunts were in Amherst in 1860, they were entertained in the Homestead. Based on that encounter, Dickinson told Higginson in 1870 that "Major Hunt interested her more than any man she ever saw. She remembered two things he said—that her great dog 'understood gravitation' & when he said he should come again 'in a year. If I say a shorter time it will be longer'" (*L* 342b). Jackson's close friend and traveling companion, Sarah Chauncey Woolsey, achieved her greatest success writing children's books with a tomboy heroine. See *What Katy-Did* (Boston: Roberts Brothers, 1872) and its sequels. See also Lois Keith, *Take Up Thy Bed and Walk: Death, Disability and Cure in Classic Fiction for Girls* (New York: Routledge, 2001).

38. Woolsey, quoted in Phillips, p. 147 ff.

39. Jackson, quoted in Phillips, p. 93.

40. Jackson, quoted in Susan Coultrap-McQuin, *Doing Literary Business: American Women Writers in the Nineteenth Century* (Chapel Hill: University of North Carolina Press,

1990), p. 151. Coultrap-McQuin discusses Higginson's influence on Jackson's early style, pp. 151–52, as does Flora Haines Apponyi, "Last Days of Mrs. Helen Hunt Jackson," *Overland Monthly and Out West Magazine* 6.33 (September 1885): 310–16.

41. Jackson's 1871 letter to Charles Dudley Warner is in Phillips, p. 200.

42. Ralph Waldo Emerson, "Preface," in *Parnassus* (Boston: Houghton, Mifflin, 1874), p. x.

43. Emerson is quoted in Higginson, "Helen Jackson," in *Short Studies of American Authors* (Boston: Lee and Shepard, 1879), p. 49. "Thought" is quoted from *Verses* 1873, pp. 121–22.

44. Jackson to Joseph Gilder and to Charles Dudley Warner, quoted in Phillips, p. 6.

45. Jackson, quoted in Phillips, p. 141.

46. Jackson, quoted in Phillips, p. 139, who offers a finely nuanced account of the evolution of Jackson's feminism and its inconsistencies.

47. Samuel Bowles's review is quoted in Jay Leyda, *The Years and Hours of Emily Dickinson*, 2 vols. (New Haven: Yale University Press, 1960), 2: 215.

48. Odell, p. 66.

49. Jackson on literary labor is in Phillips, p. 116.

50. Phillips, p. 168.

51. "October's Bright Blue Weather," *Poems* 1892, pp. 254–55.

52. Valerie Sherer Mathes, "Foreword," in Helen Hunt Jackson, *A Century of Dishonor: A Sketch of the United States Government's Dealings with Some of the Indian Tribes* (Norman: University of Oklahoma Press, 1995), p. ix.

53. Helen Jackson, cited in Higginson, "Mrs. Helen Jackson ('H. H.')," *Century Magazine* 31.2 (December 1885): 254.

54. Mathes, "Foreword," p. xiv. Theodore Roosevelt, on the other hand, later described her *Century of Dishonor* as "thoroughly untrustworthy from cover to cover." Although he credited her with a "pure and noble life" and with good intentions, he condemned her "polemic" for "hysterical indifference to facts." See *The Winning of the West*, 4 vols. (New York: G. P. Putnam's Sons, 1889–1896), 1: 93–94.

55. Helen Hunt Jackson's letter to William Jackson of December 26, 1879, quoted in Phillips, p. 229.

56. "Excited": William wrote that she had gotten the reputation of being overly agitated about Indian affairs. See William Sharpless Jackson, quoted by Helen Hunt Jackson, in Valerie Sherer Mathes, *The Indian Reform Letters of Helen Hunt Jackson, 1879–1885* (Norman: University of Oklahoma Press, 1998), p. 62.

57. Helen Hunt Jackson, *Century of Dishonor*, "Author's Note," p. 7. She sent a copy to every member of Congress at her own expense.

58. Helen Hunt Jackson's letter of May 30, 1880, to Anne Lynch Botta is quoted in Valerie Sherer Mathes, *Helen Hunt Jackson and Her Indian Reform Legacy*, p. 34. Garfield's presidency lasted just two hundred days. He was shot on July 2, lingered throughout the summer, and died on September 19, his injuries complicated by medical malpractice.

59. See Helen Hunt Jackson and Abbot Kinney, *Report on the Condition and Needs of the Mission Indians of California* (Washington, DC: Government Printing Office, 1883).

60. "Sugared my pill": Jackson's letter to Higginson is in the Thomas Wentworth Higginson Papers, Houghton Library, Harvard University. See also her letter of January 22, 1885, in Mathes, *The Indian Reform Letters of Helen Hunt Jackson*, p. 341, where it is unattributed.

61. Jackson, in Mathes, *The Indian Reform Letters of Helen Hunt Jackson*, p. 314, where it is attributed "To an Intimate Friend."

62. Michael Dorris, "Introduction," in H. H. Jackson, *Ramona* (New York: Signet, 2002), p. 1. There have been a number of useful studies challenging the novel's contribution to American Indian policy, including a talk by Susan K. Harris at the 2009 meeting of the Society for the Study of American Women Writers in Philadelphia, "Leveraging the Future: Narration, Literary Convention, and Counterfactual History in [Catharine Maria Sedgwick's] *A New-England Tale* and *Ramona.*" Harris stated that while the Dawes Act looked like a good deal at the time, it contributed to the problem it was trying to solve and that although Jackson wanted *Ramona* to do for Indians what *Uncle Tom's Cabin* did for African Americans, its effect was, at least in part, negative. For a more positive view, see John M. Gonzalez, "The Warp of Whiteness: Domesticity and Empire in Helen Hunt Jackson's *Ramona*," *American Literary History* 16.3 (Fall 2004): 437–65. He argues that *Ramona* effectively models assimilative multiculturalism rather than exclusionary difference. See also Robert McKee Irwin, "'Ramona' and Postnationalist American Studies: On 'Our America' and the Mexican Borderlands," *American Quarterly* 55.4 (December 2003): 539–67. Pointing out that Cuban patriot José Marti translated *Ramona* in 1887, Irwin faults Jackson for blindness to racial conflicts in Mexico's Northern borderlands.

63. H. H. Jackson, *Ramona*, p. 38.

64. H. H. Jackson, *Ramona*, p. 2.

65. "Genius" is *Ramona*, p. 11, "unlimited power" is p. 271, "Mexican officer and a gentleman" is p. 8. On "In the Name of the Law," see Phillips, pp. 259–60. For a reading of the Señora as both victim and victimizer, see Nathan Wolff, "Fits of Reason: The U.S. Political Romance, 1865–1900" (Ph.D. diss., University of Chicago, 2012).

66. Phillips, p. 260.

67. See Michele Moylan, "Materiality as Performance: The Forming of Helen Hunt Jackson's *Ramona*," in *Reading Books: Essays on the Material Text and Literature in America*, ed. Michele Moylan and Lane Stiles (Amherst: University of Massachusetts Press, 1996), p. 226. See also Dydia DeLyser, *Ramona Memories: Tourism and the Shaping of Southern California* (Minneapolis: University of Minnesota Press, 2005).

68. There is an extensive literature on Dickinson and Shakespeare. Memorably, Dickinson told Higginson that when she was forbidden to read because of severe eye strain in 1864 and 1865, "It was a comfort to think that there were so few real books." When "she regained her eyes" and read Shakespeare, she "thought to herself, 'Why is any other book needed?'" See "Emily Dickinson's Letters," *Atlantic Monthly* 68.408 (October 1891): 453. See also Páraic Finnerty, *Emily Dickinson's Shakespeare* (Amherst: University of Massachusetts Press, 2006).

69. See Richard B. Sewall, "Emily Dickinson's Perfect Audience: Helen Hunt Jackson," in *Dickinson and Audience*, ed. Martin Orzeck and Robert Weisbuch (Ann Arbor: University of Michigan Press, 1996), p. 202.

70. On *Forest Leaves*, see Emily Fowler Ford, cited in *Letters of Emily Dickinson*, ed. Mabel Loomis Todd, new and enlarged ed. (New York: Harper, 1931), pp. 127–28. Ford also describes a Shakespeare Club in which Dickinson participated, pp. 128–29.

71. Although Helen and Henry Root gossiped about mutual acquaintances including Susan Gilbert, Emily Dickinson is mentioned only as part of a family constellation and as Susan's friend. Moreover, in a letter written from Washington on February 26, 1855, Helen explained that she was sparing herself the trouble of calling on the Dickinson sisters while they were in Washington and that to do so would be "a great piece of hypocrisy for me," even

though they were from "dear old Amherst." By then, Helen had had a falling out with Susan and accused her of insincerity. See Helen Hunt Jackson Papers, Part 6, Ms. 0353, Box 1, Folder 5, Tutt Library, Colorado College.

72. Helen Hunt Jackson to her sister, quoted in Jay Leyda, 2: 31.

73. "Could not tell [him] much": Higginson to Dickinson *L* 333a; "much interested": Higginson to R. W. Gilder, quoted in Leyda, 2: 111.

74. On the Norcross recommendation, see the August 1873 letter to her sister in Helen Hunt Jackson Papers, Part 2, Ms 0156, Box 1, Folder 3, Tutt Library, Colorado College.

75. In about 1861, Dickinson copied both stanzas of "That after Horror" into her Fascicle 11. The quoted passage was sent to Higginson in about late 1862. See R. W. Franklin, *The Poems of Emily Dickinson: Variorum Edition*, 3 vols. (Cambridge: Harvard University Press, 1998), 1: 266. Her fascicles contain from eleven to twenty-nine poems, with an average of about twenty.

76. H. H. Jackson, "Coronation," 1892 *Poems*, pp. 98–100.

77. "There came a day": the quoted version was sent to Higginson on April 25, 1862, and differs from other versions in its profusion of commas. See *The Poems of Emily Dickinson: Variorum Edition* 1: 347.

78. Helen Hunt Jackson, "Emigravit," in *Mercy Philbrick's Choice* (Boston: Roberts Brothers, 1876), p. 296. The novel features a dozen of Mercy's verses. When Henry James reviewed it in the *Nation*, he objected to characters who functioned in a society given to "ethical hair-splitting" and expressed surprise that Jackson would make a "sternly moralistic" young woman a poetess. "These things do not at all hang together," he contended. "Poets are not a literal but an imaginative folk, devoted to seeing the charm, the joke, of things—to finding it where it may be, and slipping it in where it is not." See Henry James, "An American and an English Novel," *Nation* (December 21, 1876); reprinted in Henry James, *Literary Criticism: Essays on Literature, American Writers, & English Writers* (New York: Literary Classics of America, 1984), p. 512. Whatever its faults, the book sold well. As Coultrap-McQuin observes, Mercy "is overjoyed when she first earns money with her poems and insists that there is no difference between men and women taking money for what they can do." See *Doing Literary Business*, p. 150.

79. See Odell, p. 134.

80. *Diary*, October 10, 1876, Helen Hunt Jackson Papers, Part 1, Ms 0020, Box 5. "Mrs. Warren": probably Emily Chase Warren, wife of Gouverneur K. Warren, a civil engineer and Union Army officer, "the Hero of Little Round Top," who was a friend of Jackson's first husband. Leyda, 2: 283, misreads "Warren" and creates the misleading impression that "lovely day" is a comment on the visit rather than the weather. In general, Jackson did not use her diaries for subjective comments. They approximate appointment books, or planners, and the paragraphing of the original is clearer. Comments on weather are a staple of her diaries, in part because of concern about her health.

81. Jackson to Dickinson, Leyda, 2: 258.

82. Homeopathist Hamilton J. Cate treated Austin Dickinson in 1876 when he was suffering from malaria, but Cate was not one of Emily Dickinson's physicians.

83. There were also poems written in her later years of which she kept no copy. See Cristanne Miller, *Reading in Time: Emily Dickinson in the Nineteenth Century* (Amherst: University of Massachusetts Press, 2012). "Success" consists of eleven lines in the copies sent to Higginson and Susan Dickinson, with twelve in the other versions. It is likely that Jackson submitted a twelve-line poem to Niles.

84. The extant correspondence is convoluted and there are missing documents. *L* 813, in which Dickinson thanks Niles for "the delightful Book," is an undated draft in the Amherst College Archives and Special Collections. The question is this: is Dickinson thanking Niles for *A Masque of Poets* or for Mathilde Blind's *George Eliot*? Johnson thinks the latter and dates the manuscript mid-March 1883. Leyda, 2:307, places it in 1879, perhaps in mid-January. Because of the importance of the Dickinson-Niles interchange, I will document it further.

Letter 1: Dickinson asked Niles about J. W. Cross's life of George Eliot. This letter is lost and can be inferred from his response. Letter 2: on March 13, 1883, Niles writes that he does not expect the Cross any time soon but that they are publishing the biography by Blind. Letter 3: Dickinson sends Niles her copy of the Brontë sisters' poems. Letter 4: He returns her book, explaining that he has a copy of a later edition and that the gift is overgenerous. He asks her for a manuscript volume of her poems instead. Letter 5: Dickinson sends him "No Brigadier throughout the Year" (*Fr* 1596). Letter 6: He thanks her in a lost letter and says he likes it better than the first two she sent. Letter 7: She says forget about the others and take these three, "a Thunderstorm – a Humming Bird, and a Country Burial." She adds, "The Life of Marian Evans had much I never knew – a Doom of Fruit without the Bloom, like the Niger Fig" (*L* 814). The question remains: in *L* 813, is she thanking Niles for Blind's biography or for *A Masque of Poets*? Either context makes sense.

85. Helen Hunt Jackson, "A Critical Opinion of the Last Literary Venture," *Denver Daily Tribune*, December 8, 1878. Helen Hunt Jackson Papers, Part 1, Ms 0020, Box 6, Tutt Library, Colorado College. Jackson also used the occasion to speculate about the role of anonymity in creating demand. For the full list of contributors to *A Masque of Poets*, see Aubrey H. Starke, "An Omnibus of Poets," *Colophon* 4.16 (March 1934): 12 unnumbered pages.

86. The most likely source of the April 27, 1864, *Brooklyn Daily Union* version of "Success" is Susan Dickinson. See *Variorum* 1: 145. In reviewing "Success," Jackson also commented, "It is perhaps the only poem of them all whose authorship will never be known to the public."

87. Higginson to Mabel Loomis Todd, December 15, 1890, quoted in Leyda, 2: 111.

88. H. H. Jackson, "Horizon," in *A Masque of Poets*, p. 159.

89. Dickinson sent Higginson ninety-eight poems. Franklin includes five unsent poems in his total of 103. See *Variorum* 3: 1552.

90. Dickinson mentions her dog Carlo in letters beginning in February 1850 (*L* 34). He was her "Shaggy Ally" (*L* 280), a dog "large as myself" her father bought her (*L* 261), a Newfoundland who accompanied her on her calls and walks before she became housebound. He functions as a messenger in "What shall I do – it whimpers so – / This little Hound within the Heart" (*Fr* 237), where she mentions him by name. He contributed to her imagination in other poems such as "Again – his voice is at the door" (*Fr* 274), where the speaker remarks, "We *walk* – I leave my Dog – at home," and in "I started Early – Took my Dog – / And visited the Sea" (*Fr* 656). In early 1866, Dickinson wrote about his death to Higginson, who sympathized (*L* 314). On dogs named "Carlo" in Victorian literature, see Habegger, pp. 226, 688n.

91. Higginson's "A Plea for Culture" appeared in the *Atlantic Monthly* 19.111 (January 1867): 29–38 and is discussed in Lawrence W. Levine, *Highbrow/Lowbrow: The Emergence of Cultural Hierarchy in America* (Cambridge, MA: Harvard University Press, 1988) as an argument for cultural elitism.

92. Higginson, quoted in an 1872 letter by Lydia B. Torrey, is in Leyda, 2: 193.

93. For the Amherst *Record* on Higginson's 1873 visit, see Leyda, 2: 212.

94. Higginson's 1873 letter to his sisters is quoted in Leyda, 2: 212.

95. For "Because that you are going," see *Variorum* 3: 1135–40. I excerpt Version C.

96. The *Woman's Journal* on Dickinson's poems is quoted in Karen Dandurand, "Dickinson and the Public," in *Dickinson and Audience*, ed. Martin Orzeck and Robert Weisbuch (Ann Arbor: University of Michigan Press, 1996), p. 266. By 1875, Higginson had received some fifty poems, including "The Snake," which was published, as Dickinson complained to him, without her permission in the *Springfield Republican* in 1866 (*L* 316).

97. Higginson's letter to his sister Anna is quoted in Leyda, 2: 239. Louisa's poems also attracted admirers, but his dream of publishing a small volume as a memorial to her was never realized.

98. See Dandurand, "Dickinson and the Public," p. 265.

99. Dandurand, "Dickinson and the Public," p. 267. Higginson's letter to Anna, with whom he often discussed books and whose opinion he valued, states that about eighty people attended. Ms., Thomas Wentworth Higginson Papers, Houghton Library.

100. Dickinson's treason poem is *Fr* 1388 and exists in an alternate version sent to Susan. See *Variorum* 3: 1214 for lineation. The version to Higginson responds to the Newport ocean setting in *Malbone: An Oldport Romance* (Boston: Fields, Osgood, 1869).

101. Susan Dickinson's letter is in Leyda, 2: 48. Bowles was a close friend of both Susan and her husband Austin.

102. Higginson, "Letter to a Young Contributor," p. 410.

103. See *Variorum* 1: 375. See also Fascicle 17, in *The Manuscript Books of Emily Dickinson*, ed. R. W. Franklin, 2 vols. (Cambridge, MA: Harvard University Press, 1981), 1: 360.

104. Dickinson's correspondence with Edward Everett Hale is discussed in Alfred Habegger, *"My Wars Are Laid Away in Books": The Life of Emily Dickinson* (New York: Random House, 2001), pp. 313–15. On Newton, see Vivian R. Pollak, *Dickinson: The Anxiety of Gender* (Ithaca: Cornell University Press, 1984), pp. 38, 85–87. He told her that he wanted to live until she was a great poet.

105. On Charles Wadsworth, see Pollak, *Dickinson: The Anxiety of Gender*, chap. 3. Dickinson met him during her visit to Philadelphia in 1855, where he was the minister of the Arch Street Presbyterian Church.

106. Thomas Wentworth Higginson, "Saints and Their Bodies," in *Out-Door Papers* (Boston: Ticknor and Fields, 1863), pp. 8–9.

107. "Triumph" is quoted from *Verses* 1870, pp. 94–95. There is a discrepancy between the title page ("My Triumph") and the text; in later editions, "Triumph" prevails.

108. Dickinson wrote several bluebird poems, and Thomas Johnson speculates that Jackson is referring to "Before you thought of Spring" (*Fr* 1484), whose poet/bird "shouts for joy to nobody / But his seraphic Self." There are other candidates, such as "A prompt – executive Bird is the Jay" (*Fr* 1022) and "No Brigadier throughout the Year" (*Fr* 1596). Both can be read as satires on masculinist rhetoric. So too "After all Birds have been investigated and laid aside" can be read as an affirmation of a female-identified "Elegy of Integrity" (*Fr* 1383). Elizabeth A. Petrino usefully frames "Before you thought of Spring" in terms of autonomous, female poetic practice, as does Paul Crumbley, who locates it in terms of gift-based circulation outside the literary marketplace. See Elizabeth A. Petrino, *Emily Dickinson and Her Contemporaries: Women's Verse in America, 1820–1885* (Hanover, NH: University Press of New England, 1998), p. 183, and Paul Crumbley, *Winds of Will: Emily Dickinson and the Sovereignty of Democratic Thought* (Tuscaloosa: University of Alabama Press, 2010), pp. 140–42.

109. The quatrain is the second of two in "Upon his Saddle sprung a Bird" (*Fr* 1663). For more on Dickinson's response, see Vivian R. Pollak, "American Women Poets Reading

Dickinson: The Example of Helen Hunt Jackson," in *The Emily Dickinson Handbook*, ed. Gudrun Grabher, Roland Hagenbüchle, and Cristanne Miller (Amherst: University of Massachusetts Press, 1998), pp. 329–30. A correction: Jackson did not spend the summer of 1868 in Amherst but may have stopped by for a visit.

110. Jackson's "A Woman's Death Wound," in *Poems* (Boston: Roberts Brothers, 1892), p. 205. In *Dickinson and the Strategies of Reticence: The Woman Writer in Nineteenth-Century America* (Bloomington: Indiana University Press, 1989), Joanne Dobson observes that Jackson's poetry "is characterized by a didacticism uncongenial to the modern reader," p. 85. For another approach to this subject, see Mary Loeffelholz, "Helen Hunt Jackson and Emily Dickinson," in *From School to Salon: Reading Nineteenth-Century American Women's Poetry* (Princeton: Princeton University Press, 2004). In some poems, she argues, Jackson's didacticism is "at the vanishing point, by comparison with either earlier American women's poetry or Jackson's later social art," p. 157.

111. See Lilian Whiting's review of Dickinson's 1890 *Poems*, quoted in Buckingham, p. 28.

112. On "direct correspondence": *Springfield Daily Republican*, quoted in *Variorum Edition* 1: 53.

113. Why Tuscarora? Because of a mistake in Fitz-Greene Halleck's "Red Jacket." "Red Jacket" was a Seneca chief who sided with the British in the Revolution. Halleck addresses him as "King of Tuscarora." The poem is a satiric ode evoking the figure of James Fenimore Cooper and mocking his nationalist zeal before setting its sights on Red Jacket, who was a skilled diplomat and noted orator.

114. See "Draxy Miller's Dowry" and "The Elder's Wife," in *Saxe Holm's Stories*, Series 1 (New York: Scribner, Armstrong, 1874), pp. 1–97, 98–164.

115. On "civil wrong": see the unsigned review from around November 15, 1891, in Buckingham, p. 239.

116. See Mary J. Reid, "Julia Dorr and Some of Her Poet Contemporaries," *Midland Monthly* 3 (June 1895): 499–507. Published in Des Moines, Iowa, the *Monthly* was interested in women's issues. Reid, a regular reviewer, speculated that Dickinson's "concentration" would be attractive in the new century, as it was.

CHAPTER 2

1. Roland Barthes, "The Death of the Author" (1967), in *The Rustle of Language*, trans. Richard Howard (Berkeley: University of California Press, 1989), p. 54.

2. Mabel Loomis Todd, quoted in *Ancestors' Brocades: The Literary Discovery of Emily Dickinson: The Editing and Publication of Her Letters and Poems*, ed. Millicent Todd Bingham (New York: Dover, 1945), p. 31.

3. Mabel Todd, quoted in Richard B. Sewall, *The Life of Emily Dickinson*, 2 vols. (New York: Farrar, Straus, Giroux, 1974), 1: 220.

4. Mabel on work as salvation is in Polly Longsworth, *Austin and Mabel: The Amherst Affair and Love Letters of Austin Dickinson and Mabel Loomis Todd* (New York: Farrar, Straus, Giroux, 1984), p. 333.

5. Mabel Todd was interested in women's rights and active in women's clubs and organizations beginning in about 1888, when she spent four days at a meeting of the International Council of Women in Washington, DC. Later, she was head of the Massachusetts Federation

of Women's Clubs and founded the Amherst chapter of the Daughters of the American Revolution.

6. "Only a Shadow" by Collette Loomis was published in the *Springfield Republican* on September 24, 1859, p. 2. See the discussion in Paula Bernat Bennett, *Poets in the Public Sphere: The Emancipatory Project of American Women's Poetry, 1800–1900* (Princeton: Princeton University Press, 2003), p. 171.

7. Clara Barrus, *Whitman and Burroughs: Comrades* (Boston: Houghton Mifflin, 1931), p. 168.

8. "Fearless": the Wood County, West Virginia, Bar Association. See "Brinkerhoff-Loomis Home Page: Information About George Loomis" (accessed August 25, 2011).

9. See William Dean Howells, *Literary Friends and Acquaintance: A Personal Retrospect or American Authorship* (New York: Harper & Brothers, 1900), pp. 178, 179, 195. See also *Suburban Sketches* (New York: Hurd and Houghton, 1871).

10. Lawrence N. Powell, *New Masters: Northern Planters During the Civil War and Reconstruction* (New Haven: Yale University Press, 1980), p. xii, 115. Powell further notes, "The fact that the Massachusetts man paid his hands in full each month partly explains why so many laborers deserted him at once." The more usual practice was to defer full payment until after the crop was in, and Loomis was trusting. See also Millicent Todd, *Eben Jenks Loomis, 1828–1912: A Paper Read by His Granddaughter Millicent Todd to a Group of Friends* (Cambridge, MA: Riverside Press, 1913), pp. 28–30.

11. On Loomis as a distinguished man, see William Douglas O'Connor, quoted in *With Walt Whitman in Camden*, ed. Horace Traubel (Boston: Small, Maynard, 1906), 1: 313–14.

12. On Loomis's poetry, see *A Sunset Idyl and Other Poems* (Cambridge, MA: Riverside Press, 1903), which he dedicated "To my wife, Mary Alden Loomis, my most sympathetic reader and critic." On Sarah Morgan Bryan Piatt, see Paula Bernat Bennett, "Introduction," in *Palace-Burner: The Selected Poetry of Sarah Piatt*, pp. xxiii–lviii (Urbana: University of Illinois Press, 2001).

13. Longsworth, p. 27.

14. Mabel Todd, quoted in Longsworth, p. 37.

15. *Millicent's Life* is in the Millicent Todd Bingham Papers, MS 496D, Series II, Box 47, Sterling Memorial Library, Yale University.

16. Mabel to her parents, quoted in Jay Leyda, *The Years and Hours of Emily Dickinson*, 2 vols. (New Haven: Yale University Press, 1960), 2: 361.

17. Mabel's diary, quoted in Leyda, 2: 361.

18. Mabel, quoted in Leyda, 2: 354.

19. Todd's story "Footprints" appeared in the *Independent* 35 (September 27, 1883): 26–29. "Alleged modern artificiality" is from the first sentence of her "Preface" to *Poems by Emily Dickinson: Second Series*, ed. T. W. Higginson and Mabel Loomis Todd (Boston: Roberts Brothers, 1891).

20. Mabel, December 1, 1882, quoted in Leyda, 2: 386. Months earlier, Mabel was thrilled when she received "a box of the most exquisite flowers . . . hyacinths, heliotrope, and some odd yellow flowers which I do not know—from—who do you imagine? Miss Emily Dickinson!" Quoted in Leyda, 2: 361.

21. Mabel's journal, quoted in Leyda, 2: 376.

22. Martha Dickinson Bianchi, "T.G.D.—'Deare Childe,'" *The Wandering Eros* (Boston: Houghton Mifflin, 1924), p. 86.

23. "Wild life current" is in a letter from Austin to Mabel, about early December 1883. Quoted in Longsworth, p. 173.

24. See Lyndall Gordon, "Emily's Stand," in *Lives Like Loaded Guns: Emily Dickinson and Her Family's Feuds* (New York: Viking, 2010), pp. 197–230.

25. On Maggie Maher, an Irish immigrant, see Áife Murray, *Maid as Muse: How Servants Changed Emily Dickinson's Life and Language* (Hanover, NH: University Press of New England, 2010). Maggie testified about her knowledge of the liaison at the 1889 trial in which Lavinia accused the Todds of fraud.

26. On Millicent's childhood fear of Austin, see "Austin," from her fragmentary autobiography, quoted in Sewall, *The Life of Emily Dickinson*, 1: 297.

27. On the experiment, see Longsworth, *Austin and Mabel*, and Gordon, *Lives Like Loaded Guns*.

28. I quote Christopher Benfey, who is summarizing Peter Gay's argument. See Peter Gay, *The Bourgeois Experience Victoria to Freud: Education of the Senses* (New York: Oxford University Press, 1984), pp. 71–108, and Christopher Benfey, *The Great Wave: Gilded Age Misfits, Japanese Eccentrics, and the Opening of Old Japan* (New York: Random House, 2003), p. 192.

29. Charles E. Rosenberg, "Sexuality, Class and Role in 19th-Century America," *American Quarterly* 25.2 (May 1973): 131–53.

30. Ann Schofield, "Sin, Murder, Adultery, and More: Narratives of Transgression in Nineteenth-Century America," *American Studies* 43.2 (Summer 2002): 125. See also Laura Hanft Korobkin, *Criminal Conversations: Sentimentality and Nineteenth-Century Legal Stories of Adultery* (New York: Columbia University Press, 1998).

31. Mabel Todd, *Millicent's Life*. For more on Whitman, women writers, and motherhood, see Vivian R. Pollak, "'In Loftiest Spheres': Whitman's Visionary Feminism," in *The Erotic Whitman* (Berkeley: University of California Press, 2000), pp. 172–93.

32. Walt Whitman, "Song of Myself," in *Leaves of Grass and Other Writings*, ed. Michael Moon (New York: W. W. Norton, 2002), p. 34.

33. Mabel Todd, quoted in Leyda, 2: 438. The Dickinson family regularly read the *Century* magazine, which they associated with their friend J. G. Holland, who served as the founding editor of *Scribner's Monthly* until 1881, when *Scribner's* was redefined as the *Century*. For Emily Dickinson's friendship with Holland and his wife Elizabeth, see Chapter 6. Apparently Holland had the opportunity to publish Dickinson's poems but thought they were "not suitable . . . too ethereal." See Leyda, 2: 193.

34. Mark Twain, *Adventures of Huckleberry Finn*, ed. Thomas Cooley, 3rd ed. (New York: W. W. Norton, 1999), pp. 122–23:

ODE TO STEPHEN DOWLING BOTS, DEC'D

And did young Stephen sicken,
   And did young Stephen die?
And did the sad hearts thicken,
   And did the mourners cry?

No; such was not the fate of
   Young Stephen Dowling Bots;
Though sad hearts round him thickened,
   'Twas not from sickness' shots.

No whooping-cough did rack his frame,
    Nor measles drear, with spots;
Not these impaired the sacred name
    Of Stephen Dowling Bots.

Despised love struck not with woe
    That head of curly knots,
Nor stomach troubles laid him low,
    Young Stephen Dowling Bots.

O no. Then list with tearful eye,
    Whilst I his fate do tell.
His soul did from this cold world fly,
    By falling down a well.

They got him out and emptied him;
    Alas it was too late;
His spirit was gone for to sport aloft
    In the realms of the good and great.

35. Walter Blair, "Introduction," in *The Sweet Singer of Michigan: Poems by Mrs. Julia A. Moore* (Chicago: Pascal Covici, 1928), pp. xvi–xvii. See also *Mark Twain & Huck Finn* (Berkeley: University of California Press, 1960), in which Blair is more interested in "The Sweet Singer of Michigan" as a unique source. An excellent discussion of Twain's poetess as a stereotype is Barton Levi St. Armand, *Emily Dickinson and Her Culture: The Soul's Society* (New York: Cambridge University Press, 1984), pp. 24ff. He argues persuasively that the "Victorian Way of Death" included obituary verses on demand such as those of Emmeline Grangerford, Lydia Huntley Sigourney, and, in some instances, Dickinson.

36. Myra Jehlen, "Reading Gender in *Adventures of Huckleberry Finn*," in *"Adventures of Huckleberry Finn": A Case Study in Critical Controversy*, ed. Gerald Graff and James Phelan (Boston: Bedford/St. Martin's, 1995), p. 507.

37. Mark Twain, *Adventures of Huckleberry Finn*, ed. Cooley, 3rd ed., p. 123.

38. Edward Dickinson, quoted in *A Poet's Parents: The Courtship Letters of Emily Norcross and Edward Dickinson*, ed. Vivian R. Pollak (Chapel Hill: University of North Carolina Press, 1988), p. 35. Edward sent Emily Norcross a copy of Sedgwick's historical romance *Hope Leslie* in July 1827 shortly after it was published. He asked her to bring it with her when she came to Amherst, so that he could lend it around. For an illuminating reference to Sedgwick and the antebellum poetess tradition, see Eliza Richards, *Gender and the Poetics of Reception in Poe's Circle* (Cambridge: Cambridge University Press, 2004), pp. 77–79. See also Sedgwick at an 1848 party in Anne Lynch's New York salon attended by such literati as N. P. Willis, Margaret Fuller, Bayard Taylor, Grace Greenwood, and Horace Greeley, p. 16. In *From School to Salon: Reading Nineteenth-Century American Women's Poetry* (Princeton: Princeton University Press, 2004), pp. 13–16, 20–24, 29–31, 215n30, Mary Loeffelholz describes Sedgwick's role in the posthumous careers of Lucretia and Margaret Davidson. On Sedgwick, family, disciplinary intimacy, and culture, see also Richard H. Brodhead, *Cultures of Letters: Scenes of Reading and Writing in Nineteenth-Century America* (Chicago: University of Chicago Press, 1993). And see

also Nina Baym, *Woman's Fiction: A Guide to Novels by and about Women in America, 1820–1870* (Ithaca: Cornell University Press, 1978), pp. 63, 53–63.

39. "Peculiar" and "I am not very well acquainted" are quoted by Ellen E. Emerson, in Leyda, 2: 482. Under the pressure of feminist inquiry in the 1970s and 1980s, Dickinson's mother was increasingly written into the picture, as were her brother and sister-in-law. A strong case for Lavinia as an influence on Dickinson's thought has yet to be made.

40. Martha Dickinson Bianchi, quoted in Alfred Habegger, *"My Wars Are Laid Away in Books": The Life of Emily Dickinson* (New York: Random House, 2001), p. 589n.

41. Bianchi, quoted in Habegger, pp. 531, 532. *Recollections of a Country Girl* is in the Martha Dickinson Bianchi Papers, John Hay Library, Brown University.

42. In *The Single Hound: Poems of a Lifetime* (Boston: Little, Brown, 1914), p. 4, Bianchi prints only the last stanza of *Fr* 817, changing the dash in line 2 to a semicolon, eliminating the apostrophe in "It's," and capitalizing "single" and "identity." "ADVENTURE" is capitalized in keeping with the book's format. These choices produce a cheerier text.

43. Marietta Jameson in a letter to her son Frank, quoted in Longsworth, 121n.

44. Mabel Todd, quoted in Leyda, 2: 474.

45. Mabel Todd, in Leyda, 2: 474.

46. Roland Barthes, "A Cruel Country: Notes on Mourning," *New Yorker* (September 13, 2010): 26. Translation by Richard Howard.

47. Marietta Jameson, quoted in Leyda, 2: 471.

48. Mabel Todd, quoted in Longsworth, p. 290. David had worked day and night oblivious of the sickening heat, but it was not to be. "I knew that he was losing what up to this point is the chance of his life, for his method of observing this had never been used at an eclipse before, & all astronomers were watching." Mabel never respected him so much again.

49. Mabel Loomis Todd, "The Ascent of Fuji-San," *Nation* (October 13, 1887). Quoted in Benfey, *The Great Wave*, p. 197.

50. David Peck Todd, quoted in Bingham, *Ancestors' Brocades*, p. 31n.

51. See Longsworth, p. 201.

52. Mabel's journal entry of July 15, 1889, is quoted in Sewall, 1: 220.

53. Willa Cather, "The House on Charles Street," *Literary Review* 3 (November 4, 1922): 173. "Eminent Friendships" is Fields, in *Memories of a Hostess: A Chronicle of Eminent Friendships Drawn Chiefly from the Diaries of Mrs. James T. Fields*, ed. M. A. De Wolfe Howe (Boston: Atlantic Monthly Press, 1922). On Fields as hostess, philanthropist, poet, biographer, editor, essayist, and as Sarah Orne Jewett's beloved companion, see Rita K. Gollin, *Annie Adams Fields: Woman of Letters* (Amherst: University of Massachusetts Press, 2002); Mary Loeffelholz, "Metropolitan Pastoral: The Salon Poetry of Annie Fields," in *From School to Salon: Reading Nineteenth-Century American Women's Poetry* (Princeton: Princeton University Press, 2004), pp. 162–91; Susan K. Harris, *The Cultural Work of the Late Nineteenth-Century Hostess: Annie Adams Fields and Mary Gladstone Drew* (New York: Palgrave Macmillan, 2002).

54. Mabel, quoted in Longsworth, p. 336.

55. Mabel, quoted in Longsworth, pp. 345, 344.

56. Austin, quoted in Longsworth, p. 358.

57. Mabel quoting her cousin Lydia Coonley, in Longsworth, p. 360.

58. Thomas Niles, quoted in Bingham, *Ancestors' Brocades*, p. 53.

59. Austin, quoted in Bingham, *Ancestors' Brocades*, p. 66.

60. See *Emily Dickinson's Reception in the 1890s: A Documentary History*, ed. Willis J. Buckingham (Pittsburgh: University of Pittsburgh Press, 1989), pp. 416, 397, 477, 96.

61. Quoted in *Emily Dickinson's Reception in the 1890s*, pp. 142, 143.

62. Eben Jenks Loomis, quoted in Longsworth, p. 364.

63. See Ralph Waldo Emerson, "New Poetry," *Dial: A Magazine for Literature, Philosophy, and Religion* 1.2 (October 1840). On Emerson's gendered language, see David Leverenz, "The Politics of Emerson's Man-Making Words," *Manhood and the American Renaissance* (Ithaca: Cornell University Press, 1989), pp. 42–71. Higginson's "Preface" to the 1890 *Poems by Emily Dickinson* is reprinted in *Emily Dickinson's Reception in the 1890s*, pp. 13–14.

64. On portfolios and scrapbooks, see St. Armand, p. 5. Virginia Jackson notes that such collections often included publicly circulated materials. She critiques Higginson's emphasis on privacy. See *Dickinson's Misery: A Theory of Lyric Reading* (Princeton: Princeton University Press, 2005), p. 58.

65. "An Open Portfolio," *Christian Union* 42 (September 25, 1890): 392–93, is quoted in *Emily Dickinson's Reception in the 1890s*, pp. 3–4.

66. Thomas Wentworth Higginson, "Emerson," in *Contemporaries* (Boston: Houghton, Mifflin, 1900). A version of the essay appeared in the *Nation* in May 1882, and Higginson was knowledgeable enough about Emerson's life to be consulted by the first biographers. See Robert D. Habich, *Building Their Own Waldos: Emerson's First Biographers and the Politics of Life-Writing in the Gilded Age* (Iowa City: University of Iowa Press, 2011).

67. "Transcendentalist" is Charles Goodrich Whiting, *Springfield Republican* (November 16, 1890), quoted in Buckingham, *Reception*, p. 16; "Influence of Emerson" is "The World of New Books," *Philadelphia Press* (November 22, 1890), in Buckingham, p. 25. There are many fine studies of Emerson's influence on Dickinson's language, among them David Porter, *Dickinson: The Modern Idiom* (Cambridge, MA: Harvard University Press, 1981), and Cristanne Miller, *Emily Dickinson: A Poet's Grammar* (Cambridge, MA: Harvard University Press, 1987). I discuss Emerson's and Dickinson's theme of compensation in "Thirst and Starvation in Emily Dickinson's Poetry," *American Literature* (1979), reprinted in *Emily Dickinson: A Collection of Critical Essays*, ed. Judith Farr (Upper Saddle River, NJ: Prentice Hall, 1996), pp. 62–75.

68. See Louise Chandler Moulton, "A Very Remarkable Book," *Boston Sunday Herald* (November 23, 1890), in Buckingham, pp. 33–37.

69. Mabel Todd, in Bingham, *Ancestors' Brocades*, p. 74n.

70. "Organic lesion" is Maurice Thompson, "Miss Dickinson's Poems," *America* (January 8, 1891), in Buckingham, p. 95.

71. Thompson's letter to Higginson is quoted in Bingham, *Ancestors' Brocades*, p. 79.

72. Jay Fliegelman, *Declaring Independence; Jefferson, Natural Language & the Culture of Performance* (Stanford: Stanford University Press, 1991), p. 228n29.

73. On Dickinson's courage, see Todd, "Bright Bits from Bright Books," *Home Magazine* 3 (November 1890): 13. Quoted in Buckingham, p. 11.

74. Higginson, "Preface" 1890, quoted in Buckingham, p. 13. "Tainted" is Susan B. Rosenbaum, *Professing Sincerity: Modern Lyric Poetry, Commercial Culture, and the Crisis in Reading* (Charlottesville: University of Virginia Press, 2007). As she explains, "Sincerity has dominated both the reading and writing of Anglo-American poetry since the late eighteenth century, influencing the widespread understanding of the lyric poem as a site of private, individual expression, an aesthetic and moral refuge from the taint of commercial culture." Focusing on British romanticism and post-1945 American lyric, she shows that "by performing their 'private' lives and feelings in public, poets marketed the self, cultivated celebrity, and advanced

professional careers. Professing sincerity was a moral practice, but it was also good business," pp. 4–5.

75. Todd's prefaces are in Buckingham, pp. 236–37, 340–43, 343–48, 460, as well as some of the commentary interspersed in *Letters of Emily Dickinson*, 2 vols. (Boston: Roberts Brothers, 1894). It should also be noted that the 1894 *Letters* contains 109 previously unpublished poems. This contribution is rarely emphasized, and those wanting to pursue questions about Todd's editorial practices would be well advised to look more carefully at this edition.

76. Todd, *Letters* 1894, in Buckingham, pp. 344–45.

77. Todd, *Letters* 1894, pp. 244–45.

78. See "Grim Slumber Songs," *New York Commercial Advertiser*, January 6, 1891, in Buckingham, p. 87.

79. "Much too queer": David Peck Todd, paraphrase quoted in Bingham, *Ancestors' Brocades*, p. 51n.

80. "When a thought": Higginson, "Open Portfolio," *Christian Union*, in Buckingham, p. 6. Rhymes can create merely artificial connections, and Donald Wesling observes that in our modern idiom, "rhyme is a deception all the more suspect because it gives us pleasure." See *The Chances of Rhyme: Device and Modernity* (Berkeley: University of California Press, 1980), p. ix.

81. On thought-rhymes, see Todd, "Preface" to *Poems: Second Series*, reprinted in Buckingham, p. 237.

82. "Too intense": Higginson, "Preface" 1890, in Buckingham, p. 8.

83. Higginson's letter of April 21, 1891, is quoted in Bingham, *Ancestors' Brocades*, p. 127.

84. Charles Goodrich Whiting, *Springfield Republican*, November 8, 1891. Quoted in Buckingham, p. 231.

85. The quotations are from Todd's 1891 "Preface" to *Poems: Second Series*, in Buckingham, pp. 237–38.

86. Todd, 1891 "Preface," in Buckingham, p. 236.

87. Susan Dickinson's letter to Higginson is quoted in Bingham, *Ancestors' Brocades*, pp. 86–87.

88. "Mr. Dickinson thinks": quoted in Bingham, *Ancestors' Brocades*, pp. 114–15. On the strength of Lavinia's legal position, see Elizabeth Horan, "To Market: The Dickinson Copyright Laws," *Emily Dickinson Journal* 5.1 (Spring 1996): 88–120. See also Elizabeth Rosa Horan, "Technically Outside the Law: Who Permits, Who Profits, and Why," *Emily Dickinson Journal* 10.1 (Spring 2001): 34–54.

89. "*sub rosa*": quoted in Bingham, *Ancestors' Brocades*, p. 60; "It is hard": Bingham, *Ancestors' Brocades*, p. 62.

90. Mabel's 1894 diary entry is quoted in Bingham, *Ancestors' Brocades*, p. 285, and Longsworth, p. 386.

91. For Austin's letter, see Longsworth, p. 297. She explains that the will, dated November 3, 1887, "left his share of his father's estate (the Homestead, the meadow, certain stocks and bonds) to Vinnie, a [landscape] painting and an engraving to Mabel Todd, and all the rest of his property to Sue."

92. Austin's deathbed letter is quoted in Longsworth, p. 392.

93. Mabel on her dead master is in Gordon, p. 282.

94. "One lovely thing": Mabel's diary, December 29, 1895, quoted in Longsworth, p. 403.

95. Gordon, p. 286.

96. When a "Record of conveyance was made in the Registry of Deeds at Northampton on April 1, 1896," the Todds were unaware of it. They left for Japan several days later, where

David wanted to photograph the corona of a total solar eclipse. See "Record of conveyance": Longsworth, p. 405.

97. The *New York Tribune* review appeared on August 23, 1896, and is reprinted in Buckingham, p. 459.

98. Ned Dickinson to Lavinia, quoted in Longsworth, pp. 408–9.

99. See Higginson, "Recent Poetry," *Nation* 62 (June 4, 1896), reprinted in Buckingham, p. 457.

100. See Caroline C. Maun, "Editorial Policy in *The Poems of Emily Dickinson, Third Series*," *Emily Dickinson Journal* 3.2 (Fall 1994): 56–77. For an account of the journey, see Mabel's "unscientific account of a scientific expedition," in *Corona and Coronet* (Boston: Houghton Mifflin, 1898). As Benfey notes in *The Great Wave*, pp. 203–4, both Todds used an altered, handwritten version of "This – is the land – the Sunset washes" (*Fr* 297) to bid farewell to their hosts in Esashi.

101. See Mabel Loomis Todd, "A Mid-Pacific College," *Outlook* 54 (August 15, 1896): 285.

102. Todd, ed., *Poems by Emily Dickinson: Third Series* (Boston: Roberts Brothers, 1896), p. 38.

103. Maggie Maher's court testimony, quoted in Gordon, pp. 295–96.

104. Todd, "Introductory" to the 1894 *Letters*, quoted in Buckingham, p. 341.

105. Susan Dickinson's *Springfield Republican* obituary, "Miss Emily Dickinson of Amherst," is reprinted in Buckingham, pp. 551–52.

106. Susan Dickinson, quoted in Bingham, *Ancestors' Brocades*, p. 86.

107. "True as the grave": William Dean Howells, "Editor's Study," *Harper's New Monthly Magazine* 82 (January 1891): 318–21, reprinted in Buckingham, pp. 73–78.

108. William Dean Howells, *Mark Twain-Howells Letters: The Correspondence of Samuel L. Clemens and William Dean Howells, 1872–1910*, ed. Henry Nash Smith and William M. Gibson, with the assistance of Frederick Anderson, 2 vols. (Cambridge, MA: Harvard University Press, 1960), 2: 681. For Dickinson on Howells—"one hesitates"—see *L* 622. She linked him not to Twain but to Henry James.

109. Martha Dickinson remained single until she was thirty-six, when she married a Russian adventurer who claimed to have served in the czar's Imperial Horse Guard. For an account of Captain Alexander Emmanuel Bianchi's financial *mis*adventures, which led to his arrest in New York City in 1907 and to the couple's eventual separation and divorce, see Gordon, pp. 322–23.

110. Mabel Todd's second journal, dated "From November 10th, 1875, to March 5th, 1879," is in the Mabel Loomis Todd Papers, 496C, Series III, Box 45, Sterling Library, Yale University.

111. Todd's second journal, Mabel Loomis Todd Papers, 496 C, Series III, Box 45.

112. "We never know how high we are" is quoted from Todd, "Introductory," 1894 *Letters*, in Buckingham, pp. 342–43.

1. "Polyphonic Craftsman" is quoted from *The Poems of Marianne Moore*, ed. Grace Schulman (New York: Viking, 2003), p. 37. The undated typescript may have been part of a manuscript Moore tried unsuccessfully to publish in England in 1915.

2. "Omissions are not accidents": see the motto to *The Complete Poems* (New York: Macmillan, 1967), p. vii. See also Jeanne Heuving, *Omissions Are Not Accidents: Gender in the Art of Marianne Moore* (Detroit, MI: Wayne State University Press, 1992).

3. "Watchful" is from "The Paper Nautilus," in *The Complete Poems of Marianne Moore* (New York: Macmillan/Viking, 1967; rev. 1981), p. 121. This edition will be cited as *P*. In "Nautilus," Moore associates the mother and the artist. On being oversupervised, see Donald Hall, "Interview with Marianne Moore," *McCall's* 93.3 (December 1965): 182.

4. Mary Warner Moore paid to have the memorial book published. See *Sermons of the Rev. John R. Warner, D. D., with a Sketch of His Life by his Daughter, Mary Warner Moore* (Philadelphia: J. B. Lippincott, 1895), title page.

5. *Sermons*, "Sketch," p. 16.

6. Linda Leavell, "Kirkwood and Kindergarten," in *Critics and Poets on Marianne Moore: "A Right Good Salvo of Barks,"* ed. Linda Leavell, Cristanne Miller, and Robin G. Schulze (Lewisburg, PA: Bucknell University Press, 2005), p. 26. Leavell further comments that "John Warner's own parents were Irish immigrants; the family considered itself Scotch Irish."

7. Mary Craig Eyster began to live with her brother-in-law at the Manse after the deaths of her daughters and of her husband. In *Holding on Upside Down: The Life and Work of Marianne Moore* (New York: Farrar, Straus and Giroux, 2013), Linda Leavell suggests that George Eyster, who was the inspector of the Philadelphia mint, probably committed suicide after a series of financial disappointments. See p. 23. Mary Warner Moore later inherited her aunt's estate.

8. "When I Was Sixteen," in *The Complete Prose of Marianne Moore*, ed. Patricia C. Willis (New York: Viking, 1986), p. 662. This edition will be cited as *Pr*.

9. *Sermons*, "Sketch," p. 14.

10. Mary Institute graduates often took courses at the art school, whose offerings included painting, sculpture, sketching, and art history.

11. Mary Warner Moore, unpublished memoir, Rosenbach Museum & Library, Philadelphia.

12. Mary Warner Moore, letter of February 23, 1916, Rosenbach Museum & Library.

13. *Sermons*, "Sketch," pp. 8–9.

14. Mary Warner Moore had less confidence in her son's malleability than in her daughter's. She later interfered in his romances, arguing against one of them on the grounds of a possible hereditary taint of insanity—the John Milton Moore factor. After he married, her relations with his wife were never easy. Constance Eustis Moore was also disturbed by his continuing closeness to Marianne.

15. *Sermons*, "Sketch," p. 13.

16. For an excellent summation of some of the many sources of Moore's quoting practices, see Laura O'Connor, "Flamboyant Reticence: An Irish Incognita," in *Critics and Poets on Marianne Moore: "A Right Good Salvo of Barks,"* ed. Linda Leavell, Cristanne Miller, and Robin G. Schulze (Lewisburg, PA: Bucknell University Press, 2005), p. 179n. O'Connor notes that "almost all of Moore's critics have explored some aspect of her citational strategies." See also Elizabeth Gregory, *Quotation and Modern American Poetry: "Imaginary Gardens with Real Toads"* (Houston, TX: Rice University Press, 1996). Gregory is most interested in Moore's revision of gender and, by analogy, her revision of "hierarchies of all kinds," p. 130.

17. *Sermons*, "Sketch," pp. 18–19.

18. Marianne Moore, quoted in Charles Molesworth, *Marianne Moore: A Literary Life* (New York: Atheneum, 1990), p. 7. Moore was seven.

19. Moore, quoted in *The Selected Letters of Marianne Moore*, ed. Bonnie Costello, Celeste Goodrich, and Cristanne Miller (New York: Knopf, 1997), p. 7. See also *The Poems of Marianne Moore*, ed. Schulman, p. 3. Schulman observes that the young poetess uses a semicolon after the salutation.

20. Mary Warner Moore, quoted in *Selected Letters*, p. 6.

21. See Leavell, *Holding on Upside Down*, p. 34.

22. Leavell, *Holding on Upside Down*, pp. 35, 36.

23. Uncle Henry Warner had been managing her investments. After he died, his nephew Henry Warner Armstrong took over some of her inherited real estate, and Leavell notes that Armstrong embezzled some of the profits.

24. In Kirkwood, the children had attended a kindergarten, and in Ben Avon they attended a dame school, "Miss Lizzie's." Metzger Primary School closed its doors to boys a year after they arrived, and Warner began attending the local public school. In high school, Marianne was a student in her mother's classes.

25. In *Holding on Upside Down*, Leavell describes a lesbian partnership between Mary Norcross and Mary Moore, terminated by Norcross in the summer of 1910 because she had fallen in love with another woman. The breakup was traumatic for all involved, including Marianne. Much later, Marianne Moore wrote a moving obituary for Mary Jackson Norcross in the *Bryn Mawr Alumnae Bulletin* 28 (June 1938): 27–28, which is quoted in full in Molesworth, *Marianne Moore*, p. 300. She praises Norcross as a model of selflessness, but the reality was more complex. On the Norcross family and its influence on her development, see also *Pr* 572: "We were constantly discussing authors."

26. Moore, quoted in *Letters*, p. 19.

27. "'He Wrote the History Book'" appeared both in the *Egoist* 3 (May 1, 1916): 71 and in Moore's first book publication, *Poems* (London: Egoist Press, 1921).

28. Charles McLean Andrews (1863–1943) was an authority on American colonial history. He taught at Bryn Mawr from 1889 to 1907, at Johns Hopkins from 1907 to 1910, and at Yale from 1910 until his retirement in 1931. The "book," however, was *A History of England* (Boston: Allyn and Bacon, 1903). See Moore's letter to her mother and brother, February 11, 1906, Rosenbach: "I am John Andrews. My father wrote the English History." See also Patricia C. Willis, "'He Wrote the History Book,'" *Marianne Moore Newsletter* 5.1 (Spring 1981): 19–20. Andrews was not the only professor who urged Moore to be clearer.

29. John Williams Andrews (b. November 1898) was a fighter pilot during World War I and graduated from Yale College in 1920. He was an international news correspondent based in China before receiving his degree from Yale Law School in 1926. The younger Andrews wrote some history books too, and taught history at Yale for several years, but in addition to his law practice and government service, he was also "editor-in-chief of *Poet Lore* and a member of the Poetry Society of America." See "Strangers to Us All: Lawyers and Poetry," http://myweb.wvnet.edu/~jelkins/lp-2001/andrews.html. *The Poetry Society of America Anthology* (1946) includes his "New Wonder" but nothing by Moore. It's a terrible poem, beginning, "To me, between the all-absorbing wonders / Of birth and death, is come this woman-thing," but his forte may have been narrative, and *Poet Lore* has established a narrative poetry prize in his honor.

30. See *Daisy Miller: A Study*, in *Tales of Henry James*, ed. Christof Wegelin and Henry B. Wonham, 2nd ed.(New York: W. W. Norton, 2003), p. 5.

31. Moore's 1907 letter to her mother and brother is quoted in *Selected Letters*, p. 28. For more on the Bryn Mawr context, see Bethany Hicok, "To Work 'Lovingly': Marianne Moore

at Bryn Mawr, 1905–1909," in *Degrees of Freedom: American Women Poets and the Women's College, 1905–1955* (Lewisburg, PA: Bucknell University Press, 2008), pp. 29–30. The quotation refers to a letter by Mary Warner Moore when she chastised her daughter for not working "lovingly enough." Hicok aptly notes that the context links writing and the nurturing aspect of motherhood, which Hicok distinguishes from the biological labor of childbirth. See also Lynn D. Gordon, *Gender and Higher Education in the Progressive Era* (New Haven: Yale University Press, 1990), and Carroll Smith-Rosenberg, "The Female World of Love and Ritual: Relations Between Women in Nineteenth-Century America," *Signs* (1975), reprinted in *Disorderly Conduct: Visions of Gender in Victorian America* (New York: Oxford University Press, 1984), pp. 53–76. Among other valuable sources on the Bryn Mawr context, see Helen Lefkowitz Horowitz, *The Power and Passion of M. Carey Thomas* (New York: Alfred A. Knopf, 1994); Barbara Miller Solomon, *In the Company of Educated Women: A History of Women and Higher Education in America* (New Haven: Yale University Press, 1985); and Patricia Ann Palmieri, *In Adamless Eden: The Community of Women Faculty at Wellesley* (New Haven: Yale University Press, 1995).

32. For Henry James as Moore's favorite "literary bachelor," see also Leavell, "Marianne Moore, the James Family, and the Politics of Celibacy," *Twentieth-Century Literature* 49.2 (Summer 2003): 219–45.

33. Moore described "Marriage" as a little anthology in the "Foreword" to *A Marianne Moore Reader* (New York: Viking, 1961), p. xv. On the poem's publication history, see Robin G. Schulze, ed., *Becoming Marianne Moore: The Early Poems, 1907–1924* (Berkeley: University of California Press, 2002), p. 455. Schulze notes that "most critics agree that Moore's ruminations on the institution of marriage have their roots in the 1921 marriage of convenience of her friend Winifred Ellerman (better known as the historical novelist Bryher) to writer and editor Robert McAlmon," p. 459. For readings of the poem within this frame, see Lynn Keller and Cristanne Miller, "'The Tooth of Disputation': Marianne Moore's 'Marriage,'" *Sagetrieb* 6.3 (Winter 1987): 99–116, and David Bergman, "Marianne Moore and the Problem of Marriage," *American Literature* 60.2 (May 1988): 241–54. For the role of Bryher and H. D. in publishing the 1921 *Poems*, see Cyrena N. Pondrom, "Marianne Moore and H. D.: Female Community and Poetic Achievement," in *Marianne Moore: Woman and Poet*, ed. Patricia C. Willis (Orono, ME: National Poetry Foundation, 1990), pp. 371–402, and Jayne E. Marek, *Women Editing Modernism: "Little" Magazines & Literary History* (Lexington: University of Kentucky Press, 1995), pp. 109–11 and passim. For a discussion of Thayer's marriage proposal, see Linda Leavell, "'Frightening Disinterestedness': The Personal Circumstances of Marianne Moore's 'Marriage,'" *Journal of Modern Literature* 31.1 (Fall 2007): 64–79.

34. Moore, "Foreword," *A Marianne Moore Reader*, p. xv.

35. See Elisabeth W. Joyce, "The Collage of 'Marriage': Marianne Moore's Formal and Cultural Critique," *Mosaic* 26.4 (Fall 1993): 103–18.

36. Moore's draft is quoted in Joyce, p. 109. I interpret her concern with loss as a reflection of her family's history, but Moore does not entertain the suggestion of separation or divorce in "Marriage." Philosophically, the ur-marriage she describes is either never or forever.

37. See Cheryl Walker, *The Nightingale's Burden: Women Poets and American Culture Before 1900* (Bloomington: Indiana University Press, 1982), p. xi.

38. On the author function and Moore's relations to traditions of gendered voice, see Cristanne Miller, *Marianne Moore: Questions of Authority* (Cambridge, MA: Harvard University Press, 1995). See also Cristanne Miller, *Cultures of Modernism: Marianne Moore, Mina Loy, and*

Else Lasker-Schüler: Gender and Literary Community in New York and Berlin (Ann Arbor: University of Michigan Press, 2005).

39. On lesbian desire: Susan McCabe, for example, believes that these lines are "a personal address to Bryher as Eve." See "'Let's Be Alone Together': Bryher's and Marianne Moore's Aesthetic-Erotic Collaboration," *Modernism/Modernity* 17.3 (September 2010): 612.

40. See Heather Love, *Feeling Backward: Loss and the Politics of Queer History* (Cambridge, MA: Harvard University Press, 2007), p. 78.

41. Laurence Stapleton, *Marianne Moore: The Poet's Advance* (Princeton: Princeton University Press, 1978), p. 39. The handsome Adam passage is from Moore's *Poetry Notebook*, Rosenbach 1251/7, p. 16.

42. See Emory Holloway, ed., *The Uncollected Poetry and Prose of Walt Whitman*, 2 vols. (Garden City, New York: Doubleday, Page, 1921), 2: 102n. For further discussion of gender switching in "Once I Pass'd through a Populous City," see Vivian R. Pollak, *The Erotic Whitman* (Berkeley: University of California Press, 2000), pp. 133ff. It is not clear how much of Whitman Moore had read by 1922 when she was composing "Marriage," but in 1915 she wrote to her brother about seeing "a magnificent photograph of Whitman with autographs" on a visit to *Others* editor Alfred Kreymborg's apartment. See *Selected Letters*, p. 106.

43. Kathryn R. Kent, "The *M* Multiplying," in *Making Girls into Women: American Women's Writing and the Rise of Lesbian Identity* (Durham, NC: Duke University Press, 2003), p. 174.

44. See "'And Shall Life Pass an Old Maid By?'" in *The Poems of Marianne Moore*, ed. Schulman, p. 40.

45. See Bryher, *West* (London: Jonathan Cape, 1925), p. 35.

46. Moore's April 1921 response to Bryher is in *Letters*, p. 153.

47. Kent, p. 181.

48. Kent, p. 181.

49. Benjamin Kahan, "'The Viper's Traffic-Knot': Celibacy and Queerness in the 'Late' Marianne Moore," *GLQ: A Journal of Lesbian and Gay Studies* 14.4 (2008): 509–35.

50. On "love undying": the phrase is from "Voracities and Verities Sometimes Are Interacting," which Moore wrote not long after Mary's death. It begins, "I don't like diamonds." She had already sent the diamond brooch that was Mary's wedding gift from John Milton Moore to her close friend and patron Hildegarde Watson.

51. On the haircutting episode, see the quotation from her "brief, incomplete memoir written in 1969–70." Moore describes the severed foot of her hair as a "truncated relic" and says that it inspired the "Rape of the Lock" parody she and her friend produced. See *Letters*, p. 142n. She and Mary Frances Nearing wrote the poem during a Thanksgiving vacation when she had not returned to Carlisle as usual. It seems that hair cutting held special meaning for Moore, as Elizabeth Bishop obliquely observes in the memoir "Efforts of Affection." Bishop describes a visit to the circus, in which Moore, with lots of forethought, snips the hair of a baby elephant. She emphasizes Moore's elaborately conceived show of "criminal ingenuity." See "Efforts of Affection: A Memoir of Marianne Moore," in *Elizabeth Bishop: Poems, Prose, and Letters*, ed. Robert Giroux and Lloyd Schwartz (New York: Library of America, 2008), pp. 474–75.

52. Mary Ann O'Farrell theorizes that the blush functions as an important trope in nineteenth-century British novels because it represents involuntary desire. See *Telling Complexions: The Nineteenth-Century English Novel and the Blush* (Durham, NC: Duke University Press, 1997). See also Kenneth Burke, "She Taught Me to Blush," in *Festschrift for Marianne Moore's*

Seventy Seventh Birthday, by Various Hands, ed. Tambimuttu (New York: Tambimuttu and Mass, 1964), p. 61.

53. John Emil Vincent, *Queer Lyrics: Difficulty and Closure in American Poetry* (New York: Palgrave Macmillan, 2002), p. 109. Vincent is revising T. S. Eliot's formula in "The Three Voices of Poetry." "Queer nonidentity" is Benjamin Kahan's formula for Vincent's description. See Kahan, p. 521.

54. See M. Carey Thomas, "Present Day Problems in Teaching: An Address Delivered at Mount Holyoke College Founder's Day, October 7, 1921," *Mount Holyoke Alumnae Quarterly* 5:4 (January 1922): 193–99. Here is the sentence Moore extracts: "As in 1912, so in 1921, the very men who have generously yielded so much to women are themselves still sitting in the seats of the mighty, enthroned in all the ancient privilege of sex, and are still jealously guarding for themselves and for other men the prizes and rewards of intellect and achievement,—more pay for the same work, the most highly paid positions in all occupations, such as the best high school positions, all superintendencies, principalships, associate professorships, full professorships, head curatorships in museums, and even an unfair proportion of fellowships and scholarships, especially of the most valuable kinds, stately funerals, monuments, statues, membership in academies, medals, titles, *stars, garters, ribbons, buttons and other shining baubles*, so valueless in themselves and yet so infinitely valuable because they are symbols of recognition by their fellows and of fame richly deserved for difficult work done" (p. 195, italics mine).

55. The publication history of "Marriage" is complex, even for Moore. The *Manikin* version reproduced in Schulze, *Becoming Marianne Moore*, pp. 289–306, includes line numbers, and there are no notes. The 1924 *Observations* has notes but no line numbers in either the poem or the notes; the 1925 *Observations* has no line numbers in the text, but there are line numbers in the notes; similarly for the 1935 and 1951 *Selected Poems* and the 1967 *Complete Poems*.

56. Her striking appearance didn't hurt either.

57. Moore, *Letters*, p. 48. Carey Thomas read "To My Cup-Bearer" aloud. See Schulman, *Poems*, p. 9.

58. Georgiana Goddard King received her B.A. in English from Bryn Mawr in 1896 and her M.A. in philosophy and political science in 1897, also from Bryn Mawr. In 1907, she tried unsuccessfully to interest her own publisher, Macmillan, in Stein's *Three Lives* and blurbed the book when it was published in 1909 by Grafton at Stein's expense. On King's turn from literature to art history, and on King and Stein, see Susanna Terrell Saunders, "Georgiana Goddard King (1871–1939): Educator and Pioneer in Medieval Spanish Art," in *Women as Interpreters of the Visual Arts, 1820–1979*, ed. Claire Richter Sherman and Adele M. Holcomb (Westport, CT: Greenwood Press, 1981), pp. 209–38. See also Steven J. Meyer, *Irresistible Dictation: Gertrude Stein and the Correlations of Writing and Science* (Stanford: Stanford University Press, 2001), pp. 297–301. Meyer explains, "As early as the winter of 1907, Stein was making arrangements for King to read the tales later published as *Three Lives*, and well into the next decade she regularly sent copies of manuscripts to King to read," p. 298. See also Brenda Wineapple, *Sister Brother: Gertrude & Leo Stein* (Baltimore: Johns Hopkins University Press, 1996), p. 269. King was a poet as well as an art historian. See her dramatic poem, *The Way of Perfect Love* (New York: Macmillan, 1908). On lesbian culture at Bryn Mawr, as exemplified by Carey Thomas, see Lillian Faderman, *Odd Girls and Twilight Lovers: A History of Lesbian Life in Twentieth-Century America* (New York: Columbia University Press, 1991), pp. 17, 24, 28–31, 35, 269, 314n, and Leila J. Rupp, *A Desired Past: A Short History of Same-Sex Love in America* (Chicago: University of Chicago Press, 1999), pp. 88, 90–91, 155.

59. The entry is for May 8, 1909, with "carnnally" misspelled. Moore's spelling is usually impeccable. Lecture Notebook, Rosenbach, vii: 05:07; 1251/27.

60. On Dickinsonian irony, see also Canadian poet Bliss Carman, who in 1896 wrote that Dickinson was "full of skepticism and the gentle irony of formal unbelief," but he imagines that the function of her gentle irony is to bring us "face to face with new objects of worship." Quoted in Willis J. Buckingham, ed., *Emily Dickinson's Reception in the 1890s: A Documentary History* (Pittsburgh: University of Pittsburgh Press, 1989), pp. 504–8. Like Goddard King, Carman compares Dickinson to Swinburne, but he concludes that because of her lack of "sensuousness," she "never could have risen into the first rank of poets," p. 508. Carman's essay marked the publication of the 1896 *Poems* and appeared in the *Boston Evening Transcript* on November 21.

61. For more on the unpublished record, see Cynthia Hogue, "'The Plucked String': Emily Dickinson, Marianne Moore and the Poetics of Select Defects," *Emily Dickinson Journal* 7.1 (Spring 1998): 89–109. Hogue provides a theoretical frame for thinking about Moore's identificatory anxiety and modifies Betsy Erkkila's claim that Moore "had no desire to place herself in the literary tradition of Emily Dickinson." See Hogue, p. 89, and Erkkila, *The Wicked Sisters: Women Poets, Literary History, and Discord* (New York: Oxford University Press, 1992), p. 102. Whereas Erkkila states that Moore "found her precursors among men rather than women," Hogue suggests that "Erkkila may, in fact, be too hasty."

62. Marianne Moore's letter of December 1926 to Hart Crane is at the Beinecke Rare Book and Manuscript Library, Yale University. Crane published "To Emily Dickinson" in the *Nation* (June 29, 1927): 718.

63. Scofield Thayer, "Announcement," *Dial* 78 (January 1925): 89. Thayer was lugubrious and "Glee – The great storm is over" describes a physical or psychological shipwreck, in which "Four – have recovered the Land – / Forty – gone down together – / Into the boiling Sand" (*Fr* 685). See also *The Complete Poems of Emily Dickinson*, ed. Martha Dickinson Bianchi (Boston: Little, Brown, 1924), p. 5. The "Introduction" claims that this volume is "a final complete edition." Bianchi evidently did not believe that Dickinson was scandalous. She writes, "All truth came to Emily straight from honor to honor unimpaired. She never trafficked with falsehood seriously, never employed a deception in thought or feeling of her own," instead attributing to her "pitiless sincerity," p. vi. Yet Bianchi's *The Life and Letters of Emily Dickinson*, which was published that same year, pushes the romance theory. Her point is that Emily resisted temptation. See chap. 5, "'The End of Peace' 1853–55," in *The Life and Letters of Emily Dickinson* (Boston: Houghton Mifflin, 1924), pp. 43–51.

64. Moore, *Letters*, p. 216.

65. "The Hero" appeared in *Poetry* in June 1932, as did "The Steeple-Jack" and "The Student," under the title "Part of a Novel, Part of a Poem, Part of a Play." Her review of *Letters of Emily Dickinson* (New York: Harper & Brothers, 1931), ed. Mabel Loomis Todd, appeared in *Poetry* 41 (January 1933): 219–26.

66. "Expressionary need" is from "Pym," a story Moore published in *Tipyn o'Bob* in January 1908. Pym is a young man and an aspiring author, in a vaguely British context. He says, "There are times when I should give anything on earth to have writing a matter of indifference to me. Then add with a glance modestly askance, that it is undeniably convenient, in time of expressionary need, to be able to say things to the point. And, irrelevantly, that I like the thing for the element of personal adventure in it." See *Pr* 12–16.

67. Thomas Wentworth Higginson, "Emily Dickinson's Letters," *Atlantic Monthly* 68.408 (October 1891): 453.

68. Martha Dickinson Bianchi, "Introduction," in *The Single Hound: Poems of a Lifetime by Emily Dickinson* (Boston: Little, Brown, 1914), pp. v–xviii. The quotations are from pp. v, vi, vii, xiii, xi, x.

69. The quotations are from Bianchi, "Introduction," pp. viii, vi, xviii, xviii–xix.

70. James Warwick Price, "Three Forgotten Poetesses," *Forum* 42 (March 1912): 361–66. The quotations are from pp. 361, 365, 363. "Looked through nature" is attributed to Higginson.

71. Martha Hale Shackford, "The Poetry of Emily Dickinson," *Atlantic Monthly* 111 (January 1913): 93–97. Reprinted in *The Recognition of Emily Dickinson*, ed. Caesar R. Blake and Carlton F. Wells (Ann Arbor: University of Michigan Press, 1964), pp. 79–87. The quotations are from pp. 84 and 98.

72. Moore discusses Marsden Hartley in Donald Hall, "Interview with Marianne Moore," *McCall's* 93 (December 1965): 74ff. See also her account of a 1915 visit to photographer Alfred Stieglitz's 291 gallery, where he showed her "paintings of mountains by a man named Hartley, also some Picabias and Picassos and so on." Quoted in Linda Leavell, *Marianne Moore and the Visual Arts: Prismatic Color* (Baton Rouge: Louisiana State University Press, 1995), p. 22.

73. Marsden Hartley, "Emily Dickinson," *Dial* 65 (August 1918): 95–97. The quotations are from pp. 95, 95–96, 97.

74. Amy Lowell, "The Sisters," *North American Review* (June 1922), reprinted in *Literature by Women: The Traditions in English*, ed. Sandra M. Gilbert and Susan Gubar, 2 vols., 3rd ed. (New York: Norton, 2007), 2: 137–40. See also Erkkila, pp. 8–14, 114, 160, on "the difficulty and complexity of sisterhood as an affirming model of women's literary history," p. 8.

75. See "Emily Dickinson," in *Poetry and Poets: Essays* (Boston: Houghton Mifflin, 1930). The quotes are pp. 88, 89–90, 93. The posthumously published essay was delivered as a lecture at the Brooklyn Institute on March 20, 1918, under the general heading "Imagism Past and Present." See S. Foster Damon, *Amy Lowell: A Chronicle* (Boston: Houghton Mifflin, 1935), pp. 443–44, 444n. When Moore attended one of Lowell's readings of her poems at this time, she described it in a letter to her brother as not particularly inspiring.

76. In a 1922 letter to Mabel Loomis Todd, Lowell mentioned "a dream of mine sometime to write a life of Miss Dickinson." The letter is quoted in Damon, p. 611. According to Klaus Lubbers, "Emily's relationships with the other members of the family was to have been the main theme. Amy Lowell had already established contact with Mrs. Todd and begun to collect material." See *Emily Dickinson: The Critical Revolution* (Ann Arbor: University of Michigan Press, 1968), pp. 114, 247n34. On Lowell and Millicent Todd and Walter Bingham, see Jean Gould, *The World of Amy Lowell and the Imagist Movement* (New York: Dodd, Mead, 1975), pp. 319–20, 334.

77. "Exciting realness" is Moore paraphrasing George Frisbie Whicher's "Foreword" to *Emily Dickinson: December 10, 1830–May 15, 1886: A Bibliography* (Amherst, MA: Jones Library, 1930), pp. 9–15. For an excellent discussion of Moore's reading in preparation for the essay, see Linda Leavell, "Marianne Moore's Emily Dickinson," *Emily Dickinson Journal* 12.1 (Spring 2003): 1–20. Leavell discusses Moore's process of composition, as well as the drafts in the Rosenbach. Both Leavell and Hogue observe that Moore owned Conrad Aiken's 1924 *Selection of Emily Dickinson's Poems*, but it is not clear when she acquired it.

78. On Moore and China, see Cynthia Stamy, *Marianne Moore and China: Orientalism and a Writing of America* (Oxford: Oxford University Press, 1999).

79. "After great pain" was first published in the *Atlantic Monthly* in 1929. See "Unpublished Poems by Emily Dickinson," *Atlantic Monthly* 143.2 (February 1929): 184. On repression, see Hogue, p. 98. The manuscript is at the Rosenbach.

80. Moore published 187 prose pieces in the *Dial* alone.

81. See Charles K. Trueblood, "Review of *The Life and Letters of Emily Dickinson* by Martha Dickinson Bianchi," *Dial* 80 (April 1926): 301–11. The quotes are p. 308.

82. See Josephine Pollitt, *Emily Dickinson: The Human Background of Her Poetry* (New York: Harper, 1930), and Genevieve Taggard, *The Life and Mind of Emily Dickinson* (New York: Alfred A. Knopf, 1930). Pollitt believed that the lover was Helen Hunt Jackson's husband, basing her case largely on Dickinson's statement to Higginson, during his 1870 visit, "Major Hunt interested her more than any man she ever saw." See Pollitt, p. 120. She also put a name to Bianchi's Philadelphia preacher, the Rev. Charles Wadsworth. Taggard, meanwhile, opted for George Gould, also a preacher, Amherst College class of 1850. Taggard was influenced by "an affidavit received in 1929 from an unnamed correspondent who claimed to have it from Lavinia Dickinson 'that the man Emily Dickinson loved and renounced was Mr. George Gould . . . and . . . that Emily Dickinson's father forbad the match.'" See Taggard, p. 109.

83. The stealing trope runs in several directions. It suggests that the book is a good buy and that Todd is engaged in an illegitimate activity. While Moore slyly alludes to the property rights issue, she also reads her as "expressing a friendship" and praises her editorial exactness and scholarly zeal. Mrs. Todd, she explains, has been "more than the usual editor." See *Pr* 290.

84. Moore's comment to Williams about despising connectives is in his May 1925 *Dial* essay. See "Marianne Moore," in *The William Carlos Williams Reader*, ed. M. L. Rosenthal (New York: New Directions, 1966), p. 387. Comparing her to Dickinson, Williams notes that the poets share a "distaste for lingering" and "a too fastidious precision of thought where unrhymes fill the purpose better than rhyme," p. 386.

85. The quotation is from "The Monkey Puzzle," the paraphrase from "The Steeple-Jack."

86. See Louise Bogan, "The Poet Dickinson Comes to Life," *New Yorker* 31.34 (October 8, 1955): 178.

CHAPTER 4

1. Hughes began publishing this account in the late 1980s, and eight of the poems appeared in his *New Selected Poems* of 1994: "Chaucer," "You Hated Spain," "The Earthenware Head," "The Tender Place," "Black Coat," "Being Christlike," "The God," and "The Dogs Are Eating Your Mother." Diane Middlebrook states that "Hughes produced the individual poems over a period of twenty-five years, but apparently the possibility of organizing them into a narrative only occurred to him in 1992." See Diane Middlebrook, *Her Husband: Hughes and Plath—A Marriage* (New York: Viking, 2003), pp. 274–75.

2. Sarah Churchwell, for example, historicizes the politics of publication surrounding *Birthday Letters*, but this forty-six-page essay does not mention Moore. See "Secrets and Lies: Plath, Privacy, Publication and Ted Hughes's *Birthday Letters*," *Contemporary Literature* 42 (Spring 2001): 102–48. Concentrating on the daddy myth, she contends that the poems retell "a very familiar story," p. 122. I seek to defamiliarize the narrative. Hughes was morally allied with Moore against Plath, and with Plath against Moore, but these alliances were necessarily unstable.

3. Erica Wagner, *Ariel's Gift: A Commentary on "Birthday Letters" by Ted Hughes* (London: Faber and Faber, 2000), p. 150.

4. In introducing the abridged journals, Hughes claimed to have destroyed the journal that Plath kept during the last two or so months of her life to protect their children. He also stated that Plath's 1960–62 journal was lost at some later time. See "Foreword," *The Journals of Sylvia Plath*, ed. Frances McCullough (New York: Dial Press, 1982), p. xiii. Biographer Middlebrook observes that "reasonable people have always doubted Hughes's claims that they were missing" and that it is "possible that Ted Hughes did not destroy or lose the journals," p. 238.

5. Ted Hughes, *Birthday Letters* (New York: Farrar, Straus, Giroux, 1998), p. 3. References will be cited in the text as *BL*.

6. *The Unabridged Journals of Sylvia Plath*, ed. Karen V. Kukil (New York: Anchor, 2000), p. 406, to be cited in the text as *Unabridged*; Sylvia Plath, *The Collected Poems*, ed. Ted Hughes (New York: Harper & Row, 1981), p. 166, to be cited as *Collected*.

7. For the view that Moore was too quirky to be fully canonical, see Margaret Dickie, "Women Poets and the Emergence of Modernism," in *The Columbia History of American Poetry*, ed. Jay Parini and Brett C. Millier (New York: Columbia University Press, 1993), pp. 233–59.

8. Plath's New England heritage was mainly the product of her education; her father was a German immigrant and her mother was the daughter of Austrian immigrants.

9. Sylvia Plath, *Letters Home: Correspondence, 1950–1963*, ed. Aurelia Schober Plath (New York: Harper & Row, 1975), p. 166. Cited subsequently as *Letters*.

10. In her letter to Professor Joseph Bottkol, Moore comments on "Winter Words," "Epitaph in Three Parts," "Lament," "*Danse macabre*," "Verbal Calisthenics," "April Aubade," "Two Lovers and a Beachcomber by the Real Sea," and "Love is a Parallax." Mount Holyoke College Archives and Special Collections. Cited in the text as Holyoke Ms. For more on the contest, see Paul Alexander, *Rough Magic: A Biography of Sylvia Plath* (New York: Viking, 1991; rev., 1999, Da Capo Press Edition), pp. 154–57, 232.

11. Moore is quoted in Alexander, p. 155.

12. Moore, quoted in Alexander, p. 155.

13. Perhaps this is why she adopted the pseudonym "Marcia Moore" for "Circus in Three Rings," the poem cycle written in her senior year of college. It was the product of an independent study supervised by Alfred Fisher, who emerges later in Plath's diaries as a notorious womanizer. Marcia Brown was one of her college roommates during freshman and sophomore years and continued to be a close friend.

14. Several months later, Plath submitted her own book manuscript, *Two Lovers and a Beachcomber by the Real Sea*, to the Yale Series of Younger Poets, but nothing came of it.

15. Moore is quoted in Alexander, p. 203. She repeated this praise, some of it verbatim, in an enthusiastic notice of the published book. See *The Complete Prose*, ed. Patricia C. Willis (New York: Viking/Penguin, 1986), p. 634.

16. Plath, "Nine Letters to Lynne Lawner," *Antaeus* 28 (Winter 1978): 34.

17. All of these poems had been previously published. As Paul Alexander notes, "He changed his mind because he did not want to jeopardize the successful publication of his book," p. 204. The title page of Hughes's selected poems, published in 1994, makes it appear that at least part of "Bawdry Embraced" was in the original *Hawk* volume. As published, this was not the case, although Hughes's editor Elizabeth Lawrence encouraged him to stand firm. Probably his choice not to offend Moore was a wise one, but it appears that the omissions continued to rankle. Hughes was particularly attached to "Bawdry," which he used to conclude his privately printed *Recklings* (1966).

18. Plath, "Nine Letters," p. 32.

19. In *Barren in the Promised Land: Childless Americans and the Pursuit of Happiness* (New York: Basic Books, 1995), Elaine Tyler May discusses the pressure on women such as Plath to produce babies but also the emphasis accorded to individual achievement. See also *Homeward Bound: American Families in the Cold War Era* (New York: Basic Books, 1988). As I discuss below, Moore opposed pronatalist discourse, at least in writing about Plath, and she certainly opposed coercive pronatalism as a fact of American life.

20. Sylvia Plath, *The Bell Jar* (New York: Harper & Row, 1971), p. 77.

21. Hughes takes up Plath's true subject in the Introduction to *Johnny Panic and the Bible of Dreams* (London: Faber, 1975), p. 5. He continued to believe that Plath was making a mistake in thinking of her personal dilemma as generalizable. On Hughes as a critic of Plath in a transatlantic context, see Paul Giles, "Crossing the Water: Gunn, Plath, and the Poetry of Passage," in *Virtual Americas: Transnational Fictions and the Transatlantic Imaginary* (Durham, NC: Duke University Press, 2002), pp. 182–224.

22. Eugene F. Saxton (1888–1943) was a distinguished editor at Harper's; after his death, the fellowship was established in his honor.

23. In *Sylvia Plath: The Wound and the Cure of Words* (Baltimore: Johns Hopkins University Press, 1990), Steven Gould Axelrod offers an illuminating discussion of Plath's attempts to imitate Moore, for example, her use of syllabics and her minutely detailed descriptions of the natural world. He contends that Plath was intent on exposing the thinness of Moore's project and that she should have realized that Moore was an unlikely ally, pp. 130–39.

24. Joanne Feit Diehl, *Women Poets and the American Sublime* (Bloomington: Indiana University Press, 1990), p. 113.

25. Moore previously used the journey metaphor to describe her experience of reading poems that she considered sexually indecorous and therefore degrading. Writing to Allen Ginsberg in 1952 about a manuscript he had left with her, she remarked, "In the opening piece . . . you say, 'I wandered off in search of a toilet.' And I go with you, remember. Do I have to? I do if you take me with you in your book." See Moore, *The Selected Letters*, ed. Bonnie Costello, Celeste Goodridge, and Cristanne Miller (New York: Alfred A. Knopf, 1997), p. 499.

26. In her July 7 journal, Plath remarks, "I am evidently going through a stage in beginning writing similar to my two months of hysteria in beginning teaching last fall. A sickness, frenzy of resentment at everything, but myself at the bottom. I lie wakeful at night, wake exhausted with that sense of razor-shaved nerves. I must be my own doctor. I must cure this very destructive paralysis & ruinous brooding & daydreaming. If I want to write, this is hardly the way to behave—in horror of it, frozen by it. The ghost of the unborn novel is a Medusa-head." She also comments that she "is becoming too dependent on Ted. . . . It is as if I were sucked into a tempting but disastrous whirlpool" (*Unabridged* 401). Both Margaret Dickie Uroff, in *Sylvia Plath and Ted Hughes* (Urbana: University of Illinois Press, 1979), and Susan R. Van Dyne, in *Revising Life: Sylvia Plath's Ariel Poems* (Chapel Hill: University of North Carolina Press, 1993), discuss the intertextual aspect of their poetic production. For an illuminating discussion of Plath's dependence on Hughes as informed by her earlier dependence on her mother, see Barbara Johnson, *Mother Tongues: Sexuality, Trials, Motherhood, Translation* (Cambridge, MA: Harvard University Press, 2003).

27. In "The Literary Life," Hughes comments on Moore's unwillingness to be indebted, as exemplified by the subway coins she foisted on her guests. On this well-known eccentricity, see Elizabeth Bishop's "Efforts of Affection: A Memoir of Marianne Moore," in *Poems, Prose,*

and Letters, ed. Robert Giroux and Lloyd Schwartz (New York: Library of America, 2008), pp. 471–99.

28. Columbia University has the relevant archive, but these records show only that Plath was a successful applicant for *The Bell Jar* in 1961. Standard biographies of Plath mention at least one prior application for a Saxton grant but provide no information about the recommenders. Alexander, p. 267, states that Plath had been turned down for a poetry project when she received the award in 1961, and Anne Stevenson, in *Bitter Fame: A Life of Sylvia Plath* (Boston: Houghton Mifflin, 1989), refers to "the jinx of a long autumn of rejections," including the Saxton Fellowship, p. 147. It seems likely, then, that after she calmed down, Plath used Moore as a recommender for her poetry project, but this is speculation.

29. Ted Hughes, *New Selected Poems 1957–1994* (London: Faber and Faber, 1995), p. 41.

30. This is only part of the story. As Cristanne Miller remarks, Moore could be quite clear about "communities with which she sought to identify her work and those which she rejected." See *Marianne Moore: Questions of Authority* (Cambridge, MA: Harvard University Press, 1995), p. 32. Affection was not all.

31. See Alexander, p. 257.

32. On the subject of Plath and privacy in a Cold War context, see Deborah Nelson, *Pursuing Privacy in Cold War America* (New York: Columbia University Press, 2002). For important discussions of Moore and "questions of authority," see Rachel DuPlessis, "No Moore of the Same," *William Carlos Williams Review* 14 (1988): 6–32, and Miller, *Marianne Moore*.

33. Moore, "Foreword," *A Marianne Moore Reader* (New York: Viking, 1961), p. 552.

34. Langdon Hammer, "Plath's Lives: Poetry, Professionalism, and the Culture of the School," *Representations* 75 (Summer 2001): 61.

35. Although Adrienne Rich is not ordinarily classified as a confessional poet, there is a good case for including at least some of her work in this historically specific tradition, beginning with her breakthrough volume *Snapshots of a Daughter-in-Law* (New York: Harper & Row, 1963).

36. May Swenson, "A Matter of Diction," in *Made with Words*, ed. Gardner McFall (Ann Arbor: University of Michigan Press, 1989), p. 87.

37. Elizabeth Bishop, quoted in *Conversations with Elizabeth Bishop*, ed. George Monteiro (Jackson: University Press of Mississippi, 1996), p. 45.

38. Moore, "Silence," *The Complete Poems* (New York: Macmillan, 1967; rev. Macmillan/Viking, 1981), pp. 276n, 91.

39. As mentioned in the preceding chapter, the poet's father, John Milton Moore, had a nervous breakdown before her birth and the poet's mother returned to live with her own father in Kirkwood, Missouri. In 1887, John Milton Moore was admitted to the Athens (Ohio) Mental Hospital. Eventually, he was able to return to his family home in Portsmouth, Ohio, where he was a bookkeeper in the family business for at least some of the time. Unfortunately, he again became ill, and in 1909, suffering from paranoia and religious delusions, he was readmitted to the Athens hospital, where he died in 1925. It remains unclear how much Moore knew of his tragic history, but an obituary in the Athens newspaper describes him as an exceptional patient, learned and a gentleman.

40. Charles Molesworth, *Marianne Moore: A Literary Life* (New York: Atheneum, 1990), pp. 363–64.

41. Moore, "Blessed Is the Man," *The Complete Poems*, p. 173.

42. Moore on Plath, letter to Judith Jones, Rosenbach Museum & Library, Philadelphia.

43. I will not rehearse the various medical tragedies that led to Plath's suicide. By all accounts, including her own, Plath was highly sexed, and given its ice boxes, furnaces, and sticky fingers, "The Tour" invites a reading grounded in suppressed fantasies of self-pleasure. In a wonderful conversation on December 9, 2009, my colleague Carl Phillips developed his theory of the poem as an act of self-love, pointing out that however strange the speaker's home, she takes pride in the fact that it is hers. Phillips finds something strangely attractive in her slovenliness, crediting "The Tour" with its own vision of beauty. On poems and love, see Carl Phillips, *Poetry, Love, and Mercy* (Berkeley: University of California Press, 2010). Phillips's reading was not explicitly sexual but focused rather on the persona's refusal to adopt her visitor's values. Not to digress too far, I will nevertheless mention that Moore can be viewed as a Sedgwickian masturbating girl. Plath too. Phillips also suggested the possibility that the home is literally an asylum, the nurse literally a nurse. From this perspective, Plath can be viewed as revising the Victorian imagination of home as a haven in a heartless world, to grotesque ends.

44. Hughes reviewed *Emily Dickinson's Poetry: Stairway of Surprise* by Charles R. Anderson in *The Listener* in 1963 and edited a selection of Dickinson's poems in 1968. See the next chapter for the politics of this intervention.

45. Moore arrived in England in early August 1964 and sailed for home in early October. She was traveling with her friends the Browne sisters, Frances and Norvelle, and wrote to her brother describing a number of satisfying social gatherings. Examining her correspondence, I have not been able to discover a reference to the party at which Hughes was present. Biographer Elaine Feinstein has suggested to me in an e-mail that the party is likely to have been given by Charles Monteith, Hughes's editor at Faber and Faber. In 1964, Faber also published Moore's *The Arctic Ox*, a cause for celebration.

46. "Ocean 1212-W," in *Johnny Panic and the Bible of Dreams*, p. 26.

47. Moore, "Marriage" and "Silence," *Collected Poems*, pp. 69 and 95.

48. Barbara Johnson points out that, more often than not, *Birthday Letters* "tell us that Hughes was keeping to himself any mention of how differently he and his wife were experiencing something. In other words, he is telling the *reader* something he did not tell his wife." *Mother Tongues*, p. 171. This is true.

49. Hughes, quoted in Wagner, *Ariel's Gift*, p. 40.

50. Moore, "The Pangolin," *Complete Poems*, pp. 119, 120.

CHAPTER 5

1. The 1941 *Herald* interchange is reprinted in Lois Ames, "Notes Toward a Biography," in *The Art of Sylvia Plath: A Symposium*, ed. Charles Newman (Bloomington: Indiana University Press, 1970), p. 158. The manuscript, on Boston University Stationary, was annotated by Plath's mother on the verso and has scansion marks and feet. Beinecke Rare Book and Manuscript Library, Yale University. The "Good Sport" page published "Letters from Members" of the Good Sport Club. After filling out a coupon, the children received a red and white pin. In a line below her poem, Plath thanks Margaret Ford, the editor, for hers.

2. Quoted in *Letters Home by Sylvia Plath: Correspondence 1950–1963*, ed. Aurelia Schober Plath (New York: Harper & Row, 1975), p. 25. To be cited parenthetically in the text as *Letters*.

3. Paul Alexander, *Rough Magic: A Biography of Sylvia Plath* (New York: Da Capo, 2003), p. 44.

4. On "Sunrise and Sunset," see Andrew Wilson, *Mad Girl's Love Song: Sylvia Plath and Life Before Ted* (New York: Scribner, 2013), p. 46.

5. "I Thought That I Could Not Be Hurt" is in "Introduction," *Letters*, pp. 33–34. See also p. 33 for "little strategy of 'popularity.' "

6. Wilbury Crockett is quoted in Wilson, pp. 83–84.

7. *The Unabridged Journals of Sylvia Plath*, ed. Karen V. Kukil (New York: Anchor Books, 2000), p. 20. To be cited in the text as *Unabridged*.

8. See "Sunday at the Mintons'," in *Johnny Panic and the Bible of Dreams: Short Stories, Prose, and Diary Excerpts* (New York: Harper, 2000). "Domestic duties" is p. 311, "a colossus" is p. 317, "triumphant, feminine giggle" is p. 319. On Plath as disruptive, see James Matthews, *Voices: A Life of Frank O'Connor* (New York: Atheneum, 1983), pp. 289–90.

9. "Admonition" in *Letters Home* should not be confused with another early poem, a villanelle called "Admonition*s*," warnings being a subject to which the emerging Plath is drawn. For a clear statement of the difference between the poems, see Stephen Tabor, *Sylvia Plath: An Analytical Bibliography* (Westport, CT: Meckler, 1987). In *Letters Home*, the birthday poems are titled "Admonition," "Parallax," and "Verbal Calisthenics" (pp. 110–11). "Parallax" is not to be confused with "Love Is a Parallax," a poem on which Marianne Moore commented when she judged the Glascock Poetry Contest at Mount Holyoke in 1955. See chap. 4, "Moore, Plath, Hughes." In Sylvia Plath, *The Collected Poems*, ed. Ted Hughes (New York: Harper & Row, 1981), they are titled "Trio of Love Songs" and identified by the numbers 1, 2, and 3. This title originates with Plath, who used it in her senior year poetry sequence, *Circus in Three Rings*. For the contents of *Circus*, see Sylvia Plath Papers, Lilly Library, Indiana University. In discussing the erotics of "Admonition," I cite the four-stanza version in *The Collected Poems*, p. 315, which is almost identical with the typescript I examined in the Lilly Library. This edition will be cited parenthetically in the text as *Collected*.

10. "Admonition" extends the erotics of such Dickinson poems as "Sang from the Heart, Sire" (*Fr* 1083) and "Split the Lark – and you'll find the Music" (*Fr* 905). In "Sang from the Heart," the poet represents herself as a self-murdered bird. She writes with her blood, and her death is mandated by her song. Because of this dubious origin, for which she offers an insincere apology, the song is "Awkward – faltering." "Split the Lark" is a more ironic endorsement of poet-murder. Both poems hearken back to Wordsworth's "We murder to dissect." In "The Tables Turned," he cautions against misguided attempts to contain, discipline, and master the great heart of nature: "Sweet is the lore which Nature brings; / Our meddling intellect / Misshapes the beauteous forms of things:—/ We murder to dissect. / / Enough of Science and of Art; / Close up those barren leaves; / Come forth, and bring with you a heart / That watches and receives." See *Lyrical Ballads, 1798 [by] Wordsworth & Coleridge*, ed. W. J. B. Owen, 2nd ed. (London: Oxford University Press, 1969).

In its conditional if-then structure, "Admonition" also draws on "If you were coming in the Fall" (*Fr* 356). First published in the 1890 *Poems* and reprinted in 1924, 1930, and 1937 editions edited by Martha Dickinson Bianchi, it was included in a list of readings distributed at Smith College in 1953 to honors candidates in English, including Plath. They used *Poems First and Second Series*, ed. Mabel Loomis Todd and T. W. Higginson, intro. Carl Van Doren (Cleveland, OH: World Publishing, 1948).

11. Sylvia Plath Papers, Indiana University, Box 9, Folder 4.

12. On the Dickinson imitations, see Marjorie Perloff, "Sylvia Plath's 'Sivvy' Poems: A Portrait of the Poet as Daughter," in *Sylvia Plath: New Views on the Poetry*, ed. Gary Lane (Baltimore: Johns Hopkins University Press, 1979), pp. 163–64; Margaret Dickie Uroff, *Sylvia*

Plath and Ted Hughes (Urbana: University of Illinois Press, 1979), pp. 66, 84; Steven Gould Axelrod, *Sylvia Plath: The Wound and the Cure of Words* (Baltimore: Johns Hopkins University Press, 1990), p. 127; Gayle Wurst, *Voice and Vision: The Poetry of Sylvia Plath* (Geneva, Switzerland: Editions Slatkine, 1999), p. 182; Wurst, "'We See—Comparatively—': Reading Rich/Reading Plath/Reading Dickinson," in *Profils Américains* 8, ed. Antoine Cazé (Montpellier, France: Presses de l'Université Paul Valéry, 1996), p. 105; Christina Britzolakis, *Sylvia Plath and the Theatre of Mourning* (Oxford: Oxford University Press, 1999), p. 76. Britzolakis rightly observes that "Dickinson constituted a significant if equivocal exception to the New Critical devaluation of women poets."

13. Plath's letter of March 11, 1959, is from "Nine Letters to Lynne Lawner," *Antaeus* 28 (Winter 1978): 46.

14. On Aurelia's youthful dreams of being a creative writer, see Alexander, pp. 19, 21, 24. See also Linda Heller, "Aurelia Plath: A Lasting Commitment," *Bostonia [Boston University Alumnae Magazine]* (Spring 1976): 36.

15. The quotes are from Alexander, p. 14.

16. Perloff, p. 157.

17. Alexander, pp. 12–13.

18. Lydia Clara Bartz was the sister of Otto Plath's friend Rupert Bartz, whom he seems to have met at Northwestern College in Watertown, Wisconsin. After graduating from church-affiliated Northwestern College in 1910, Otto entered the Wisconsin Lutheran Seminary in Wauwatosa. Religious fundamentalism, however, was not consistent with his developing passion for Darwin and for science. When he left the seminary, his immigrant grandparents, who had financed his education with the expectation that he would become a minister, were so displeased that they struck his name from the family bible. Otto then earned a Master of Arts degree in German at the University of Washington in Seattle in 1912. He and Lydia Bartz were married in Spokane on August 7, 1912. A letter written by Aurelia to her granddaughter Frieda describing the marriage is quoted in Wilson, p. 17. According to this account, "Lydia had been what was then termed 'delicately raised' and educated along very idealistic lines. She was not prepared for the physical side of marriage at all. So when she and Otto were married, the two found they had decidedly different attitudes (too bad they didn't discuss all this before!) and the upshot was that Lydia left Otto after three weeks and returned to her family. The two people never saw each other again—ever!" There is a less detailed, slightly different account in *Letters Home*.

19. The quotation is from Langdon Hammer, "Plath's Lives: Poetry, Professionalism, and the Culture of the School," *Representations* 75.1 (Summer 2001): 66. On Dickinson as a "constant" in Plath's early reading: Aurelia's unpublished manuscript is quoted in Wurst, "'We See—Comparatively—,'" p. 107. See also Axelrod, *Sylvia Plath*, p. 126.

20. "Verbal Calisthenics," by "Sylvia Plath, '55," also appeared in the *Smith Review* (Spring 1954): 3.

21. *Letters of Ted Hughes*, ed. Christopher Reid (London: Faber and Faber, 2007), pp. 215–16.

22. The poems included in the anthology Plath constructed for Wilbury Crockett are "Presentiment – is that long shadow – on the Lawn" (*Fr* 487); "He ate and drank the precious Words" (*Fr* 1593); and "The Sky is low – the Clouds are mean" (*Fr* 1121). See also Plath, "And Summer Will Not Come Again," *Seventeen* (August 1950): 275–76.

23. As Christina Britzolakis has noted, Teasdale was a poet "beloved" by women of Aurelia Plath's generation. Steven Gould Axelrod speculates that through Teasdale, Plath "sought

access to Dickinson's complex grammar of feelings by means of the intermediary's comparative simplifications." At the same time, he suggests, "she wished to explore more fully Teasdale's own characteristic association of love-loss with death." See Britzolakis, *Sylvia Plath*, p. 70; Axelrod, *Sylvia Plath*, p. 154. According to Carolyn Kizer, Teasdale appeals to the perennial adolescent in us and she certainly appealed to the teenage Plath. "Think of that crew of self-pitiers, not-very-distant," Kizer wrote, "Who carried the torch for themselves and got first-degree burns, / Or the sad sonneteers, toast-and teasdales we loved at thirteen." See "Pro Femina," in *Knock Upon Silence* (Garden City, NY: Doubleday, 1965). The poem was first published in 1963 in *Poetry* and has been widely reprinted.

24. Material in this paragraph is taken from Alexander, pp. 66, 78–79, 80–81, 90–91; Cohen's Dickinson letter, Plath's description of him, and his analysis of their relationship are quoted in Lynda K. Bundtzen, *Plath's Incarnations: Woman and the Creative Process* (Ann Arbor: University of Michigan Press, 1983), pp. 66–67, 67–68, and passim. On Cohen's semi-bohemian radicalism and antiwar politics, see Linda W. Wagner-Martin, *Sylvia Plath: A Biography* (New York: Simon and Schuster, 1987), passim.

25. Bundtzen, p. 74.

26. Plath on Dick Norton is quoted in Bundtzen, pp. 74, 69. See also Bundtzen's intriguing analysis of "Admonition" as a response to Norton's letters describing his dissection of cadavers. She describes Plath as defeating him intellectually in verse "with one of her Emily Dickinson imitations," pp. 78–79. Bundtzen also reads Norton as the original for Henry in "Sunday at The Mintons'." She explains, "One of Plath's strategies for dealing with her anger at Norton is to cast him in her story as a smug, scientific, domineering and 'always right' older brother to Elizabeth Minton, the dreamy, intuitive alter ego for Plath herself," p. 77.

27. Cohen's letters are cited in Bundtzen, pp. 73, 69. On the psychology of overidealization in fatherless daughters, see Nancy Chodorow, *The Reproduction of Mothering: Psychoanalysis and the Sociology of Gender* (Berkeley: University of California Press, 1978), p. 118. According to Chodorow, overidealization comports with demonization, when an idealized male, modeled on an insufficient father figure, is endowed with "sadistic or punitive characteristics."

28. Richard L. Sassoon's letter to Plath is quoted in Wilson, p. 247.

29. Sassoon, quoted in Wilson, p. 247.

30. Sassoon's self-analysis is quoted in Wilson, pp. 246–47.

31. See R. L. Sassoon, "Diagram," *Chicago Review* 17.4 (1965): 110–11.

32. "Gordon has the body, but Richard has the soul," Plath wrote to her mother (*Letters* 229). On the trip through Germany, see "The Munich Mannequins" (*Collected* 262–63).

33. In her analysis of the poet as daughter, Perloff shrewdly observes that Plath appears to have written to her mother most extensively during her courtship with Hughes and in the first year of her marriage: "One has in any case, the impression that falling in love and marrying made it possible for Sivvy to be equally loving toward her mother; the loss of Ted created exactly the reverse situation." See Perloff, p. 177.

34. For a nuanced, sympathetic study of the ways in which Plath and Hughes mutually influenced each other as poets, see Heather Clark, *The Grief of Influence: Sylvia Plath and Ted Hughes* (New York: Oxford University Press, 2011).

35. As mentioned, "Parallax" and "Verbal Calisthenics" were published in the *Smith Review*, Spring 1954. The retyped versions of "Admonition" and "Verbal Calisthenics" are in the Sylvia Plath Collection, Mortimer Rare Book Room, Smith College Library.

36. See "Among the Bumblebees," in *Johnny Panic and the Bible of Dreams*, p. 324.

37. "Among the Bumblebees," pp. 320–22, 327.

38. As she explained to her brother Warren, Plath had been offered "$50 to $75 for a poem on a work of art" by the "New York magazine, *Art News*" (*Letters* 35), and as she mentioned to her mother, she had been auditing a course on modern art (*Letters* 336). In her *Journals*, she attributes both "On the Decline of Oracles" and "The Disquieting Muses" to her engagement with de Chirico's paintings, diaries, and aesthetic theories. Further, when Plath read "The Disquieting Muses" on a BBC radio program in 1962, she commented, "All through the poem I have in mind the enigmatic figures in this painting—three terrible, faceless dressmaker's dummies in classical gowns, seated and standing in a weird, clear light that casts the long strong shadows characteristic of de Chirico's early work." Quoted in Christina Britzolakis, "Conversation amongst the Ruins: Plath and de Chirico," in *Eye Rhymes: Sylvia Plath's Art of the Visual*, ed. Kathleen Connors and Sally Bayley (New York: Oxford University Press, 2007), p. 176.

39. Aurelia is on record as objecting to "The Disquieting Muses." Reading biographically, she explained later that the daughter she trusted had used her unfairly: "The fact is Sylvia never took ballet lessons. I did—and told her about my delight, especially during the ballet recital, when, at nine, I was a member of the chorus of about thirty other 'fireflies.' On the dimly lit stage, as, in our winged costumes, we danced, tiny 'blinking flashlights' in each hand, I felt myself exalted, for I knew that in the front row my parents were sitting with eyes for me alone—I was for *them* the prima ballerina!" See Aurelia Plath, "Letter Written in the Actuality of Spring," in *Ariel Ascending: Writings About Sylvia Plath*, ed. Paul Alexander (New York: Harper & Row, 1984), p. 215.

40. Plath, "Nine Letters to Lynne Lawner," p. 47.

41. Plath's false pregnancy inspired "Metaphors," a witty nine-line poem in syllabics. See *Collected*, p. 116.

42. Hughes's letter to Olwyn is in *Letters of Ted Hughes*, p. 166. He also mentioned Dickinson to John Fisher, his former schoolmaster at Mexborough Grammar School, saying he would like to send Dickinson's collected works to the school if he were rich enough. See *Letters*, p. 167.

43. Hughes's August 1960 letter to Aurelia requesting the three-volume Johnson edition of Dickinson's *Poems* is quoted in *Letters of Ted Hughes*, pp. 169–70.

44. Hughes enclosed twelve dollars in his May 1962 letter asking Aurelia to send the one-volume *Complete Poems*, edited by Johnson. The unpublished manuscript is in Correspondence, Box 6a, Lilly Library, Indiana University.

45. Hughes, "Emily Dickinson's Poetry," *Listener* 70 (September 12, 1963): 394. He was reviewing the British edition of Charles R. Anderson's *Emily Dickinson's Poetry: Stairway of Surprise*, published by Holt, Rinehart and Winston in 1960 and by Heinemann in 1963. The quote is the last stanza of "It was not Death, for I stood up" (Johnson 510, Franklin 355). Hughes uses the line "It was not Death" and then "It was not poetic death" in "Isis," *Birthday Letters*, p. 112.

46. Emerson's "Merlin" is quoted on Anderson's title page. The back cover blurb by Johnson says, "I think of the book as a companionpiece and capstone of my editions." "Finite infinity" is quoted from *The Complete Poems of Emily Dickinson*, ed. Johnson, p. 691, number 1695.

47. Anderson, *Emily Dickinson's Poetry*, pp. 46, ix–xi, 167. The page numbers refer to the American edition.

48. Millicent Todd Bingham, blurb, back cover, *Emily Dickinson's Poetry: Stairway of Surprise*. "Tensions" is Anderson, p. 285, in his last paragraph.

49. On nimble believing, see James McIntosh, *Nimble Believing: Dickinson and the Unknown* (Ann Arbor: University of Michigan Press, 2000). Hughes quotes her 1882 letter to Otis P. Lord (*L* 750). Dickinson's reworking of the "Master" construct informs her inquiry and she addresses Lord as "Papa." All the quotes are from Hughes's review.

50. Among Hughesians, the book *Shakespeare and the Goddess of Complete Being* (London: Faber and Faber, 1992) garners high praise, but Hughes himself was concerned about its diffuseness and obscurity. More accessible and from the point of view of gender critique more relevant is the book's seed, Hughes's "Introduction" to *A Choice of Shakespeare's Verse* (London: Faber and Faber, 1971), which spells out Shakespeare's supposed sexual dilemma. The essay tantalizes with its mix of commitments and evasions, bold statements and mysterious blanks. Titled "The Great Theme: Notes on Shakespeare," it represents Shakespeare as a tragic hero and is included in *Winter Pollen: Occasional Prose*, ed. William Scammell (London: Faber and Faber, 1994), pp. 103–21. For more on Hughes and Shakespeare, see Terry Gifford, *Ted Hughes* (London: Routledge, 2009), and Jonathan Bate, "Hughes on Shakespeare," in *The Cambridge Companion to Ted Hughes*, ed. Terry Gifford (Cambridge: Cambridge University Press, 2011), pp. 135–49. Dickinson also idolized Shakespeare, but for different reasons.

51. *A Choice of Emily Dickinson's Verse* (London: Faber and Faber, 1968), p. 17. "That Love is all there is" is a four-line quatrain whose text derives from a lost manuscript. Franklin explains that the original, "signed 'Emily' and sent to Susan Dickinson," was published by Martha Dickinson Bianchi in *The Single Hound* (1914). She had the manuscript "as late as 1937, when she lent it for exhibition." See Franklin, *Variorum* 3: 1505.

52. Hughes, *A Choice of Emily Dickinson's Verse*, pp. 14–15.

53. Maria Stuart, "Dickinson in England and Ireland," in *The International Reception of Emily Dickinson*, ed. Domhnall Mitchell and Maria Stuart (London: Continuum, 2009), p. 213.

54. For an elegant recreation of Assia's dilemma, see Yehuda Koren and Eilat Negev, *Lover of Unreason: Assia Wevill, Sylvia Plath's Rival and Ted Hughes's Doomed Love* (New York: Carroll & Graf, 2007). When Hughes was editing Dickinson, Assia's 1969 suicide was still to come. It was more grisly than Plath's because she took their four-year-old daughter Shura down with her, but by this time Hughes was somewhat numbed—as he explained to her sister Celia Chaikin, he was "in a daze." He also described Assia as "my true wife and the best friend I ever had." See *Letters*, p. 290. The quotes are from "Dreamers," *Birthday Letters*, pp. 158, 157, in which Assia is othered as a femme fatale. Underscoring this theme, *Birthday Letters* rather consistently flirts with national stereotypes.

55. *Letters of Ted Hughes*, May 19, 1966, pp. 257–58. Hughes offered to change the notes that were to appear in the American *Ariel* if anything he had said gave Aurelia "the slightest qualm," but he tended to overpromise, and a letter several months later makes it clear that the *Ariel* train, notes and all, had already left the station. See also pp. 259–60.

56. Hughes to Anne Sexton in August 1967, following her visit to England, *Letters*, p. 275. Despite his primitivism, or pseudoprimitivism, Hughes was relentlessly social, although in this letter he cautions Sexton against worrying about reviews, even positive ones, and in the most charming terms. "They deprive you of your own anarchic liberties—by electing you into the government. Also, they separate you from your devil, which hates being observed, and only works happily incognito. Also, they deprive you of your detachment from the scene into which you are injecting your work, by making you a visible part of the scene. Also, they satisfy ambition, which only works from a radical discontent and public neglect." *Letters*, p. 276.

57. Hughes, *Birthday Letters*, p. 183.

58. The initial print run was 2,825, and a year later there was a paperback of 6,000. Paperbacks were reprinted in 1970, 1974, 1979, 1984, 1986, 1988, and 1990. Prominent reviews included one by Margaret Drabble, headlined "Queen of Calvary," *Listener* (August 1, 1968). See also "Sovereign Self" by Elizabeth Jennings, *New Statesman* (August 16, 1968).

59. "That Moment," *Collected Poems: Ted Hughes*, ed. Paul Keegan (New York: Farrar, Straus and Giroux, 2003), p. 209. It introduces the *Crow* sequence.

60. The "Manzi" notebook is at the Lilly Library, Indiana University, Box 11, Folder 4.

61. Plath believed that Whitman, for example, could not honor sufferers in their separateness. Reading *Leaves of Grass and Selected Prose* in 1954, she dutifully underlined phrases such as "Victorian taboo" and "democratic idealism" in the "Introduction" by Sculley Bradley. But reading "I Sing the Body Electric," Plath responded "NO" when the speaker asks, "Have you ever loved the body of a woman? / Have you ever loved the body of a man? / Do you not see that these are exactly the same to all in all nations and times all over the earth?" Her "NO" is written beside this last line. Reading "Song of Myself," she did not believe the poet when he wrote, "I was the man, I suffered, I was there." "Fake," she wrote in the margin. Whitman offered "easy solvent[s]," was "affected," "too easy." When she read, "The suicide sprawls on the bloody floor of the bedroom, / I witness the corpse with its dabbled hair, I note where the pistol has fallen," she commented, "But doesn't understand." Plath's Whitman "never can see 'world out of joint,'" and she recoiled from his optimism. Lines such as "All goes onward and upward, nothing collapses, / And to die is different from what any one supposed" infuriated her. Reading "What behaved well in the past or behaves well to-day is not such a wonder, / The wonder is always and always how there can be a mean man or an infidel" (Section 22), she responded, "No wonder at all." Plath's Whitman was a "supreme egotist," his optimism too voluntary. The defiant "swagger" and "galloping rhythms" of his lines brought out the hostile reader in her, and she mocked him with "No doubter he" and "never gives *experience* of doubting." In Dickinson, Plath was alert to the authority of involuntary experience. See *Leaves of Grass and Selected Prose*, ed. Sculley Bradley (New York: Rinehart, 1953), Small Special Collections Library, University of Virginia.

62. On Bishop as a lesbian, see Lorrie Goldensohn, *Elizabeth Bishop: The Biography of a Poetry* (New York: Columbia University Press, 1992), p. 63. On lesbian invisibility, see Terry Castle, *The Apparitional Lesbian: Female Sexuality and Modern Culture* (New York: Columbia University Press, 1993).

63. See Marianne Moore, "Archaically New," in *Trial Balances*, ed. Ann Winslow (New York: Macmillan, 1935), pp. 82–83. Moore praises Bishop for "the rational, considering quality of her work" and for "the natural unforced ending." Reprinted in *Elizabeth Bishop and Her Art*, ed. Lloyd Schwartz and Sybil P. Estess (Ann Arbor: University of Michigan Press, 1983), pp. 175–76.

64. On lesbianism and oral sex in "The Rabbit Catcher," see Jacqueline Rose, "No Fantasy Without Protest," in *The Haunting of Sylvia Plath* (Cambridge, MA: Harvard University Press, 1991), p. 138, and pp. 135–143, passim. On April 10, 1992, the *Times Literary Supplement* published Hughes's letter objecting to Rose's psychoanalytic reading. He claimed, "The gross assault on Sylvia Plath's sexual identity made in this interpretation is totally INADMISSIBLE" (capitals his). In *The Silent Woman: Sylvia Plath & Ted Hughes* (New York: Alfred A. Knopf, 1994), Janet Malcolm suggests that "Rose's reading does not seem very remarkable in today's climate of acceptance of both enacted and imagined homosexuality; the bisexual component of human sexuality is a commonplace of post-Freudian thought," p. 178. See also Rose's

summary of her quarrel with Hughes and his partisans, "This Is Not a Biography," *London Review of Books* 24.14 (August 2002): 12–15.

65. "You make me puke": Plath, *The Bell Jar* (New York: Harper Collins, 1999), p. 220.

66. See Karen Maroda, "Sylvia and Ruth," *Salon.com* (November 29, 2004). See also Ruth Tiffany Barnhouse, *Homosexuality: A Symbolic Confusion* (New York: Seabury, 1977). For the homophobic context in which Barnhouse treated and came to love Plath, see Sherrie A. Inness, *The Lesbian Menace: Ideology, Identity, and the Representation of Lesbian Life* (Amherst: University of Massachusetts Press, 1997). And for a classic account of the incoherence of "modern homo/heterosexual definition," see Eve Kosofsky Sedgwick, *Epistemology of the Closet* (Berkeley: University of California Press, 1990).

67. Plath's letter to Gordon Lameyer is quoted in Carl Rollyson, *American Isis: The Life and Art of Sylvia Plath* (New York: St. Martin's, 2013), p. 67. The original is at the Lilly Library and is dated April 6, 1954.

68. Dr. Ruth Tiffany Barnhart Beuscher had seven children.

69. "Marilyn Monroe appeared to me last night in a dream as a kind of fairy godmother. . . . She gave me an expert manicure. I had not washed my hair, and asked her about hairdressers, saying no matter where I went, they always imposed a horrid cut on me. She invited me to visit her during the Christmas holidays, promising a new, flowering life" (*Unabridged* 513–14).

70. Bishop and Swenson met at Yaddo in 1950. See Swenson's "Somebody Who's Somebody," in *Dear Elizabeth: Five Poems & Three Letters to Elizabeth Bishop*, "Afterword" by Kirstin Hotelling Zona (Logan: Utah State University, 2000), pp. 12–14. For Swenson's response to Plath, see "Sylvia Plath: A Recollection," in *Made with Words*, ed. Gardner McFall (Ann Arbor: University of Michigan Press, 1997), pp. 172–74. The initials are used in Plath's manuscript. Several days later, referring to her as "May," Plath describes Swenson as "freckled, in herself, a tough little nut." She amplifies: "I imagined the situation of two lesbians: the one winning a woman with child from an apparently happy marriage. Why is it impossible to think of two women of middle-age living together without Lesbianism the solution, the motive?" (*Unabridged* 528).

71. Plath, "Context," *London Magazine* 1.11 (February 1962). Reprinted in *Johnny Panic and the Bible of Dreams*, pp. 65–67. *London Magazine* invited eighteen poets to participate. Hughes chose not to respond to this question but rather to mention his indebtedness to Yeats, Coleridge, Mayakovsky, Wordsworth, and Blake. His essay "Context" is reprinted in *Winter Pollen: Occasional Prose*, ed. William Scammell (London: Faber, 1994), pp. 1–3. He acknowledges no American influences, while Plath wrote feelingly about "the hurt and wonder of loving," a subject in which her education continued. In November 1962, which was a peculiarly hurting time, Plath wrote to Stevie Smith describing herself as a "desperate Smith-addict" and suggesting that they get together. See the "delightfully Smithish" reply in Jack Barbera and William McBrien, *Stevie: A Biography of Stevie Smith* (New York: Oxford University Press, 1987), pp. 242–43. "Wild as a cat" is from "The New Age." See Smith, *Collected Poems*, ed. James MacGibbon (New York: New Directions, 1983), p. 308. Smith is the only British poet she cites.

72. "Filling Station," in *Elizabeth Bishop: Poems, Prose, and Letters*, ed. Robert Giroux and Lloyd Schwartz (New York: Library of America, 2008), pp. 124, 123.

73. See Mary Douglas, *Purity and Danger: An Analysis of Concepts of Pollution and Taboo* (London: Routledge & Kegan Paul, 1966), p. 2. On Douglas, social taboos, and the boundaries

of the body, see Judith Butler, "Bodily Inscriptions, Performative Subversions," in *Gender Trouble: Feminism and the Subversion of Identity* (New York: Routledge, 1990), pp. x, 131–34.

CHAPTER 6

1. "Confused migration": "The Burglar of Babylon," in *Elizabeth Bishop: Poems, Prose, and Letters*, ed. Robert Giroux and Lloyd Schwartz (New York: Library of America, 2008), p. 90. Cited in the text as *Poems*.

2. For Robert Lowell on Dickinson and Plath as touchstones of female poetic genius, see *Words in Air: The Complete Correspondence Between Elizabeth Bishop and Robert Lowell*, ed. Thomas Travisano with Saskia Hamilton (New York: Farrar, Straus and Giroux, 2008), p. 513.

3. Bishop to Lowell, in *Words in Air*, January 1972, p. 702. See also Ian Hamilton, "A Conversation with Robert Lowell," *Review* 26 (Summer 1971): 10–29. Lowell was quoted as saying, "Few women write major poetry. Can I make this generalization? Only four stand with our best men: Emily Dickinson, Marianne Moore, Elizabeth Bishop and Sylvia Plath."

4. Bishop to Lowell, *Words in Air*, pp. 134, 141, 143.

5. On Swenson: Bishop to Lowell, *Words in Air*, p. 110.

6. Swenson's letter of September 14, 1953, is quoted in Kirstin Hotelling Zona, *Marianne Moore, Elizabeth Bishop, & May Swenson: The Feminist Poetics of Self-Restraint* (Ann Arbor: University of Michigan Press, 2002), p. 100. She argues persuasively that Swenson was intrigued and exasperated by Bishop's sexual reserve.

7. On erotic waste: "While Someone Telephones" was written at Yaddo in the summer of 1949. It is the third of the blandly titled series "Four Poems." See *Bishop: Poems, Prose, and Letters*, p. 59.

8. Bishop may be suggesting that it is easier for men to be relaxed than for women, or she may be suggesting that to relax would be to discover an androgynous self as a same-sex love. Succinctly, Lorrie Goldensohn states that "love poetry was a minefield for Bishop." See "Bishop's Posthumous Publications," in *The Cambridge Companion to Elizabeth Bishop*, ed. Angus Cleghorn and Jonathan Ellis (New York: Cambridge University Press, 2014), p. 191.

9. On Lota, see Carmen L. Oliveira, *Rare and Commonplace Flowers: The Story of Elizabeth Bishop and Lota de Macedo Soares*, trans. Neil K. Besner (New Brunswick, NJ: Rutgers University Press, 2002).

10. Lines from Bishop's draft of "The Shampoo" are quoted in Victoria Harrison, *Elizabeth Bishop's Poetics of Intimacy* (Cambridge: Cambridge University Press, 1993), p. 70.

11. See Harrison, p. 71.

12. For Bishop's August 1953 letter to Swenson, see Harrison, p. 71.

13. For Bishop's September 1955 letter to Swenson, see Harrison, p. 71.

14. "Painful distances" is Lloyd Schwartz, "Foreword," *Rare and Commonplace Flowers*, p. x.

15. "Born guilty": Bishop, quoted in *Words in Air*, p. 673.

16. Bishop's draft of the Plath essay is in the Elizabeth Bishop Papers, Archives and Special Collections, Vassar College Libraries. In *Elizabeth Bishop: Life and the Memory of It* (Berkeley: University of California Press, 1993), p. 504, Brett C. Millier describes it as a commissioned review, "a painfully edited two pages of theorizing about writers and their letters."

17. Poet Anne Hussey's compelling account is in *Remembering Elizabeth Bishop: An Oral Biography*, ed. Gary Fountain and Peter Brazeau (Amherst: University of Massachusetts Press, 1994), p. 276.

18. Hussey, p. 276.

19. Bishop to Lowell, *Words in Air*, p. 767.

20. Bishop to Hussey, *Remembering*, p. 276.

21. Previously, as Langdon Hammer notes, Bishop's work had appeared only in school magazines, "which were student run, nonpaying, and all-female." See "Useless Concentration: Life and Work in Elizabeth Bishop's Letters and Poems," *American Literary History* 9.1 (Spring 1997): 165. Moore, he suggests, represented "the practice of composition that made the small number of Bishop's poems a sign of her ambition," p. 166.

22. See Lynn Keller, "Words Worth a Thousand Postcards: The Bishop/Moore Correspondence," *American Literature* 55.3 (October 1983): 429. Keller points out, "This was not the first time [Moore] had taken it upon herself to retype one of Bishop's poems; she had done so with 'The Weed,' and the correspondence files contain several other poems she apparently recopied and probably 'improved' slightly. With 'Roosters,' however, her changes are drastic," p. 423. There have been many lively accounts of the deference dance in which Bishop and Moore mutually engaged, some of them emphasizing the tensions in the relationship more than others. See David Kalstone, *Becoming a Poet: Elizabeth Bishop with Marianne Moore and Robert Lowell*, ed. Robert Hemenway (New York: Farrar, Straus, and Giroux, 1989); Lorrie Goldensohn, *Elizabeth Bishop: The Biography of a Poetry* (New York: Columbia University Press, 1992); Betsy Erkkila, *The Wicked Sisters: Women Poets, Literary History, and Discord* (New York: Oxford University Press, 1992); Joanne Feit Diehl, *Elizabeth Bishop and Marianne Moore: The Psychodynamics of Creativity* (Princeton: Princeton University Press, 1993); Susan McCabe, *Elizabeth Bishop: Her Poetics of Loss* (University Park: Pennsylvania State University Press, 1994).

23. The Moores' poem "The Cock" is reprinted in Kalstone, *Becoming a Poet*, pp. 265–69. For Bishop's response, see *One Art: Letters / Elizabeth Bishop*, pp. 96–97. For Moore's defense of their drastic changes, see *The Selected Letters of Marianne Moore*, ed. Bonnie Costello, Celeste Goodridge, and Cristanne Miller (New York: Alfred A. Knopf, 1997), p. 404. For "Roosters," see *Elizabeth Bishop: Poems, Prose, and Letters*, ed. Robert Giroux and Lloyd Schwartz, pp. 27–31.

24. Moore is quoted in Bishop, "Efforts of Affection," in *Elizabeth Bishop: Poems, Prose, and Letters*, p. 484.

25. Bishop, "Efforts of Affection," p. 477.

26. Bishop, "Efforts of Affection," p. 477. "Nine Nectarines and Other Porcelain" was first published in *Poetry* in November 1934 and then included in the 1935 *Selected Poems* introduced by T. S. Eliot. The "zoo" joke alludes to Moore's animal poems. See also the facsimile in *A-Quiver with Significance: Marianne Moore, 1932–1936*, ed. Heather Cass White (Victoria, BC: ELS Editions, 2008), pp. 91–94, which makes it easier to understand what Bishop admired than does the truncated version in Moore's *Complete Poems* (New York: Macmillan, 1967; rev. Macmillan/Viking, 1981). For example: "From manifold / small boughs, productive as the / magic willow that grew / above the mother's grave and threw / on Cinderella what she wished, / a bat is winging," p. 92.

27. Bishop, "Efforts of Affection," p. 487.

28. Bishop, "Efforts of Affection," p. 489.

29. Bishop, "Efforts of Affections," p. 489.

30. On going into herself, see Elodie Osborn, *Remembering*, p. 232. See also Helen Vendler on Bishop as an "encapsulated, isolated child" who "could turn off." In *Remembering*, Vendler describes the affect as defensively "chilly," p. 332.

31. The letter to Loren MacIver describing compulsive writing is in *One Art: Letters / Elizabeth Bishop*, p. 209.

32. Elizabeth Bishop, "Love from Emily," *New Republic* 125.9 (August 27, 1951): 20–21. Reprinted in *Elizabeth Bishop: Poems, Prose, and Letters*, ed. Robert Giroux and Lloyd Schwartz (New York: Library of America, 2008), pp. 689–91. She was reviewing *Emily Dickinson's Letters to Dr. and Mrs. Josiah Gilbert Holland*, ed. Theodora Van Wagenen Ward (Cambridge, MA: Harvard University Press, 1951). Ward is identified on the title page as their granddaughter.

33. See the unpublished manuscript "Sunday at Nine," Muriel Rukeyser Papers, Library of Congress, Part I, Box 42. The one-hour program devoted to Dickinson aired on August 7, 1949, on FM California radio station KDFC. It was the first of a four-part series combining words and music. Rukeyser read fourteen poems from *Bolts of Melody: New Poems of Emily Dickinson*, ed. Millicent Todd Bingham (New York: Harper & Brothers, 1945).

34. Alfred Habegger, *"My Wars Are Laid Away in Books": The Life of Emily Dickinson* (New York: Random House, 2001), p. 308.

35. Some of the Holland letters had already been published in Mabel Loomis Todd's 1931 *Letters of Emily Dickinson*, including *L* 185. Ward explains, "Owing to the unfortunate disappearance of the manuscripts of the [twenty-nine] published letters after they were returned to my grandmother, my study of them has been limited to the printed text." See *Emily Dickinson's Letters to Dr. and Mrs. Josiah Gilbert Holland*, p. vi. In *"My Wars Are Laid Away in Books,"* Appendix 5, Habegger suggests a redating of *L* 185 to August 1858, with a question mark. Based on the biographical paradigm I explored in *Dickinson: The Anxiety of Gender* (Ithaca: Cornell University Press, 1984), I prefer the earlier date because of its greater proximity to the marriage of Austin and Sue, the poet's brother and sister-in-law. Their marriage in July 1856 was an important turning point in Dickinson's erotic imagination. Additionally, Dickinson's letters become more elliptical in the late 1850s, and the "Don't tell" letter is comparatively detailed.

36. Thomas H. Johnson, "Affectionately, Emily," *New York Times Book Review* (April 22, 1951): 6. See also Josephine Young Case, "This is a peculiarly happy collection of letters; and it has been fortunate in its editing. Clearly this has been a labor of love for Mrs. Ward; but it is also a labor of careful scholarship. The introduction, the commentary between the letters, the notes explaining references in the letters (insofar as Emily's hieroglyphic style can be explained), the appendices on handwriting and paper, are models of brevity and grace." *New England Quarterly* 24.4 (December 1951): 546–48.

37. George F. Whicher, "More Light on Emily," *New York Herald Book Review* (April 29, 1951): 6.

38. Grace B. Sherrer, "Emily Dickinson's Letters to Dr. and Mrs. Josiah Gilbert Holland," *American Literature* 23.3 (November 1951): 382.

39. *New Yorker* 27.33 (September 29, 1951): 123.

40. Richard Chase, "Letters to the World," *Nation* (April 21, 1951): 380.

41. Henry W. Wells, "Contradictions of Life and Art," *Saturday Review of Literature* (September 29, 1951): 17–18. Wells suggested rather casually that Dickinson may have "loved man or woman, one or many," while also stating that too much attention had been paid to her romantic frustrations at the expense of her artistry.

42. I have consulted more than a dozen reviews. In addition to those already mentioned, see Walter Harding, "'Dazzling Snapshots of the Human Spirit,'" *Chicago Sunday Tribune* (May 6, 1951): 5. Harding, a Thoreau scholar, does not mention Wadsworth and comments on the poetic qualities of Dickinson's prose: "The letters are as individualistic as her poetry, and

they are close in spirit to it. Indeed, many paragraphs need only a different typographical set-up to become poetry, and in some spots Emily herself made that change." Thus contemporary questions of genre and of letter-poems are already present in reviews of the Holland *Letters*. For example, the *New York Times Book Review* identifies Thomas H. Johnson as the prospective editor of "Dickinson's *papers*" (italics mine) (April 22, 1951): 6.

43. Theodora Van Wagenen Ward, "The Background," *Emily Dickinson's Letters to Dr. and Mrs. Josiah Gilbert Holland*, p. 18.

44. Elizabeth Holland, quoted in Millicent Todd Bingham, *Ancestors' Brocades: The Literary Discovery of Emily Dickinson* (New York: Dover, 1945), p. 193.

45. See Harriet Merrick Hodge Plunkett, *Josiah Gilbert Holland* (New York: Charles Scribner's: 1894), pp. 25–26. Plunkett was a close family friend whose moderately feminist biography was written with Elizabeth Holland's assistance.

46. See *Emily Dickinson's Letters to Dr. and Mrs. Josiah Gilbert Holland*, pp. 90–91.

47. On Elizabeth Chapin Holland's early life and education, see Theodora Van Wagenen Ward, "The Background," p. 8.

48. See J. G. Holland, "Fleta Gray," *Home Journal* 13.163 (March 24, 1849): 1. The editor comments, "With a little more finish, this would have been one of the very finest poems of the time." See also Holland, "Land of the North," *Home Journal* 4.154 (January 20, 1849): 2.

49. See Elizabeth Holland, quoted in "Background," *Emily Dickinson's Letters*, p. 13. The baby, Arthur Gilbert Holland, did not survive early childhood. See Harry Houston Peckham, *Josiah Gilbert Holland in Relation to His Times* (Philadelphia: University of Pennsylvania Press, 1940), p. 48. A daughter, Julia, was stillborn. In all, Elizabeth Holland gave birth to five children in the ten years from 1849 to 1859.

50. "Three Weeks on a Cotton Plantation" was published anonymously in the *Springfield Daily Republican*, beginning on Wednesday, September 26, 1849, p. 2. The sketches include a sentimental deathbed scene which unites the races around the loss of a beloved child, in this regard anticipating the death of Little Eva in Harriet Beecher Stowe's *Uncle Tom's Cabin*. They culminate in emotional and economic disaster for the sympathetic white family depicted in this fictionalized account of slavery "under its fairest aspects." The seven sketches had been presumed lost and I am grateful to Kristine Helbling of Olin Library, Washington University, for helping to locate them. See J. G. Holland, "Three Weeks on a Cotton Plantation," edited and introduced by Vivian R. Pollak, *The Emily Dickinson Journal* 24.1 (2015): 72–95.

51. See J. G. Holland, "To the Rev. Henry Ward Beecher," in *Titcomb's Letters to Young People, Single and Married* (New York: C. Scribner, 1858), pp. v, viii.

52. I continue to believe that J. G. Holland was one of the two editors she had in mind when she wrote Higginson in April 1862, "Two Editors of Journals came to my Father's House, this winter – and asked me for my Mind – and when I asked them 'Why,' they said I was penurious – and they, would use it for the World" (*L* 261). A later comment by Holland refers to Dickinson's poems as too delicate for publication. In 1861–62, his judgment was better. The other editor must have been Samuel Bowles.

53. *Reveries of a Bachelor; A Book of the Heart* (New York: Baker and Scribner, 1850) by "Ik Marvel" (Donald Grant Mitchell) was one of Dickinson's favorite books in the 1850s. For a discussion of Dickinson's bachelor persona in letters to Susan Gilbert, see Pollak, *Dickinson*, p. 65n. See also Vincent J. Bertolini, "Fireside Chastity: The Erotics of Sentimental Bachelor-hood in the 1850s," in *Sentimental Men: Masculinity and the Politics of Affect in American Culture*, ed. Mary Chapman and Glenn Hendler (Berkeley: University of California Press, 1999), pp. 19–42. Bertolini explains, "Bachelors and fireplaces go together in the antebellum

period. The scene of the solitary lounging bachelor dreaming before the glowing embers, lost in that mood of feelingful reminiscence and imaginative projection that the nineteenth century called 'revery,' is common in the narrative literature of the period. Not merely a literary motif or familiar setting, the bachelor's fireside revery is a widely diffused cultural topos. . . . Bachelorhood was an obsessive preoccupation of antebellum American culture, and the bachelor, a highly problematized social identity, was the frequent topic of stories, plays, magazine pieces, poetry, and songs, as a rapid check of publication records from the period immediately reveals." For later permutations of the bachelor as a cultural topos, see Eve Kosofsky Sedgwick, *Epistemology of the Closet* (Berkeley: University of California Press, 1990), and George Chauncey, *Gay New York: Gender, Urban Culture, and the Making of the Gay Male World, 1890–1940* (New York: Basic Books, 1999). See also Katherine V. Snyder, *Bachelors, Manhood, and the Novel, 1850–1925* (Cambridge: Cambridge University Press, 1999).

54. See "The Day undressed – Herself" (*Fr* 495), "The Wind begun to rock the Grass" (*Fr* 796), "Truth – is as old as God" (*Fr* 795), and "Away from Home are some and I" (*Fr* 807). R. W. Franklin suggests that "The Day undressed – Herself" may have been sent to Elizabeth alone; "Truth – is as old as God" was addressed "Doctor" and signed "Emily." The provisionally dated 1862 letter (*L* 269) may be earlier. If so, there is a five-year gap in the extant correspondence aside from the poems. Thomas Johnson observes that Dickinson's tone does not suggest a break when the letters pick up again in November 1865. I agree. See *L* 311n.

55. See Allen C. Guelzo, "Holland's Informants: The Construction of Josiah Holland's 'Life of Abraham Lincoln,'" *Journal of the Abraham Lincoln Association* 23.1 (Winter 2002): 1. See also Guelzo, "Introduction," in *Holland's Life of Lincoln* (Lincoln: University of Nebraska Press, 1998). Samuel Bowles marketed the book by subscription and it was translated into several languages, which may explain Dickinson's reference to Holland's "foreign accent" (*L* 311).

56. Probably quoting Elizabeth, Plunkett states, "'He did not entertain exhilarating views of woman's place in intellectual advancement, yet to the individual woman no one could be more tender, more helpful, more considerate.'" See p. 49, *Life of Josiah Gilbert Holland*. For more on Holland and women writers, see Mary Loeffelholz, "Really Indigenous Productions: Emily Dickinson, Josiah Holland, and Nineteenth-Century Popular Verse," in *A Companion to Emily Dickinson*, ed. Martha Nell Smith and Mary Loeffelholz (Malden, MA: Blackwell, 2008), pp. 183–204. She describes him as "one of the several editorial friends and acquaintances of Emily Dickinson who did not take up the cause of publishing her poetry," p. 183.

In Berlin, Elizabeth had consulted the eminent eye specialist Albrecht von Graefe, who warned her to expect diminished vision for the rest of her life. Unfortunately, his prediction was borne out, but as Dickinson remarked, Elizabeth took a "cheerful view of Woe" (*L* 521). She had always been an enthusiastic hostess and after the move to New York in the fall of 1872, she and "Gilbert" entertained writers such as Kate Field, "H. H." (Helen Hunt Jackson), Frances Hodgson Burnett, Bret Harte, Charles Dudley Warner, and Richard Henry Stoddard in their newly constructed Park Avenue home.

57. The quotation is from *Emily Dickinson's Letters to Dr. and Mrs. Josiah Gilbert Holland*, p. 96. See also "Longing is like the Seed," *The Poems of Emily Dickinson: Variorum Edition*, ed. R. W. Franklin (Cambridge, MA: Harvard University Press, 1998), 3: 1125.

58. The copy Dickinson sent to Higginson has variant line breaks. See Franklin, *The Poems of Emily Dickinson: Variorum Edition*, 3: 1124–26. The copy she kept for herself has a penciled word variant, "Zone" for "Clime." On "Longing is like the Seed" as an instrument

of flirtation with Higginson, see Brenda Wineapple, *White Heat: The Friendship of Emily Dickinson & Thomas Wentworth Higginson* (New York: Random House, 2008), p. 189.

59. On "Longing is like the Seed" and other definition poems, see Sharon Cameron, *Lyric Time: Dickinson and the Limits of Genre* (Baltimore: Johns Hopkins University Press, 1979), p. 34.

60. Henry James, *The Notebooks of Henry James*, ed. F. O. Matthiessen and Kenneth B. Murdoch (New York: Oxford University Press, 1947), p. 47.

61. R. D. Gooder, "Introduction," in Henry James, *The Bostonians* (New York: Oxford University Press, 1998), p. xxiv. The classic account of Boston marriage is Lillian Faderman, *Surpassing the Love of Men: Romantic Friendship and Love Between Women from the Renaissance to the Present* (New York: Morrow, 1981). She explains: "The term 'Boston marriage' was used in late nineteenth-century New England to describe a long-term monogamous relationship between two otherwise unmarried women. The women were generally financially independent of men, either through inheritance or because of a career. They were usually feminists, New Women, often pioneers in a profession. They were also very involved in culture and in social betterment, and these female values, which they shared with each other, formed a strong basis for their life together. Their relationships were in every sense, as described by a Bostonian, Mark De Wolfe Howe, the nineteenth-century *Atlantic Monthly* editor, who had social contact with a number of these women, 'a union—there is no truer word for it.' Whether these unions sometimes or often included sex we will never know, but we do know that these women spent their lives primarily with other women, they gave to other women the bulk of their energy and attention, and they formed powerful emotional ties with other women. If their personalities could be projected to our times, it is probable that they would see themselves as 'women-identified-women,' i.e. what we would call lesbians, regardless of the level of their sexual interests." See Faderman, *Surpassing the Love of Men*, part 2, chap. 4.

62. The description of Bishop is from the *New Republic*, p. 20. For convenience, I quote from the version of the essay in *Elizabeth Bishop: Poems, Prose, and Letters*.

63. "I'd love to be a bird or a bee" is quoted from Ward, p. 33. The letter dated Autumn 1853, followed by a question mark. In *Letters*, edited by Johnson and Ward, the question mark disappears (*L* 133). Dickinson was twenty-two when she wrote the "sentimental" letter from which Bishop quotes; she mentions having written an earlier letter and not sending it, because she feared it was too "lofty." "'This Mortal' essays immortality" quotes 1 Corinthians 15:54; Dickinson suggests that she would like to be able to fly to her friends and that her heaven is filled with them.

64. For a classic example of hidden emotion in Bishop's poetry, see "Sestina," *Poems*, pp. 120–21, where the child-artist's expressions of feeling have gone underground. "Sestina" picks up the cooking stove image in the autumn 1853 letter discussed above (*L* 133). On lies and sentimentality, see Valerie Rohy, "Love's Substitutions: Elizabeth Bishop and the Lie of Language," in *Impossible Women: Lesbian Figures & American Literature* (Ithaca: Cornell University Press, 2000), pp. 117–43.

65. George Herbert is one of Bishop's most frequently acknowledged influences. On his continuing and powerful presence in her life and work, see Jeredith Merrin, *An Enabling Humility: Marianne Moore, Elizabeth Bishop, and the Uses of Tradition* (New Brunswick, NJ: Rutgers University Press, 1990), chap. 2 and passim. Attempts to tease out Herbert's influence on Dickinson are somewhat inconclusive, but in *Bolts of Melody: New Poems of Emily Dickinson*, p. 125, Millicent Todd Bingham included two stanzas of Herbert's "Mattens" Dickinson had copied from the 1876 *Springfield Republican*. The *New Yorker* quickly pointed out Bingham's

mistaken attribution, in "The Talk of the Town" (June 16, 1945): 15. In *Emily Dickinson's Home: Letters of Edward Dickinson and His Family* (New York: Harper, 1955), p. 572, Bingham offers an account of her error, explaining that Dickinson intermingled Herbert's words with her own characteristic dashes. See also Judith Farr, *The Passion of Emily Dickinson* (Cambridge, MA: Harvard University Press, 1992), pp. 326–27, who links this episode to Dickinson's visual experiments and to Herbert's shape poems, noting that "the dash, for Victorians, was the most used and abused of punctuation marks . . . [and] the closest to a brushstroke," p. 328.

66. In "Arrival at Santos" (*Poems* 65–66), "Miss Breen" is described as "about seventy, / a retired police lieutenant, six feet tall, / with beautiful bright blue eyes and a kind expression." The actual Miss Breen was the head of the women's jail in Detroit. See Bishop's letter to Lowell in *One Art*, p. 225. Breen, who had retired to Glens Falls, explained shyly that she had solved several murders and been written up in *True Detective Stories*. As Brett Millier notes, "Miss Breen received her second widest bit of notoriety from Elizabeth. . . . The local paper in Glens Falls noted with pleasure the poem's publication in the *New Yorker* of June 21, 1952," *Life*, p. 239. Millier suggests that "what Elizabeth got from this brief acquaintance was a vision of an accomplished and successful lesbian life, not at all secretive or ashamed, at a time when she was herself at a major transition, a moment of courageous 'growth and redirection' unprecedented in her life." This may be so, but there is still considerable coding at play in Bishop's published and unpublished poetry and prose even after this time.

67. "Unseemly Deductions" was published in the *New Republic* 127.7 (August 18, 1952): 20. See Rebecca Patterson, *The Riddle of Emily Dickinson* (Boston: Houghton Mifflin, 1951). On the typescript of the review, Bishop wrote, "Never published. They changed editors or something." Elizabeth Bishop Collection, Vassar College Libraries. In a slightly different form, the essay became part of the official Bishop canon in *Prose*, ed. Lloyd Schwartz (New York: Farrar, Straus and Giroux, 2011), pp. 264–65. In *Prose*, the review ends with a joke, rather than with "this infuriating book": "Or, as a poetic friend of mine better summarized it: 'Kate Scott! / Great Scot!'" Bishop is quoting May Swenson.

68. On the de-eroticized American Sappho, see Thomas Wentworth Higginson, "Sappho," *Atlantic Monthly* 28 (July 1871): 83–93. See also Gloria Shaw Duclos, "Thomas Wentworth Higginson's Sappho," *New England Quarterly* 57.3 (September 1984): 403–11. "Wild love" for "fair girls and young men" is from an 1896 review in *Godey's Magazine* of "Sappho and Other Princesses of Poetry," cited in Willis J. Buckingham, *Emily Dickinson's Reception in the 1890s: A Documentary History* (Pittsburgh: University of Pittsburgh Press, 1989), p. 454. The reviewer, Rupert Hughes, encourages us to "note the large pantheism and fellowship with Nature of Emily Dickinson's fieldward muse."

69. Erkkila, pp. 10, 13. See also Amy Lowell, "The Sisters," *North American Review* (June 1922). Twentieth-century linkings of Dickinson and Sappho include Louis Untermeyer, who is cited on *Riddle*'s jacket copy, describing Dickinson as "with the possible exception of Sappho, the greatest woman poet of all time." See also Untermeyer, quoted in *The Poems of Emily Dickinson*, ed. Martha Dickinson Bianchi and Alfred Leete Hampson (Boston: Little, Brown, 1941), p. x. For a theoretical essay on Sappho's importance to twentieth-century women writers, especially Renée Vivien and H. D., see Susan Gubar, "Sapphistries," *Signs* 10.1 (Autumn 1984): 43–62. On pp. 45–46, she quotes Edith Sitwell's 1944 letter to Oxford classicist Maurice Bowra complaining that "most women's poetry 'is *simply awful*—incompetent, floppy, whining, arch, trivial, self-pitying.'" For a fuller version of the letter, which characterizes the best of Dickinson as "deep and concentrated, but fearfully incompetent," see *Edith Sitwell: Selected Letters 1919–1964*, ed. John Lehmann and Derek Parker (New York: Vanguard, 1970), p. 116. For more on

the tradition, see also Joan DeJean, *Fictions of Sappho, 1546–1937* (Chicago: University of Chicago Press, 1989); Yopie Prins, *Victorian Sappho* (Princeton: Princeton University Press, 1999); and Virginia Jackson, *Dickinson's Misery: A Theory of Lyric Reading* (Princeton: Princeton University Press, 2005), which discusses Anne Carson's Dickinson-associated Sappho and its generic extensions, pp. 118–22. See too Carson's translation, *If Not, Winter: Fragments of Sappho* (New York: Alfred A. Knopf, 2002), p. 191.

70. Patterson, p. 147.

71. Patterson, pp. 147–48.

72. "Baffling problem in human behavior": Jacket copy, *Riddle*.

73. Reviews of *Riddle*: *Nation* 173 (December 29, 1951): 573; George F. Whicher, "Riddle or Reconstruction," *New York Herald Tribune Book Review* (November 9, 1951): 21; *New York Times* (November 4, 1951): 3; *San Francisco Chronicle* (December 2, 1951): 18; Richard Chase, "Seeking a Poet's Inspiration," *Saturday Review of Literature* 34 (December 1, 1951): 26; *New Yorker* 27 (January 12, 1952): 86; Grace B. Sherrer, "Review of *The Riddle of Emily Dickinson* by Rebecca Patterson," *American Literature* 24.2 (May 1952): 255–58; R. P. Blackmur, "A Plea for the Essay," *Kenyon Review* 14.3 (Summer 1952): 530–34; Laurence Perrine, "Emily's Beloved Friend," *Southwest Review* 37 (Winter 1952): 81–83; Myron Ochshorn, "In Search of Emily Dickinson," *New Mexico Quarterly* 23.1 (Spring 1953): 94–106; Nicholas Joost, "The Pain That Emily Knew," *Poetry* 80.4 (July 1952): 242–45; John Ciardi, "Review of *The Riddle of Emily Dickinson* by Rebecca Patterson," *New England Quarterly* 25.1 (March 1952): 93–98. Thanks to Bonnie Carr O'Neill and Randy Robertson for their help in this search.

74. On Bishop and her 1940s psychiatrist Ruth Foster, see Brett C. Millier, *Elizabeth Bishop: Life and the Memory of It* (Berkeley: University of California Press, 1993), pp. 180, 181, 194, 201, 227, 228. Foster treated Bishop in 1944–45 and the spring of 1946. When she died in September 1950, she was also treating Bishop's friends Louise Crane and Tommy Wanning. See the letter to Moore in *One Art*, p. 206, describing Foster as "so good and kind, and certainly [she] helped me more than anyone in the world." Dr. Ruth Foster is not to be confused with Dr. Anny Baumann, a general practitioner who treated Bishop beginning in 1947 for alcoholism, asthma, and depression. Ruth Foster died on September 29, 1950, in her home at 110 E. 87th Street, where she had her office. Her *New York Times* obituary describes her as a psychiatrist and psychoanalyst. She was born in Boston, where her father was an attorney, graduated from the Winsor School there, attended Goucher College in 1921–23, and in 1931 graduated from the University of Maryland Medical School. Foster was unmarried.

75. Bishop, "The U.S.A. School of Writing," *Poems, Prose, Letters*, p. 456.

76. Lillian Faderman, *Odd Girls and Twilight Lovers: A History of Lesbian Life in Twentieth-Century America* (New York: Columbia University Press, 1991), pp. 119, 138.

77. On Bishop's strategic retreat, see Camille Roman, *Elizabeth Bishop's World War II–Cold War View* (New York: Palgrave, 2001), p. 7. Roman comments, p. 2, on her personal struggle with Bishop's "political decisions and personal choices."

78. Valerie Traub, *The Renaissance of Lesbianism in Early Modern England* (Cambridge: Cambridge University Press, 2002), pp. 13–14.

79. See also Bishop to Alexandra Johnson, in *Conversations with Elizabeth Bishop*, ed. George Monteiro (Jackson: University Press of Mississippi, 1996), pp. 98–99: "I was very isolated as a child and perhaps poetry was my way of making familiar what I saw around me. . . . I never intended to 'be' a poet, as I think people set out to do today. I never wanted to think about any label."

80. Sylvia Plath, *The Unabridged Journals*, p. 322.

81. On closets, see Bishop to Frank Bidart, *Remembering*, p. 327.

82. On advice for the lovelorn in Seattle, see *Conversations with Elizabeth Bishop*, p. 44.

83. Allen Ginsberg, "A Supermarket in California," in *Howl and Other Poems* (San Francisco: City Lights Books, 1956), pp. 29–30. Bishop, "The U.S.A. School of Writing," *Poems, Prose, Letters*, p. 452.

84. The "U.S.A." quotations are from pp. 449, 450, 449, 450, 452.

85. The "U.S.A." drafts are in Archives and Special Collections, Vassar College Libraries. "Dated and unpleasant things" is *One Art*, p. 75; "Modern love" is *Poems, Prose, Letters*, p. 452.

86. "Entire brains of the place": *Poems, Prose, Letters*, p. 453.

87. Bishop's letters to Katharine White and hers to Bishop are in *Elizabeth Bishop and "The New Yorker": The Complete Correspondence*, ed. Joelle Biele (New York: Farrar, Straus and Giroux, 2011). The quotations are from pp. 183, 186, 187–88. Despite William Shawn's caveat, I can't cite other examples of correspondence school fiction and would be grateful for leads. But see Galway Kinnell, "The Correspondence School Instructor Says Goodbye to His Poetry Students," in *A New Selected Poems* (New York: Houghton Mifflin, 2001), p. 53. For an illuminating reading of "The U.S.A. School" as an example of Bishop's despair over writing and its products, see Gillian C. White, " 'We Do Not Say Ourselves Like That in Poems': The Poetics of Contingency in Wallace Stevens and Elizabeth Bishop" (Ph.D. diss., Princeton University, 2006). White sees the story as responding to 1930s culture, while I am more concerned with its mid-career implications.

88. *Conversations with Elizabeth Bishop*, pp. 11, 52.

89. Quoted in Goldensohn, *Elizabeth Bishop*, p. xvii.

90. Gertrude Stein, "The Good Anna," in *Three Lives* (New York: Viking Penguin, 1990), p. 36.

91. Bishop's copy of Walt Whitman, *Leaves of Grass: From the Text of the Edition Authorized and Editorially Supervised by His Literary Executors, Richard Maurice Bucke, Thomas B. Harned, and Horace L. Traubel*, ed. Emory Holloway (Garden City, NY: Doubleday, Page, 1926), is in the Elizabeth Bishop Collection, Houghton Library, Harvard University. Houghton Library also has her copy of Thomas H. Johnson's Dickinson *Variorum*, about which more later. "The Americans" line from the 1855 "Preface" is in *Leaves of Grass and Other Writings*, ed. Michael Moon (New York: W. W. Norton, 2002), p. 616; *Leaves of Grass*, ed. Holloway, p. 488.

92. "Poets to Come" first appeared in *Leaves of Grass* 1860, as number 14 in "Chants Democratic," with variations. For example, Whitman stated, "I expect that Kanadians, a hundred, and perhaps many hundred years from now, in winter, in the splendor of the snow and woods, or on the icy lakes, will take me with them, and permanently enjoy themselves with me." See *Leaves of Grass, 1860: The 150th Anniversary Facsimile Edition*, ed. Jason Stacy (Iowa City: University of Iowa Press, 2009), pp. 186–87.

93. Bishop to Frani Blough and Margaret Miller, *One Art*, p. 75.

94. Bishop to Ashley Brown in 1966, reprinted in *Conversations*, p. 20.

95. Bishop to Anne Stevenson, January 8, 1964, Special Collections, Olin Library, Washington University in St. Louis.

96. For more on Bishop's markings in *Leaves of Grass*, see Joanne Feit Diehl, *Women Poets and The American Sublime* (Bloomington: Indiana University Press, 1990), p. 92. Diehl observes that the young Elizabeth Bishop admired in Whitman "a prudence suitable for immortality" and that Bishop marked this seminal line from the 1855 "Preface" in her copy of *Leaves of Grass*.

97. Bishop's notebooks, including the 1934–36 notebook containing the "Flags and Banners" motif, are in Archives and Special Collections, Vassar College Libraries. Poems quoted are "Song of the Banner at Daybreak" and "Delicate Cluster," in *Leaves of Grass*, ed. Moon, pp. 243, 271.

98. Whitman, "Poets to Come," *Leaves of Grass*, ed. Moon, p. 14.

99. Bishop, *Notebooks 1934–36*, Vassar College Libraries.

100. Quotations from "Faces" are in *Leaves of Grass*, ed. Moon, pp. 389, 390, 390; "breathing plain of snow" is "The Imaginary Iceberg," Bishop, *Poems*, p. 4.

101. "Parent leaf" is *Notebooks 1934–36*; "Name it 'friendship'" is *Notebooks 1934–37*, Folder 3. "The Map" is *Poems*, p. 3.

102. Bishop's March 21, 1972, letter to Lowell is in *One Art*, p. 563 and *Words in Air*, p. 708.

103. Lowell's letter claims that he avoided using even more damaging material, but many other reviewers took him to task for his poaching, which had its precedent in William Carlos Williams's *Paterson*. See Lowell, *Words in Air*, pp. 713–14. See also *The Critical Response to Robert Lowell*, ed. Steven Gould Axelrod (Westport, CT: Greenwood Press, 1999). For deep background on Bishop's response, see the nuanced discussion of Lowell's use of *her* letters in Kalstone, *Becoming a Poet*, pp. 232–39.

104. Sewall, *The Life of Emily Dickinson*, 1: 233.

105. Bishop, quoted in Eileen McMahon, "Elizabeth Bishop Speaks About Her Poetry," in *Conversations*, p. 108. See also her 1977 interview with George Starbuck, reprinted in *Conversations*, p. 97: "I know I wish I had written a great deal more. Sometimes I think if I had been born a man I probably would have written more. Dared more, or been able to spend more time at it. I've wasted a great deal of time." Bishop made the point to Bidart as well. "Late in her life, in a mood of anger, self-doubt, and bitterness, she told me that she felt she would have written much more had she been a man. She brought up how little she had written in contrast to Lowell (his *Selected Poems* had just come out. . . .). I can't quote her words exactly, but she felt that certain kinds of directness and ambition—because of her gender—had been denied her, had been impossible." See Bidart, "Elizabeth Bishop," *Threepenny Review* 58 (Summer 1994): 6.

106. A double gender poem, "I showed her Hights" is quoted from *The Poems of Emily Dickinson: Variorum Edition*, ed. Thomas H. Johnson, 3 vols. (Cambridge, MA: Harvard University Press, 1955), where it appears as number 446. This poem's variant version is "He showed me Hights," which Franklin uses in his *Reader's Edition* while excluding "I showed her Hights," which is featured by itself in Johnson's 1960 *The Complete Poems of Emily Dickinson*. There are several other Dickinson poems which exist in double gender versions, for example "I robbed the Woods" (Johnson 41; Franklin 57), "Going to Him! Happy letter!" (Johnson 494; Franklin 277), "The Stars are old, that stood for me" (Johnson 1249; Franklin 1242), and "Her Losses make our Gains ashamed" (Johnson 1562; Franklin 1602). On doubling and gender, see Pollak, *Dickinson: The Anxiety of Gender*, p. 136, where I describe how Dickinson transforms her specific loss of an actual woman into the symbolic loss of any lover. The Rich quote is in "'I am in Danger—Sir,'" in *Necessities of Life: Poems, 1962–65* (New York: W. W. Norton, 1966), p. 33.

107. Undated birthday card, Elizabeth Bishop Letters to Frank Bidart, 1971–1978, Houghton Library.

108. "Snide remarks" and "Poetress": Bishop to Lowell, December 2, 1956, *One Art*, p. 333 and *Words in Air*, pp. 189–90.

109. Randall Jarrell's review of Dickinson and Bishop appeared in "The Year in Poetry," *Harper's* October 1955. Reprinted in Jarrell, *Kipling, Auden & Co: Essays and Reviews 1935–1964* (New York: Farrar, Straus and Giroux, 1980), p. 244. See also Bishop's letter to Jarrell in *One Art*, p. 312, (over)praising him: "I always agree with you in matters of taste." Bishop's letter to Lowell is in *One Art*, p. 333 and *Words in Air*, pp. 189–90.

110. "If you were coming in the Fall" is Johnson number 511, Franklin 356, and is quoted from the Johnson *Variorum*. It was one of the sources for Plath's "Admonition," as I discussed in Chapter 5. Lowell copied it into his notebooks, 1939–43. See Steven Gould Axelrod, "Appendix A," in *Robert Lowell: Life and Art* (Princeton: Princeton University Press, 1978), p. 246. Lowell also responded to "Because I could not stop for Death," which was famously (mis)praised by his mentor Allen Tate, who was using a corrupt version of the text that omitted the fourth stanza, as was Lowell and everyone else until Johnson straightened things out. For Tate's essay "New England Culture and Emily Dickinson," see *Symposium* 3 (April 1932): 206–26; reprinted in *The Recognition of Emily Dickinson*, ed. Caesar R. Blake and Carlton F. Wells (Ann Arbor: University of Michigan Press, 1968), pp. 153–66.

111. "Now I knew I lost her" is Johnson number 1219, Franklin 1274, and is quoted from the Johnson *Variorum*. Rebecca Patterson reads it as about "a woman visiting in the house next door," Kate Scott Turner Anthon, while contemporary critics read it as about Sue. Here is Patterson: "Emily wept over her lost idol. All summer she had deceived herself with the notion that her friend was suffering equally. Now that she saw Kate's laughing face again, it was obviously no such matter," p. 207.

112. Magically, "The last Night that She lived" is Johnson 1100, Franklin 1100, a rare coincidence of numbers, and is quoted from the Johnson version. Although Bishop did not mark the poem in her copy, she identified strongly with Dickinson's problem of belief in herself and in other people.

113. Bishop, quoted in Millier, *Elizabeth Bishop*, pp. 62–63. "We play at Paste" is Johnson 320, Franklin 282. Bishop first read Dickinson when she was twelve, "but in an early edition, and . . . didn't like it much." See *Conversations*, p. 88. The early edition may have been *The Single Hound*, ed. Martha Dickinson Bianchi (Boston: Little, Brown, 1914). See also *Conversations*, p. 20, in which she recalls that about the time she started going to summer camp she "met some more sophisticated girls who already knew Emily Dickinson and H. D. and Conrad and Henry James. One of them gave me Harriet Monroe's anthology of modern poets. That was an important experience."

114. "We play at Paste" is Johnson number 320 and is quoted from the Johnson *Variorum*.

115. Bishop, quoted in *Conversations*, p. 54, and Bishop, quoted in *Elizabeth Bishop and Her Art*, ed. Lloyd Schwartz and Sybill P. Estess (Ann Arbor: University of Michigan Press, 1983), pp. 318–19, 324.

116. "Exchanging Hats" was published in *New World Writing* 9 (April 1956): 128–29. See also Frank O'Hara's "The Day Lady Died," in *The Handbook of Heartbreak: 101 Poems of Lost Love and Sorrow*, ed. Robert Pinsky (New York: Rob Weisbach Books, 1998), pp. 76–79.

117. "Memories of Uncle Neddy" was published in the *Southern Review* 13 (Fall 1977): 786–80. See "Memories of Uncle Neddy," *Poems, Prose, Letters*, pp. 618, 624, 628. On "avernal": in a letter to Ilse and Kit Barker, June 5, 1956, Bishop says that she likes "anxious" better. Princeton University Library, Mss. On privileging heteronormativity in the name of the idealized child, see Lee Edelman, *No Future: Queer Theory and the Death Drive* (Durham, NC: Duke University Press, 2004).

118. "Art is art" is in *Conversations*, p. 54; "human being" is "The Country Mouse," *Collected Prose*, p. 33.

119. "Time passing" is "The U.S.A. School of Writing," p. 459. For Jimmy's first appearance, see "The Sea and Its Shore," *Poems, Prose, Letters*, p. 179. "Mr. Margolies" is there too. "The Sea" was published in *New Letters in America*, ed. Horace Gregory and Eleanor Clark (New York: W.W. Norton, 1937), pp. 19–25. In both stories, Jimmy has trouble with his teeth, which make him nervous and sick; Bishop recycles the description of his complaint.

CONCLUSION

1. On word frequency, see the link to the "Emily Dickinson Lexicon," *Emily Dickinson Archive: An Open-Access Website for the Manuscripts of Emily Dickinson*, edickinson.org.

2. See "cubit" in Noah Webster, *An American Dictionary of the English Language* (1844), at edickinson.org. For Dickinson's fourteen letters to Webster's granddaughter Emily Ellsworth Fowler (Ford), a girlhood friend, see *The Letters of Emily Dickinson*, ed. Thomas H. Johnson and Theodora Ward, 3 vols. (Cambridge, MA: Harvard University Press, 1958).

3. Gillian C. White, *Lyric Shame: The "Lyric" Subject of Contemporary American Poetry* (Cambridge, MA: Harvard University Press, 2014), p. 1.

4. See "intimacy" in Webster, *An American Dictionary* (1844).

5. For an example of Mabel Loomis Todd in poet mode when Dickinson knew her, see Polly Longsworth, *Austin and Mabel: The Amherst Affair and Love Letters of Austin Dickinson and Mabel Loomis Todd* (New York: Farrar, Straus, Giroux, 1984), p. 177.

Works Cited

What follows is a list of published sources. Archival material is cited in the endnotes to each chapter.

Abbott, John S. C. *The Mother at Home; or the Principles of Maternal Duty*. New York: American Tract Society, 1833.

Alexander, Paul. *Rough Magic: A Biography of Sylvia Plath*. New York: Viking, 1991. Revised 1999, Da Capo Press Edition.

Allen, Gay Wilson. *The Solitary Singer: A Critical Biography of Walt Whitman*. New York: New York University Press, 1955.

Ames, Lois. "Notes Toward a Biography." In *The Art of Sylvia Plath: A Symposium*, edited by Charles Newman, 155–73. Bloomington: Indiana University Press, 1970.

Anderson, Charles R. *Emily Dickinson's Poetry: Stairway of Surprise*. New York: Holt, Rinehart and Winston, 1960; London: Heinemann, 1963.

Andrews, Charles McLean. *A History of England*. Boston: Allyn and Bacon, 1903.

Apponyi, Flora Haines. "Last Days of Mrs. Helen Hunt Jackson." *Overland Monthly and Out West Magazine* 6.33 (September 1885): 310–16.

Axelrod, Steven Gould, ed. *The Critical Response to Robert Lowell*. Westport, CT: Greenwood Press, 1999.

———. *Robert Lowell: Life and Art*. Princeton: Princeton University Press, 1978.

———. *Sylvia Plath: The Wound and the Cure of Words*. Baltimore: Johns Hopkins University Press, 1990.

Banning, Evelyn I. *Helen Hunt Jackson*. New York: Vanguard, 1973.

Barbera, Jack, and William McBrien. *Stevie: A Biography of Stevie Smith*. New York: Oxford University Press, 1987.

Barnhouse, Ruth Tiffany. *Homosexuality: A Symbolic Confusion*. New York: Seabury, 1977.

Barrus, Clara. *Whitman and Burroughs: Comrades*. Boston: Houghton Mifflin, 1931.

Barthes, Roland. "A Cruel Country: Notes on Mourning." Translated by Richard Howard. *New Yorker* (September 13, 2010): 26.

———. "The Death of the Author." In *The Rustle of Language*, translated by Richard Howard, 49–55. Berkeley: University of California Press, 1989.

———. *Mourning Diary Oct. 26, 1977–Sept. 15, 1979*. New York: Hill and Wang, 2010.

Bate, Jonathan. "Hughes on Shakespeare." In *The Cambridge Companion to Ted Hughes*, edited by Terry Gifford, 135–49. Cambridge: Cambridge University Press, 2011.

Baym, Nina. *Woman's Fiction: A Guide to Novels by and About Women in America, 1820–1870*. Ithaca, NY: Cornell University Press, 1978.

Benfey, Christopher. *The Great Wave: Gilded Age Misfits, Japanese Eccentrics, and the Opening of Old Japan.* New York: Random House, 2003.

Bennett, Paula Bernat, ed. *Palace-Burner: The Selected Poetry of Sarah Piatt.* Urbana: University of Illinois Press, 2001.

———. *Poets in the Public Sphere: The Emancipatory Project of American Women's Poetry, 1800–1900.* Princeton: Princeton University Press, 2003.

Bergman, David. "Marianne Moore and the Problem of Marriage." *American Literature* 60.2 (May 1988): 241–54.

Berlant, Lauren. *The Female Complaint: The Unfinished Business of Sentimentality in American Culture.* Durham, NC: Duke University Press, 2008.

———. "Introduction: The Intimate Public Sphere." In *The Queen of American Goes to Washington City: Essays on Sex and Citizenship,* 1–22. Durham, NC: Duke University Press, 1997.

Bertolini, Vincent J. "Fireside Chastity: The Erotics of Sentimental Bachelorhood in the 1850s." In *Sentimental Men: Masculinity and the Politics of Affect in American Culture,* edited by Mary Chapman and Glenn Hendler. Berkeley: University of California Press, 1999.

Bianchi, Martha Dickinson. *The Life and Letters of Emily Dickinson.* Boston: Houghton Mifflin, 1924.

———, ed. *The Single Hound: Poems of a Lifetime.* Boston: Little, Brown, 1914.

———. "T.G.D.—'Deare Childe.'" In *The Wandering Eros.* Boston: Houghton Mifflin, 1924.

Bidart, Frank. "Elizabeth Bishop." *The Threepenny Review* 58 (Summer 1994): 6.

Bingham, Millicent Todd, ed. *Ancestors' Brocades: The Literary Discovery of Emily Dickinson: The Editing and Publication of Her Letters and Poems.* New York: Dover, 1945.

———. *Emily Dickinson's Home: Letters of Edward Dickinson and His Family.* New York: Harper, 1955.

Bishop, Elizabeth. *The Complete Poems, 1927–1979.* New York: Farrar, Straus and Giroux, 1983.

———. "Efforts of Affection: A Memoir of Marianne Moore." In *The Collected Prose,* edited by Robert Giroux, 121–56. New York: Farrar, Straus, and Giroux, 1984. Reprinted in *Elizabeth Bishop: Poems, Prose, and Letters,* edited by Robert Giroux and Lloyd Schwartz New York: Library of America, 2008.

———. *Elizabeth Bishop and "The New Yorker": The Complete Correspondence,* edited by Joelle Biele. New York: Farrar Straus and Giroux, 2011.

———. *Elizabeth Bishop: Poems, Prose, and Letters,* edited by Robert Giroux and Lloyd Schwartz. New York: Library of America, 2008.

———. "Love from Emily." *New Republic* 125.9 (August 27, 1951): 20–21.

———. *One Art: Letters / Elizabeth Bishop.* Edited by Robert Giroux. New York: Farrar, Straus, Giroux, 1994.

———. "Travelling, A Love Poem (or just Love Poem?)." In *Edgar Allan Poe & The Juke-Box: Uncollected Poems, Drafts, and Fragments,* edited by Alice Quinn, 162. New York: Farrar, Straus and Giroux, 2006.

———. "Unseemly Deductions." *New Republic* 127.7 (August 18, 1952): 20.

———. "The U.S.A. School of Writing." In *Collected Prose,* 35–49.

———. *Words in Air: The Complete Correspondence Between Elizabeth Bishop and Robert Lowell.* Edited by Thomas Travisano with Saskia Hamilton. New York: Farrar, Straus and Giroux, 2008.

Blackmur, R. P. "A Plea for the Essay." *Kenyon Review* 14 (1952): 530–34.

Blair, Walter. "Introduction." In *The Sweet Singer of Michigan: Poems by Mrs Julia A. Moore*, xvi–xvii. Chicago: Pascal Covici, 1928.

———. *Mark Twain & Huck Finn*. Berkeley: University of California Press, 1960.

Blake, Caesar, and Carlton Wells, eds. *The Recognition of Emily Dickinson*. Ann Arbor: University of Michigan Press, 1964.

Bogan, Louise. *Achievement in American Poetry 1900–1950*. Chicago: Henry Regnery, 1951.

———. *Emily Dickinson: Three Views [by] Archibald MacLeish, Louise Bogan [and] Richard Wilbur*. Amherst, MA: Amherst College, 1960.

———. "The Poet Dickinson Comes to Life." *New Yorker* 31.34 (October 8, 1955): 178.

Bourdieu, Pierre. *Distinction: A Social Critique of the Judgement of Taste*. Translated by Richard Nice. Cambridge, MA: Harvard University Press, 1984.

"Brinkerhoff-Loomis Home Page: Information About George Loomis." http://www.genea logy.com/ftm/l/o/o/Roeliff-L-Loomis/WEBSITE-0001/UHP-0072.html.

Britzolakis, Christina. "Conversation Amongst the Ruins: Plath and de Chirico." In *Eye Rhymes: Sylvia Plath's Art of the Visual*, edited by Kathleen Connors and Sally Bayley, 167–82. New York: Oxford University Press, 2007.

———. *Sylvia Plath and the Theatre of Mourning*. New York: Oxford University Press, 1999.

Brodhead, Richard H. *Cultures of Letters: Scenes of Reading and Writing in Nineteenth-Century America*. Chicago: University of Chicago Press, 1993.

Brooks, Gwendolyn. *Report from Part One*. Detroit: Broadside, 1972.

Brunner, Edward. *Cold War Poetry*. Urbana: University of Illinois Press, 2001.

Bryher [Winifred Ellerman]. *West*. London: Cape, 1925.

Buckingham, Willis J., ed. *Emily Dickinson's Reception in the 1890s: A Documentary History*. Pittsburgh: University of Pittsburgh Press, 1989.

Buell, Lawrence. *Emerson*. Cambridge, MA: Harvard University Press, 2003.

Bundtzen, Lynda K. *Plath's Incarnations: Woman and the Creative Process*. Ann Arbor: University of Michigan Press, 1983.

Burke, Kenneth. "She Taught Me to Blush." In *Festschrift for Marianne Moore's Seventy Seventh Birthday, by Various Hands*, edited by Tambimuttu, 61. New York: Tambimuttu and Mass, 1964.

Burr, Zofia. *Of Women, Poetry, and Power: Strategies of Address in Dickinson, Miles, Brooks, Lorde, and Angelou*. Urbana: University of Illinois Press, 2002.

Butler, Judith. *Gender Trouble: Feminism and the Subversion of Identity*. New York: Routledge, 1990.

Cameron, Sharon. *Choosing Not Choosing: Dickinson's Fascicles*. Chicago: University of Chicago Press, 1992.

———. *Lyric Time: Dickinson and the Limits of Genre*. Baltimore: Johns Hopkins University Press, 1979.

Capps, Jack. *Emily Dickinson's Reading, 1836–1886*. Cambridge, MA: Harvard University Press, 1966.

Carson, Anne, trans. *If Not, Winter: Fragments of Sappho*. New York: Alfred A. Knopf, 2002.

Case, Josephine Young. "Emily Dickinson's Letters to Dr. and Mrs. Josiah Gilbert Holland." *New England Quarterly* 24.4 (December 1951): 546–48.

Castle, Terry. *The Apparitional Lesbian: Female Sexuality and Modern Culture*. New York: Columbia University Press, 1993.

Cather, Willa. "The House on Charles Street." *The Literary Review* 3 (November 4, 1922): 173–74.

Cavitch, Max. *American Elegy: The Poetry of Mourning from the Puritans to Whitman*. Minneapolis: University of Minnesota Press, 2007.

Chase, Richard. "Letters to the World." *Nation* (April 21, 1951): 380.

———. "Seeking a Poet's Inspiration: Review of *The Riddle of Emily Dickinson* by Rebecca Patterson." *Saturday Review of Literature* 34 (December 1, 1951): 26.

Chauncey, George. *Gay New York: Gender, Urban Culture, and the Making of the Gay Male World, 1890–1940*. New York: Basic Books, 1999.

Chodorow, Nancy. *The Reproduction of Mothering: Psychoanalysis and the Sociology of Gender*. Berkeley: University of California Press, 1978.

Churchwell, Sarah. "Secrets and Lies: Plath, Privacy, Publication and Ted Hughes's *Birthday Letters*." *Contemporary Literature* 42 (Spring 2001): 102–48.

Ciardi, John. *Mid-Century American Poets*. New York: Twayne, 1950.

———. "Review of *The Riddle of Emily Dickinson* by Rebecca Patterson." *New England Quarterly* 25.1 (March 1952): 93–98.

Clark, Heather. *The Grief of Influence: Sylvia Plath and Ted Hughes*. New York: Oxford University Press, 2011.

Cody, John. *After Great Pain: The Inner Life of Emily Dickinson*. Cambridge, MA: Harvard University Press, 1971.

Costello, Bonnie. *Elizabeth Bishop: Questions of Mastery*. Cambridge, MA: Harvard University Press, 1991.

Coultrap-McQuin, Susan. "'Very Serious Literary Labor': The Career of Helen Hunt Jackson." In *Doing Literary Business: American Women Writers in the Nineteenth Century*, 137–66. Chapel Hill: University of North Carolina Press, 1990.

Crane, Hart. "To Emily Dickinson." *Nation* 124 (June 29, 1927): 718.

Crumbley, Paul. *Winds of Will: Emily Dickinson and the Sovereignty of Democratic Thought*. Tuscaloosa: University of Alabama Press, 2010.

Damon, S. Foster. *Amy Lowell: A Chronicle*. Boston: Houghton Mifflin, 1935.

Dandurand, Karen. "Dickinson and the Public." In *Dickinson and Audience*, edited by Martin Orzeck and Robert Weisbuch, 255–77. Ann Arbor: University of Michigan Press, 1996.

DeJean, Joan. *Fictions of Sappho, 1546–1937*. Chicago: University of Chicago Press, 1989.

DeLyser, Dydia. *Ramona Memories: Tourism and the Shaping of Southern California*. Minneapolis: University of Minnesota Press, 2005.

Dickie, Margaret. "Women Poets and the Emergence of Modernism." In *The Columbia History of American Poetry*, edited by Jay Parini and Brett C. Millier, 233–59. New York: Columbia University Press, 1993.

Dickinson, Emily. *Bolts of Melody: New Poems of Emily Dickinson*. Edited by Mabel Loomis Todd and Millicent Todd Bingham. New York: Harper, 1945.

———. *The Complete Poems of Emily Dickinson*. Edited by Martha Dickinson Bianchi. Boston: Little, Brown, 1924.

———. *The Complete Poems of Emily Dickinson*. Edited by Thomas H. Johnson. London: Faber and Faber, 1960.

———. *Emily Dickinson's Letters to Dr. and Mrs. Josiah Gilbert Holland*. Edited by Theodora Van Wagenen Ward. Cambridge, MA: Harvard University Press, 1951.

———. *The Letters of Emily Dickinson*. Edited by Thomas H. Johnson and Theodora Ward. 3 vols. Cambridge, MA: Harvard University Press, 1958.

———. *Letters of Emily Dickinson*. Edited by Mabel Loomis Todd. New York: Harper, 1931.

———. *The Manuscript Books of Emily Dickinson.* Edited by R. W. Franklin. 2 vols. Cambridge, MA: Harvard University Press, 1981.

———. *Poems by Emily Dickinson.* Edited by Mabel Loomis Todd and T. W. Higginson. Boston: Roberts Brothers, 1890.

———. *Poems by Emily Dickinson: Second Series.* Edited by T. W. Higginson and Mabel Loomis Todd. Boston: Roberts Brothers, 1891.

———. *Poems by Emily Dickinson: Third Series.* Edited by Mabel Loomis Todd. Boston: Roberts Brothers, 1896.

———. *The Poems of Emily Dickinson.* Edited by Martha Dickinson Bianchi and Alfred Leete Hampson. Boston: Little, Brown, 1937.

———. *The Poems of Emily Dickinson.* Edited by Martha Dickinson Bianchi and Alfred Leete Hampson. Boston: Little, Brown, 1941.

———. *The Poems of Emily Dickinson: Centenary Edition.* Edited by Martha Dickinson Bianchi and Alfred Leete Hampson. Boston: Little, Brown, 1930.

———. *The Poems of Emily Dickinson: Including Variant Readings Critically Compared with All Known Manuscripts.* Edited by Thomas H. Johnson. 3 vols. Cambridge, MA: Harvard University Press, 1955.

———. *The Poems of Emily Dickinson: Reading Edition.* Edited by R. W. Franklin. Cambridge, MA: Harvard University Press, 1999.

———. *The Poems of Emily Dickinson: Variorum Edition.* Edited by R. W. Franklin. 3 vols. Cambridge, MA: Harvard University Press, 1998.

———. "Unpublished Poems by Emily Dickinson." *Atlantic Monthly* 143.2 (February 1929): 184.

Diehl, Joanne Feit. *Elizabeth Bishop and Marianne Moore: The Psychodynamics of Creativity.* Princeton: Princeton University Press, 1993.

———. *Women Poets and the American Sublime.* Bloomington: Indiana University Press, 1990.

Dobson, Joanne. *Dickinson and the Strategies of Reticence: The Woman Writer in Nineteenth-Century America.* Bloomington: Indiana University Press, 1989.

Douglas, Ann. *The Feminization of American Culture.* New York: Alfred A. Knopf, 1977.

Douglas, Mary. *Purity and Danger: An Analysis of Concepts of Pollution and Taboo.* London: Routledge & Kegan Paul, 1966.

Drabble, Margaret. "Queen of Calvary." *Listener* 80.2053 (August 1, 1968): 150.

Duclos, Gloria Shaw. "Thomas Wentworth Higginson's Sappho." *New England Quarterly* 57.3 (September 1984): 403–11.

DuPlessis, Rachel. "No Moore of the Same." *William Carlos Williams Review* 14 (1988): 6–32.

Edelman, Lee. *No Future: Queer Theory and the Death Drive.* Durham, NC: Duke University Press, 2004.

Edelstein, Tilden G. *Strange Enthusiasm: A Life of Thomas Wentworth Higginson.* New Haven: Yale University Press, 1968.

Ehrlich, Paul R. *The Population Bomb.* New York: Ballantine Books, 1968.

Elkins, James R. "John Williams Andrews." *Strangers to Us All: Lawyers and Poetry.* College of Law, West Virginia University, 2009. http://myweb.wvnet.edu/~jelkins/lp-2001/andrews.html.

Emerson, Ralph Waldo. "New Poetry." *Dial: A Magazine for Literature, Philosophy, and Religion* 1.2 (October 1840): 220–32.

———. *Parnassus.* Boston: Houghton, Mifflin, 1874.

Erkkila, Betsy. *The Wicked Sisters: Women Poets, Literary History, and Discord*. New York: Oxford University Press, 1992.

Faderman, Lillian. *Odd Girls and Twilight Lovers: A History of Lesbian Life in Twentieth-Century America*. New York: Columbia University Press, 1991.

———. *Surpassing the Love of Men: Romantic Friendship and Love Between Women from the Renaissance to the Present*. New York: Morrow, 1981.

Fagley, Richard Martin. *The Population Explosion and Christian Responsibility*. New York: Oxford University Press, 1960.

Farr, Judith. *The Passion of Emily Dickinson*. Cambridge, MA: Harvard University Press, 1992.

Finnerty, Páraic. *Emily Dickinson's Shakespeare*. Amherst: University of Massachusetts Press, 2006.

Fliegelman, Jay. *Declaring Independence: Jefferson, Natural Language and the Culture of Performance*. Stanford: Stanford University Press, 1991.

Fountain, Gary, and Peter Brazeau, eds. *Remembering Elizabeth Bishop: An Oral Biography*. Amherst: University of Massachusetts Press, 1994.

Gardner, Isabella. *The Collected Poems*. Brockport, NY: BOA, 1990.

Gardner, Thomas. *A Door Ajar: Contemporary Writers and Emily Dickinson*. New York: Oxford University Press, 2006.

Gay, Peter. "An Erotic Record." In *The Bourgeois Experience Victoria to Freud: Education of the Senses*, 71–108. New York: Oxford University Press, 1984.

Gifford, Terry. *Ted Hughes*. London: Routledge, 2009.

Gilbert, Sandra M., and Susan Gubar, eds. *Literature by Women: The Traditions in English*. 2 vols. 3rd ed. New York: W. W. Norton, 2007.

———. *The Madwoman in the Attic: The Woman Writer and the Nineteenth-Century Literary Imagination*. New Haven: Yale University Press, 1979.

———. *No Man's Land: The Place of the Woman Writer in the Twentieth Century*. 3 vols. New Haven: Yale University Press, 1988–1994.

Giles, Paul. "Crossing the Water: Gunn, Plath, and the Poetry of Passage." In *Virtual Americas: Transnational Fictions and the Transatlantic Imaginary*, 182–224. Durham, NC: Duke University Press, 2002.

Ginsberg, Allen. "A Supermarket in California." *Howl and Other Poems*, 29–30. San Francisco: City Lights Books, 1956.

Goldensohn, Lorrie. "Bishop's Posthumous Publications." In *The Cambridge Companion to Elizabeth Bishop*, edited by Angus Cleghorn and Jonathan Ellis, 183–96. New York: Cambridge University Press, 2014.

———. *Elizabeth Bishop: The Biography of a Poetry*. New York: Columbia University Press, 1992.

Gollin, Rita K. *Annie Adams Fields: Woman of Letters*. Amherst: University of Massachusetts Press, 2002.

Gonzalez, John. "The Warp of Whiteness: Domesticity and Empire in Helen Hunt Jackson's *Ramona*." *American Literary History* 16.3 (Fall 2004): 437–65.

Gordon, Lyndall. *Lives Like Loaded Guns: Emily Dickinson and Her Family's Feuds*. New York: Viking, 2010.

Gordon, Lynn D. *Gender and Higher Education in the Progressive Era*. New Haven: Yale University Press, 1990.

Gould, Jean. *The World of Amy Lowell and the Imagist Movement*. New York: Dodd, Mead, 1975.

Gouldner, Alvin W. *The Future of Intellectuals and the Rise of the New Class*. New York: Seabury, 1979.

Gregory, Elizabeth. *Quotation and Modern American Poetry: "Imaginary Gardens with Real Toads."* Houston, TX: Rice University Press, 1996.

Gubar, Susan. "Sapphistries." *Signs* 10.1 (1984): 43–62.

Guelzo, Allen C. "Holland's Informants: The Construction of Josiah Holland's 'Life of Abraham Lincoln.'" *Journal of the Abraham Lincoln Association* 23.1 (Winter 2002): 1–53.

———. "Introduction." In *Holland's Life of Lincoln*. Lincoln: University of Nebraska Press, 1998.

Guillory, John. *Cultural Capital: The Problem of Literary Canon Formation*. Chicago: University of Chicago Press, 1993.

Habegger, Alfred. *"My Wars Are Laid Away in Books": The Life of Emily Dickinson*. New York: Random House, 2001.

Habich, Robert D. *Building Their Own Waldos: Emerson's First Biographers and the Politics of Life-Writing in the Gilded Age*. Iowa City: University of Iowa Press, 2011.

Hall, Donald. "Interview with Marianne Moore." *McCall's* 93 (December 1965): 74ff.

Hamilton, Ian. "A Conversation with Robert Lowell." *Review* 26 (Summer 1971): 10–29.

Hammer, Langdon. "Plath's Lives: Poetry, Professionalism, and the Culture of the School." *Representations* 75 (Summer 2001): 61–81.

———. "Useless Concentration: Life and Work in Elizabeth Bishop's Letters and Poems." *American Literary History* 9.1 (Spring 1997): 162–80.

Harding, Walter. "'Dazzling Snapshots of the Human Spirit.'" *Chicago Sunday Tribune* (May 6, 1951): 5.

Harris, Susan K. *The Cultural Work of the Late Nineteenth-Century Hostess: Annie Adams Fields and Mary Gladstone Drew*. New York: Palgrave Macmillan, 2002.

———. "Leveraging the Future: Narration, Literary Convention, and Counterfactual History in [Catharine Maria Sedgwick's] *A New-England Tale and Ramona*." Meeting of the Society for the Study of American Women Writers. Philadelphia, October 2009.

Harrison, Victoria. *Elizabeth Bishop's Poetics of Intimacy*. New York: Cambridge University Press, 1993.

Hart, Ellen Louise, and Martha Nell Smith, eds. *Open Me Carefully: Emily Dickinson's Intimate Letters to Susan Huntington Dickinson*. Ashfield, MA: Paris Press, 1998.

Hartley, Marsden. "Emily Dickinson." *Dial* 65 (August 1918): 95–97.

Heller, Linda. "Aurelia Plath: A Lasting Commitment." *Bostonia [Boston University Alumnae Magazine]* (Spring 1976): 36–37.

Heuving, Jeanne. *Omissions Are Not Accidents: Gender in the Art of Marianne Moore*. Detroit: Wayne State University Press, 1992.

Hicok, Bethany. "'To Work 'Lovingly': Marianne Moore at Bryn Mawr, 1905–1909." In *Degrees of Freedom: American Women Poets and the Women's College, 1905–1955*, 29–56. Lewisburg, PA: Bucknell University Press, 2008.

Higginson, Thomas Wentworth. *Cheerful Yesterdays*. Boston: Houghton, Mifflin, 1898.

———. "Emerson." In *Contemporaries*, 1–22. Boston: Houghton, Mifflin, 1900.

———. "Emerson." *Nation* 34.879 (May 4, 1882): 375–76.

———. "Emily Dickinson's Letters." *Atlantic Monthly* 68.408 (October 1891): 444–56.

———. "Helen Hunt Jackson." *Nation* 41.1051 (August 20, 1885): 150–51.

———. "Helen Jackson." In *Short Studies of American Authors*, 40–50. Boston: Lee and Shepard, 1879.

————. "Letter to a Young Contributor." *Atlantic Monthly* 9 (April 1862): 401–11.

————. *Malbone: An Oldport Romance.* Boston: Fields, Osgood, 1869.

————. "Mrs. Helen Jackson ('H. H.')." *Century Illustrated Magazine:* 31.2 (December 1885): 251–58; revised, *Contemporaries*, 142–67. Boston: Houghton, Mifflin, 1899.

————. "A New Poetess." *Woman's Journal* 51 (December 24, 1870): 405.

————. "An Open Portfolio." *Christian Union* 42 (September 25, 1890): 392–93.

————. "Ought Women to Learn the Alphabet?" *Atlantic Monthly* 3 (February 1859): 137–50.

————. *Out-Door Papers.* Boston: Ticknor and Fields, 1863.

————. "A Plea for Culture." *Atlantic Monthly* 19.111 (January 1867): 29–38.

————. "Preface." In *Poems by Emily Dickinson*, edited by Mabel Loomis Todd and T. W. Higginson. Boston: Roberts Brothers, 1890.

————. Review of *Verses* by H. H. *Atlantic Monthly* 27.161 (March 1871): 400.

————. "Sappho." *Atlantic Monthly* 28 (July 1871): 83–93.

————. Thomas Wentworth Higginson Papers. Houghton Library, Harvard University.

————. "To the Memory of H.H." *Century Illustrated Magazine* 32.1 (May 1886): 47.

Hogue, Cynthia. "'The Plucked String': Emily Dickinson, Marianne Moore and the Poetics of Select Defects." *Emily Dickinson Journal* 7.1 (Spring 1998): 89–109.

————. *Scheming Women: Poetry, Privilege, and the Politics of Subjectivity.* Albany: State University of New York Press, 1995.

Holland, J. G. "Fleta Gray." *Home Journal* 13.163 (March 24, 1849): 1.

————. "Land of the North." *Home Journal* 4.154 (January 20, 1849): 2.

————. "Three Weeks on a Cotton Plantation," edited and introduced by Vivian R. Pollak. *Emily Dickinson Journal* 24.1 (2015): 72–95.

————. *Titcomb's Letters to Young People, Single and Married.* New York: C. Scribner, 1858.

Horan, Elizabeth. "To Market: The Dickinson Copyright Laws." *Emily Dickinson Journal* 5.1 (Spring 1996): 88–120.

Horan, Elizabeth Rosa. "Technically Outside the Law: Who Permits, Who Profits, and Why." *Emily Dickinson Journal* 10.1 (Spring 2001): 34–54.

Horowitz, Helen Lefkowitz. *The Power and Passion of M. Carey Thomas.* New York: Alfred A. Knopf, 1994.

Howe, Julia Ward. "The Salon in America." In *Is Polite Society Polite? And Other Essays*, 113–29. New York: Lamson, Wolffe, 1895.

Howe, M. A. De Wolfe, ed. *Memories of a Hostess: A Chronicle of Eminent Friendships Drawn Chiefly from the Diaries of Mrs. James T. Fields.* Boston: Atlantic Monthly Press, 1922.

Howe, Susan. *The Birth-Mark: Unsettling the Wilderness in American Literary History.* Hanover, NH: University Press of New England, 1993.

————. *My Emily Dickinson.* Berkeley, CA: North Atlantic Books, 1985.

Howells, William Dean. *Editor's Study.* Edited by James W. Simpson. Troy, NY: Whitston, 1983.

————. *Literary Friends and Acquaintance: A Personal Retrospect of American Authorship.* New York: Harper & Brothers, 1900.

————. *Mark Twain-Howells Letters: The Correspondence of Samuel L. Clemens and William Dean Howells, 1872–1910.* Edited by Henry Nash Smith and William M. Gibson, with the assistance of Frederick Anderson. 2 vols. Cambridge, MA: Harvard University Press, 1960.

————. *Suburban Sketches.* New York: Hurd and Houghton, 1871.

Hughes, Ted. *Birthday Letters.* New York: Farrar, Straus, Giroux, 1998.

————, ed. *A Choice of Emily Dickinson's Verse.* London: Faber and Faber, 1968.

————, ed. *A Choice of Shakespeare's Verse*. London: Faber and Faber, 1971.

————. *Collected Poems: Ted Hughes*. Edited by Paul Keegan. New York: Farrar, Straus, and Giroux, 2003.

————. "The Great Theme: Notes on Shakespeare." In *Winter Pollen: Occasional Prose*, edited by William Scammell, 103–21. London: Faber and Faber, 1994.

————. *The Hawk in the Rain*. New York: Harper, 1957.

————. *Letters of Ted Hughes*. Edited by Christopher Reid. London: Faber and Faber, 2007.

————. *New Selected Poems 1957–1994*. London: Faber and Faber, 1995.

————. Review of *Emily Dickinson's Poetry: Stairway of Surprise* by Charles R. Anderson. *Listener* 70 (September 12, 1963): 394.

————. *Shakespeare and the Goddess of Complete Being*. London: Faber and Faber, 1992.

————. Ted Hughes Papers. Woodruff Library, Emory University.

Hunt, E. B. *Union Foundations: A Study of American Nationality as a Fact of Science*. New York: D. Van Nostrand, 1863.

Inness, Sherrie A. *The Lesbian Menace: Ideology, Identity, and the Representation of Lesbian Life*. Amherst: University of Massachusetts Press, 1997.

Irwin, Robert McKee. "'Ramona' and Postnationalist American Studies: On 'Our America' and the Mexican Borderlands." *American Quarterly* 55.4 (December 2003): 539–67.

Ives, Ella Gilbert. "Emily Dickinson: Her Poetry, Prose and Personality—Their Distinction and Growing Fame." *Boston Evening Transcript* (October 5, 1907): 3.

Jackson, Helen Hunt. "The Abbot Paphnutius." *Scribner's Monthly* 1.2 (December 1870): 170–72.

————. *Bathmendi*. *St. Nicholas: An Illustrated Magazine for Young Folks* 12.2 (May–October 1885): 508–12.

————. *Bathmendi: A Persian Tale*. Boston: Loring, 1867.

————. *A Century of Dishonor: A Sketch of the United States Government's Dealings with Some of the Indian Tribes*. Foreword by Valerie Sherer Mathes. Norman: University of Oklahoma Press, 1995.

————. "Coronation." *Atlantic Monthly* 23.136 (February 1869): 241–42.

————. "A Critical Opinion of the Last Literary Venture." *Denver Daily Tribune* (December 8, 1878). Colorado College Special Collections, MS 0020, Box 6, HHJ 1.

————. *Diary*. October 19, 1876. Helen Hunt Jackson Papers, Part 1, Ms 0020, Box 5.

————. "Freedom." *Scribner's Monthly* 10.6 (October 1875): 709–10.

————. *Glimpses of California and the Missions*. Boston: Little, Brown, 1903.

————. "The Indian's Cross and Star." *New York Independent* 35.1802 (June 1883): 1.

————. *A Masque of Poets*. *Mercy Philbrick's Choice*. 1876. Reprint, New York: AMS Press, 1970.

————. *Mercy Philbrick's Choice*. Boston: Roberts Brothers, 1876.

————. "Nebulae." *Galaxy* 17.2 (February 1874): 282.

————. *Poems*. Boston: Roberts Brothers, 1892.

————. *Ramona*. "Introduction" by Michael Dorris. New York: Signet, 2002.

————. *Saxe Holm's Stories*. Series 1. New York: Scribner, Armstrong, 1874.

————. "Too Much Wheat." *New York Independent* (November 6, 1884).

————. "Tribute." In *Verses*, 58–59. Boston: Fields, Osgood, 1870.

————. *Verses*. Boston: Roberts Brothers, 1873.

Jackson, Helen, and Abbot Kinney. *Report on the Condition and Needs of the Mission Indians of California*. Washington, DC: United States Office of Indian Affairs, Government Printing Office, 1883.

Jackson, Virginia. *Dickinson's Misery: A Theory of Lyric Reading*. Princeton: Princeton University Press, 2005.

———. "'The Story of Boon'; or, The Poetess." *ESQ* 54.1–4 (2008): 241–68.

James, Henry. "An American and an English Novel." *Nation* (December 21, 1876). Reprinted in *Literary Criticism: Essays on Literature, American Writers, & English Writers*, 511–15. New York: Literary Classics of the United States, 1984.

———. *The Bostonians*, edited by R. D. Gooder. New York: Oxford University Press, 1998.

———. *Daisy Miller*. In *Tales of Henry James*, edited by Christof Wegelin and Henry B. Wonham, 2nd ed., 3–51. New York: W. W. Norton, 2003.

The *Notebooks of Henry James*. Edited by F. O. Matthiessen and Kenneth B. Murdoch. New York: Oxford University Press, 1947.

Janssen, Marian *Not at All What One Is Used To: The Life and Times of Isabella Gardner*. Columbia: University of Missouri Press, 2010.

Jarrell, Randall. "The Year in Poetry." *Harper's* (October 1955). Reprinted in Jarrell, *Kipling, Auden & Co: Essays and Reviews 1935–1964*, 244. New York: Farrar, Straus and Giroux, 1980.

Jehlen, Myra. "Reading Gender in *Adventures of Huckleberry Finn*." In *"Adventures of Huckleberry Finn": A Case Study in Critical Controversy*, edited by Gerald Graff and James Phelan, 505–17. Boston: Bedford/St. Martin's, 1995.

Jennings, Elizabeth. "Sovereign Self." *New Statesman* 76 (August 16, 1968): 205–6.

Johnson, Barbara. *Mother Tongues: Sexuality, Trials, Motherhood, Translation*. Cambridge, MA: Harvard University Press, 2003.

Johnson, Thomas H. "Affectionately, Emily." *New York Times Book Review* (April 22, 1951): 6.

Joost, Nicholas. "The Pain That Emily Knew." *Poetry* 80 (1952): 242–45.

Joyce, Elisabeth W. "The Collage of 'Marriage': Marianne Moore's Formal and Cultural Critique." *Mosaic* 26.4 (Fall 1993): 103–18.

Juhasz, Suzanne, Cristanne Miller, and Martha Nell Smith, eds. *Comic Power in Emily Dickinson*. Austin: University of Texas Press, 1993.

Kahan, Benjamin. "'The Viper's Traffic-Knot': Celibacy and Queerness in the 'Late' Marianne Moore." *GLQ: A Journal of Lesbian and Gay Studies* 14.4 (2008): 509–35.

Kalstone, David. *Becoming a Poet: Elizabeth Bishop with Marianne Moore and Robert Lowell*. Edited by Robert Hemenway. New York: Farrar, Straus, and Giroux, 1989.

Keith, Lois. *Take Up Thy Bed and Walk: Death, Disability and Cure in Classic Fiction for Girls*. New York: Routledge, 2001.

Keller, Lynn. "Words Worth a Thousand Postcards: The Bishop/Moore Correspondence." *American Literature* 55.3 (October 1983): 405–29.

Keller, Lynn, and Cristanne Miller. "'The Tooth of Disputation': Marianne Moore's 'Marriage.'" *Sagetrieb* 6.3 (Winter 1987): 99–116.

Kelley, Mary. *Learning to Stand and Speak: Women, Education, and Public Life in America's Republic*. Chapel Hill: University of North Carolina Press, 2006.

Kent, Kathryn R. "The *M* Multiplying." In *Making Girls into Women: American Women's Writing and the Rise of Lesbian Identity*, 167–208. Durham, NC: Duke University Press, 2003.

Kertesz, Louise. *The Poetic Vision of Muriel Rukeyser*. Baton Rouge: Louisiana State University Press, 1980.

King, Georgiana Goddard. *The Way of Perfect Love*. New York: Macmillan, 1908.

Kinnell, Galway. "The Correspondence School Instructor Says Goodbye to His Poetry Students." In *A New Selected Poems*. New York: Houghton Mifflin, 2001.

Kizer, Carolyn. "Pro Femina." In *Knock upon Silence*. Garden City, NY: Doubleday, 1965.

Koren, Yehuda, and Eilat Negev. *Lover of Unreason: Assia Wevill, Sylvia Plath's Rival and Ted Hughes's Doomed Love*. New York: Carroll & Graf, 2007.

Korobkin, Laura Hanft. *Criminal Conversations: Sentimentality and Nineteenth-Century Legal Stories of Adultery*. New York: Columbia University Press, 1998.

Leavell, Linda. E-mails to the author. May 16, 2009; May 27, 2009.

———. "'Frightening Disinterestedness': The Personal Circumstances of Marianne Moore's 'Marriage'." *Journal of Modern Literature* 31.1 (Fall 2007): 64–79.

———. *"Holding on Upside Down": The Life and Work of Marianne Moore*. New York: Farrar, Straus, and Giroux, 2013.

———. "Kirkwood and Kindergarten." In *Critics and Poets on Marianne Moore: "A Right Good Salvo of Barks,"* 25–39. Lewisburg, PA: Bucknell University Press, 2005.

———. *Marianne Moore and the Visual Arts: Prismatic Color*. Baton Rouge: Louisiana State University Press, 1995.

———. "Marianne Moore, the James Family, and the Politics of Celibacy." *Twentieth-Century Literature* 49.2 (Summer 2003): 219–45.

———. "Marianne Moore's Emily Dickinson." *Emily Dickinson Journal* 12.1 (Spring 2003): 1–20.

Leavell, Linda, Cristanne Miller, and Robin G. Schulze, eds. *Critics and Poets on Marianne Moore: "A Right Good Salvo of Barks."* Lewisburg, PA: Bucknell University Press, 2005.

Lee, Hermione. *Edith Wharton*. New York: Alfred A. Knopf, 2007.

Leverenz, David. "The Politics of Emerson's Man-Making Words." In *Manhood and the American Renaissance*, 42–71. Ithaca, NY: Cornell University Press, 1989.

Levine, Lawrence W. *Highbrow/Lowbrow: The Emergence of Cultural Hierarchy in America*. Cambridge, MA: Harvard University Press, 1988.

Leyda, Jay, ed. *The Years and Hours of Emily Dickinson*. 2 vols. New Haven: Yale University Press, 1960.

Loeffelholz, Mary. *From School to Salon: Reading Nineteenth-Century American Women's Poetry*. Princeton: Princeton University Press, 2004.

———. "Really Indigenous Productions: Emily Dickinson, Josiah Gilbert Holland and Nineteenth-Century Popular Verse." In *A Companion to Emily Dickinson*, edited by Martha Nell Smith and Mary Loeffelholz, 183–204. Malden, MA: Blackwell, 2008.

Longsworth, Polly. *Austin and Mabel: The Amherst Affair and Love Letters of Austin Dickinson and Mabel Loomis Todd*. New York: Farrar, Straus, Giroux, 1984.

Loomis, Collette. "Only a Shadow." *Springfield Republican* (September 24, 1859): 2.

Loomis, Eben Jenks. *A Sunset Idyl and Other Poems*. Cambridge, MA: Riverside Press, 1903.

Love, Heather. *Feeling Backward: Loss and the Politics of Queer History*. Cambridge, MA: Harvard University Press, 2007.

Lowell, Amy. "Emily Dickinson." In *Poetry and Poets: Essays*, 88–108. Boston: Houghton Mifflin, 1930.

———. "The Sisters." *North American Review* (June 1922). Reprinted in *Literature by Women: The Traditions in English*, edited by Sandra M. Gilbert and Susan Gubar, 3rd ed., vol. 2, 137–40. New York: W. W. Norton, 2007.

Lowell, Robert. *Words in Air: The Complete Correspondence Between Elizabeth Bishop and Robert Lowell*. Edited by Thomas Travisano with Saskia Hamilton. New York: Farrar, Straus and Giroux, 2008.

Lubbers, Klaus. *Emily Dickinson: The Critical Revolution*. Ann Arbor: University of Michigan Press, 1968.

Malcolm, Janet. *The Silent Woman: Sylvia Plath and Ted Hughes*. New York: Alfred A. Knopf, 1994.

Marek, Jayne E. *Women Editing Modernism: "Little" Magazines & Literary History*. Lexington: University Press of Kentucky, 1995.

Maroda, Karen. "Sylvia and Ruth." *Salon* 29 (November 2004). http://www.salon.com/2004/11/29/plath_therapist/.

Martin, Robert K. *The Homosexual Tradition in American Poetry*. Austin: University of Texas Press, 1979.

Mathes, Valerie Sherer. *Helen Hunt Jackson and Her Indian Reform Legacy*. Austin: University of Texas Press, 1990.

———, ed. *The Indian Reform Letters of Helen Hunt Jackson, 1879–1885*. Norman: University of Oklahoma Press, 1998.

Matthews, James. *Voices: A Life of Frank O' Connor*. New York: Atheneum, 1983.

Maun, Caroline C. "Editorial Policy in *The Poems of Emily Dickinson, Third Series*." *Emily Dickinson Journal* 3.2 (Fall 1994): 56–77.

May, Elaine Tyler. *Barren in the Promised Land: Childless Americans and the Pursuit of Happiness*. New York: Basic Books, 1995.

———. *Homeward Bound: American Families in the Cold War Era*. New York: Basic Books, 1988.

McCabe, Susan. *Elizabeth Bishop: Her Poetics of Loss*. University Park: Pennsylvania State University Press, 1994.

———. "'Let's Be Alone Together': Bryher's and Marianne Moore's Aesthetic-Erotic Collaboration." *Modernism/Modernity* 17.3 (September 2010): 607–37.

McIntosh, James. *Nimble Believing: Dickinson and the Unknown*. Ann Arbor: University of Michigan Press, 2000.

Melhem, D. H. "Gwendolyn Brooks and Emily Dickinson." *Emily Dickinson International Society Bulletin* 7.1 (May/June 1995): 14–15, 17.

Merrin, Jeredith. *An Enabling Humility: Marianne Moore, Elizabeth Bishop, and the Uses of Tradition*. New Brunswick, NJ: Rutgers University Press, 1990.

Messmer, Marietta. *Reading Emily Dickinson's Correspondence: "A Vice for Voices."* Amherst: University of Massachusetts Press, 2001.

Meyer, Steven J. *Irresistible Dictation: Gertrude Stein and the Correlations of Writing and Science*. Stanford: Stanford University Press, 2001.

Michelson, Peter. "Sentiment and Artifice: Elizabeth Bishop and Isabella Gardner." *Chicago Review* 18.3/4 (1966): 188–96.

Middlebrook, Diane. *Her Husband: Hughes and Plath—A Marriage*. New York: Viking, 2003.

Miller, Cristanne. *Cultures of Modernism: Marianne Moore, Mina Loy, and Else Lasker-Schüler: Gender and Literary Community in New York and Berlin*. Ann Arbor: University of Michigan Press, 2005.

———. *Emily Dickinson: A Poet's Grammar*. Cambridge, MA: Harvard University Press, 1987.

———. *Marianne Moore: Questions of Authority*. Cambridge, MA: Harvard University Press, 1995.

———. *Reading in Time: Emily Dickinson in the Nineteenth Century*. Amherst: University of Massachusetts Press, 2012.

Millier, Brett C. *Elizabeth Bishop: Life and the Memory of It*. Berkeley: University of California Press, 1993.

Molesworth, Charles. *Marianne Moore: A Literary Life*. New York: Atheneum, 1990.

Monteiro, George, ed. *Conversations with Elizabeth Bishop*. Jackson: University Press of Mississippi, 1996.

Moore, Marianne. "Archaically New," review of *Trial Balances*, edited by Ann Winslow. In *Elizabeth Bishop and Her Art*, edited by Lloyd Schwartz and Sybil P. Estess, 175–76. Ann Arbor: University of Michigan Press, 1983.

———. *Collected Poems*. New York: Macmillan, 1951.

———. *The Complete Poems of Marianne Moore*. 1967. Revised, New York: Macmillan, 1981.

———. *The Complete Prose of Marianne Moore*. Edited by Patricia C. Willis. New York: Viking, 1986.

———. *A Marianne Moore Reader*. New York: Viking, 1961.

———. Mary Norcross Obituary. *Bryn Mawr Alumnae Bulletin* 28 (June 1938): 27–28.

———. *Observations [by] Marianne Moore*. New York: Dial Press, 1924.

———. *Poems*. London: The Egoist Press, 1921.

———. *The Poems of Marianne Moore*. Edited by Grace Schulman. New York: Viking, 2003.

———. Review of *Letters of Emily Dickinson*, edited by Mabel Loomis Todd. *Poetry* 41 (January 1933): 219–26.

———. Review of *North and South* by Ann Winslow. In *Elizabeth Bishop and Her Art*, edited by Lloyd Schwartz and Sybil P. Estess, 175–76. Ann Arbor: University of Michigan Press, 1983.

———. *The Selected Letters of Marianne Moore*. Edited by Bonnie Costello, Celeste Goodridge, and Cristanne Miller. New York: Alfred A. Knopf, 1997.

———. *Selected Poems by Marianne Moore*. New York: Macmillan, 1935.

Morris, Timothy. *Becoming Canonical in American Poetry*. Urbana: University of Illinois Press, 1995.

Morse, Jonathan. "Bibliographical Essay." In *A Historical Guide to Emily Dickinson*, edited by Vivian R. Pollak, 255–74. New York: Oxford University Press, 2004.

———. "J. G. Holland's Moral Politics." *Journal of Popular Culture* 12 (1978): 127–37.

Mossberg, Barbara Antonina Clarke. *Emily Dickinson: When a Writer Is a Daughter*. Bloomington: Indiana University, 1982.

Moylan, Michele. "Materiality as Performance: The Forming of Helen Hunt Jackson's *Ramona*." In *Reading Books: Essays on the Material Text and Literature in America*, edited by Michele Moylan and Lane Stiles, 223–47. Amherst: University of Massachusetts Press, 1996.

Murray, Áife. *Maid as Muse: How Servants Changed Emily Dickinson's Life and Language*. Hanover, NH: University Press of New England, 2010.

Nelson, Deborah. *Pursuing Privacy in Cold War America*. New York: Columbia University Press, 2002.

Ngai, Sianne. *Ugly Feelings*. Cambridge, MA: Harvard University Press, 2005.

Obituary of Ruth Foster. *New York Times* (September 30, 1950): 12.

Ochshorn, Myron. "In Search of Emily Dickinson." *New Mexico Quarterly* 23 (1953): 94–106.

O'Connor, Laura. "Flamboyant Reticence: An Irish Incognita." In Leavell et al., 165–83.

Odell, Ruth. *Helen Hunt Jackson [H. H.]*. New York: D. Appleton Century, 1939.

O'Farrell, Mary Ann. *Telling Complexions: The Nineteenth-Century English Novel and the Blush*. Durham, NC: Duke University Press, 1997.

O'Hara, Frank. "The Day Lady Died." In *The Handbook of Heartbreak: 101 Poems of Lost Love and Sorrow*, edited by Robert Pinsky, 75. New York: Rob Weisbach Books, 1998.

Oliveira, Carmen L. *Rare and Commonplace Flowers: The Story of Elizabeth Bishop and Lota de Macedo Soares*. Translated by Neil K. Besner. New Brunswick, NJ: Rutgers University Press, 2002.

Ostriker, Alicia Suskin. *Stealing the Language: The Emergence of Women's Poetry in America*. Boston: Beacon Press, 1986.

Palmieri, Patricia Ann. *In Adamless Eden: The Community of Women Faculty at Wellesley*. New Haven: Yale University Press, 1995.

Patterson, Rebecca. *The Riddle of Emily Dickinson*. Boston: Houghton Mifflin, 1951.

Peckham, Harry Houston. *Josiah Gilbert Holland in Relation to His Times*. Philadelphia: University of Pennsylvania Press, 1940.

Peel, Robin. "The Ideological Apprenticeship of Sylvia Plath." *Journal of Modern Literature* 27.4 (Summer 2004): 59–72.

Perloff, Marjorie. "Sylvia Plath's 'Sivvy' Poems: A Portrait of the Poet as Daughter." In *Sylvia Plath: New Views on the Poetry*, edited by Gary Lane, 163–64. Baltimore: Johns Hopkins University Press, 1979.

Perrine, Laurence. "Emily's Beloved Friend." *Southwest Review* 37 (Winter 1952): 81–83.

Petrino, Elizabeth A. *Emily Dickinson and Her Contemporaries: Women's Verse in America, 1820–1885*. Hanover, NH: University Press of New England, 1998.

Phillips, Carl. *Poetry, Love, and Mercy*. Berkeley: University of California Press, 2010.

Phillips, Kate. *Helen Hunt Jackson: A Literary Life*. Berkeley: University of California Press, 2003.

Plath, Aurelia. "Letter Written in the Actuality of Spring." In *Ariel Ascending: Writings about Sylvia Plath*, edited by Paul Alexander, 214–17. New York: Harper & Row, 1984.

Plath, Sylvia. "And Summer Will Not Come Again." *Seventeen* (August 1950): 275–76.

———. *Ariel*. New York: Harper & Row, 1971.

———. *The Bell Jar*. New York: Harper Collins, 1999.

———. *The Collected Poems*. Edited by Ted Hughes. New York: Harper & Row, 1981.

———. *The Colossus and Other Poems*. London: Heinemann, 1960.

———. *Johnny Panic and the Bible of Dreams: Short Stories, Prose, and Diary Excerpts*. New York: Harper, 2000.

———. *The Journals*. Edited by Frances McCullough. New York: Dial Press, 1982.

———. *Letters Home: Correspondence, 1950–1963*. Edited by Aurelia Schober Plath. New York: Harper & Row, 1975.

———. "Nine Letters to Lynne Lawner." *Antaeus* 28 (Winter 1978): 31–51.

———. *The Unabridged Journals*. Edited by Karen V. Kukil. New York: Anchor, 2000.

———. "Verbal Calisthenics." *Smith Review* (Spring 1954): 3.

Plunkett, Mrs. H. M. *Josiah Gilbert Holland*. New York: C. Scribner's, 1894.

Pollak, Vivian R. "American Women Poets Reading Dickinson: The Example of Helen Hunt Jackson." In *The Emily Dickinson Handbook*, edited by Gudrun Grabher, Roland Hagenbüchle, and Cristanne Miller, 323–41. Amherst: University of Massachusetts Press, 1998.

———. *Dickinson: The Anxiety of Gender*. Ithaca, NY: Cornell University Press, 1984.

———. "Dickinson and the Poetics of Whiteness." *Emily Dickinson Journal* 9.2 (2000): 84–95.

———. *The Erotic Whitman*. Berkeley: University of California Press, 2000.

———, ed. *A Historical Guide to Emily Dickinson*. New York: Oxford University Press, 2004.

————, ed. *A Poet's Parents: The Courtship Letters of Emily Norcross and Edward Dickinson*. Chapel Hill: University of North Carolina Press, 1988.

————. "Thirst and Starvation in Emily Dickinson's Poetry." *American Literature* 51.1 (March. 1979): 33–49. Reprinted in *Emily Dickinson: A Collection of Critical Essays*, edited by Judith Farr, 62–75. Prentice Hall: Upper Saddle River, NJ, 1996.

Pollitt, Josephine. *Emily Dickinson: The Human Background of Her Poetry*. New York: Harper, 1930.

Pondrom, Cyrena N. "Marianne Moore and H. D.: Female Community and Poetic Achievement." In *Marianne Moore: Woman and Poet*, edited by Patricia C. Willis, 371–402. Orono, ME: National Poetry Foundation, 1990.

Porter, David. *Dickinson: The Modern Idiom*. Cambridge, MA: Harvard University Press, 1981.

Powell, Lawrence N. *New Masters: Northern Planters During the Civil War and Reconstruction*. New Haven: Yale University Press, 1980.

Price, James Warwick. "Three Forgotten Poetesses." *Forum* 42 (March 1912): 361–66.

Prins, Yopie. *Victorian Sappho*. Princeton: Princeton University Press, 1999.

Reid, Mary J. "Julia Dorr and Some of Her Poet Contemporaries." *Midland Monthly* 3 (June 1895): 499–507.

Renehan, Edward J., Jr. *The Secret Six: The True Tale of the Men Who Conspired with John Brown*. New York: Crown, 1995.

Review of *Verses* by H. H. *Nation* 12.298 (March 16, 1871): 183–84.

Rich, Adrienne. *Necessities of Life: Poems 1962–1965*. New York: W. W. Norton, 1966.

————. *Snapshots of a Daughter-in-Law*. New York: Harper & Row, 1963.

————. "'Vesuvius at Home': The Power of Emily Dickinson." In *On Lies, Secrets, and Silence: Selected Prose 1966–1978*, 157–83. New York: W. W. Norton, 1979.

Richards, Eliza. *Gender and the Poetics of Reception in Poe's Circle*. Cambridge: Cambridge University Press, 2004.

Rohy, Valerie. "Love's Substitutions: Elizabeth Bishop and the Lie of Language." In *Impossible Women: Lesbian Figures & American Literature*, 117–43. Ithaca, NY: Cornell University Press, 2000.

Rollyson, Carl. *American Isis: The Life and Art of Sylvia Plath*. New York: St. Martin's Press, 2013.

Roman, Camille. *Elizabeth Bishop's World War II–Cold War View*. New York: Palgrave Macmillan, 2001.

Roosevelt, Theodore. *The Winning of the West*. Vol 1. New York: G. P. Putnam's Sons, 1889.

Rorty, Richard. *Achieving Our Country: Leftist Thought in Twentieth-Century America*. Cambridge, MA: Harvard University Press, 1998.

Rose, Jacqueline. "No Fantasy Without Protest." In *The Haunting of Sylvia Plath*, 114–64. Cambridge, MA: Harvard University Press, 1991.

————. "This Is Not a Biography." *London Review of Books* 24.16 (August 2002): 12–15.

Rosenbaum, Susan B. *Professing Sincerity: Modern Lyric Poetry, Commercial Culture, and the Crisis in Reading*. Charlottesville: University of Virginia Press, 2007.

Rosenberg, Charles E. "Sexuality, Class and Role in 19th-Century America." *American Quarterly* 25.2 (May 1973): 131–53.

Rukeyser, Muriel. *The Collected Poems of Muriel Rukeyser*. Edited by Janet E. Kaufman and Anne F. Herzog. Pittsburgh: University of Pittsburgh Press, 2005.

————. "Josiah Willard Gibbs." *Physics Today* 2.2 (February 1949): 6.

————. *The Life of Poetry*. Ashfield, MA: Paris Press, 1996.

————. "Thoreau and Poetry." In *Henry David Thoreau: Studies and Commentaries*, edited by Walter Harding, George Brenner, and Paul A. Doyle, 103–17. Rutherford, NJ: Fairleigh Dickinson University Press, 1972.

————. *Willard Gibbs.* Garden City, NY: Doubleday, Doran, 1942.

Rupp, Leila J. *A Desired Past: A Short History of Same-Sex Love in America.* Chicago: University of Chicago Press, 1999.

Sánchez-Eppler, Karen. *Dependent States: The Child's Part in Nineteenth-Century American Culture.* Chicago: University of Chicago Press, 2005.

Sassoon, R. L. "Diagram." *Chicago Review* 17.4 (1965): 110–37.

Saunders, Susanna Terrell. "Georgiana Goddard King (1871–1939): Educator and Pioneer in Medieval Spanish Art." In *Women as Interpreters of the Visual Arts, 1820–1979*, edited by Claire Richter Sherman and Adele M. Holcomb, 209–38. Westport, CT: Greenwood Press, 1981.

Scharnhorst, Gary. *Kate Field: The Many Lives of a Nineteenth-Century American Journalist.* New York: Syracuse University Press, 2008.

Schofield, Ann. "Sin, Murder, Adultery, and More: Narratives of Transgression in Nineteenth-Century America." *American Studies* 43.2 (Summer 2002): 123–34.

Schulman, Grace. "A Conversation with Marianne Moore." *Quarterly Review of Literature* 16.1/2 (1969): 154–71.

Schulze, Robin G., ed. *Becoming Marianne Moore: The Early Poems, 1907–1924.* Berkeley: University of California Press, 2002.

————. "'Injudicious Gardening': Marianne Moore, Gender, and the Hazards of Domestication." In Leavell et al., 74–89.

Schwartz, Lloyd. "Foreword." In Carmen L. Oliveira, *Rare and Commonplace Flowers: The Story of Elizabeth Bishop and Lota de Macedo Soares*, translated Neil K. Besner, ix–x. New Brunswick, NJ: Rutgers University Press, 2002.

Sedgwick, Catharine Maria. *Hope Leslie; or, Early Times in the Massachusetts.* Edited by Mary Kelley. New Brunswick, NJ: Rutgers University Press, 1987.

————. *A New England Tale; or Sketches of New-England Character and Manners.* New York: E. Bliss & E. White, 1822.

————. *Redwood: A Tale.* New York: E. Bliss & E. White, 1824.

Sedgwick, Eve Kosofsky. *Epistemology of the Closet.* Berkeley: University of California Press, 1990.

Senier, Siobhan. *Voices of American Indian Assimilation and Resistance: Helen Hunt Jackson, Sarah Winnemucca, and Victoria Howard.* Norman: University of Oklahoma Press, 2001.

Sewall, Richard B. "Emily Dickinson's Perfect Audience: Helen Hunt Jackson." In *Dickinson and Audience*, edited by Martin Orzeck and Robert Weisbuch, 217–32. Ann Arbor: University of Michigan Press, 1996.

————. *The Life of Emily Dickinson.* 2 vols. New York: Farrar, Straus, Giroux, 1974.

Sexton, Anne. *Anne Sexton: A Self-Portrait in Letters.* Edited by Linda Gray Sexton and Lois Ames. Boston: Houghton Mifflin, 1991.

Shackford, Martha Hale. "The Poetry of Emily Dickinson." *Atlantic Monthly* III (January 1913): 93–97. Reprinted in *The Recognition of Emily Dickinson*, edited by Caesar R. Blake and Carlton F. Wells, 79–87. Ann Arbor: University of Michigan Press, 1964.

Sherrer, Grace B. "Emily Dickinson's Letters to Dr. and Mrs. Josiah Gilbert Holland." *American Literature* 23.3 (November 1951): 380–82.

———. "Review of *The Riddle of Emily Dickinson* by Rebecca Patterson." *American Literature* 24.2 (May 1952): 255–58.

Sielke, Sabine. *Fashioning the Female Subject: The Intertextual Networking of Dickinson, Moore, and Rich*. Ann Arbor: University of Michigan Press, 1997.

Sitwell, Edith. *Edith Sitwell: Selected Letters 1919–1964*. Edited by John Lehmann and Derek Parker. New York: Vanguard, 1970.

Smith, Stevie. *Collected Poems*. Edited by James MacGibbon. New York: New Directions, 1983.

Smith-Rosenberg, Carroll. "The Female World of Love and Ritual: Relations Between Women [in Nineteenth-Century A]merica." *Signs* 1.1 (Autumn 1975): 1–29. Reprinted in *Disorderly [Conduct: Visions of Gend]er in Victorian America*, 53–76. New York: Oxford University [Press]

[,] *Manhood, and the Novel, 1859–1925*. Cambridge: Cambridge [University Press]

[   ] *Unbound: Paper, Process, Poetics*. New York: Oxford University [Press]

[   ] *Company of Educated Women: A History of Women and Higher [Education.* New]Haven: Yale University Press, 1985.

[N]ew England Women's Club from 1868 to 1893. Boston: Lee and

[   ]*e and China: Orientalism and a Writing of America*. Oxford: [   ]9.

[M]*oore: The Poet's Advance*. Princeton: Princeton University [Press]

[   ]f Poets." *Colophon* 4.16 (March 1934).

[   ]*Dickinson and Her Culture: The Soul's Society*. New York: [   ]984.

[   ]" In *Three Lives*, 1–56. New York: Viking Penguin, 1990.

[o]k at *Ariel: A Memoir of Sylvia Plath*. New York: Harper's

[   ]odern Woman" (excerpted from a commencement address, [   ]*Home Companion* (September 1955).

[   ]*of Sylvia Plath*. Boston: Houghton Mifflin, 1989.

[   ]*Cabin*. Edited by Elizabeth Ammons. 2nd ed. New York:

[   ]d and Ireland." In *The International Reception of Emily [Dickinson*, edited by]Mitchell and Maria Stuart, 204–33. London: Continuum,

[   ]" In *Made with Words*, edited by Gardner McFall, 86–90. [   ]an Press, 1989.

[   ]y." In *Dear Elizabeth: Five Poems & Three Letters to [Aunt Consuelo*, edited]by Kirstin Hotelling Zona. Logan: Utah State Univer-[sity Press]

[   ]In *Made with Words*, edited by Gardner McFall, 172–[   ]igan Press, 1997.

Ta[   ]*cal Bibliography*. Westport, CT: Meckler, 1987.

Ta[   ]*f Emily Dickinson*. New York: Alfred A. Knopf, 1930.

"If you would not be forgotten, as soon as you are dead & rotten, either write things worth reading, or do things worth writing."

Benjamin Franklin

Tate, Allen. "New England Culture and Emily Dickinson." *Symposium* 3 (April 1932): 206–26. Reprinted in *The Recognition of Emily Dickinson*, edited by Caesar R. Blake and Carlton F. Wells, 153–66. Ann Arbor: University of Michigan Press, 1968.

Teasdale, Sara. *Collected Poems*. New York: Macmillan, 1937.

———. *Dark of the Moon*. New York: Macmillan, 1926.

Thayer, Scofield. "Announcement." *Dial* 78 (January 1925): 89.

Thomas, M. Carey. "Present Day Problems in Teaching: An Address Delivered at Mount Holyoke College Founder's Day, October 7, 1921." *Mount Holyoke Alumnae Quarterly* 5:4 (January 1922): 193–99.

Thoreau, Henry D. *Journal 1851–52*. Edited by John C. Broderick. Princeton: Princeton University Press, 1981.

Todd, Mabel Loomis. "The Ascent of Fuji-San." *Nation* 45.1163 (October 13, 1887): 291–92.

———. *Corona and Coronet: Being a Narrative of the Amherst Eclipse Expedition to Japan, in Mr. James's Schooner-Yacht Coronet, To Observe the Sun's Total Obscuration, 9th August, 1896*. Boston: Houghton Mifflin, 1898.

———. "Footprints." *New York Independent* 35 (September 27, 1883): 26–29.

———, ed. *Letters of Emily Dickinson*. 2 vols. Boston: Roberts Brothers, 1894.

———, ed. *Letters of Emily Dickinson: New and Enlarged Edition*. New York: Harper & Brothers, 1931.

———. "A Mid-Pacific College." *Outlook* 54 (August 15, 1896): 285.

———, ed. *Poems by Emily Dickinson: Third Series*. Boston: Roberts Brothers, 1896.

Todd, Mabel Loomis, and Millicent Todd Bingham, eds. *Bolts of Melody: New Poems of Emily Dickinson*. New York: Harper & Bros., 1945.

Todd, Mabel Loomis, and T. W. Higginson, eds. *Poems by Emily Dickinson*. Boston: Roberts Brothers, 1890.

———, eds. *Poems by Emily Dickinson: Second Series*. Boston: Roberts Brothers, 1891.

Todd, Millicent. *Eben Jenks Loomis, 1828–1912: A Paper Read by His Granddaughter Millicent Todd to a Group of Friends*. Cambridge, MA: Riverside Press, 1913.

Traub, Valerie. *The Renaissance of Lesbianism in Early Modern England*. Cambridge, MA: Cambridge University Press, 2002.

Traubel, Horace, ed. *With Walt Whitman in Camden*. Boston: Small, Maynard, 1906.

Trueblood, Charles K. Review of *The Life and Letters of Emily Dickinson* by Martha Dickinson Bianchi. *Dial* 80 (April 1926): 301–11.

Twain, Mark. "An Adventure of Huckleberry Finn: With an Account of the Famous Grangerford-Shepherdson Feud." *Century Illustrated Magazine* 29.2 (December 1884): 268–79.

———. *Adventures of Huckleberry Finn*. Edited by Thomas Cooley. 3rd ed. New York: W. W. Norton, 1999.

———. *Mark Twain on Female Suffrage, 1867: Four Satirical Letters to the Press/ Here Gathered and Introduced by Edward Connery Lathem*. Hanover, NH: Dartmouth College, 2006.

Uroff, Margaret Dickie. *Sylvia Plath and Ted Hughes*. Urbana: University of Illinois Press, 1979.

Van Dyne, Susan R. *Revising Life: Sylvia Plath's Ariel Poems*. Chapel Hill: University of North Carolina Press, 1993.

Vincent, John Emil. *Queer Lyrics: Difficulty and Closure in American Poetry*. New York: Palgrave Macmillan, 2002.

Wagner, Erica. *Ariel's Gift: A Commentary on "Birthday Letters" by Ted Hughes*. London: Faber and Faber, 2000.

Wagner-Martin, Linda W. *Sylvia Plath: A Biography*. New York: Simon and Schuster, 1987.

Walker, Cheryl, ed. *American Women Poets of the Nineteenth Century: An Anthology*. New Brunswick, NJ: Rutgers University Press, 1992.

———. *Masks Outrageous and Austere: Culture, Psyche, and Persona in Modern Women Poets*. Bloomington: Indiana University Press, 1991.

———. *The Nightingale's Burden: Women Poets and American Culture Before 1900*. Bloomington: Indiana University Press, 1982.

Warner, Charles Dudley. *My Summer in a Garden*. Boston: Houghton, Mifflin, 1870.

Warner, Rev. John R. *Sermons of the Rev. John R. Warner, D. D., with a Sketch of His Life by His Daughter, Mary Warner Moore*. Philadelphia: J. B. Lippincott, 1895.

Wasserstrom, William, ed. *A Dial Miscellany*. Syracuse, NY: Syracuse University Press, 1963.

———. *The Time of the Dial*. Syracuse, NY: Syracuse University Press, 1963.

Webster, Noah. *An American Dictionary of the English Language: Exhibiting the Origin, Orthography, Pronunciation, and Definition of Words*. New York: Harper, 1844.

Wells, Anna Mary. *Dear Preceptor: The Life and Times of Thomas Wentworth Higginson*. Boston: Houghton Mifflin, 1963.

Wells, Henry W. "Contradictions of Life and Art." *Saturday Review of Literature* (September 29, 1951): 17–18.

Werner, Marta L. *Emily Dickinson's Open Folios: Scenes of Reading, Surfaces of Writing*. Ann Arbor: University of Michigan Press, 1995.

———. *Radical Scatters: Emily Dickinson's Fragments and Related Texts, 1870–1886*. Ann Arbor: University of Michigan Press, 1999.

———, and Jen Bervin, eds. *The Gorgeous Nothings*. New York: New Directions, 2013.

Wesling, Donald. *The Chances of Rhyme: Device and Modernity*. Berkeley: University of California Press, 1980.

Wheeler, Lesley. *The Poetics of Enclosure: American Women Poets from Dickinson to Dove*. Knoxville: University of Tennessee Press, 2002.

Whicher, George Frisbie. "Foreword." In *Emily Dickinson: December 10, 1830–May 15, 1886: A Bibliography*. Amherst, MA: Jones Library, 1930.

———. "More Light on Emily." *New York Herald Book Review* (April 29, 1951): 6.

———. "Riddle or Reconstruction." *New York Herald Tribune Book Review* (November 9, 1951): 21.

Whipple, Edwin P. "Some Recent Women Poets." *Scribner's Monthly* 10.1 (May 1875): 100–106.

White, Gillian C. *Lyric Shame: The "Lyric" Subject of Contemporary American Poetry*. Cambridge, MA: Harvard University Press, 2014.

———. "'We do not say ourselves like that in poems': The Poetics of Contingency in Wallace Stevens and Elizabeth Bishop." Ph.D. diss., Princeton University, 2006.

White, Heather Cass, ed. *A-Quiver with Significance: Marianne Moore, 1932–1936*. Victoria, BC: ELS Editions, 2008.

Whitman, Walt. *Leaves of Grass, 1860: The 150th Anniversary Facsimile Edition*. Edited by Jason Stacy. Iowa City: University of Iowa Press, 2009.

———. *Leaves of Grass and Other Writings*. Edited by Michael Moon. New York: W. W. Norton, 2002.

———. *Leaves of Grass and Selected Prose*. Edited by Sculley Bradley. New York: Rinehart, 1953.

———. *Leaves of Grass: From the Text of the Edition Authorized and Editorially Supervised by His Literary Executors, Richard Maurice Bucke, Thomas B. Harned, and Horace L. Traubel*. Edited by Emory Holloway. Garden City, NY: Doubleday, Page, 1926.

———. *The Uncollected Poetry and Prose of Walt Whitman*. Edited by Emory Holloway. 2 vols. Garden City, NY: Doubleday, Page, 1921.

Whitman, William. *The Dancing Galactic Bear*. Trumansburg, NY: Crossing Press, 1974.

Williams, William Carlos. "Marianne Moore." *Dial* 78 (May 1925). Reprinted in *The William Carlos Williams Reader*, edited by M. L. Rosenthal, 384–93. New York: New Directions, 1966.

Willis, Patricia C. "'He Wrote the History Book.'" *Marianne Moore Newsletter* 5.1 (Spring 1981): 19–20.

———, ed. *Marianne Moore: Woman and Poet*. Orono, ME: National Poetry Foundation, 1990.

Wilson, Andrew. *Mad Girl's Love Song: Sylvia Plath and Life Before Ted*. New York: Simon and Schuster, 2013.

Wineapple, Brenda. *Sister Brother: Gertrude & Leo Stein*. Baltimore: Johns Hopkins University Press, 1996.

———. *White Heat: The Friendship of Emily Dickinson & Thomas Wentworth Higginson*. New York: Alfred A. Knopf, 2008.

Wolff, Nathan. "Fits of Reason: the U.S. Political Romance, 1865–1900." Ph.D. diss., University of Chicago, 2012.

Woolsey, Sarah Chauncey. *What Katy-Did*. Boston: Roberts Brothers, 1872.

Wordsworth, William, and Samuel Taylor Coleridge. *Lyrical Ballads, 1798*. Edited by W. J. B. Owen. 2nd ed. London: Oxford University Press, 1969.

Wurst, Gayle. *Voice and Vision: The Poetry of Sylvia Plath*. Geneva, Switzerland: Editions Slatkine, 1999.

———. "'We See—Comparatively—': Reading Rich/Reading Plath/Reading Dickinson." *Profils Américains* 8. Edited by Antoine Cazé, 101–25. Montpellier, France: Presses de l'Université Paul Valéry, 1996.

Zona, Kirstin Hotelling. *Marianne Moore, Elizabeth Bishop, and May Swenson: The Feminist Poetics of Self-Restraint*. Ann Arbor: University of Michigan Press, 2002.

Index of Dickinson's Poems and Letters

The abbreviation *Fr* refers to the number assigned in *The Poems of Emily Dickinson: Reading Edition,* ed. R. W. Franklin (Cambridge, MA: Harvard University Press, 1999). In several instances there are variant first lines.

The abbreviation *L* refers to the number assigned in *The Letters of Emily Dickinson,* ed. Thomas H. Johnson and Theodora Ward, 3 vols. (Cambridge, MA: Harvard University Press, 1958).

POEMS

A Counterfeit – a Plated Person (*Fr* 1514), 71–72
A narrow Fellow in the Grass (*Fr* 1096), 277n96
A precious – mouldering pleasure – 'tis (*Fr* 569), 233
A prompt – executive Bird is the Jay (*Fr* 1022), 277n108
A Shady friend – for Torrid days (*Fr* 306), 223
A Wind that rose though not a Leaf (*Fr* 1216), 202
After all Birds have been investigated and laid aside (*Fr* 1383), 277n108
After great pain, a formal feeling comes (*Fr* 372), 148
Again – his voice is at the door (*Fr* 274), 276n90
Awake ye muses nine, sing me a strain divine (*Fr* 1), 66
Away from Home are some and I (*Fr* 807), 309n54

Beauty crowds me till I die (*Fr* 1687), 132
Because I could not stop for Death (*Fr* 479), 58, 196–197, 268nn23–24, 315n110
Because that you are going (*Fr* 1314), 57–58, 277n95
Before I got my eye put out (*Fr* 336), 55
Before you thought of Spring (*Fr* 1484), 277n108
Bind me – I still can sing (Fr 1005), 200, 202

Could mortal Lip divine (*Fr* 1456), 202

Elysium is as far as to (*Fr* 1590), 81, 83
Endow the Living – with the Tears (*Fr* 657), 171
Exultation is the going (*Fr* 143), 202

Further in Summer than the Birds (*Fr* 895), 174

Glee – The great storm is over (*Fr* 685), 291n63
Going to Him! Happy letter (*Fr* 277), 314n106
Growth of Man – like Growth of Nature (*Fr* 790), 205

LETTERS

General Index

For Dickinson's poems and letters, see the separate index. For letters, poems, and prose by Muriel Rukeyser, Helen Hunt Jackson, Mabel Loomis Todd, Marianne Moore, Sylvia Plath, Ted Hughes, and Elizabeth Bishop, see the subentries.

Aaron, Daniel, 161
Abbott, Jacob, 32, 272n35
Abbott, Rev. John S. C., 32
Alexander, Paul, 174, 180
Allen, Gay Wilson: *The Solitary Singer*, 250
Ames, Lois, 297n1
Amherst College, 31, 32, 43, 67, 72; David Todd at, 72, 73; Eben Loomis and, 76; Higginson lecture at, 57
Anderson, Charles R.: *Emily Dickinson's Poetry: Stairway of Surprise*, 200–202, 297n44
Andrews, Caroline (Caro), 95
Andrews, Charles McLean, 125, 287n28
Andrews, John, 125, 287n29
Apponyi, Flora Haines, 273n40
Arvin, Newton, 161
Atlantic Monthly, 23, 30, 48, 77, 144, 310n61
Auden, W. H., 158, 178
Axelrod, Steven Gould, 162, 178, 299–300n23

Banfield, Ann, 37
Barker, George, 268n23
Barnhouse, Dr. Ruth Tiffany (Beuscher, Ruth), 165–166, 207–208
Barrus, Clara, 76
Barthes, Roland, 72, 93
Bartz, Lydia Clara, 299n18
Bate, Jonathan, 302n50
Bates, Arlo, 96
Baxter, Warner, 42
Beecher, Rev. Henry Ward, 225
Benfey, Christopher, 280n28, 282n49, 285n100

Bennett, Paula Bernat, 18, 75; *Poets in the Public Sphere*, 18
Bergman, David, 288n33
Berryman, John, 168
Bertolini, Vincent J., 308–309n53
Bervin, Jen, 269n42
Bianchi, Martha Dickinson (niece of E.D.), 114, 285n109, 291n63; *Complete Poems*, 11; *Life and Letters*, 148; *Recollections of a Country Girl*, 90; *The Single Hound*, 90, 139, 142–143; "T.G.D.—'Deare Childe'," 279n22; *The Wandering Eros*, 279n22
Bible/biblical imagery, 11, 50, 122, 134, 150, 223
Bidart, Frank, 240, 253
Bingham, Millicent Todd, 79, 85, 87, 114, 201; *Ancestors' Brocades*, 94; *Bolts of Melody*, 5, 310n65; *Eben Jenks Loomis 1828–1912: A Paper Read by His Granddaughter Millicent Todd to a Group of Friends*, 279n10
bisexuality, 207, 239
Bishop, Elizabeth, 6, 11–12, 16–17, 21, 33, 211–212; described as lesbian by Plath, 206, 240; on Dickinson's emotional neediness, 17, 219; Dickinson's letters and, 219, 230–233; lesbian relationship with Lota de Macedo Soares, 212–214, 215, 238; Moore as literary mother, 213, 215–216; notebooks of, 246–247, 248, 257, 313n96; photographs of, *218*, *238*, *251*; Plath's rivalry with, 206; in psychotherapy, 237, 312n74; unfinished review of Plath's *Letters Home*, 214, 215; on women poets, 211, 253–254, 305n3
Bishop, Elizabeth, letters of, 214, 217–218, 243, 244, 245–246, 250, 261

Hunt, Murray, 33
Hunt, Warren Horsford ("Rennie"), 33
Hussey, Anne, 214

intimacy, 2, 37, 119, 124, 213; invited and
repelled, 3, 145, 266; Plath's warning
against, 177; shame linked to, 264–265
Ives, Ella Gilbert, 21

Jackson, Helen Hunt, 11, 14–15, 17, 36–38,
265–266; biography of, 30–33; collective
memory and, 65–70; death of, 68; Dickinson's relationship with, 43–45, 47–52, 47;
as Indian rights advocate, 39–43; photographs of, 35, 46; poetry career of "H.H.,"
23–30
Jackson, Helen Hunt, letters of, 22, 36, 37,
40–41, 44–45, 50–53, 65–66, 277n108
Jackson, Helen Hunt, poems of: "The Abbot
Paphnutius," 25–26; "Ariadne's Farewell,"
36; "Coronation," 23, 25, 36, 48; "Decoration Day," 271n13; "Dedication," 29–30;
"Emigravit," 50; "Freedom," 271n13;
"Horizon," 55; "The Indian's Cross and
Star," 271n13; "Joy," 28, 36; "My Legacy,"
36; "October's Bright Blue Weather," 33,
38–39, 272n36; Poems, 68, 272n36, 273n51,
275n76, 278n110; "Quatrains," 55; The
Story of Boon, 26, 28, 271n14; "Thought,"
36; "Too Much Wheat," 271n13;
"Tribute," 23–24, 25, 270n3; "Triumph,"
64–65, 277n107; Verses, 24, 26, 29; "A
Woman's Death Wound," 55, 66
Jackson, Helen Hunt, prose of: Bathmendi: A
Persian Tale, 23, 25, 26, 270n1; A Century of
Dishonor, 40, 273n54; "Draxy Miller's
Dowry," 68, 278n114; "The Elder's Wife,"
278n114; The Indian Reform Letters of Helen
Hunt Jackson, 1879–1885, 273n56, 273n60,
274n61; A Masque of Poets and, 52–55;
Mercy Philbrick's Choice, 15, 50, 51, 66, 68,
275n78; Ramona, 15, 40–43, 65, 274n62;
Report on the Condition and Needs of the
Mission Indians of California, 40; Saxe
Holm Stories, 37–38, 68
Jackson, Virginia, 26; Dickinson's Misery, 19
Jackson, William Sharpless, 38, 44
James, Alice, 16; The Diary of Alice James,
269n37
James, Henry, 77, 137, 180, 223, 229–230,
275n78; The Bostonians, 229; Daisy Miller,
125–126

Jameson, Marietta, 93
Jarrell, Randall, 168, 253–254
Jehlen, Myra, 88
Johnson, Thomas H., 221, 237, 277n108,
301n46; The Complete Poems of Emily Dick-
inson, 199, 200, 301n43, 301n44, 314n106;
Emily Dickinson: An Interpretive Biography,
13; The Poems of Emily Dickinson: Variorum
Edition, 11, 12, 13, 21, 152, 253, 254, 255,
268n24
Jones, Judith, 169–170

Kahan, Benjamin, 131, 132
Keats, John, 145, 192
Keller, Lynn, 215
Kennedy, John F., assassination of, 211
Kent, Kathryn, 131, 132
King, Georgiana Goddard, 137, 290n58
Kipling, Rudyard, 136
Korobkin, Laura Hanft: Criminal Conversa-
tions, 86

Lameyer, Gordon, 190–191
language, affective power of, 18
Lathrop, George Parsons, 53
Lawner, Lynne, 158–159, 178, 197
Lazarus, Emma, 144
Leavell, Linda, 119, 124, 286n6; Holding On
Upside Down, 124, 287n25
Leonowens, Anna, 26, 271n14
lesbian desire, 126, 156, 287n25, 310n61;
Bishop's Dickinson and, 233–240, 253; in
Bishop's life and works, 241–250; "Boston
marriage," 230, 310n61; Dickinson and, 14;
Moore and, 129, 137, 156; Plath and, 16,
206–210
Levy, Amy, 144
Lincoln, Abraham, 227
literary culture, New England, 5
literary history: discontinuous ("spasmodic"),
3; gendering of, 18
Loeffelholz, Mary: From School to Salon, 18
Longfellow, Henry Wadsworth, 32, 223
Longsworth, Polly, 75, 78
Loomis, Collette, 75–76, 77
Loomis, Eben Jenks, 73, 75, 76, 81, 104; on
book of Dickinson's poems, 98; Sunset Idyl
and Other Poems, 279n12; Whitman and,
77, 87, 98
Loomis, George, 76
Loomis, Mahlon, 76

Plath, Sylvia (*continued*)
"Sunday at the Mintons'", 176, 300n26;
"The Tour," 170, 297n43; "Two Lovers
and a Beachcomber by the Real Sea,"
294n10; "Verbal Calisthenics," 176, 189,
192, 203, 294n10; "Winter Words," 294n10
Plath, Sylvia, prose of: "Among the
Bumblebees," 193–194; *The Bell Jar*,
160–161, 178, 188, 207, 296n28; *Johnny
Panic and the Bible of Dreams*, 272n36,
295n21, 297n46, 298n8, 300n36, 304n71;
Journals, 165, 301n38; "Ocean 1212-W," 171;
Unabridged Journals, 184, 197, *198*,
206–209
Plath, Warren, 156, 181, *185*, 194, 301n38
Poe, Edgar Allan, 247, 248
*Poems of Emily Dickinson: Including Variant
Readings Critically Compared with All
Known Manuscripts* (Johnson, ed.), 11, 12,
13, 21, 152, 199, 200, 253, 254, 255, 268n24
Pollak, Vivian R.: *A Historical Guide to Emily
Dickinson*, 9
Pollitt, Josephine, 34, 150, 293n82; *Emily
Dickinson: The Human Background of Her
Poetry*, 34
Pope, Alexander: "The Rape of the Lock,"
133, 289n51
Pound, Ezra, 140, 215–216
Powell, Lawrence N., 77, 279n10; *New
Masters*, 77
Price, James Warwick, 144
Prouty, Olive Higgins, 184

Ransom, John Crowe, 166
Reconstruction, 26, 28, 77
Reid, Mary J., 68, 278n116
Rich, Adrienne, 17, 160, 197, 252, 253, 296n35;
"I Am in Danger," 13, 269n32, 314n106;
Necessities of Life: Poems 1962–1965, 13;
Snapshots of a Daughter-in-Law, 268n32;
"'Vesuvius at Home': The Power of Emily
Dickinson," 13–14
Roberts Brothers (publisher), 11, 53, 96, 107
Roethke, Theodore, 168, 209
Roman, Camille: *Elizabeth Bishop's World
War II—Cold War View*, 239
Root, Henry, 43, 274n71
Rorty, Richard, 5
Rose, Jacqueline, 207, 303–304n64
Rosenberg, Charles E.: "Sexuality, Class and
Role in 19th-Century America," 86

Rossetti, Christina, 160, 197, 204
Rukeyser, Lawrence B., 12, 268n27
Rukeyser, Muriel, 3, 4–5, 17; on Dickinson
and hymnody, 11–12; father's disinher-
itance of, 12, 268n27; on genius and
troubles of Dickinson, 7–8; loves of, 5, 8;
photograph of, *8*; "Sunday at Nine" radio
program, 219, 307n33
Rukeyser, Muriel, poems of: "Easter Eve
1945," 5, 268n23; *Elegies*, 6; "Eyes of
Night-Time," 268n23; *Orpheus*, 6; "Song"
("A voice flew out of the river as morning
flew"), 268n23; "To Enter That Rhythm
Where the Self Is Lost," 268n23
Rukeyser, Muriel, prose of: *The Life of Poetry*,
4, 6, 7–8, 10; *Theory of Flight*, 6; "Thoreau
and Poetry," 14, 269n34; *Willard Gibbs*, 8,
10

St. Armand, Barton Levi, 88
Sappho, 89, 160, 197, 233–234, 311n69
Sassoon, Richard, 189–190; "The Diagram,"
190
Sassoon, Siegfried, 189
Schofield, Ann: "Sin, Murder, Adultery, and
More," 86
science, 5, 28, 37, 90, 177, 181, 299n18
Scribner's Monthly, 25, 28, 29, 36, 227
Sedgwick, Catharine Maria, 89, 281n38; *Hope
Leslie*, 281n38
separate spheres ideology, 159
Sergeant, Elizabeth Shepley, 139
Sewall, Richard B., 43, 250, 251; *The Life of
Emily Dickinson*, 250
Sexton, Anne, 168, 204, 302n56
sexual politics, 4, 241
Shackford, Martha Hale, 144–145
Shakespeare, William, 42–43, 145, 202, 223,
302n50
shame, 25, 169, 208, 245, 265, 311n66; Dick-
inson and, 1–3, 9, 133, 194, 195, 224, 227,
264, 314n106 ; Jackson and, 21, 40, 271n13
Shawn, William, 243–244, 313n87
Sherrer, Grace B., 221–222
Shoemaker, Mary Craig, 122
Sielke, Sabine, 18; *Fashioning the Female
Subject*, 18
Sitwell, Edith, 160, 179, 197, 311n69
slavery, 25, 26, 28, 75, 308n50
Smith, Stevie, 209, 304n71

Whicher, George, 221, 222, 237
White, Gillian, 265
White, Katharine, 243–244
Whiting, Charles Goodrich, 104
Whitman, Walt, 4, 6, 14, 16, 36, 75, 199, 217,
    289n42; "As I Ebb'd with the Ocean of
    Life," 80, 246; in Bishop's "The U.S.A.
    School of Writing," 212, 243–250; circle of,
    77, 87, 98; "Crossing Brooklyn Ferry,"
    246, 249; Ginsberg's homage to, 240;
    Leaves of Grass, 87, 245, 246, 248, 303n61,
    313n92, 313n96; "Once I Pass'd through a
    Populous City," 130; poets of future
    addressed by, 18, 245, 247–248, 313n92;
    Selected Prose, 303n61; "Song of Myself,"
    87, 246, 303n61; *Two Rivulets*, 87
Whitman, William Key: "To a Fox Girl on
    Her Birthday," 156

Whittier, John Greenleaf, 148
Wilde, Oscar, 136
Wilder, Herbert, 77
Wilder, Mary ("Mollie") Alden, 73, 76, 77,
    95, 114
Wilder, Mary Wales Fobes Jones, 77, 75, 95,
    114
Williams, Oscar, 268n23
Williams, William Carlos, 140, 151, 293n84,
    314n103
Wineapple, Brenda, 229
Wolosky, Shira, 9
Woman's Journal, 24, 58
women's suffrage, 57
Woolsey, Sarah, 33, 272n37
Wordsworth, William, 145, 298n10
Wurst, Gayle, 178

Zabel, Morton, 140, *142*

Acknowledgments

This book has been a joy to write and the people who encouraged me along the way were so helpful that I can't thank them enough. Here are some of those who read for me: Carolyn Allen, Charles Altieri, Paula Bennett, Kathleen Connors, Jed Deppman, Jane Eberwein, Betsy Erkkila, Lillian Faderman, Suzanne Juhasz, Benjy Kahan, Karen Kilcup, Linda Leavell, David Leverenz, Bill Maxwell, Frances McCue, Bob Milder, Cristanne Miller, Jonathan Morse, Anca Parvulescu, Elizabeth Petrino, Bob Pollak, Ken Price, Katherine Rogers-Carpenter, Lloyd Schwartz, Alexandra Socarides, Heather Treseler, Sara van den Berg, Kellie Wells, and Shira Wolosky. Bob Pollak tells me he feels appreciated, so I won't attempt to thank him further for his generosity on research trips to Bloomington, Indiana, to Amherst and Northampton, to Colorado Springs and San Francisco, to Boston and Washington, D.C., to Philadelphia and New York and elsewhere, and ever at home.

There were many opportunities to present parts of this work in progress, and I want to send a collective thanks to conference organizers for letting me try out my ideas in many places, including Hawaii, Norway, Japan, England, and France. Nevertheless, I can't resist the chance to express particular appreciation to Donald Pease at Dartmouth College; to David Leverenz and the Americanists in the English Department at the University of Florida; to Martha Nell Smith at the University of Maryland; to Marsha Bryant and the organizers of the "Lifting Belly High" conference in Pittsburgh; to Elisabeth Däumer for a spectacular Muriel Rukeyser conference at Eastern Michigan University in Ypsilanti; and to Elizabeth Gregory for a memorable experience at the Twenty-First Century Marianne Moore Conference in Houston.

Here at Washington University in St. Louis, my research assistants Kate Bloomquist and Yuki Tanaka deserve a shout-out, as does Betha Whitlow of our Visual Resources Center, who worked closely with me on digitizing the images. Thanks, too, to the indefatigable staff at Olin Library, including Kris

Helbling, who extends herself above and beyond the call of duty on a daily basis. Awesome librarians elsewhere include Karen Kukil of Smith College, Jessy Randall of Colorado College, Dean Rogers at Vassar, and Peter K. Steinberg of the digital Plath world (sylviaplath.info). English Department chairs David Lawton, Vince Sherry, and Wolfram Schmidgen often smoothed my way, as did Provost Ed Macias and Dean Barbara Schaal. Steve Zwicker, I value your good advice. Other friends such as narratologist Emma Kafalenos and fascicle-expert Eleanor Elson Heginbotham saw me through the inevitable rough patches, as did the members of the St. Louis Whitman Fellowship on both sides of the Mississippi River. At Penn Press, Jerry Singerman was the best of shrewd and reassuring editors. I thank Hannah Blake and Erica Ginsburg for their insights and good humor.

For hospitality and emotional support, Ed Pollak and Fiona Lee were steadily amazing, while Steve Pollak remains unsurpassed for telephone artistry. I thank my Philadelphia granddaughter Julia Pollak for a vital telephone intervention, and I thank my Franklin, Michigan, grandchildren Mia and Alex, who were ever charming sports and traveling companions. To my students over the years on both coasts and in the Midwest, you made it all possible. You made it into an intimate delight.

I thank Oxford University Press for permission to reproduce a revised version of my article "Moore, Plath, Hughes and 'The Literary Life,'" which appeared in *American Literary History* 17.1 (Spring 2005): 95–117. I am also pleased to acknowledge several awards from the Maxwell C. Weiner Humanities Faculty Research fund, Washington University, as well as a timely publication subvention from the College of Arts and Sciences and the English Department, Washington University.

"Polyphonic Craftsman, Coated Like a Zebra, Fleeing Like the Wild Ass, Mourning Like a Dove," from THE POEMS OF MARIANNE MOORE by Marianne Moore, edited by Grace Schulman, copyright © 2003 by Marianne Craig Moore, Executor of the Estate of Marianne Moore. Used by permission of Viking Books, an imprint of Penguin Publishing Group, a division of Penguin Random House LLC.

"Trio of Love Songs" [(2): 20 l.], [(3): 16 l.] from THE COLLECTED POEMS OF SYLVIA PLATH, EDITED by TED HUGHES. Copyright © 1960, 1965, 1971, 1981 by the Estate of Sylvia Plath. Editorial material copyright © 1981 by Ted Hughes. Reprinted by permission of HarperCollins Publishers.

Citations from Dickinson's letters and poems are acknowledged as follows:

Reprinted by permission of the publishers and the Trustees of Amherst College from THE LETTERS OF EMILY DICKINSON, edited by Thomas H. Johnson, Associate Editor, Theodora Ward, Cambridge, Mass.: The Belknap Press of Harvard University Press. Copyright © 1958 by the President and Fellows of Harvard College. Copyright © renewed 1986 by the President and Fellows of Harvard College. Copyright © 1914, 1924, 1932, 1942 by Martha Dickinson Bianchi. Copyright © 1952 by Alfred Leete Hampson. Copyright © 1960 by Mary L. Hampson.

Reprinted by permission of the publishers and the Trustees of Amherst College from THE POEMS OF EMILY DICKINSON, edited by Thomas H. Johnson, Cambridge, Mass.: The Belknap Press of Harvard University Press, Copyright © 1951, 1955 by the President and Fellows of Harvard College. Copyright © renewed 1979, 1983 by the President and Fellows of Harvard College. Copyright © 1914, 1918, 1919, 1924, 1929, 1930, 1932, 1935, 1937, 1942, by Martha Dickinson Bianchi. Copyright © 1952, 1957, 1958, 1963, 1965, by Mary L. Hampson.

Reprinted by permission of the publishers and the Trustees of Amherst College from THE POEMS OF EMILY DICKINSON; VARIORUM EDITION, edited by Ralph W. Franklin, Cambridge, Mass.: The Belknap Press of Harvard University Press, Copyright © 1998 by the President and Fellows of Harvard College. Copyright © 1951, 1955 by the President and Fellows of Harvard College. Copyright © renewed 1979, 1983 by the President and Fellows of Harvard College. Copyright © 1914, 1918, 1919, 1924, 1929, 1930, 1932, 1935, 1937, 1942 by Martha Dickinson Bianchi. Copyright © 1952, 1957, 1958, 1963, 1965 by Mary L. Hampson.

Reprinted by permission of the publishers and the Trustees of Amherst College from THE POEMS OF EMILY DICKINSON; READING EDITION, edited by Ralph W. Franklin, Cambridge, Mass.: The Belknap Press of Harvard University Press, Copyright © 1998, 1999 by the President and Fellows of Harvard College. Copyright © 1951, 1955 by the President and Fellows of Harvard College. Copyright © renewed 1979, 1983 by the President and Fellows of Harvard College. Copyright © 1914, 1918, 1919, 1924, 1929, 1930, 1932, 1935, 1937, 1942 by Martha Dickinson Bianchi. Copyright © 1952, 1957, 1958, 1963, 1965 by Mary L. Hampson.